Jack Dillon

ALSO BY MARK ALLEN BAKER
AND FROM MCFARLAND
___

Johnny Kilbane: The Boxing Life of a Featherweight Champion (2024)

Tony Canzoneri: The Boxing Life of a Five-Time World Champion (2023)

Willie Pep: A Biography of the 20th Century's Greatest Featherweight (2022)

Lou Ambers: A Biography of the World Lightweight Champion and Hall of Famer (2021)

The World Colored Heavyweight Championship, 1876–1937 (2020)

*Between the Ropes at Madison Square Garden:
The History of an Iconic Boxing Ring, 1925–2007* (2019)

The Fighting Times of Abe Attell (2018)

Battling Nelson, the Durable Dane: World Lightweight Champion, 1882–1954 (2017)

Jack Dillon
*A Biography
of Boxing's Giant Killer*

MARK ALLEN BAKER

McFarland & Company, Inc., Publishers
Jefferson, North Carolina

ISBN (print) 978-1-4766-9590-7
ISBN (ebook) 978-1-4766-5557-4

LIBRARY OF CONGRESS CATALOGING DATA ARE AVAILABLE

Library of Congress Control Number 2025000425

© 2025 Mark Allen Baker. All rights reserved

No part of this book may be reproduced or transmitted in any form or by any means, electronic or mechanical, including photocopying or recording, or by any information storage and retrieval system, without permission in writing from the publisher.

Front cover image: Jack Dillon (author collection).

Printed in the United States of America

*McFarland & Company, Inc., Publishers
Box 611, Jefferson, North Carolina 28640
www.mcfarlandpub.com*

Thomas Allen (November 30, 1938–October 24, 2023),
a loving husband, father, and grandfather
who understood the value of dedication and hard work
and the merits of craftsmanship

In memory of Matthew Robert Baker (1970–2021)

Table of Contents

Acknowledgments ix
Preface 1
Introduction: A Champion in Perpetuity 3

ONE. The Birth of a Giant Killer 7
TWO. A New Decade, 1910 25
THREE. One Prolific Pugilist, 1911 39
FOUR. A Championship Claim, 1912 54
FIVE. Never Better, 1913 70
SIX. Indestructible, 1914 82
SEVEN. Head East, 1915 98
EIGHT. Fisticuffs in Flatbush, 1916 112
NINE. World War I, 1917 128
TEN. A Bearcat Redux, 1918 143
ELEVEN. Bearcat Blues, 1919 154
TWELVE. Comeback, 1920 163
THIRTEEN. The Roaring Twenties Begin, 1921–1922 172
FOURTEEN. From Boxing to Breadlines, 1923–1942 183

Appendix A: Ernest Coulter Price, a.k.a. Jack Dillon—Boxing Record 197
*Appendix B: Official Records of Associated Members of
   the International Boxing Hall of Fame* 217
Chapter Notes 219
Bibliography 233
Index 235

Acknowledgments

Mark Twain once quipped, "To get the full value of joy you must have someone to divide it with." I am blessed to have many. My gratitude to everyone associated with this title at McFarland.

Those who know me understand my proud association with the International Boxing Hall of Fame in Canastota, New York. My service has been rewarding because of so many wonderful individuals associated with the museum, especially Edward P. Brophy, executive director. I would also like to acknowledge Jeffrey S. Brophy for his outstanding research and ongoing friendship.

This book would not have been possible without the assistance of the Library of Congress. Chronicling America, a website providing access to select digitized newspaper pages and produced by the National Digital Newspaper Program, was another outstanding source. Adding to my periodical research was Newspapers.com by Ancestry.com, which filled the gaps left behind by other sources.

The International Boxing Research Organization (IBRO) was organized in May 1982 for the express purpose of establishing an accurate history of boxing, compiling complete and accurate boxing records, facilitating the dissemination of boxing research information, and cooperating in safeguarding the idiosyncratic research efforts of its members by application of the rules of scholarly research. They have been successful because when they are needed, they are there. Thank you to my fellow IBRO members.

Living in the historic state of Connecticut, I am fortunate to have a great support system. My gratitude to the independent bookstores in Connecticut for supporting local authors, especially Bank Square Books in Mystic.

Larry Dasilva (Nutmeg TV), Wayne Norman (WILI–AM), Roger Zotti (*The Resident*, IBRO), the Authors Guild, IBRO, *Journal Inquirer*, Lou Eisen (*Ring Talk*), Joshua Brewer (*86Boxing*), *USA Boxing News* (Alex and John Rinaldi, Kirk Lang), Christy Martin, Pat Orr, and Dan Tortora (*Wake Up Call*), and *Round 14* (Rick and Tony), thank you for your inspiration and advocacy of my work.

There are many talented individuals in and around the sport of boxing who don't get the credit they deserve. Recognizing this, the state of Connecticut created its own Boxing Hall of Fame located inside Mohegan Sun Casino and Resort in Uncasville. I wish to express my appreciation to everyone associated with the organization for their support, especially Jimmy Burchfield, Johnny Callas, Joe Cusano, Steve Ike, Mike Mazzulli, and Don Trella.

Strength and inspiration were drawn from my friends and family. My thanks to friends Dana Beck and Brian Brinkman, Mary DeSimone, Dennis E. DiGiovanni, Rick Kaletsky, Ann and Mark Lepkowski, and Jim Risley.

To my Florida and Indiana family, Marilyn Allen Baker; Aaron, Sharon, Elliott, and Tyler Baker; Elizabeth, Mark, Paisley, and Monroe Taylor; and Rebecca Baker: thank you for your love and support. To Richard Long, my wonderful father-in-law, who has always been a second in my corner: I am grateful for your support.

In loving memory of Ford William Baker, James Buford Bird, Flavil Q. Van Dyke III, Deborah Jean Long, David Arthur Mumper, Nancy L. Allen, Richard Alan Long, Thomas P. Allen, Matthew Robert Baker, Frederic Stapleton III, and Thomas Allen.

To my wife, Alison, I send a quote from Friedrich Nietzsche: "It is not a lack of love, but a lack of friendship that makes unhappy marriages."

Preface

"It's not the size of the dog in the fight, it's the size of the fight in the dog." Mark Twain said it; Ernest Coulter Price, a.k.a. Jack Dillon, lived it. A head taller and 15 to 20 pounds heavier than most of his opponents, Dillon did not appear human. He was Superman three decades before the superhero was created. No man was too big for "Jack the Giant Killer." Everyone was merely another opponent, which meant they could be defeated.

Audacious, powerful, and precocious, Jack Dillon could intimidate an adversary with a mere glance. His powerful uppercuts and thunderous left hand were a prelude to destruction. Guarding all aspects of vulnerability, he was intensely private, purposefully reticent, and routinely unresponsive to questions. Battling at the peak of his career, during the no-decision era, his silence would both help and hurt him. As boxing's version of Greta Garbo, he wanted to be left alone.

If becoming an elite pugilist during the no-decision era were not demanding enough, the prolific pugilist also faced World War I (1917–18), Prohibition (1920–33), the stock market crash of 1929, and the Great Depression (1929–39). Mix in a plethora of health problems, not to mention legal issues, and you have an unbelievable life sustained by perseverance. Prohibition, in particular, proved a challenging time for Dillon. His unfortunate fall from grace was swift and piteous.

As the sole person to serve the International Boxing Hall of Fame as an author, historian, chairperson, sponsor, volunteer, and biographer, I felt inspired, as I did with my biographies of Oscar "Battling" Nelson, Abe Attell, Lou Ambers, Willie Pep, Tony Canzoneri, and Johnny Kilbane, to write an account of the obscure and too-often-overlooked life of Jack Dillon.

More than a year in the making, this book is largely based on contemporaneous newspaper accounts of events in the life of Ernest Coulter Price. In addition to the main text, it includes appendices of career-related information, including a selected boxing record.

In this, my 29th book, seventh biography, and 12th boxing title, I am thankful for the chance to explore the life of this nonpareil pugilist. There have been many great pugilists in the rich history of the sport, but only one—Dillon—was compared to the great Jack Dempsey.

Introduction:
A Champion in Perpetuity

> *"Now, ladies and gentlemen, I want to introduce to you one of the greatest men the ring game ever had; a man whose work was an honor to himself and the sport that he represented; a fighter from the ground up, and one who probably was robbed of the honor of being the champion of them all when fate ruled him 'through' just when he was ready, and could have beaten the best man in the world at any weight. I take great pleasure in introducing to you Jack Dillon, the scrappiest ring bearcat that ever lived."*—Introduction of fight spectator Jack Dillon, September 10, 1920

In a weight-sensitive sport, Jack Dillon was considered an anomaly. Size was irrelevant; besides, it was only an issue if the pugilist accepted it as such. He refused. Compact and sturdily build, yet nimble, Dillon not only defeated opponents—he humiliated them. It was flawless execution without a word ever spoken. And it was the soundtrack to his prolific and unparalleled career.

Ernest Coulter Price hailed from the picturesque state of Indiana. Nestled in the heart of the American Midwest, Hoosier residents had a passion for overcoming adversity, and the Price family was no different. Losing his father before the age of six, Ernest, along with his three brothers, experienced an abrupt introduction to adulthood: Employment replaced education—before the conclusion of high school—as their paramount goal. Life, as they knew it, was about survival. If that meant swabbing engine grease or delivering messages on a cold winter day, that was fine.

Following in the steps of his two older brothers, Chester and Russell, Ernest pursued pugilism as an avocation. He soon learned that the sport could be dangerous. In 1905, Chester, the eldest of the brothers, died from injuries sustained while boxing. But accepting mortality was one thing, ignoring it another. Russell and Ernest chose the latter. Retribution, they were convinced, meant remaining in the ring. As for Paul, the youngest, he would witness his brothers' identity transformation from grade school.

The inherent ring skills of the Price boys was undebatable. Of the two eldest boys, Ernest, as Jack Dillon, appeared to find a career, while older brother Russell, a.k.a. Tommy Dillon, discovered a short-term revenue solution. Stealing a moniker from a successful racehorse was convenient if not logical: it masked Ernest and Russell's identities while creating a winning association. While it was easy to separate the pugilist from the horse, Russell's moniker led some to confuse him with Tommy Dillon, a local entrepreneur and boxing referee. Nonetheless, the Dillon boys were born.

Jack and Tommy were inseparable during the early years of their professional boxing career. Together they trained, sparred, argued, and created a small business empire. There were times, like in 1909, when they fought the same opponent (Pat Lark) and even appeared on the same fight card (December 22). Jack's abilities and popularity quickly overshadowed his brother's, however.

Thrust into the spotlight, Jack Dillon made it clear: The fighter's public life was one thing, his private life another. Therefore, the latter was off limits. He seemed inscrutable to some, yet his reticence proved wise, as greater openness likely would have hurt him, or even exhibited his vulnerability. Were there skeletons in the closet? It appeared that way. In rare instances, a glimpse into his private life found its way into the public domain. It came out that Dillon had a stepson (Ralph) born around 1907, for instance, and a wife, Grace M. Dillon—Grace Schwartzman was previously married to W.J. Reed in 1906—whom he married in 1914.

Dillon abhorred exhibiting emotion in public, but in his private life, there were times when the youngster was reckless with his words and his actions, as many of his former managers attested.

Fighting during the "no-decision era" was like playing baseball without bases. It bred mediocrity. Yet many boxers took pride in performance and polished their skills—a quality performance could yield improved earnings. For those with talent, who saw the sweet science as a career, they never knew where they stood in the big picture of pugilism. Without organizations (American Boxing Association was founded in 1915), valid rankings, and communication tools—*The Ring* magazine wouldn't exist until 1922—title claims were common and often unsubstantiated. Prizefighting, illegal in many states and subject to interpretation, was also considered unbefitting conduct. Nevertheless, the Dillon boys took Indiana pugilism by a storm.

Although Indianapolis was called home, comparatively speaking, it was a minor market in the world of prizefighting. As the twentieth century began, a Midwest boxer could issue challenges and claim a title, and few noticed. Since radios weren't widely used until the late 1920s, a boxer's reputation was made, or broken, by word of mouth or via a newspaper. Izzy Brill, a popular matchmaker, took over Jack Dillon's affairs in August 1908. This would begin a seemingly never-ending process of fight management (roughly two dozen), that in retrospect proved detrimental to his career: it slowed his development, limited his fight options, and decreased his revenue potential. The sole person genuinely qualified was Sam Murbarger, who would later confirm the intractable difficulties managing the pugilist; incidentally, his perspective mirrored that of his predecessors.

Jack Dillon's first big break was a 20-round victory over George "K.O." Brown in November 1910. Afterwards, the 117-pound winner had a smile on his face and $63 in his pocket. It was the first milestone in a prolific boxing career that would include more than 240 bouts. Leo Houck became the first elite boxer to meet Jack Dillon, and did so on New Year's Day 1912. A victory over the Lancaster brawler allowed Dillon to claim his first title. For 82 days, he relished the middleweight championship before suffering a 20-round loss to elite boxer Frank Klaus.

Defeating Battling Levinsky over 12 rounds, on April 14, 1914, Jack Dillon claimed the light heavyweight championship. He defended it once before the newly formed American Boxing Association officially recognized Dillon as the light heavyweight champion on November 15, 1915. The following year, he successfully defended the title against Levinsky, over 15 rounds.

Weight meant nothing to Jack Dillon. Transforming himself from welterweight to middleweight, he dominated his opposition. But it was as a light heavyweight where he appeared invincible. And when he looked up, there wasn't a heavyweight alive who didn't fear for his life.

In one of the greatest fights not only of 1916, but of the decade, Jack Dillon defeated Frank Moran on June 29, 1916. It was nothing short of a magnificent performance as Dillon, having been suppressed early in the fight, proceeded to soundly defeat the heavyweight contender. On that day there existed no better fighter in the world than Jack Dillon. It was the ring artist's magnum opus.

Although Jack Dillon continued to dispose of heavyweights, the physical damage he endured was taking its toll, especially on his legs. It became a race against time to draw out Jess Willard, the world heavyweight champion. It was a logical provocation, even if it was ignored. The Pottawatomie Giant made only one official title defense prior to 1919, defeating Frank Moran on March 25, 1916, at Madison Square Garden. Both of the titleholder's actions were insulting to the Hoosier pugilist. At the pinnacle of Jack Dillon's career, he was denied an opportunity to become the world heavyweight champion and to unequivocally confirm his sobriquet as "Jack the Giant Killer."

The greatest disadvantage facing any elite fighter was vulnerability; Dillon understood this and lived his public life accordingly. Yet to make the illusion of invulnerability a reality—every champion's dream—required forsaking distractions. Not just one diversion but all of them, both in and out of the ring. Unfortunately, Jack Dillon could not do so, and his fall from grace would be quick, ignominious, and disturbing.

A 12-round loss to Battling Levinsky, on October 24, 1916, revealed his declining prowess, even if those who faced him and lost, such as Ed "Gunboat" Smith, felt otherwise. Two defeats (1917 and 1918) to Harry Greb, another peerless pugilist, convinced Jack Dillon that his skills had diminished. The psychological damage to Dillon was more than he could overcome. It was time to take a slow ride—if possible, during World War I—into the sunset while grabbing as much coin as he could.

The Walker Law, passed in 1920, reestablished legal boxing in New York state and set the stage for others to follow. It also gave pugilists like Dillon a glimmer of hope that they could regenerate their careers. But in Jack Dillon's case, the tank was empty.

Riding out his ring reputation followed, as did Prohibition (1920–33), the stock market crash of 1929, and the Great Depression (1929–39)—three factors that replaced the American Dream with a focus on day-to-day existence. If there was anything a pugilist understood it was survival, a condition that had no boundaries. Yet, laws—or rules, if you will—regulated the actions of the majority and set parameters. To some, challenging this line of demarcation, especially during Prohibition, became part of their existence. Jack Dillon was one such individual.

The man who could beat the best the ring had to offer—and would have defeated Jess Willard—could not beat his toughest nemesis, John Barleycorn. Nor could he alter the physical damage he had taken in the ring. His move to Hialeah, Florida, offered a brief respite, but the cloud of misfortune followed. A shadow of the man he used to be, Jack Dillon lived in a small weather-beaten shanty, not far from the Hialeah racetrack, where he peddled liquid refreshments. Holding his life in check as long as he could, he had to be institutionalized at the State Hospital at Chattahoochee, in April 1942. Jack Dillon, who had legally changed his name in 1931, died on August 7, 1942. He was buried in the institution's cemetery.

Chapter One

The Birth of a Giant Killer

"It's not the size of the dog in the fight, it's the size of the fight in the dog."
—Mark Twain

The thought of Jack Dillon, claimant to the world light heavyweight championship, being matched against Jess Willard, world heavyweight champion, ignited boxing fans around the world. In February 1916, the mental picture of two icons of the ring of contrasting size battling each other was enigmatic to fathom. Was it a fairy tale come true? One look at Jess Willard could convince anyone that he could grind Jack's bones to make his bread. Yet, size could be deceiving, as the *Washington Times* noted:

> Matching Jack Dillon with Jess Willard may not be so very wrong. Allow that the world's champion [Willard] will have some 60 pounds advantage, some foot in height in his favor, and several inches advantage in reach, that does not mean that he will have any easy time disposing of Dillon. The Indianapolis slugger is a mixer. He is bound to get inside of Willard's left now and then, and after he has landed some of his pile-driving rights and lefts up against the champion's midrib, the latter may not look a bit bigger than his antagonist.[1]

Billed as the Pottawatomie Giant, Jess Willard stood a tall six feet, six inches and weighed 245 pounds, and he was reputed to have killed a man with a single blow; his strength was undeniable. His physical presence alone was enough to send fear through the common man. Still, Jack Dillon was no ordinary man. Unintimidated by adversaries, he fought similar to a ravenous caged lion.

Society, having evolved over the years, favored three classic characters: the modish villain, the antihero, and the underdog. In support of the perceived underdog, boxing fans were quick to recall a previous giant killer, as the *Washington Times* confirmed:

> Dillon against Willard will remind ring followers of the days when Joe Walcott made the biggest men of the ring "come down to him." Walcott did it by slugging. Hardly five feet in height and never weighing 150 pounds in his life, he knocked out real heavyweights as if they had been welters. Dillon is much after the style of Walcott. He is short and heavily built. He can take a punch to land one. Since emerging into the light heavyweight class, he has done better than he ever did as a middleweight. Willard is going to have a heap of trouble winning from the Indianapolis man.... Despite his weight, height, and reach, he [Willard] will have small advantage over Dillon, for the latter is a real fighter, not a shadow of a man.[2]

Though society finds comfort, sustenance, and indeed continuity in its myths, nothing can diffuse it more quickly than reality. Once Dillon posted an impressive record that supported his dominance over some mighty big men, no one could argue the probability of a Dillon victory. Magic beans or not, he was "Jack, the Giant Killer."

The State of Indiana

As the United States of America evolved, so too did the land that would eventually be called the State of Indiana. Not long after the formation of the country, the region was defined as the Northwest Territory, followed by the Indiana Territory, before being reduced to its current size. On December 11, 1816, President James Madison approved Indiana's admission into the union as the 19th state, and nine years later the state capital was moved from Corydon (a town in the southern part of the state) to Indianapolis (centrally located). Many European immigrants, such as Germans, Irish, and English, primarily from the Northeast, migrated west to settle in Indiana in the early nineteenth century.

The Price Family Ancestry

John D. Price was born on September 17, 1806, in Ohio.[3] He married Sarah Beckhorn Price on March 14, 1830, in Montgomery, Ohio.[4] The pair settled in Owen County, in the southeastern portion of Indiana, where they raised a large family—two boys (James and Winfield) and four girls (Julia, Hannah, Mary, and Sarah)—on their farm.[5]

John and Sarah Price welcomed Winfield Scott Price (Jack Dillon's father) on November 20, 1854.[6] As the second son, he was 12 years younger than his brother James. Much would be asked of the children, as there was always work to be done on the family farm. Instilling the value of hard work with a touch of patriotism was of prime importance to John and Sarah Price.

Winfield Scott Price was named after Winfield Scott (1786–1866), a.k.a. "Old Fuss and Feathers." Scott was a hero during the War of 1812 and became supreme commander of the United States Army from 1841 until 1861. Although he ran for the office of U.S. president as the Whig candidate in 1852, Scott was defeated by Democrat Franklin Pierce. To Winfield Scott Price, the association added a touch of immediate respect, and he enjoyed it.

During the American Civil War (1861–5), or the war between the northern U.S. states (known as the Union) and the Confederate States of America (11 Southern states), Indiana sided with the former.[7] Supportive of the Union cause—Indiana's governor was an advocate of President Abraham Lincoln—the citizens of the state immediately reacted: Forever patriotic, and born competitive, so many residents volunteered for service that many were turned away.

Young Winfield Scott Price watched as his older brother, James A. Price, marched to war with the Union Army (10th Indiana Volunteer Infantry). The entire family routinely prayed for an expedient ending to the conflict and the safe return home for James. With little choice, Winfield Scott Price quickly matured, while doing his best to fill in for his brother's family obligations. Carrying with him his father's views, which were translated from President Lincoln, Winfield's values fell more to the conservative side.[8]

Winfield Price fell in love with a local girl named Amanda Jane Sigler (1863–1931), and the pair were married on November 20, 1884, in Clinton, Indiana.[9] The couple resided at 415 N. Columbia in Frankfort, Indiana. Winfield was employed as a clerk at a grocery store. Their marriage would yield four sons, Chester B. Price (1887–1905), Russell C. Price (1889–1967), Ernest C. Price (1891–1942), and Paul W. Price (1896–1933).[10]

Taking a closer look at Frankfort: A trio of brothers—John, William, and Nicholas Pence—settled on the land on which Frankfort now stands in the early nineteenth century. Located in Clinton County, the city is situated approximately 40 miles northwest of Indianapolis.[11] Later, the altruistic family donated 60 acres of land that led to the formation of a county seat in 1830. Thanks to the controversial—and may I add financially disastrous—Indiana Mammoth Internal Improvement Act (1836) that led to the construction of canals, railroads, roads, and state-funded public schools, many areas thrived. And one of those was Frankfort, an ideal location to raise a family.

Winfield Scott Price died on February 25, 1896, while Amanda was pregnant with their last child.[12] As a result, the family departed Frankfort. By 1900, the clan was living in a rented home at 314 North Capitol Avenue in Indianapolis (Ward 6), Indiana.

Life wasn't simple for Amanda Price. As head of the household, she was caring for her family while trying to make ends meet. While the older boys were at school, she looked after her youngest son, Paul; took in lodgers; and even cared for other children. Four boys without a father yielded the typical behaviors, such as fighting for their mother's attention, not to mention fighting with one another. As rambunctious teenagers, they were undisciplined and aloof. Russell and Ernest had a rough edge to them, conceivably as a protection mechanism. As soon as the older boys could, they worked and contributed to the needs of the family. Carrying with them their father's values, albeit to various degrees, they loved and respected their mother. Knowing work was in his future, Ernest left the education system during his first year of high school. "I went to school until I was 13 years old, and the gold was gone, I had to go to work, so I got a job at the Panhandle Railroad shops, wiping the grease off of engines," Dillon stated.[13] This was not unusual for the time, as less than 10 percent of youths living in the United States had high school diplomas in 1910.[14] Not clearly conservative or liberal, the youngsters were both. Later, as Ernest matured, he favored the latter ideology. In a rare interview, Dillon reflected to the *Indianapolis Star*:

Messenger-boy jobs were sought by many Hoosier youngsters. This is the Postal Telegraph Office in Indianapolis, Indiana (1908) (Library of Congress, LC-USZ62-29117, b&w film copy negative).

> I always liked athletics and after working hours Russell Price, my brother, and myself would go out to the shed, which we had rigged up a gymnasium, and box for a couple hours each evening. I worked at the shops about a year and then went to A.D.T. as a messenger boy. We had a set of gloves over there and between runs we would go down in the basement and box. I cleaned up all the boys around the office and then one day they used a ringer on me, who turned out to be Bobby Long, a professional featherweight boxer, who was considered a comer at the time. Well, he didn't show me up and after I had learned who he was it gave me the first knowledge that I could really fight.[15]

Following a series of odd jobs, Ernest landed a role as a stable boy at Dillon Stables, which typically quartered at the fairgrounds.[16] Far from intimidating in stature, he convinced his employer he could handle the duties.[17] It was strenuous work for the youngster, yet it had its benefits; he loved animals and didn't mind the physical labor. He quickly developed a muscular physique, with his strength and coordination improving. The first to notice was his brother Russell, his regular sparring partner.

The Tragic Ring Death of Chester Price, 1905

It was a parent's worst nightmare: the death of a child. Yet, the Price family was dealt such a blow on May 28, 1905. The *Indianapolis News* reported:

Two outstanding views of downtown Indianapolis in 1907. The bottom image is West Market Street, with the Gayety Theatre located to the right (top: Library of Congress, LC-DIG-det-4a10065, digital file from original; bottom: Library of Congress, LC-DIG-det-4a22241, digital file from original).

> Chester Price, an amateur pugilist, who was sparring in a friendly bout at the Apollo Athletic Club room, at 245½ West Washington Street, yesterday afternoon, died before nightfall as the result of a brain hemorrhage, that to have been caused by a blow over the right temple. His sparring partner during the practice bout was Raymond Metcalf, the 19-year-old son of patrolman Charles P. Metcalf, of 205 Hiawatha Street.[18]

It was surmised the blow that caused the hemorrhage originated from a different location and that excessive exertion combined with the shock produced by a cold bath at the Apollo Club brought on the hemorrhage. The newspaper continued:

> Price, who was 18 years old, was formerly a Postal Telegraph messenger boy, and he worked for a time as a bellboy in the Claypool Hotel.... His mother lives in the Martens Flats, at

315 North Senate Avenue.... Detectives Manning and Simon, who investigated the case, said they were of the opinion that the death was purely accidental.[19]

With the amateur wrestling and boxing scene flourishing in Indianapolis, it wasn't long before Ernest Coulter Price opted to become a pugilist. Despite the death of his brother, he was drawn to the ring. Whether it was the opportunities and rewards it presented, or a way to avenge his brother's death, he was up for the challenge.[20] However, Ernest desired an alias—for two reasons: The first was that Ernest Coulter Price didn't sound like the name of a fighter, and the second had to do with family. Pugilism was not a respected occupation, and he wanted to protect his family—his mother—from humiliation. Thus, Ernest Price became Jack Dillon. The alias was taken from Sidney Dillon, a popular three-year-old trotter that happened to be quartered where he worked. His brother Russell Price, also interested in the fight game, became Tommy Dillon. It wouldn't take long for the boys to transform their barn into a gymnasium. During Jack's superior development, Tommy, also a prolific professional fighter, was by his side; moreover, as Jack's primary sparring partner and confidant, he was irreplaceable. He wasn't as clever as Jack in the ring, but he would prove valuable outside it. Family matters, forever confidential, were rarely shared with the public. Fighting at smokers, clubs, benefits, and bootleg battles allowed Jack Dillon to discreetly hone his skills while picking up pocket cash. And it didn't take long for those who understood pugilism to admire his potential.

Boxing in 1907

Under the subtitle "Tommy Burns' Rise to Pinnacle is Chief Feature of Year," columnist Rex Lardner summed up boxing for *The South Bend Tribune*:

> Boxing's history for the year 1907 was an eventful one and the game in spite of its struggles for existence advanced. Several states where it flourished put final quietus on it but in the principal centers it is in good shape. Noah Brusso's rise under his nom de guerre of Tommy Burns to the pinnacle of fistiana was the chief feature of the year in the ring.... Another feature was the complete squelching of foreign fighters in their attempts to wrest Burns' title from him.... Among the middleweights there is ruction. Ketchel, Ryan, Papke, Kelly and Langford all claim a share of the title and there are really others who think they might be included. Langford appears to be the equal if not the superior of any of them, but the old convenient: "color line" saves possible disgrace to one of the contenders.... Joe Gans is the chief among the lightweights and probably will die that way.... Abe Attell is America's champion featherweight ... and Johnny Coulon is given the title of bantamweight.[21]

Hoping to continue to attract people to Indianapolis, the city wasn't shy about shaping its citizenry. Entering the year 1908, *Indianapolis Star* noted:

> Indianapolis businessmen, standing on the threshold of New Year of 1908, make plea for each citizen to lay aside his grouch, strangle evil gossip of his neighbor, scatter sunshine, put his shoulder to the wheel and push hard for the good of the city until 1908 is ended.[22]

As the end of the first decade of the twentieth century was nearing, the population of Indianapolis continued to increase, reaching more than 220,000 in 1908.[23] The city was thriving in virtually every aspect, and that included boxing.

From the Beginning—1908 and 1909

1908

"I am trying, however feebly, to make men better, as well as to get better laws, better administration of the laws; and the first is by far the most important."—Theodore Roosevelt[24]

Jack Dillon began his professional boxing career under the watchful eye of Wick Davidson. Having established a relationship when Dillon was an amateur and bootleg boxer, it seemed like a good fit. The fighter made it clear he wasn't interested in a lengthy amateur career; in other words, pugilism to him was all about the coin. As a fight manager, Davidson handled a number of pugilists and worked out of assorted Indianapolis haunts including Schober's billiard room, on 118 West Ohio Street, or clubs, such as the Apollo Club at 212½ North Delaware Street. A speculator at heart, his strength was his local contacts, including those with the press.[25]

The first week of April found Jack Dillon, known locally for his quick hands at age 17, training with Willie Parson. The youngster was scheduled to meet Jimmy Kelly over six rounds on April 18. Boxing was dynamic, however, and things could mutate at a moment's notice. Back in March, Kid Brown, a popular Indianapolis pugilist who hailed from nearby Fortville, wanted an opportunity to engage with Dillon, or in other words replace Kelly, and got it—it helps to be handled by the same fight manager. Kid Brown and Jack Dillon "went six hard rounds" at the Marion Club.[26] The event, which included two boxing bouts and one wrestling match, proved entertaining.

Although quiet compared to others his age, Dillon exhibited no lack of confidence, as the *Indianapolis Star* reported:

> Jack Dillon, the newcomer to the local fight fraternity of glove wielders, who weighs 128 pounds, is out with a challenge to meet any boy in the middle West who can make his weight. Dillon's first professional bout took place a few weeks ago when he held Kid Brown of Fortville to a six-round draw.[27]

Speaking of Brown, it appeared as if he and Dillon would rematch on May 28. The 10-round bout was discreetly scheduled to be held at Crystal Theater in Martinsville. However, when Sheriff Bain caught wind that the fight was being advertised "for blood," matters quickly changed.[28] Such an event was forbidden by law, and the local administrator made it very clear that he would uphold the rules and regulations.

To stay in shape, and to showcase his skills, Jack Dillon participated in various local shows, as the *Indianapolis Star* noted:

> Jack Dillon and Young Saylor, two of the most promising boxers at their weights in the city, put up one of the most interesting friendly exhibition bouts ever seen in this city last night when the two donned the big gloves at the Apollo Athletic Club. For four rounds the youngsters kept the fur flying. It was only a workout, as both are under the same manager. Both boys in action looked to be possessed of real class and they will no doubt make good next fall.[29]

Dillon also sparred with other local boxers—many preparing for larger shows—to pick up pocket cash. Another alternative form of income, albeit illegal and unpredictable, was bootleg boxing matches.

Bootleg Boxing

On August 5, 1908, Jack Dillon accepted a challenge from Ben Harper to meet at a secluded spot north of Indianapolis. Word traveled like the wind, and it wasn't long before streetcars filled with fight fans were headed out of town for the nine o'clock battle. Not surprisingly, the excitement created by a banned bootleg battle far surpassed that generated by a legal exhibition. Upon reaching the end of the line, fans departed their form of transportation. Guides led them by foot to a remote wooded area. They found a ring there, lit by torches, set up in a clearing. Following a considerable delay, both participants were seen entering the area. The *Indianapolis Star* described the action, or lack of:

> Still the fight did not start. Dillon looked about the crowd and remarked that it did not look like it had money enough for him to fight for. He said he wanted $10 to the loser and $15 to the winner. Soon the referee with the purse money, which proved to be $20, made his appearance. Harper's backer placed $10 more as a side bet for the match, and Dillon failed to cover the bet. He said there was not enough money in sight for him to fight. He wanted $35 for the winner. There was not that much in the crowd, and Harper offered to fight him for nothing, so as not to disappoint the crowd. Dillon still refused and, after considerable debating, or, as the assembled sportsmen called it, "ragging," it was officially announced that the fight would not be held.[30]

To say those in attendance were upset would be an understatement. Adding to the discomfort was the long trek back through the dark, swampy woods. When one of the departing fans mentioned that he would pay an additional dollar should the participants opt for a bare-knuckle brawl, it briefly excited the crowd. However, that sensation was quelled by regret when the offer failed.

Told every boxing manager had limitations, Jack Dillon agreed to have Izzy Brill, a popular matchmaker, take over his affairs in August.[31] The action would begin an endless transition of new fight management (roughly two dozen), that in retrospect proved detrimental to his career. It would stall his development, limit his fight options, and decrease his revenue potential. Even Sam Murbarger, the only person genuinely qualified for the position, would later confirm the intractable difficulties managing the pugilist; incidentally, his perspective mirrored that of his predecessors.

Brill had Dillon working out with James "Young" Milburn Saylor at the Hoosier Gymnastic Club. Similar to Dillon, Saylor exhibited considerable potential and had even met, and lost, to Johnny Kilbane, a promising Midwest featherweight. On August 25, Jack Dillon picked up a copy of the *Indianapolis Star* and immediately turned to page 8. There he found a three-column-wide photograph of himself—touché, Izzy—under the title "Local Boxer Said to Be Comer." One of the two paragraphs beneath his image read:

> His style of milling is far different from any of the local boys, similar to that of Battling Nelson's. He sails right into an opponent with his head down, using his boring-in tactics with good effect. He carries a sleep-producing pill in either mitt and can take punishment without winning.[32]

Thrilled to see himself prominently displayed at the top of the sports section, Dillon could not have been happier. Nor could Brill, who was no stranger to such forms of job security.

Advertised as a sparring exhibition, Jack Dillon knocked out Jack Laffy (Laffey) in the fourth round of a scheduled six-round battle. The September 19 event was held at the Marion Club. Choosing discretion over detail, accounts of the fight were brief. Local boxing remained cautious in the way they were presenting their events to avoid police interference. The line of demarcation between prizefighting and exhibitions was as small as a grain of salt.

Following two bouts—victories over Lem Potter and Tom DeLane on October 5 and 27, respectively—in October, Jack Dillon packed his bags for an exhibition in Muskogee, Oklahoma, scheduled for November 3.[33]

Upon returning to Indiana, Dillon defeated Pat Lark on November 13, in Indianapolis, before traveling to Dayton, Ohio, where he drew Teddy Malone (Tony Mullane) over 10 rounds.

Finishing out the year by defeating Tommy Clark on December 19 at the Marion Club, Dillon had few regrets. Both fighters scaled at 130 pounds. It was 10 fast-paced rounds, with both fighters refusing to give ground. As the *Indianapolis Star* noted, "Both were in good shape, and they went at each other hammer and tongs from the opening tap of the bell to the finish."[34]

1909

"If they will play fair I will play fair, but if they won't then I reserve all my rights to do anything I find myself able to do."—William Howard Taft, president of the United States (1909–13)

In 1908, Joe Gans, a 3–1 favorite, hit the canvas multiple times in a knockout loss to Battling Nelson out in Colma, California (July 4); Billy Papke gave Stanley Ketchel a vicious beating over 11 rounds during a controversial knockout victory in Vernon, California (September 7); Ketchel avenged his loss to Papke by knocking him out in the 11th round in Vernon, California (November 26); and Jack

Two images of Ray Bronson (August 1887–January 1948), who was a welterweight contender and one of the most popular pugilists in Indianapolis (circa 1912).

Johnson became the first Black heavyweight champion by knocking out Tommy Burns in Sydney, Australia (December 26).

As for the underpinning of these actions, it was a year of race and retribution. Johnson, the world heavyweight champion, so dominated his weight class that a "white hope" heavyweight championship was created in anticipation of discovering a qualified Caucasian challenger. Nelson avenged his previous loss—via a disqualification in the longest fight in modern boxing history (42 rounds)—to Gans. Ketchel took vengeance for his defeat by brutally beating Papke to such an extent that his own wife failed to recognize him. And California, where boxing was legal (as was serving alcohol), proved that the sport of boxing could thrive given befitting, though that could strike some as debatable, conditions.

As the preeminent sport, boxing was a crystal ball into the future. Unfortunately, not everyone viewed it as such.

Regional boxing markets, such as Indianapolis, varied on their perspective of the sweet science. Two days into the new year, newspapers such as the *Indianapolis News* were already noting the demand for Indianapolis boxers:

> There is a strong demand for the services of several Indianapolis boxers. Ray Bronson has accepted an offer from a Dayton, Ohio, fight club to meet featherweight champion Abe Attell there January 13, at 128 pounds, and all now remains is for Attell to sign articles.[35]

While Bronson, who debuted professionally in 1905, was the most promising local fighter at the time, Abe Attell never agreed to an initial set of articles, nor was he an easy person to negotiate with. Newspaper pieces similar to this were typically printed as favors to promotors or fight managers, with hopes of arousing public interest or gauging demand. And they occasionally worked. Abe Attell would make it to Dayton—it was a rarity to get him to fight outside California—but he would fight Frank White, not Ray Bronson.

The Indianapolis Miners' Convention, which attracted thousands of people, was held in Indianapolis during the month of January. Ever since boxing exhibitions became a staple at mining camps, the popularity of the sport among miners increased. Thus, it was no surprise that an attractive boxing promotion was conducted in the Auditorium on January 22. The *Indianapolis Star* provided a preview:

> No tickets will be sold and the mine workers who will be here to attend the big convention will be the only persons who will have the opportunity of seeing what will undoubtedly be the most interesting bouts seen staged in this city since the "lid" was clamped down. A treat is surely promised for the miners, and they will be envied by hundreds of lovers of the glove game, who must be contented with hanging around, waiting for the result, like the street Arab at the ball park.[36]

Jack Dillon, referred to as "the crack local lightweight," was scheduled to meet Joe McAree (McCrea) in one of the six-round preliminaries.[37] Although this would be a catchweight battle, both Indianapolis club fighters would scale around the 130 mark.[38]

Winning the first bout of the year would have been far better for Jack Dillon had it not been via a disqualification. Even so, a victory was a victory, and the exposure would benefit his career. Immediately impressing spectators with his actions, Dillon appeared invincible. Regrettably, the excitement of the battle concluded when a frustrated McAree was disqualified for fouling in the fourth round. As the *Indianapolis News* noted:

> These boys started at a sizzling clip and the first round was unusually fast. McAree carried a hard punch, and he dazed Dillon once or twice when he landed. Dillon was the stronger, however, and McAree had little chance after the opening round.[39]

As a result of his success, Jack Dillon was booked to meet Kid Sims (Simms) in a four-round preliminary on February 3. Although Simms, who began strong, was viewed as having potential, Dillon soon altered his status with a third-round knockout. Under the auspices of the Indianapolis Athletic Club, the regular

Wednesday evening boxing shows, of which this event was a part, were held at the Auditorium and typically began at 8:30 at night. Admission was $1.50 (reserved) and $1.00 (general).

Dillon's aggressiveness in the ring could be mirrored outside it. The teenager could be blunt, edgy, hostile, resentful, and unforgiving. As Dillon lost patience with his manager, Izzy Brill, whom he believed was moving him along at a snail-like pace, it was time for a change. Dillon felt his skills had earned him better bookings, and Brill wasn't delivering. Thus, Dillon signed under Cecil Day, a popular local sportsman.[40]

Day, who owned a gymnasium located at 901 West Twenty-Seventh Street in Indianapolis, put Dillon on an aggressive training schedule. Working diligently to match his fighter against Charles Humphries, a popular local fighter, Day succeeded. The pair squared off for a scheduled 10-round battle inside the Marion Club on February 20. An enthusiastic crowd of 500 spectators turned out for the benefit and witnessed Jack Dillon delivering his adversary with ease in the second round. Both the attendance and performance were impressive. The most popular event of the evening was a racist affair called a battle royal. Six Black men took part in the fight to the finish.[41]

One way to gauge the skills of a boxer was the respect of his peers. The *Indianapolis Star* noted:

> The Indianapolis Athletic Club promoter is seeking a good, strong 130-pound boxer to tackle Jack Dillon, the undefeated Indianapolis fighter who of late has proven "class" in all of his ring encounters.[42]

The dilemma, especially in a boxing market such as Indianapolis, confirmed the respect Jack Dillon had already achieved. In late February, Pat Lark, Ray Bronson's sparring partner, substituted for Tommy Dawson, who was originally slated to meet Dillon on March 3. The bout was a six-round semi-windup, at the 30-round boxing card being held at the Auditorium. Meanwhile, Ray Bronson was off to New Orleans to meet Freddie Welsh, the talented United Kingdom boxer.[43] Speaking of Bronson, Jack Dillon had signed to meet the lightweight contender at the gymnasium in Hartford City, Indiana, on March 12.

In an attempt to drive ticket sales for the regular Wednesday evening boxing show at the Auditorium, the press opted for this slant: "The six-round bout scheduled between Jack Dillon and Pat Lark promises additional interest because of the rivalry between the Hoosier Athletic Club and the Bronson Club, of which the boys are respective members. Dillon is giving several pounds to Lark."[44] Despite the hype, Dillon's bout against Lark proved little more than target practice. Dominating the six-round points victory, Dillon danced around Lark's rushes while pummeling his countenance like a carpenter over a 16-penny nail. Yet, to Lark's credit, he made distance.

To stay sharp for his upcoming clash against Ray Bronson, Jack Dillon participated in a four-round exhibition against Kid Griffin (Griffith) the following day

(March 4). And that was precisely what the affair was. Granted, the word "exhibition" was commonly used to mask an unlawful boxing match, but this encounter appeared to be little more than a display of skills and accuracy. It was doubtful Dillon would have agreed to a meaningful contest the day after he fought Lark. The engagement was for the Retail Hardware Association Convention being held in Indianapolis. A large faction of the "tin men" found spots inside the Grand Lodge Hall of the Knights of Pythias building to witness an entertaining evening that included everything from comedy to pugilism. Dillon toyed with his challenger, who took a terrible beating during the affair.

Ray Bronson: The Real Deal

With more than 40 professional bouts as experience, John Ray Bronson was a talented pugilist with a winning record. True, the five-four lightweight was coming off a disappointing 13-round loss, via TKO (technical knockout), to elite boxer Freddie Welsh, but he would be prepared for Jack Dillon. As the most popular pugilist in Indianapolis, he exhibited nothing but potential, and he had earned it.

Ray Bronson and Jack Dillon had much in common: Both were former messenger boys, loved animals and worked with them (Bronson was a blacksmith), developed their physiques courtesy of their occupations, turned to pugilism to pick up extra cash (Bronson began his professional career in 1905), and fought out of Indianapolis.

An ebullient crowd, estimated at 350, turned out to witness Ray Bronson battle Jack Dillon inside the gymnasium in Hartford City, Indiana.[45] As anticipated, both Indiana boxers were warmly greeted. Measuring distances and acclimating themselves to the pace of the fight in the first two rounds, both fighters were cautious. Dillon picked up the pace in the third and was delivering multiple blows for each punch received. Bronson, try as he might, could not dance away from Dillon's precision strikes. Relying on a solid right uppercut, Dillon appeared in control during the opening rounds.

Noting the sixth and final frame, *Star Press* reported:

> The sixth round proved to be Bronson's, although Dillon made a game fight for it. Bronson landed several telling blows that completely stopped Dillon, showing so much superiority that it was conceded that he would probably have put Dillon away in a few more rounds, had he desired. No decision was given, although Bronson will probably receive the long end of the purse of $150. Dillon will get $50 for the fight he put up, and his future contests will be watched by local fight followers, with whom he made a hit on account of the cleverness which he displayed in the fight tonight.[46]

Was Dillon fatigued during the final rounds? It appeared that way. Did Bronson win by a shade? Likely, as many spectators were left with that impression. The legal outcome was a no decision; however, most record books claim it was a draw.

Giving himself a few days of rest, Jack Dillon replaced Lee Patterson, who was scheduled to meet Bobby Long, in a four-round semi-windup bout on March 31. The battle was part of the regular Wednesday boxing show held at the Auditorium in Indianapolis. As part of an established Auditorium rule, no decisions were given. That said, the *Indianapolis News* claimed, "Dillon outweighed Long several pounds and their exhibition was of the friendly kind, with Dillon clearly the superior."[47]

A Line of Demarcation

Speaking of rules, identifying the difference between a legal boxing exhibition and an illegal prizefight was no simple task. Noting that a boxing card being advertised—at the Mitchell Club on April 2—appeared similar to the latter, the local police felt it was time for them to witness the competition for themselves. The event included Jack Dillon. Thus, Lieutenant Sandmann and company decided to occupy a portion of the ringside seats. The *Indianapolis Star* detailed:

> They were there with the expressed intention of enforcing the law regarding boxing shows. Ten-ounce gloves were used throughout, instead of the six-ounce ones as is generally the rule. Consequently, the preliminaries, which would have been fast, became inoffensive pillow fights.... A crowd of 500 persons, including the police, witnessed the revised card [participants, gloves, rounds per bout, etc.] and 200 more walked away when the announcement of the change was made.[48]

Dillon, who could have walked away, did not. Alterations or not, he was there to fight. The newspaper continued:

> Jack Dillon took on "Kid" Gray. They were booked for eight rounds. It was cut to six and then stopped in the second when Jack floored the "Kid" with a hearty wallop to the mouth that drew blood. It was announced that Gray had hurt his hand. Even if the bout had been eight rounds it likely would not have gone the limit.[49]

Without comment, Jack Dillon returned home. Scheduled to meet Terry Nelson, of Chicago, on April 28 inside the Auditorium, Dillon remained optimistic that boxing would sort out its legality issues.[50] It could not, and due to the recent police intervention, this event was canceled.

One way to avoid police intercession was to conduct the sport in smaller venues, such as the Knights of Columbus. Exclusive membership meant limited access. On May 10, the local order of the club witnessed Jack Dillon take a five-round decision over Young Conners. The referee for the bout was none other than Izzy Brill. Regrettably, even the restricted exposure aroused police interest. It was time to get out of town.

Next stop, Terre Haute, Indiana, where Jack Dillon knocked out Jimmy Kid Sullivan in the third round of a preliminary battle on May 28. As the *Indianapolis News* saw it:

> Sullivan's seconds tried to end it earlier by throwing in the sponge first, and later the towel, but Sullivan insisted on fighting. He repeatedly covered up his head with his hands

and Dillon pounded away at him, sending him down repeatedly for almost the count. When he was finally counted out, he was unable to get up without assistance.[51]

In one of those "say it ain't so" moments, the referee of the main event counted wrong, and instead of the bout (Andy Bezenah versus Freddie Cole) going 10 rounds, it went 11.

Back in Terre Haute, Jack Dillon was scheduled for a 10-round battle against Tommy Scanlon, a popular local fighter, on July 2. Despite a gallant display, Scanlon was no match for Dillon. Noting their fighter's fatigue and inability to protect himself, Scanlon's seconds threw up the towel in the sixth round. Having been dropped three times that term, Scanlon looked relieved. According to the *Brazil Daily Times*:

> The semi-wind up between Tommy Scanlon of Brazil [Indiana] and Jack Dillon, led off in a way that promised to be interesting. The men agreed to fight in the clinches, and this proved a disadvantage to Scanlon since Dillon had him bested in this department of the game.[52]

Jack Dillon returned home, with his next bout set for July 22, when he would head to Anderson, Indiana, or about 35 miles northeast of Indianapolis. In the meantime, he trained at The Carnation Club, a modern workout center that included everything a boxer desired to optimize his training. From a 16-foot ring to a variety of free weights, it was a boxer's paradise. The *Indianapolis Star* noted:

> These are busy days at the Carnation Club, where boxers are getting trim for their respective bouts, Jack Dillon, the most promising young lightweight this city has had for some time, is working daily with his sparring partners Nate Fob [Farb] and Jimmy Watts, in preparation for his go with [Everett] Barber Reeves of Anderson at that place July 22.[53]

The winner of this bout was said to be matched against Ray Bronson. However, that proved more of an enticement than reality.

Entering the Grand Opera House in Anderson, Jack Dillon, noticeably heavier than his opponent, pounded Everett Reeves like a throw rug during spring cleaning. Dillon, who announced his weight at 137 pounds, or 13 pounds heavier than Reeves, used every ounce to his advantage. The referee, noting the punishment Reeves was taking, had little choice but to stop it in the fifth round. As the *Indianapolis News* noted:

> Considering the difference in weight and the fact that the unbeaten Dillon was far more experienced, the showing of Reeves pleased his army of Anderson followers who completely filled the Grand Opera House.[54]

When Ray Bronson was matched for a 20-round bout against Packey McFarland—a fight scheduled for September 12 in New Orleans—a training camp needed to be selected and prepared. Walter Owens, who was handling the training camp for Bronson, selected White City Park, owned by the Broad Ripple Transit Company. The facility, which was recovering from a catastrophic fire the previous year, was capable of hosting the camp on a beach area near their

Downtown Anderson, Indiana, located just over 43 miles northeast of Indianapolis. According to the U.S. Census Bureau, it had a population of 22,476 in 1910.

enormous concrete pool. With large crowds anticipated to watch Bronson train, it appeared the ideal location. As for the ideal sparring partner, during the daily four-round exhibition, Jack Dillon's name was the first mentioned. The youngster jumped at the opportunity. And, as kismet might have it, his decision paid dividends.

On August 25, Jack Dillon was inked to meet Jack Redmond, of New Orleans, in a 10-round semi-windup to the Bronson–McFarland battle being held at the West Side Athletic Club. Redmond was an adroit fighter who had been in the ring with Ad Wolgast and Eddie McGoorty. It was Bronson who suggested to the promoters that his sparring partner could handle the bout, and they agreed. Sid Cox, who was now handling Dillon's affairs, hoped to land his fighter a warm-up bout prior to the event. Was this Jack Dillon's big break? Dillon wasn't sure, but the exposure was huge, and he intended to deliver the finest performance of his career.

Typical of large promotions, alterations were made: When the date of the bout was amended to September 19, Jack Redmond was unable to make it, and an alternative needed to be selected.

Ray Bronson and Jack Dillon arrived in New Orleans on September 14. Immediately they were greeted with the news: a large crowd was anticipated on September 19 at the West Side Athletic Club, which seated six thousand. Three days later, Dillon learned he would meet Kid Sparks, who was Packey McFarland's sparring partner—the pairing not unusual for this era of boxing. Although Dillon would have rather met Redmond, Sparks made more sense. At this point Dillon wasn't prepared to meet a talent like Redmond.

It was quick, but far from painless, as the *Indianapolis News* reported:

> Kid Sparks, of Louisville, McFarland's trainer, and Jack Dillon, of Indianapolis, sparring partner of Bronson, furnished the single preliminary. Dillon battered Sparks to pieces in one- and one-half rounds, knocking him to the floor three times. On the third occasion he took the final count.[55]

In the main event, the undefeated Packey McFarland, who held victories over Freddie Welsh and Jimmy Britt, was held to a draw by Ray Bronson. After the verdict was announced, both participants were greeted with a 15-minute standing ovation.

Although Dillon dominated his opponent—not to mention turned a few heads—he suffered an unspecified strain that required an operation. Once recovered from his injury, Dillon began working himself into shape at Ray Bronson's club at 39½ South Illinois Street in Indianapolis. Both he and Young Donnelly planned to assist Bronson's training for a potential match against Ad Wolgast.

Jack Dillon was next matched against Jimmy Cooley. The six-round bout, initially scheduled for December 3, was to be held at the Mitchell Athletic Club. However, it was postponed due to Dillon's injury. At one point, it looked as if Jack Dillon would meet Ford Munger in Saginaw, Michigan, at the Valley Athletic Club, but the governor banned the bout.

In his final bout of the year, on December 21, Jack Dillon fought six challenging rounds to defeat Jimmy Cooley. Even though Dillon had the edge, both boxers were on their feet at the finish. As the *Indianapolis News* reported:

> The boys boxed hard from the first gong, and they were swinging fast at the final bell. Dillon was the cleverer and his judgement of distance was better. Cooley was in fair form,

Ernest Coulter Price was born on February 2, 1891, in Frankfort, Indiana. He stood five feet, seven and a half inches and was as handsome as he was talented (circa 1910).

and he early demonstrated that he carried a punch that was to be respected. Dillon never stopped, however, and forced the boxing throughout. After Dillon turned loose in the second round, Cooley's only chance to win was with a lucky punch.[56]

It was a gratifying way to finish the year.

In late December, John Tracey, an Indianapolis heavyweight, who had advised Dillon in past bouts, was signed to condition the fighter for his future bouts. As a former sparring partner of Marvin Hart, Tracey understood the fight game and worked well with both Dillon and his manager, Nate Farb.[57]

Though boxing often taught a youth self-discipline, tenacity, and physical fitness, not everyone at the turn of the century saw it that way. Many viewed it as an outlet for hostile behavior and a primitive form of communication catering to the illiterate. It was ironic: city gentry, who publicly abhorred the sport, often purchased the most expensive tickets. They condemned it at social functions, yet privately were certain to attend the fight and sit in the very best seats. It was a contradiction.

For most participants, it was a schooling in life, but for those who excelled at the sport, it could be a professional path out of poverty. And that thought appealed to many.

For Jack Dillon, age 18, boxing created boundless self-confidence. He enjoyed knowing that he wasn't only as good as an opponent, but better. Where it would take the talented teenager was anybody's guess at this stage of his life. As the decade concluded, Jack Dillon, with close to two years of experience and more than 20 professional fights, exhibited nothing but promise. Undefeated—granted, he had drawn a few and come razor close to defeat in his bout against Ray Bronson—he had faced primarily novice pugilists, a.k.a. tomato cans, or those trying to decide if they had a future in the sport. Still, the activity was vital to his development. And the teenager seldom failed to make an impression. Dillon's bout against Bronson, by far the most talented adversary he had faced, provided him a blast of assurance while increasing his market exposure. By sparring with Bronson, he picked up valuable training, and even a spot on a major fight card. If there was a criticism of the fighter, and there was, it was his tendency to dispose of fight managers like tissues. Frustrated by the development process, he wanted more out of the fight game, and he wanted it now. Jack Dillon required someone who understood his needs and knew how to meet them. He exuded an abundance of aplomb, but his immaturity surfaced at times, reminding people of his age. Keeping him in check and focused on the task at hand might cost a fight manager his job, yet that was what the youngster required.

Chapter Two

A New Decade, 1910

"Believe you can and you're halfway there."—Theodore Roosevelt

Invigorated by a new year, Jack Dillon felt great. A new training facility, the Dillon Athletic Club, located at Thirty-Third Street and Sutherland Avenue in Indianapolis, along with a new manager, Clint Truesdale, unquestionably contributed to his excitement. Assisting him for his initial battle of 1910 were Larry Donavan and Willie Fitzgerald. The personnel were in place as the members of Team Dillon readied themselves for a trip to Newport, Kentucky—about 100 miles as the crow flies—to greet Jasper Roberts on January 31.[1] Reducing his fight frequency to one or occasionally two bouts a month gave Dillon more time to heal and prepare for his competition. And according to vernacular, "the extra time looked good on him."

Fight Articles

First things first: Fight articles for the Dillon-Roberts contest were signed on January 18, 1910. In a rare glimpse into the world of pugilism, the *Cincinnati Enquirer* printed the agreement:

Articles of agreement entered into by and between Jasper Roberts, of Cincinnati, Ohio, party of the first part, and Jack Dillon, of Indianapolis, Indiana, party of the second part.
  *It is agreed by both parties that they shall fight a scheduled ten-round bout before the Clifton Athletic Club, of Newport, Kentucky, on the evening of January 31, 1910.
  *It is agreed and understood by both parties that they shall fight at 145 pounds ringside.
  *Both parties agree to post twenty-five ($25) dollars as appearance money with the sporting editor of THE CINCINNATI ENQUIRER by January 21, 1910, which amount is to be forfeit in case of the failure of either party to appear to go on before the said club.
  *Both parties agree to fight at straight rules.
  *Both parties agree to the use of bandages.
  *Both parties agree to the use of the regulation five-ounce gloves.
  *It is further agreed and understood by both that the referee shall be named not later than January 28, 1910.
  *Clint H. Truesdale, for Jack Dillon.
  *Harry Keitz, for Jasper Roberts.
  *Witness: J.M. Monahan.
  *It is hereby understood by and between the above parties of the first, and second part

The very first prediction, made by manager Clint Truesdale, that Jack Dillon was on his way to becoming a champion (*The Indianapolis Star*, April 4, 1910).

> that they are to receive from the Clifton Athletic Club forty (40) percent of the gross receipts that accrue from the attendance at said club on the night of January 31, 1910, and that said receipts are to be divided between the parties of the first and second parts as may be hereafter agreed upon.
>
> *In acknowledgement of the above conditions the manager of the said club has hereunto affixed his name on the 18th day of January 1910. —Wm. Wulftange.[2]

As one reads through the stipulations, it is easy to understand how some clauses could become potential sticking points during negotiation. On to the fight.[3]

Jack Dillon delivered a short right hand with such force that many ringside at the Clifton Athletic Club couldn't believe their eyes. Instantly, it was lights out for Jap Roberts in the second round. The *Cincinnati Post* noted the action:

> Roberts had the best of the first round, landing repeatedly with his left, and Dillon went to his corner groggy. Before the close of the second round, which was full of action, Dillon pushed Roberts away with his left and quickly landed his right to the point of the jaw and Roberts went down and out.[4]

Returning home, Jack Dillon was scheduled for a rematch against Jimmy Cooley at the Mitchell Athletic Club on February 8. The highly anticipated eight-round bout promised to be entertaining and was. Looking far better than in his previous match with Dillon (December 21, 1909), Cooley was in fine physical condition, and his punches, specifically his uppercuts, were noticeably improved. As the *Indianapolis Star* reported:

> The first round was fairly even with Dillon shooting a left to the nose at the bell. The boys set a faster pace in the second round and Dillon sent a hard right to the head that slowed Cooley a bit. Dillon had a shade in this round, but Cooley came back strong and evened matters with a left and right to the head. Dillon had the better of the work at close range and before the bell gained a lead on Cooley. The boys did not lose a bit of time in the fourth round, and Cooley, who was outgeneraled in this session lost his head and was rushed through the ropes. Dillon had the shade in this round, but in the fifth Cooley sent a stiff left to the jaw and made a better showing at close range.[5]

Dillon, who had a weight advantage, used it when he could. Unlike in their first bout, Cooley was able to slow Dillon's assaults. It was a fast-paced crowd-pleaser that many saw even.

The month of February ended up a bust for Jack Dillon. His management failed to find a promoter to take Dillon's bout against Willie Fitzgerald, his sparring partner. However, March appeared better: Dillon was about to encounter a fistic memory he would forever remember.

A Visit from James J. Corbett

What a thrill it was for fans to see James J. Corbett, the former heavyweight champion and stage actor, in person. The only man ever to defeat John L. Sullivan rolled into Indianapolis during the final week of February. In addition to appearing at the Colonial Theatre, Corbett trained at the Marion Club. As James J. Jeffries's principal second for his battle against Jack Johnson at Reno on July 4, not to mention a man of the stage, he too wanted to be in tip-top condition. At age 43, Corbett, who scaled at 184½, looked impressive. As the *Indianapolis Star* noted:

> Mr. Corbett said he will be glad to have Charles Olson and Jack Dillon play handball with him at the Marion Club this week. He also intimated that he may put on the gloves with Dillon for a little fun.[6]

True to his word, Corbett did spar three short and uneventful exhibition rounds with Dillon. Asked about Jeffries's chances against Johnson, world heavyweight champion Corbett replied: "Can Jeff win? Well, I should say he can. All he needs is to get down to brass tacks. That colored man has lots of the real article, but if it ever comes to a case of winning on gameness he is gone."[7]

Replacement Therapy

Jack Dillon was intensely training for his battle against Willie Fitzgerald. Originally scheduled for February 13, at the Grand Opera House in Anderson, Indiana, it was rescheduled for March 8. To answer your question before you ask:

Yes, Fitzgerald was working with Dillon, and this could be a quid pro quo for his services. Dillon also needed the money, however, and spectator interest was high.

Dillon, along with his manager, departed Indianapolis the night before the contest. Both were in good spirits and ready to meet at 142 pounds. The referee for the bout was Marion Scott, from Indianapolis. Anticipation was high as the *Indianapolis Star* reported:

> About 200 local boxing fans are expected to journey to Anderson to witness the contest and arrangements have been made for special cars to run from Anderson to this city after the show to bring the fans home.... Dillon and his manager expect to invade the South for matches in about two weeks.[8]

Within hours, Team Dillon was greeted with disbelief: Willie Fitzgerald was unable to meet Jack Dillon owing to the death of his father. Therefore, a substitute for the eight-round match had to be found. After extending their thoughts and prayers to Fitzgerald, Team Dillon waited patiently for the solution. Joe Hennings, promoter at the Grand Opera House, quickly scrambled to find an adequate opponent. And he succeeded. Enter Ray Bronson, who would take Fitzgerald's place. For fight fans—no offense to Fitzgerald—it was like a dream come true. And when it was over, not a soul was disappointed.[9]

Eight fast and furious rounds had fans on the edge of their seats. The *Muncie Evening Press* provided the details:

> In the second round Dillon drew blood from Bronson's mouth by a heavy uppercut and in the third round Dillon had decidedly the better of things until near the end of the round when Bronson floored Dillon. During the fourth round with several heavy uppercuts Dillon staggered and finally floored Bronson, but Bronson held on like a bulldog until the gong sounded. In the fifth round the men fought doggedly and with great determination. In the sixth and seventh rounds neither had a shade the better of the other. In the eighth round Bronson fought with his head down as though trying for a knockout but the gong sounded before he could find an opening.[10]

About 1,500 fans watched, many in shock, as both fighters separately hit the canvas—later, both fight managers dismissed the significance of the knockdowns. It was one of those battles in which it looked in every round like a knockout was imminent. It was, in other words, a rousing eight rounds of boxing where spectators were afraid to sit in their chairs.[11]

Ad Wolgast, the lightweight champion, was showing in a vaudeville act at the Empire Theatre in Indianapolis on March 30, 1910. He was scheduled to box a three-round exhibition with Jack Dillon on March 29; however, Young Donnelly took his place. Dillon's manager heard a rumor that his fighter intended to land a knockout against Wolgast. Dillon, who smirked when asked about it, denied the gossip. Could it have it been true? You betcha!

Focused on defeating Rube May, the Michigan welterweight champion, on April 2, Dillon avoided distractions, one of which was food. The pair were doing battle at 142 pounds, which meant Dillon had three pounds to trim before the following Saturday evening.

It took no more than half a contest, or five rounds, for Jack Dillon to beat Rube May into submission. Far too strong for the Michigan champion, the Hoosier pugilist saw to it that May took a nine count in each round leading up to the fifth. Landing practically at will, Dillon had his adversary's body scarred from body punches, while the blood flowed from May's nose like a waterfall. Though the victory wasn't disputed, the ending was. The first version was, when it was clear that May was helpless, the referee stopped the bout, while the other had May down, but not out, awaiting the conclusion of the count. Regardless, Dillon dominated the affair. Of the 1,500 in attendance, none questioned the termination.

Upon his return home from Anderson, Clint Truesdale, Jack Dillon's manager, declared that his boy would "be the welterweight champion of the country in less than a year."[12] This was likely the first extrapolation of the fighter's success.

By the second week of April, Dillon was signed to meet Dick Fitzpatrick. The battle was to take place at the Grand Opera House in Anderson on April 21.[13] The *Indianapolis Star* noted:

> Dick Fitzpatrick has fought Jimmy Clabby, Honey Mellody, Mike Twin Sullivan, Martin Duffy, and former champion Joe Thomas.... Fitzpatrick and Dillon are to weigh in at 3 p.m. day of contest at 148 pounds.... Dillon is working out with Ray Bronson, the local candidate for the lightweight championship belt.[14]

Despite the résumé of Fitzpatrick, he was no match for Jack Dillon, as the *Indianapolis News* detailed:

> Dick Fitzpatrick, of Chicago, was given a severe beating by Jack Dillon, of Indianapolis, at Anderson last night. After the third round Jack outfought his heavier opponent and Fitz seemed contented to stay the ten rounds. Ray Bronson's coaching was very much in evidence, as he kept Dillon cool all the time. Jack had an opportunity in the ninth round, when he had Fitz groggy, but could not put his opponent down.[15]

About 1,500 witnessed a superb evening of boxing. The *Anderson Herald* reported: "Dillon after the fight remarked that Fitzpatrick took more punishment than any other man he ever met. Dillon did not think he had Fitzpatrick going [close to a knockout] in any round."[16] As a result of this performance, along with his victory over Rube May, Jack Dillon was offered a match before the Windsor Athletic Club of Canada, the date and opponent to be determined.

Teen Tragedies

Oscar Wilde once quipped, "There are only two tragedies in life: one is not getting what one wants, and the other is getting it." How true this would prove for Jack Dillon. Was it easy to forget Jack Dillon was a teenager? Yes. He was at that stage where his maturity was effortlessly altered by his experiences, and many times without regard to consequence. The 19-year-old pugilist planned to continue a reduced fight schedule during the month in order to dedicate more time to his athletic club and his friends. Speaking of the latter, a teenager with idle

Ray Bronson's "horseshoe punch" illustrated by Bronson (left) and Dillon (right): Step 1—Sparring for an opening; Step 2—Going into a clinch, while using your open right to push your opponent's left backward, while your left foot is outside his left foot; Step 3—Coming out of a clinch while spinning your opponent to the right, setting up the left hand; Step 4—Delivering a solid left hook, while blocking his left (Bottom graphic, *The Indianapolis Star*, May 29, 1910).

time was like a loaded gun. His revolving door of fight managers understood this, even if they could do little about it. Assisting Ray Bronson with his training, Dillon continued to refine his own skills. He also added Bronson's horseshoe punch to his arsenal.

Dillon was scheduled to meet Howard Morrow, of Benton Harbor, Michigan, on May 30. The Memorial Day bout was to take place at the Grand Opera House in Anderson. Both fighters agreed to scale at 145 pounds for the eight-round contest (it was originally scheduled for 10 rounds). As a protégé of Tommy Ryan, the former middleweight champion of the world, Morrow was anticipated to be a challenge, and he delivered. The bout was ruled a draw, and none of the two thousand spectators complained. It was an evenly matched battle with a slight edge in favor of Morrow.

Scheduled to meet Ray Bronson in Evansville, Indiana, on June 8, Jack Dillon was replaced by Kid Dalton. The action made sense: Rather than tussle with Bronson, a familiar figure, he preferred to train for his battle against Freddie Hicks, of

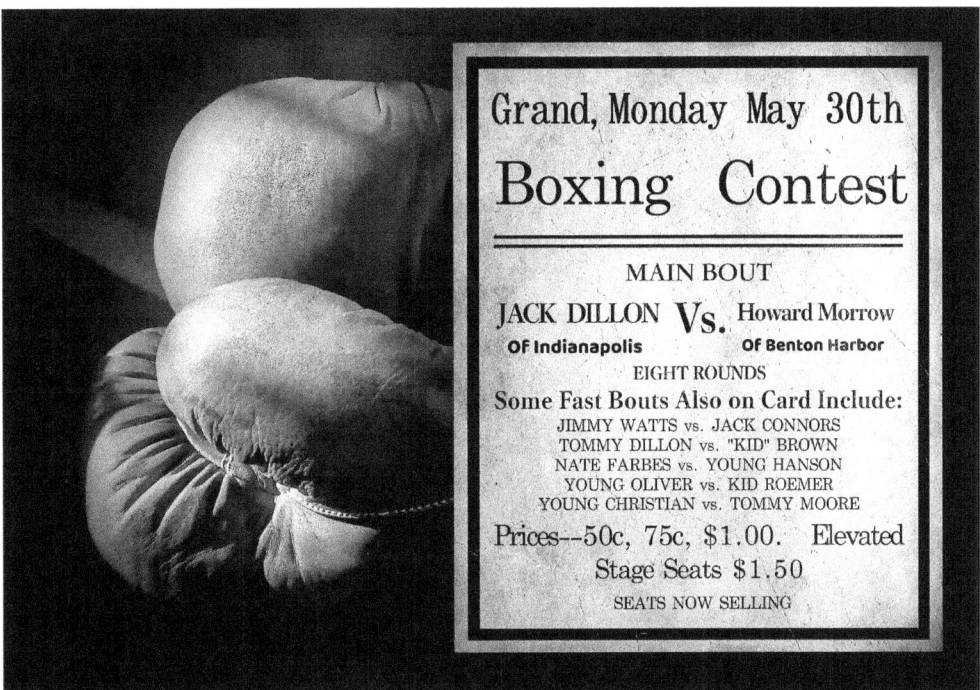

A handbill from May 30, 1910, for Jack Dillon's battle against Howard Morrow. Russell Price, a.k.a. Tommy Dillon, also appeared on the fight card. Nate Farb's name was misspelled.

Detroit. The pair were scheduled for 15 rounds, a distance Dillon had yet to experience, on June 20 at Newark, Ohio. Hicks, having fought in the city before, had become popular with fans and could fill a large portion of the Auditorium. And he did, as one thousand spectators turned out for the event. The *Indianapolis Star* detailed the action:

> In only one round was Hicks the better, in the 11th, when he landed two hard right-hand hooks on Dillon's jaw and shot two more to the wind, which made Dillon wince, and he fought a bit wild for a few seconds, but was the same careful fellow afterward. In the seventh round in a hot mix-up, it is alleged that Dillon hit low, and Hicks fell to the floor. Hicks outweighed his opponent by six pounds.[17]

As the aggressor throughout the prolonged contest, Dillon put his reach advantage to proficient use. Although he denied fouling Hicks in the seventh, it was later proven to be true—frustration undeniably played a role. Be that as it may, the Detroit fighter was given two minutes to recover during the round; incidentally, the *Indianapolis Star* viewed the incident as knockout victory for Dillon.[18]

As Dillon made distance against Hicks, his superior conditioning showed. However, it was becoming clear that the 19-year-old was outgrowing the welterweight division. His manager was convinced it was a matter of time before he stepped up to middleweight. The *Indianapolis Star* noted:

> One look at Dillon bears out the fact that he is a fighter. He is strong as an ox, built of the Jeffries style. He is good looking, with large blue eyes, an unassuming and gentlemanly mannered pugilist, in and out of the ring, and a credit to the boxing game.[19]

Jack Dillon continued working with fighters at his club, even refereeing bouts. Promising his manager that he would be ready to meet Jack Ryan in Anderson on July 28, he was taken at his word. Fighting out of Chicago, Ryan agreed to meet Dillon in a 10-round journey at 148 pounds. The bout would close the boxing season in Anderson.

Far from living up to expectation, Jack Ryan, who exhibited minimal enthusiasm during the first round, faded like the evening sun. A few light jabs to Dillon's muzzle represented his effective offensive over the first two rounds. Saved by the bell at the end of the fifth round, he could barely walk to his corner. *Indianapolis News* noted:

> After the first, which was about even, everything went Dillon's way. Ryan was shaken up badly in the second round, and from then on to the end of the fifth he hung on frantically. Dillon punished him heavily, but could not keep him at arm's length long enough to put him out. In the sixth he caught the Windy City boy coming in, and it was all over.[20]

The following day, Jack Dillon was in Muncie, Indiana, assisting Freddie Cole in his preparation for a bout against Ad Wolgast, the world's premier lightweight, on August 9. The pair would be working out of the Magic City Athletic Club in Muncie. It was time well spent as Cole went six no-decision rounds against the Michigan Wildcat. Dillon wasn't slated to do battle again until August 31, when he would face Jack Morgan at Germania Hall in Indianapolis.[21]

Gone Too Far

A boxing exhibition could transform into a prizefight—a subjective opinion—instantly, leaving police little time to react and stop an event. And it could happen at any stage of a boxing card. For example, confirmation by the authorities came during an early battle (Young McGee and Young Donnelly) on the August 31 card that included Jack Dillon. It was McGee's loss of blood that convinced Captain Crane of the Indianapolis police department to intervene and end the event.

The *Indianapolis News* provided the details:

> The final event of the evening, an eight-round bout between Jack Dillon and Jack Morgan, was called off after the police walked away with the referee, the announcer and most of the available seconds. Matchmaker Buck Carroll, for the Mitchell Club, announced that the two men would probably box at Muncie in the middle of September. Most of the interest in the program centered on this one contest, and the crowd was greatly disappointed when the announcement was made. Morgan and Dillon had already entered the ring and had been introduced when the decision was made known.[22]

Police intervention was the risk fight promoters—and fans for that matter—

took during the advent of the no-decision era. On many previous occasions the authorities looked—vision easily impaired via a pecuniary enticement—the other way, but the city of Indianapolis was currently enforcing the laws on prizefighting. Jack Dillon, none too happy with this event and the pace of his career, hired Jimmy Walters as his new manager.

Having never fought in Pennsylvania, Jack Dillon was booked to meet Jim Perry, one of the better middleweight contenders, on September 17, at Old City Hall in Pittsburgh. This would be Dillon's debut as a middleweight. Billed as a great match, it proved to be exactly that. The *Pittsburgh Post-Gazette* provided an overview:

> The main bout ... was a hummer. Both boys started off in whirlwind fashion. Perry tried for the head and Dillon fought for the body. In the first round the fighting was even, but from this time on Perry used a left to the nose that worried Dillon. In the second Perry landed hard on Dillon's nose and the blow started it bleeding. Perry kept jabbing his left to the nose and had Dillon fighting wild in the fifth. Perry landed three straight lefts to Dillon's nose without a return. Dillon was so surprised at the onslaught that he could not guard himself. He came out of the daze in a second or two and swung right and left for the body, Perry getting out of danger. In the sixth round Perry kept his left working and had Dillon's head bobbing from one side to the other. At the close of the bout both boys were mixing it in good style in the center of the ring.[23]

The bout was called a draw.[24] Welcome to the Keystone State, Mr. Dillon.

Excessive Demands

Selfishness and avarice are the cause of many troubles, and it shocked few that these conditions found a home in boxing. For the first time, word hit the newspapers that Jack Dillon had "refused" to sign articles and had "made demands" that were "so excessive" that the club in question, Magic City Athletic Club, could "not think of granting them."[25] Money was the issue. The organization wanted to reschedule Dillon's match against Jack Morgan. Behind the scenes there had been indications that Dillon was a bit demanding, but this was the first public evidence. Was this the reason he disposed of fight managers like wrapping paper on Christmas morning? Perhaps a part of it, but matchmaking also played into the action.

A week after his bout with Jim Perry, Jack Dillon inked articles for a 12-round contest in Winnipeg, Manitoba, Canada. Jack Herrick, claimant to the Canadian middleweight championship, would meet Indiana's undefeated premier welter at 152 pounds, on October 3. The event was staged by the Red River Athletic Club. Dillon, along with his manager, left for the contest on September 30.

During the first six rounds, the momentum shifted between fighters. After the sixth round, however, Herrick began to fade. At this point Dillon increased the pace and put the Canadian in a defensive position. The *Indianapolis News* reported, "At the close of the bout it was generally conceded that two more rounds would have finished Herrick."[26] It was a solid performance by the Hoosier pugilist.

When an offer to do battle against George Chip on October 21 at Old City Hall in Pittsburgh surfaced, Jack Dillon immediately accepted. Both fighters were excited about the opportunity. Chip, who had the ability to mold his offensive skills to an opponent, understood that battling the Indianapolis prospect would certainly challenge his skills. Managed by Jimmy Dime of New Castle, Pennsylvania, Chip was in good hands and no doubt would be prepared to greet Dillon.[27]

The Death of Stanley Ketchel

On October 15, 1910, Stanisław Kiecal, a.k.a. Stanley Ketchel, 24, the Michigan Assassin, was murdered at a ranch in Conway, Missouri. The pugilist was staying on the ranch of R.P. Dickerson, a friend. The dining room was built into an old porch, near a door leading into the house. While Ketchel was having breakfast, a man came through the door of the house with a rifle in his hands and commanded the pugilist, "Throw up your hands." The *Salt Lake Herald-Republican* detailed:

> The pugilist, not realizing the seriousness of the situation, smiled, and started to arise [his back facing the man], and walk toward the man [Walter Hurtz]. Before he turned completely around the man fired. The ball entered the pugilist's body below the right shoulder, coursed upward and entered the lung. The pugilist fell to the floor. The nearest physician was at Conway [40 miles east of Springfield, Missouri]. It was 45 minutes before he arrived. It was hours before the special train arrived from here [Springfield]. By that time Ketchel was in bad shape. Soon after the shooting Ketchel lost consciousness, but not before he had said that Hurtz had shot him. An hour before he died Ketchel regained consciousness, but his condition soon took a decided change for the worse. Stanley Ketchel, middleweight champion pugilist of the world, died here [Springfield, Missouri] tonight [October 15, 1910] at 7:05 o'clock.[28]

Ketchel was a natural fighter who compiled a professional record of 52–4–4, with four no decisions. A staggering 49 of his victories were by way of knockout. In a career that lasted 2,596 days, or seven years, one month, and eight days, the Michigan Assassin became one of the—if not *the*—greatest middleweights of all time.[29] His tragic loss left an enormous void in the sport, and while many would claim the vacant middleweight title, filling Ketchel's shoes would be an impossibility.

Ketchel claimed the world middleweight title in 1907. It wasn't until he defeated Billy Papke on November 26, 1908, however, that he was given universal recognition. It was the third time the pair had met.

Upon Ketchel's death, Papke was the first to lay claim to the title—it made sense, at least to him, since he had defeated Ketchel in their second fight—but he faded in performance (losing seven of his next 14 contests) before determining that he could no longer make 158 pounds ringside. Contending for the title at this point were Jack Dillon, Georges Carpentier, George Chip, Gus Christie, Jimmy Clabby, Mike Gibbons, Leo Houck, Frank Klaus, Harry Lewis, Frank Mantell, Eddie McGoorty, Dave Smith, and Jeff Smith. The scramble for the championship was on. As the group thinned due to attrition or fighters outgrowing the weight class, the claims decreased in number.[30]

George Chip

Born on August 25, 1888, in Scranton, Pennsylvania, Jurgis Čepulionis (a.k.a. George Chip) was of Lithuanian decent. Hardworking, he sought a career as a professional boxer in 1909, rather than mining the anthracite-filled hills of Pennsylvania. As Chip fought out of hamlets such as Greensburg, Herminie, Johnstown, Latrobe, Madison, and Pittsburg(h), it became immediately evident that it was a worthwhile career choice. Similar to Jack Dillon, whom he would meet a dozen times in his career, the Battling Miner was on pace toward a championship.

Jurgis Čepulionis, a.k.a. George Chip (August 25, 1888–November 6, 1960), was a Lithuanian American boxer who was the world middleweight champion from 1913 to 1914. Chip, who fought Dillon a dozen times, came to be known as a heavy puncher with an impressive knockout ratio (Library of Congress, LC-DIG-ggbain-12181, digital file from original negative).

And he would become world middleweight champion on October 11, 1913, by defeating Frank Klaus. As a heavy puncher with an impressive knockout ratio, Chip cast a large shadow for a pugilist who stood five feet, eight inches.

Jimmy Walters, Dillon's manager, felt compelled to issue this challenge the day before his fighter met George Chip:

> Since the death of champion [Stanley] Ketchel there has been considerable talk as to who should be regarded as the champion middleweight of the world. Experts everywhere seemed inclined to share the honor between Billy Papke and Frank Klaus—and this despite the fact that Jack Dillon is ready and willing to meet either of them.[31]

It was a brazen move by Walters, but a correct one. Since Ketchel had been murdered less than a week prior, one could question the timing, but Walters felt pressured to draw out Papke or Klaus and was even willing to post a forfeit to bind a match.

In a six-round fight before the National Club in Pittsburgh, Jack Dillon was given a newspaper decision over George Chip. Dillon dominated the first three rounds. When he caught Chip, who was avoiding him like the plague, he pummeled him from multiple angles. Appearing as if he was going for broke in the third frame, Dillon had Chip dazed. The Battling Miner was saved by the bell, however.

The second half of the battle was far different. Dillon, winded from the first three sessions, slowed. Both boxers traded punches in the fourth and fifth rounds, but neither fighter was in any danger. *Indianapolis Star* detailed the final round:

> The sixth and last round was wild, each man trying for a knockout, and on several occasions. Dillon landed blows which, had he had his old-time steam behind, would have brought home the money. But he could not put his man down. Chip, however, was taking no chances and hugged every time he had a chance. While no decision could be given in Pennsylvania it was the silent verdict of the newspaper men who witnessed the bout that Dillon had far best of it.[32]

This was Chip's 23rd professional bout. Though he was three years older than his Hoosier rival, he had more than a dozen fewer battles. Jack Dillon was the best opponent he had faced thus far in his career.

In his last bout of the month, Jack Dillon met Billy Berger, the East Pittsburgh Bearcat, in his hometown on October 29. The bout was scheduled for six rounds at Old City Hall. The *Indianapolis Star* described the action:

> Undismayed by the falling of a tier of seats which injured 50 people, 12 seriously, Jack Dillon of Indianapolis went in against Billy Berger at the Northern Club Show in Old City Hall here tonight and in the last two rounds had the Pittsburgh boy groggy and breaking ground. Dillon's seconds contend the last round was cut 20 seconds to save Berger from a knockout.[33]

A tier of seats collapsed during one of the semifinals, and while it delayed the action, the main event was not canceled. Berger, who held his own against Frank Klaus, was no match for the aggressiveness of Dillon—and exceptionally lucky he didn't collapse via a finishing blow.

Jack Dillon, along with manager Jimmy Walters, left for Winnipeg, Manitoba, Canada, on November 8. The pugilist was scheduled to rematch with Jack Herrick over the 12-round distance. The pair had last met on October 3; incidentally, Dillon was given the newspaper verdict in that no decision.

Attracting a large crowd, the bout failed to live up to expectations. Since a decision could not be awarded by law, it was ruled a draw. Otherwise, Dillon would have added another victory to his résumé. The *Indianapolis News* noted:

> There was little doing in the way of hard fighting until the fifth round, when the boxers mixed it in lively fashion. Dillon showed that he was the master of Herrick, notwithstanding that he weighed considerably less than his opponent. In the closing rounds Dillon was the aggressor, and he had Herrick hanging on at the finish.[34]

On November 28, Jack Dillon, in his last bout of the month, went the 20-round journey against George "Knockout" Brown, of Chicago. It was the longest fight of Dillon's young career. And he earned the decision. Taking command early, he led throughout the battle. Dillon was disappointed, however, in his failure to put his adversary away. Undergoing a miserable beating, Brown

Georgios "George" A. Contas, a.k.a. George "Knockout" Brown (August 25, 1890–September 21, 1971), was a Greek American middleweight boxer from Chicago, Illinois (Library of Congress, LC-DIG-ggbain-12860, digital file from original negative).

was saved by the bell in the 15th round; nevertheless, his perseverance impressed everyone. Since making weight bothered him, this would likely be Dillon's last bout at under 150 pounds. In the wake of the fight, Dillon decided to rest for two weeks.[35]

In his final bout of the year, Jack Dillon met Eddie McGoorty, of Oshkosh, on December 16. The bout took place in Fond du Lac, Wisconsin. Initially scheduled for January 1911, one wonders if the extra time might have worked better for Dillon. McGoorty prevailed and won the 10-round decision, much to the discontent of Dillon's friends, who considered the contest a draw. *The Times* noted:

> McGoorty had the best of the battle for seven rounds. In the fifth and sixth, Dillon showed a flash of form and drove McGoorty into the ropes repeatedly under a shower of blows.

Up to the fifth round Dillon had not landed a clean blow. McGoorty got in bad in the last round when he resorted to butting tactics. McGoorty was far more clever in straight boxing.[36]

Dillon's nose took a pounding in the first round, and it aggravated him for the remainder of the contest. With both a reach and weight advantage, McGoorty outgeneraled his opponent. It was Jack Dillon's first professional loss.

Walters, Dillon's manager, admitted telling his fighter to be cautious in the first five rounds, and he regretted it afterwards. Robbed of the decision, at least from his perspective, Dillon was disconcerted.

The Color Line

While many white fighters wanted nothing to do with Sam Langford, a Black boxer, in a boxing ring, Jack Dillon was not one of them. Dillon stated, "The eligibility of Langford as a candidate for middleweight honors rests solely on his ability to make weight. If he can do 158 pounds ringside, he is not only entitled to fight for the title but is really the first man that should get consideration, if we consider fighting ability alone."[37] Dillon hinted that Billy Papke was a coward for drawing the color line. Dillon, who would have loved the opportunity to meet Langford, thought Papke should put up his title so that either he or Langford, battling at 158 pounds, had a fair shot at the championship. Papke ignored the comments.

Fifteen bouts, a majority representing a victory or an exceptional performance, placed Jack Dillon in the contender column. Notable new experiences included: boxing outside the United States, battling at the distance of 20 rounds, boxing in the states of Wisconsin and Pennsylvania, fighting while a section of a venue collapsed, fighting opponent George Chip, opening an athletic club, and officially losing a professional bout. And a dream come true: Although it was for a short period of time, the teenage pugilist had the opportunity to spar with James J. Corbett, the former heavyweight champion. Dillon's manager, Clint Truesdale, departed, and Jimmy Walters was brought onboard. But how long would Walters last in light of his advice during the McGoorty bout?

Chapter Three

One Prolific Pugilist, 1911

> "The country is governed for the richest, for the corporations, the bankers, the land speculators, and for the exploiters of labor. The majority of mankind are working people. So long as their fair demands—the ownership and control of their livelihoods—are set at naught, we can have neither men's rights nor women's rights. The majority of mankind is ground down by industrial oppression in order that the small remnant may live in ease."—Helen Keller, *Rebel Lives*

The *Indianapolis News* noted:

> The 1910 records of Ray Bronson, Jack Dillon, and Young Saylor, the bright lights of Hoosier pugdom, have caused the promoters of the fistic game to card these youngsters for their headline events. Considering that Indianapolis is beyond the deadline as a fight town, it is doubtful if any other city in the country can show as good a bunch of boxers.[1]

Pittsburgh, with more than double the population of Indianapolis and growing much faster, was a strong demographic for pugilism. As a manufacturing epicenter for steel, it drew people from all over the world to its industrial jobs. Having fought there three times in 1910, Jack Dillon would open his year in the metropolis, inside Old City Hall. Repaired following the collapse of its seating tier, the venue was positioned to host another exciting year of boxing. Fighting under the aegis of the Northern Club, Jack Dillon met Harry Mansfield, a talented English middleweight (fighting out of Philadelphia), on January 2. Normally a teenager of few words, Dillon decided to engage the press; after all, he was turning 20 years old the following month. The *Pittsburgh Press* noted his self-assurance:

> I don't think that a man should yell about getting the worst of a decision, said Dillon last night, but in that McGoorty affair I think it was handed to me. I was never in distress, and I had McGoorty on queer street in the fifth and sixth. He came back and outboxed me in the last three rounds and got the decision. Now I want a match with Klaus and recognize that I will have to go some with Mansfield to get it. That means the English Hebrew [Harry Mansfield] will have a very busy six rounds on Monday night.[2]

And busy it was for Harry Mansfield, a.k.a. Harry Ginsburg, who lost the six-round no-decision newspaper verdict to Jack Dillon. The Englishman was out of shape, and Dillon capitalized on his languidness.

Proof that Mansfield had done his homework, even if it wasn't enough, came in the opening round when he targeted Dillon's nose to begin the flow of crimson.³ Possessing an irritating short hook, the Englishman penetrated Dillon's defense early in the bout. Later, Dillon was successful at countering his adversary's assaults, and the alterations sufficed to gain him the advantage.

Harry Gilmore, who handled the matchmaking for the Red River Athletic Club in Winnipeg, inked Jack Dillon to a rematch with Eddie McGoorty. The 12-round bout was to be held in Winnipeg on January 11. Dillon, who was outweighed by 12 pounds during their initial bout, hoped to even things up in the weight department.⁴

Called a draw by law, Jack Dillon and Eddie McGoorty, who were both standing at the end of the journey, put on an exciting display. The Hoosier took command early but could not muster a knockout blow. McGoorty, who drew blood from his rival's nose for a third of the bout, worked behind an accurate left jab. Both fighters maintained an effective defense. At the conclusion, many were under the impression that Dillon had a shade better of the battle.⁵

Continuing in the rematch mindset, Jack Dillon agreed to meet with George Chip. The 15-round conflict was to be held at the Gymnastic Club at Dayton, Ohio, on January 25. The *Indianapolis Star* reported:

> Dillon left for Dayton last night [January 24, 1911] accompanied by his Manager Jimmy Walters, Nate Farb and Harry Donahue, who will be in his corner in tonight's battle. Dillon and Chip are to weigh in this afternoon at 154 pounds and a large crowd of local boxing enthusiasts will go to Dayton to see the bout.⁶

A young Edward Martin "Eddie" McGoorty (July 31, 1889–November 2, 1929) was one of the hardest punching middleweight American boxers (circa 1910) (Library of Congress, LC-DIG-ggbain-11842, digital file from original negative).

It was a well-earned decision over George Chip, as Jack Dillon took control and never looked back. Chip's nose bled from the third round onward, and he was dropped to a nine count in the 13th round by a stiff Dillon right hand. After the fight, the *Indianapolis Star* reported Dillon's remarks:

> Chip is one of the toughest fighters in the country, an iron-jawed fellow with a good record, and to knock him out you must land a lucky punch. Chip was there to stay tonight, and I would have scored a clear knockout had he not held on for dear life throughout the entire fifteen rounds.... I give Chip credit. He is a game fighter and can stand the gaff, for he took a world of punishment. I have not a scratch on me, have I?[7]

There was a maturity associated with his comments that had been absent two years prior. Older, stronger, and even more confident, Jack Dillon was in a healthy place mentally and physically.

Oh, Those Eyes

Forever trying to increase circulation, the *Indianapolis Star* ran a four-column picture of Jack Dillon's "hypnotic eyes." The newspaper noted:

> Dillon is one of the fighters who are a charter member of the "Don't Worry Club." In the ring and out of it he takes everything as a matter of course and with a little more experience he should become the greatest lightweight in the country.[8]

How Dillon used his mesmerizing azure optics wasn't clear, but as long as his optics produced a victory, or sold more newspapers, they would be a topic of conversation. And from what some had noted, his baby blues appeared to have a spellbinding impact over certain females. Dillon's reach, which measured at 72½ inches, was also another advantage. Exceeding that of a number of heavyweights, the distance greatly contributed to the effectiveness of his long-range artillery.[9]

Following the Chip contest, Dillon planned to meet Bob Moha in Milwaukee

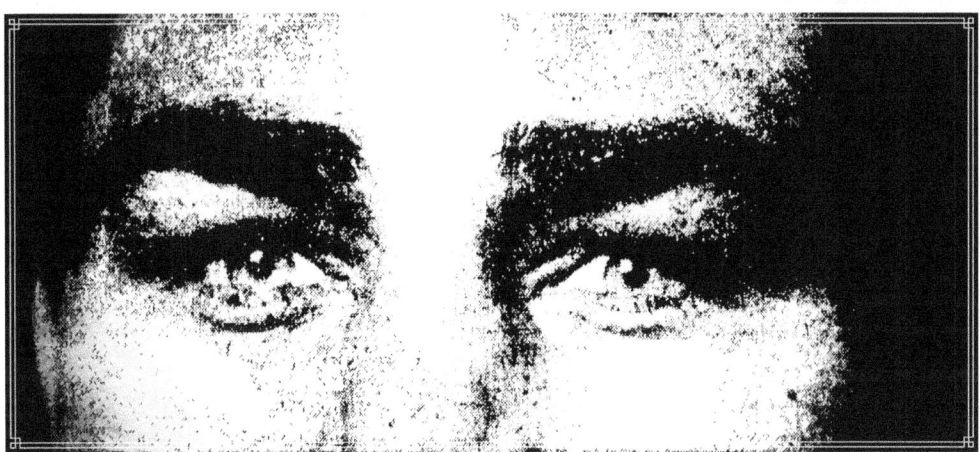

The hypnotic eyes of Ernest Coulter Price, a.k.a. Jack Dillon (*The Indianapolis Star*, January 29, 1911).

and Jimmy Gardner and Frank Klaus in Pittsburgh, but that would change. He would make it to Pittsburgh, but face Mike Glover on February 4 and Young Loughrey on February 18. Combined, these two talented pugilists had more than 100 victories against fewer than 50 losses.

Heading back to Steel City two days before his six-round bout with Mike Glover, Dillon was in good spirits. It was his 20th birthday, and he planned on adding a victory over Mike Glover as a gift to himself. His confidence showed in his comments to the local press: "I expect to take Glover's measure in about three rounds. He's tough but I am going better than ever now, and I will not be satisfied with anything less than a knockout."[10]

That said, outstanding footwork and strong defense enabled Mike Glover to stay six rounds against Jack Dillon. It was honors even at the conclusion of the no decision. Dillon, far too cautious early, became more aggressive in the final three rounds. It saved him from a defeat. Some, including the *Pittsburgh Post*, had a different view:

> Mike Glover, the Boston middleweight, outpointed Jack Dillon, the Hoosier champion, last night in their six-round bout before the northern Club at Old City Hall, in one of the best bouts seen here this year. Although Dillon forced the fighting nearly all the time the Hub miller proved far too clever for him and landed about four blows to every clean one received.[11]

Returning briefly to Indianapolis, Jack Dillon was featured at the Empire Theatre all week for two shows, 2:15 p.m. and 3:15 p.m., in an event called *The Best of Burlesque, The Jolly Girls and Jack Dillon*. The middleweight was meeting challengers and conducting three-round exhibitions. It was a convenient way for Dillon to line his pockets, spar, and view some eye candy. Bear in mind: The handsome and talented pugilist was only 20 years old. Pardon the androcentrism.

Next to test Jack Dillon's skills was veteran Young Loughrey, of Philadelphia, a hard-hitting and competitive middleweight. Dillon dominated during the first half of the bout. During the third and fourth rounds it looked as though a bloodied Loughrey was in trouble, yet he made it to the closing bell. Insisting on infighting, Loughrey took a beating. Jack Hanlon, Loughrey's manager, thought Dillon looked 170 pounds, rather than the 154 he scaled, and he wasn't shy about proclaiming it to the press. Hanlon's protest was quelled, however, when Dillon's manager offered—very well shoved the money in Hanlon's mug—to bet him $500 that Dillon wouldn't tip more than 157.[12]

Dillon's Training Quarters and Boxing School

The *Indianapolis Star* announced the news:

> Frank Cantwell [a promoter] has opened up new training quarters on East Washington Street for Jack Dillon, which is one of the finest and largest gymnasiums of its kind in the city. Dillon moved his old quarters to the new clubrooms yesterday [February 15, 1911],

where he started to prepare himself for his coming matches. Cantwell says Dillon's new training quarters has a 600-seating capacity and it will be run on a membership basis. When completed it will be handsomely equipped and will be known as Dillon's training quarters and boxing school.[13]

Finishing up the month on February 22 in Indianapolis, Jack Dillon met veteran Jimmy Gardner, of Boston. As a fighter who knew how to win—the pugilist won more than five times as many battles as he lost—Gardner was a draw for the Virginia Avenue Auditorium. Both fighters scaled at 154. With his deft defensive skills and scientific boxing, Gardner impressed fight fans yet fell short of a victory. Dillon proved far too much for the veteran. From the first to the last round, the Hoosier dominated the fast-milling match. Viewing the 10-round no decision, many of the five thousand in attendance favored Dillon.

The *Indianapolis News* acknowledged Gardner's comments:

> After the bout Gardner said he did not anticipate such a hard fight when he came here. He said Indianapolis had a "great kid" in Dillon, and that he was one of the hardest hitters he had ever met. Gardner praised Dillon for being a fair and square fighter, recalling an incident when Gardner slipped to the floor and Dillon backed away.[14]

Teenage Delinquency

At what point does young and reckless evolve to mature and accountable? Jack Dillon found out. On February 24, 1911, Jack Dillon, 20, was one of five men charged with having contributed to the delinquency of a teenage girl. The affidavits were filed by James E. Carroll, 1834 North Rural Street, father of Sarah E. Carroll, 16 years old. The *Indianapolis Star* listed the remaining four men:

> They are ... James Walters, 28 years old, Lorraine hotel, poolroom owner on South Illinois Street; Nathan Farb, son of Sain Farb, professional bondsman, 1016 South Capitol Avenue; Louis Farb, brother of Nathan Farb, and Alex Goldman, alias "Kid" Nig, 524 South Illinois Street. All but Goldman gave bond for their appearance before Judge Stubbs of Juvenile Court today.[15]

All five charged denied the allegations in the affidavits filed against them. And all five disclaimed any knowledge of the charges. Later, on September 28, 1911, all were found guilty and fined $10 and costs by Judge Markey in Criminal Court.[16]

Jack Dillon's self-confidence could extend beyond the ring. At times he could be audacious, careless, and inconsiderate. Blaming it on immaturity was an excuse that had a time limit.

Picking Up the Pace

To forget about his problems, Dillon turned to the ring. Participating in eight fights in 40 days, there was barely enough time to do his laundry.

On March 4, Jack Dillon met Billy Berger, the popular South Side of

Pittsburgh millworker, at Old City Hall in Pittsburgh. The pair had last met in October of the previous year. Berger was a popular contender for the middleweight title but lacked an impressive performance to solidify his status. Dillon knew the six-round contest would be a challenge, and he was correct. Coming out of his corner strong, the Hoosier took the first two rounds. Dropping Berger in the third round at least four times, victory appeared imminent. Berger refused to stay down, however. In the fifth round, Berger appeared rejuvenated—Lord knows what magic was performed in his corner—and he managed to win this round and the one that followed. Despite Berger's splendid turnaround, it was not enough for a victory nod in the no decision. Of the contest, Dillon remarked, "No man I have ever met would have stood up under the punishment I gave Berger."[17]

As a result of this bout, many fistic experts regarded Jack Dillon as the probable successor to Stanley Ketchel's crown. As the *Buffalo Courier* noted:

> Dillon belongs in the school of mixers made famous by Ketchel and Billy Papke. He knows nothing but fight. He is forever carrying the battle to his opponents. Not once has he ever been forced to break ground or back away from an opponent. With terrific punches to the body and that famous Ketchel swing to the jaw, he relentlessly carries the battle to the other man and beats him into submission.[18]

Afterwards, Leo Houck, who was scheduled to meet Dillon, called off the contest. This gave the Hoosier a much-appreciated break. His upcoming fight was a 10-round bout against Jimmy Mellody at Brazil, Indiana, on March 14. That's Jimmy Mellody, not to be confused with William "Honey" Mellody of Boston. Since nobody was certain who Jimmy Mellody was, it was possibly a quid pro quo bout.[19] The night of the contest many insisted Mellody was Kid Stone of Indianapolis. Nevertheless, Dillon sent him to Dreamland in the third round: moreover, Dillon was even insolent enough to tell Mellody it was going to be his last round. In reality, the contest was nothing more than a quick workout for Dillon, who was scheduled to meet Young Loughrey the following evening in Indianapolis.

Jack Dillon met Young Loughrey at the Auditorium on March 15. One day removed from his knockout victory over Jimmy Mellody, Dillon looked confident but didn't press his agenda until the final few rounds. Was he counting rounds? No doubt, but it wasn't the first time. Most saw the 10-round no decision as a draw.

Mike "Twin" Sullivan

Capturing the welterweight championship of the World on April 23, 1907, Mike Sullivan had soundly defeated William "Honey" Mellody over 20 rounds. But that was well over three years in the past. Unable to make weight, he vacated the title in late fall of 1908. Sullivan's meteoric rise to fame was courtesy of an impressive knockout percentage and battling some of the greatest boxers of his era: Joe Gans, while he was the reigning lightweight champion; contender and future welterweight champion Harry Lewis; and numerous other welterweight contenders. Not only had Sullivan entered the ring against Joe Gans three times before his 31st professional battle, but he had the guts to face Stanley Ketchel for the middleweight crown in 1908.

Fewer than 10 bouts from hanging up the gloves, Mike Sullivan faced Jack Dillon over the 10-round route in Buffalo, New York, on March 17, 1911. Dillon went right to work and for five rounds pounded Sullivan's midriff like a cook over a flank steak. Sullivan had little choice but to start avoiding his younger adversary. Chasing after Sullivan, Dillon wouldn't allow him a moment's rest. As the rounds counted off, Sullivan began using his legerdemain in attempt to slow Dillon, but it got him little more than a warning from the referee. The Hoosier pug was far more than the veteran could handle during the no-decision contest.

Mike "Twin" Sullivan (September 23, 1878–October 31, 1937) was credited with taking the welterweight championship of the world on April 23, 1907, by defeating William "Honey" Mellody in Los Angeles in a 20-round bout.

The *Buffalo News* called it this way:

> A new boxer of great promise arose on the Eastern horizon last night before the International Athletic Club, when Jack Dillon, the pride of Hoosierdom, made a pugilistic meal off Mike [Twin] Sullivan. Dillon is one of the quickest, coolest, and most phlegmatic fighters that has shown in the squared circle in this vicinity for some time. He gives absolutely no signs of emotion at any time, is never angry, never loses his head. He just settles down steadily to work, following out what is evidently a prearranged plan of campaign, and he follows it quite as a matter of course and independent of what the other fellow may do.[20]

It was an accurate observation.

Returning home, Dillon planned on taking a little personal time. One goal he mentioned was to have a nose operation to improve his breathing. As usual, if he wasn't training at his club, he was refereeing a local contest. The pugilist would meet Billy Clark in a six-round bout in Pittsburgh on April 1.

Working out of Philadelphia, Clark was a light heavyweight slugger who tackled some heavy hitters, including Terry Martin and Frank Klaus. As one of those fighters who wasn't graceful but packed a punch, Dillon had to be on his toes. As the *Pittsburgh Post-Gazette* reported:

> Billy Clark of Philadelphia was outclassed by Dillon last night at Old City Hall, and in the fourth round was knocked out. Clark was beaten from the very start twice in the same round [first round] taking the count of eight and nine, respectively, and going down for the final time in the fourth. Dillon walloped him so hard he had to be carried to his corner.[21]

With no time to waste, Dillon was on his way to Boston to tackle Frank Mantell, a talented boxer who won three times as many bouts as he lost and had more than 50 professional battles under his belt. With an imposing physique—Mantell's back resembled a road map—the Pawtucket pug was cut similar to a bodybuilder. Three rounds of circumspect boxing opened the 12-round contest at the Armory A.A., before both fighters began to ignite. Adhering to his fight plan, Dillon advanced straight to the body. It slowed Mantell but wasn't enough to put him away. Dominating the final four rounds, Dillon was awarded the points victory.

Returning to Indiana, Jack Dillon faced Billy Mayfield at Crawfordsville on April 10 and Jack Stevens at Mt. Vernon, a.k.a. Evansville, on April 12. Both fights ended in first-round knockouts. While Mayfield resembled a boxer, Stevens did not. As the *Evansville Press* detailed:

> It took Jack Dillon, the Indianapolis boy who claims the middleweight belt, just two ugly frowns, a couple of motions, a blow to the stomach and a biff to the nose to scare, bluff—at any rate defeat Jack Stevens, the touted wonder of Terre Haute.... When the two came together there were four blows and Stevens fell, assuming the attitude of a heathen Chinaman in idolatrous prayer. He refused to get up. When the count was tolled off, he arose. A little blood ran from his nose, but he was seemingly all right. On the car [ride] home he was very lively.[22]

While it resembled theater, it was doubtlessly a favor. Naturally, the 300 in attendance were disappointed, yet it was an opportunity to view the Indianapolis pugilist in a small venue. Making no comment, Jack Dillon left for Pittsburgh on April 18. He was scheduled to meet Jimmy Gardner over six rounds on April 22.

Slowing Down

Regardless of his record, Dillon found it necessary to adjust his fight frequency. And he planned to do so after his final two bouts in April, Jimmy Gardner on April 22 and George Chip on April 28.

The *Pittsburgh Press* noted:

"Never again." This was the refrain warbled by hundreds of sports as they filed out of Duquesne Garden last night after witnessing a glove event between Jack Dillon, of Indianapolis, and Jimmy Gardner, of Lowell, Mass.... They were far from being pleased over the display of scrapping shown by these worthies.... Somehow or other, it didn't look like either man was "out for keeps."[23]

Jimmy Gardner, of Lowell, Massachusetts, lasted six rounds but fought in one, the sixth. Gardner, having recently defeated Frank Klaus, was forced to contend defensively for a majority of the bout courtesy of Dillon's aggressive infighting.[24] Since Gardner's punches lacked the steam to do any damage, the Hoosier's strategy was spot on.

In the pair's third meeting, Jack Dillon had the better of George Chip in a 10-round no-decision bout. The fight was held at the Fair Grounds Casino in Terre Haute, Indiana. Both fighters tipped at 158. The *Star Press* observed, "Dillon closed Chip's right eye early, bloodied his mouth and twice sent him through the ropes."[25] Dillon assiduously tried to put away Chip in the ninth and 10th rounds but failed. Determined to make distance, the Pittsburgh pugilist succeeded.

Granted, for most pugilists it was an era where you took fights when you could get them. But before the fall season ignited in October, Jack Dillon needed to be more selective with his battles. In a cost-per-punch world, contenders had the edge. The trick was to squeeze every cent you could out of a promoter; after all, fighting once for a dollar was better than three times.

As was sometimes the case, the hype for an event proved more impressive than the contest. On May 3, Jack Dillon, who tipped at 154, met Wild Bill Moha, who scaled at 172, in the Auditorium at Indianapolis. As the announcer stated a variety of excuses for Moha's girth, Dillon stared down his opponent without saying a word. The *Indianapolis Star* noted, "Moha, who is a roly-poly bear-like person with Jack Johnson arms and Sam Langford stature, moved about with exceeding grace until Dillon showed the extent of his power in his 'kicks.'"[26] Both fighters vigorously fought, with Dillon forcing the fighting at each stage. Only in the eighth round did Moha shine, and it wasn't enough to gain the verdict; consequently, the 10-round no decision was seen as a draw.

Jack Dillon tangled with the familiar face of Jack Herrick, "the Fighting Tiger," of Kewanee, Illinois, over six rounds at the Pittsburgh Athletic Association's Clubhouse on May 20. The *Indianapolis Star* reported:

> While Dillon was Herrick's master throughout the six rounds, Herrick fought like a tiger, sending in right and left jabs and swings like a triphammer. Dillon was the cleverer of the two, however. He floored Herrick twice with right swings to the jaw. But Herrick was on his feet like lightening and tearing into his opponent.... At the end of six rounds, Dillon had not a mark on his face. Herrick was badly bruised about the jaw and his eyes were puffed out. While there was no decision rendered by the referee, the newspapers gave the fight to Dillon.[27]

This bout completed a trilogy for the pair.

The month of May closed with Dillon busy training for his bout against Ralph

Young Erne, of Philadelphia—not to be confused with Young Erne, a.k.a. Hugh Frank Calvin, the Philadelphia pugilist—scheduled for 10 rounds at Petty Auditorium in Muncie, Indiana, on June 5. Would there be value in the extra training? It appeared that way.

Ralph "Young" Erne took a terrible beating against Jack Dillon. Robbed of a knockout by the final bell, Dillon appeared remorseful for his adversary. For example, in the second round when he dropped Erne to the canvas with a left hook, he didn't capitalize on the situation. At the closing bell, Erne's face was covered in crimson, as the cuts he sustained bled like a leaking kitchen sink and his left eye was virtually closed. The 10-round no decision proved little more than a solid workout for Dillon.

For his final match in June, Jack Dillon faced Paddy Lavin, of Buffalo, on June 21, at the Auditorium in Indianapolis. Both boys went at it hammer and tongs. Although Lavin gave away eight pounds to Dillon, his alacrity combined with cleverness enabled him to make distance. For his part, the Hoosier delivered a splendid display and had his opponent at his mercy a few times. And even though he couldn't deliver Lavin, Dillon was superb. The *Indianapolis Star* noted, "Lavin's much touted left was in evidence numerous times, but the jabs and uppercuts did not seem to distress Dillon in the least."[28] Though Lavin held his own, the 10-round no decision leaned toward Dillon.

Despite the fact that Jack Dillon was matched with

Bob Moha (1890–1959) (birth name Robert Mucha), a.k.a. Milwaukee Caveman, was a Milwaukee-based middleweight boxer who contended for the title. He fought Harry Greb six times and Jack Dillon five times (Library of Congress, LC-DIG-ggbain-11849, digital file from original negative).

Advertisement for Jack Dillon's 10-round battle against Bob Moha on May 3, 1911. This was the pair's first meeting (*The Indianapolis Star*, April 30, 1911).

Jimmy Howard for a bout in Memphis, Tennessee, he opted instead to rematch with Bob Moha, in Buffalo. The *Indianapolis News* summed up the event:

> Jack Dillon, of Indianapolis, and Wild Bill Moha, of Milwaukee, fought a vicious ten-round draw last night [July 3]. Moha, seeming a little bigger and stronger, was on the aggressive, but Dillon fought him off like a wildcat and gave him as good as he sent. Neither man had an advantage at any time. In the 10th both tried hard for knockouts, but neither could put it across. Both men bled freely, but neither was off his feet at any time. A decision either way would have been an injustice to the other man.[29]

With fewer than 25 professional battles, Moha clashed like a far more experienced fighter. Unlike their first meeting back in May, this was a contest between two men each determined to destroy the other.

Although Dillon's name had traveled a substantial distance, when you gain the attention of a prominent West Coast promoter such as Jimmy Coffroth, a career could be altered overnight. It was Coffroth, along with James "Big Jim" Kennedy, who attracted the popular pugilists—boxers such as James J. Corbett, Bob Fitzsimmons, and James J. Jeffries—to the San Francisco area. It was also "Sunny Jim" who quickly outshined many of the promoters on the East Coast when it came to conducting world title fights. Coffroth was now eyeing Dillon as a possible opponent for Billy Papke in a championship match. However—and it was a big however—Jack Dillon had to first defeat Frank Klaus. For Dillon, whose engines seldom reached full speed until the 10th round, this could be a dream come true: longer battles, a.k.a. larger purses. The outstanding issue: matching with Klaus.

Taking time to digest his fight offers, Dillon turned to training, refereeing, and promoting shows for the Dillon Club at Walhalla Hall. He had been toying with the idea of adding his services to an international tour but remained undecided. The money was there, but Dillon was concerned about the time requirements and maintaining his contender status. His next fight, scheduled for August 23, was against Glenn Coakley, of Fort Wayne, Indiana. After that, Dillon planned on meeting Eddie McGoorty, either in Indianapolis or New Orleans (it would be the latter), on September 4. At that point, he would evaluate how to handle the final three months of the year, which optimistically included a match with Frank Klaus.

Jack Dillon headed to the charming city of Vincennes, Indiana, population 15,000, located on the lower Wabash River in the southwestern part of the state, virtually halfway between Evansville and Terre Haute. At Lakewood Park, he fought 10 no-decision rounds with novice Glenn Coakley, of Fort Wayne. Hampered by a sore left arm, Coakley's defensive skills carried him the entire journey. Although no decision was given, Dillon patently outpointed his adversary. To Coakley's credit, a solid right sent Dillon briefly to his knees in the second round. It was more of an off-balance drop than anything else.[30]

Hitting the Boil-ing Point

The *Indianapolis News* reported:

> Jack Dillon, of Indianapolis, with a newly lanced boil on his right arm, made such a poor attempt at fighting Eddie McGoorty, of Oshkosh, Wisconsin, at the New Orleans Athletic Club last night [September 4] that referee Harry Stout stopped the bout at the end of the fourth round, awarding McGoorty the decision. They were to have boxed ten rounds. Both are light middleweights.[31]

By cutting the fight short, the referee placed himself, not to mention both fighters, in peril. An estimated two thousand fans were convinced they were defrauded and began hurling threats at the participants. When large mobs formed outside the venue, the police had to be contacted to intervene. It was a contest that never should have taken place.

The *Times-Democrat* detailed:

> He [Dillon] couldn't fight, and after stalling through three rounds, said so. Referee Harry Stout led him to the center of the ring, bared his afflicted arm as evidence, and explained the situation to the crowd ... the excitement ran at a high pitch. Nothing was done, however, after a few minutes the crowd filed out.[32]

Later, the club offered a partial (half the price of admission) refund to ticket holders. Meanwhile, Dillon returned home to convalesce from his injury.

A Familiar Fall

By the beginning of October, Jack Dillon was ready to reenter the ring. Scheduled to meet Jack Graham over 10 rounds in Vincennes on October 4, he felt confident. Bad luck, however, would again rear its ugly head.

The *Evansville Courier and Press* reported:

> The ten-round contest between Jack Dillon, of Indianapolis and Jack Graham, of Kansas City, Missouri, which was billed for Lakewood Park last evening was stopped by police in the fourth round and the crowd gave its approval as Graham was found to be entirely out of Dillon's class. For two rounds Graham was allowed to go unpunished. In the third he was floored with almost every blow of Dillon. The fourth round was barely begun when the interference from the police came.[33]

Since familiarity normally yielded a favorable outcome, rematches were common for Jack Dillon. The pugilist met Jack Herrick on October 20 at Magyar Haz in South Bend. It was the pair's fourth meeting. An even match entering the seventh round, there was plenty of action. That was when the tide turned in favor of Dillon, who pummeled Herrick's face into a bloody mess. How Herrick managed to make distance was anybody's guess. Both fighters worked on a percentage basis, and since turnout was small, their take was minimal.

Realizing he had four more bouts scheduled before the end of the month, Jack Dillon was forced to make schedule adjustments. He moved his October 31 bout against George "K.O." Brown to November 11 and postponed his battle against Leo Houck—he could not make the midnight train to Boston. From South Bend, he headed to Philadelphia to meet a local fighter by the name of Barney Williams. The six-round bout was conducted under the auspices of the American Athletic Club on October 23.

The *Indianapolis Star* noted:

> Dillon floored Williams three times in the first round and had him on the floor for 24 seconds of the round with three punches. The first damaging right landed on the cheekbone, and the other two on the jaw. After the first round Williams, who recuperated during the intermission, became cautious and covered up at all times. Dillon was so anxious to land a knockout punch that he became wild.[34]

Years later, Jack Dillon would truly appreciate this lackluster victory.

On October 24, Jack Dillon, along with six other pugilists, was indicted by a Posey County grand jury on charges of assault and battery, a.k.a. engaging in boxing contests. The others charged were Jack Brennan, Glenn Coakley, George Coogan, Neal Hendricks, and Jack Stevens. Most were arrested and released on a $250 bond. The entire purpose of these indictments was to test the legality of the fight game.[35] It failed.[36]

Unfazed by the legal vicissitudes, Jack Dillon hammered Ralph Erne for six rounds at Old City Hall in Pittsburgh on October 28. The no-decision fight was unquestionably in favor of Dillon. For a bloodied Erne, it was simply a matter of survival, both inside the ring and out—he put $100 in his pocket for his effort.

Dillon returned to Indianapolis, where he met Eddie McGoorty over 10 rounds at the Auditorium on November 1. Since this was the fourth time the pair had met, there was little mystery as to how they would battle one another. Despite a strong start by McGoorty—his accurate lefts and uppercuts accounted for plenty of damage—he faded fast. Dillon, who was the aggressor throughout, gradually modified his defense to counter McGoorty's efforts. As for the Wisconsin fighter, he took only the third round, thanks to a powerful uppercut to the Hoosier's jaw that nearly put him out. The no decision fell in favor of Dillon.

Ten days later it was off to Pittsburgh, where Jack Dillon met George "K.O." Brown over a six-round journey at Old City Hall. Outboxing his opponent, Dillon had Brown struggling to see by the end of the third round—both of Brown's eyes were sliced and bleeding. Continuing to go to the body—left hooks to the body a recipe to destroy most fighters—Brown took two punches for each delivered. The no decision fell in favor of Dillon.[37]

When Buck Crouse couldn't meet his engagement with George Chip, Jack Dillon agreed to fill in. The pair engaged over 12 rounds at the Auditorium in Youngstown, Ohio, on November 22. As their fourth meeting, no introductions were required. The no decision went to the limit with the advantage falling in favor of Dillon. In both the ninth and 10th rounds, Dillon had Chip wavering, but he could not put him away.

Frank Klaus

Born on December 30, 1887, to German American parents in Turtle Creek, Pennsylvania, near Pittsburgh, Frank Klaus was the son of a coal miner. Following in his father's footsteps, he worked in the mines, and in doing so developed an exceptional physique. By winning an amateur boxing tournament at a local athletic club, he turned heads. And it wasn't long before he was approached about pursuing an amateur career.

Success as a nonprofessional led to an obvious transition: Klaus began a professional boxing career in 1905. It was a rocky start at first, but Pittsburgh was a fight town, and soon he made the proper contacts to advance his skills. Developing fast, he was a contender for the division title by the spring of 1909. Victories over Harry Lewis, Billy Papke, and Porky Dan Flynn brought him to Stanley Ketchel, world middleweight champion, on March 23, 1910. Taking a six-round newspaper victory over the Michigan Assassin was the confidence he yearned for. When Stanley Ketchel died, on October 15, 1910, Klaus began a path of destruction through the division—Jack Dillon encountered near the end of the trail—that eventually led to him claiming the title.

Jack Dillon, who could care less about location, met Frank Klaus on December 7 in Pittsburgh. The pair would conduct their six-round business at the

Old Town Hall in front of a partisan group of spectators. The *Pittsburgh Post* described the contest in this manner:

> Jack Dillon and Frank Klaus tried to settle their differences last night, but failed. In one of the greatest six-round battles that was ever fought in this city the two middleweights slammed each other around the ring before the American Club at Old City Hall, but when the final gong had sounded there wasn't a thing to choose between them. Dillon landed the most punches and had the East Pittsburgher bleeding during the last two rounds, but Klaus evened matters up by the sledgehammer blows he sent home to Dillon's face and body. Klaus was the aggressor most of the distance, though Dillon only backed ground in one or two instances—in the third round when the bear cat ripped home some terrific slams to the stomach.[38]

As for the view published in the *Indianapolis Star*:

> Here's to the new middleweight champion of the world. If any pugilist in the ring disputes Jack Dillon's claim, he must crawl through the ropes and fight it out. Following his fight last night Dillon laid claim to the crown left by Stanley Ketchel, and until he is defeated Dillon has a perfect right to pose as the champion.[39]

The six-round no decision leaned toward Jack Dillon. But he was in Pittsburgh, which meant he wasn't going to steal a victory.

On December 14, Jack Dillon learned that he would meet Leo Houck, of Lancaster, Pennsylvania, on New Year's afternoon. The six-round affair would be held at the Auditorium in Indianapolis.

Redefining the word prolific, Jack Dillon fought in 30 bouts and officially lost once. His longest battle was 15 rounds, while his shortest contests came in the form of back-to-back first-round knockouts. Dillon's primary competitor was Frank Klaus, who had more than 80 battles' worth of experience. Having a passion for well-known adversaries, Dillon had already met George Chip, Jack Herrick, and Eddie McGoorty four times—familiarity, at this echelon, was all about maintaining a proficiency level. Having fought his heart out against Frank Klaus, Jack Dillon deserved the victory. However, it was his opponent's hometown, over a short journey. And frankly speaking, not a surprise. In retrospect, he should have thought more about the possible consequences of accepting the offer. The question now was: How would the outcome of this contest impact Coffroth's offer to have Dillon come to California and fight Klaus in a distance battle?

Chapter Four

A Championship Claim, 1912

"The man who is swimming against the stream knows the strength of it."
—Woodrow Wilson, newly elected president of the United States

A Turning Point

Like a diver approaching the edge of a cliff, Jack Dillon could feel the exhilaration in his gut. His dream of becoming a *recognized* world champion was drawing closer.[1] All he had to do was perform to the best of his ability and the opportunities should materialize. And proof came the first day of a new year.

Leo Houck

Leo Florian Hauck, born on November 4, 1888, in Lancaster, Pennsylvania, began a professional boxing career in 1904. Lancaster—located about 70 miles as the crow flies from Philadelphia, Pennsylvania—wasn't a major fight market, but it did host entertaining fight cards at places such as Lancaster Athletic Club, Maennerchor Hall, Jack Milley's Club, and Prince Street Hall. And these venues were where Leo Houck honed his skills. Learning quickly, Houck met Jack Britton three times; Young Erne three times; Harry Lewis three times; Young Otto, Jimmy Gardner, Frank Klaus three times; Battling Levinsky three times; and George Chip before facing Jack Dillon on New Year's Day, January 1, 1912. Skilled, Houck was competitive at multiple weight classes. As he had held the middleweight title since May 3, 1911, when he defeated Harry Lewis, Leo Houck wasn't concerned about facing Jack Dillon, even if it was in Indianapolis. But, in retrospect, he should have been.

Jack Dillon versus Leo Houck— Claimed Middleweight Championship of the World

Leo Houck was decisively beaten and there wasn't a soul who left the Auditorium on New Year's Day who doubted the identity of the new middleweight champion of the world.

Following the contest, Louis H. Durlacher, Houck's manager, spoke to the *Indianapolis News*:

> Houck could not continue. It would have been criminal to send him back for that seventh round, for he would have been knocked out cold and he might have been killed. As it is I do not believe he is seriously injured, but his left side is swollen. Another round of such an attack as Dillon made might have had grave results, for he had Houck beaten. If it had been a contest for the championship Dillon would have won, the title without any question. He won a clean victory over Houck, and it is the first time that Houck has ever suffered a decisive defeat. Jack Dillon, in my opinion, is the middleweight champion of the world. There is not a man in the game today who can defeat him at his weight.[2]

Dillon played to his strength—strategic infighting—unleashing solid combinations to the stomach mixed with short uppercuts. As the fight progressed, the Lancaster Thunderbolt had little choice but to hold—at arm's length, he succumbed to numerous violent lefts, one of which sliced his mouth in the fourth. Houck was trounced by the end of the sixth round; his corner thought he had broken a rib.[3] With the victory, Jack Dillon became the only man who ever made Houck give up.[4] That and claimant to the middleweight championship of the world.

As the *Indianapolis Star* affirmed:

> Here's how Dillon stands today: Buck Crouse and Hugo Kelley are the only middleweights of any consequence whom Dillon has never met. Kelley may be able to fight again, but he balks on entering the ring. Crouse was all but knocked out last night by George Chip, whom Jack Dillon has defeated so many times it has become a joke. Chicago "Knockout" Brown was beaten by a dub on the coast, and the much-heralded French champion was beaten by another dub in New York. Frank Klaus sidestepped a match with Eddie McGoorty recently, and that brings it down to the question, can Eddie McGoorty make the weight? He made it last time he met Dillon, and he got a fine, large beating. So, you will have to take your hats off to Jack Dillon, middleweight champion of the world. Chicago papers please copy.[5]

Deluged with fight offers from as far away as Europe, Jack Dillon was a wanted man. Even Thomas McCarey, renowned West Coast fight promoter, was hoping to entice Dillon to head west for a championship battle.[6] As his management waded through the complex opportunities, Dillon planned to increase his fight frequency. One could question the strategy shift, as the pugilist fought better if he had time to heal between bouts. As Dillon saw it, though, the coin was there—why not take it?

On January 10, Jack Dillon's six-round mill at Duquesne Garden in Pittsburgh was called off when Bob Moha, a.k.a. "Cave Man," tipped the scale at a hefty 183 pounds. Moha's manager had convinced everyone, especially the press, that his fighter was in tip-top condition. He was not. Dillon, following numerous opponent substitutions, eventually met Billy Griffith at Old City Hall in Pittsburgh on January 20.[7]

Few, if any, were convinced that Billy Griffith, an Erie welterweight who was outweighed by 10 pounds, would last six rounds against the Hoosier champion.

Yet, despite a hellacious beating, Griffith survived the distance. As the *Pittsburgh Post* reported:

> Dillon was the aggressor throughout, and in the closing round sent Griffith to the floor with rights and lefts to the jaw that had solid backing. But Griffith was game and kept up his dancing, taking care to keep out of the danger zone. Dillon did his best to beat down his adversary's defense, and only partially succeeded. A well-directed left to the jaw sent the Erie fighter to the floor for the count of seven and a moment later he was sent again to the floor, but the bell saved him. Dillon tried his best to put Griffith away in the final round, but the latter managed to hang on, although sent to the floor twice. The crowd shouted itself hoarse at Griffith's ability to last the limit.[8]

Indeed, it was a mismatch; however, it was entertaining, and, in the end, nobody demanded their money back.

Vindication for Leo Houck's loss to Jack Dillon hit the press on January 24:

> An x-ray examination today [in Philadelphia, Pennsylvania] proved that Leo Houck did not quit his fight with Jack Dillon in Indianapolis. It showed three broken ribs, and he won't be able to fight for two months. He is going to Paris.[9]

A rematch appeared inevitable, at least from Houck's perspective. Until then, as Vincent van Gogh once quipped, "the French air clears up the brain and does one good."

Howard Wiggam, whose claim to fame was acting as a sparring partner for Bob Fitzsimmons during his vaudeville tour, was scheduled to meet Jack Dillon over 10 rounds on January 26. The bout was part of the entertainment being provided to the miners attending their national convention being held in the city. Having solicited area promoters for months— importunate indeed, yet later it would prove justified—to appear on this fight card, Wiggam succeeded. The *Evansville Journal* ran this three-sentence summary, the day after the fight, under the title "Dillon Puts the Kibosh to Wiggam":

Leo Florian Hauck (November 4, 1888–January 21, 1950), a.k.a. Lancaster Thunderbolt, began boxing in 1902 as a flyweight and fought successfully in every weight division up to heavyweight (Library of Congress, LC-DIG-ggbain-18239, digital file from original negative).

Four. A Championship Claim, 1912

In Indianapolis on Friday night Jack Dillon put Howard Wiggam out in the second round of a scheduled ten round fight. Dillon knocked Wiggam through the ropes with a right to the chin and Wiggam quit. Wiggam was seen in Evansville a year and a half ago when he lost a ten-round decision to Kid Hoy, the negro welterweight.[10]

An impressive crowd of five thousand spectators filled every available space in Tomlinson Hall. Claiming Wiggam was not knocked out, but slightly injured, those sitting ringside wanted the battle to continue. It would not. Noting the damage, one of the fighter's seconds wisely tossed a sponge into the ring. Accepting the capitulation, Dillon quickly headed to the dressing room.

Later, it was learned that there was something behind Wiggam's endless fight solicitations: He had "lost a little daughter a short time ago and was unable to pay funeral expenses. He took the fight with Dillon, one of the hardest hitters in the business, to pay off the debt and to provide a few meals for his family."[11]

Hoping to stay sharp for an anticipated big money West Coast bout, Jack Dillon took five contests during the short month of February. And to little surprise, there were a few familiar faces: Billy Berger on February 1, Jimmy Gardner just two days later, Paddy Lavin on February 8, George Chip on February 10, and Grant Clark (Clarke) on February 22. With the exception of Clark, there were no tomato cans on the schedule. Training at the Bronson-Dillon Club kept the pugilist loose—sustaining a relaxed, confident, and fluid feel—and at home. He would celebrate his 21st birthday on February 2.

It was off to Youngstown, Ohio, where Jack Dillon mixed with Billy Berger, of Pittsburgh, over a scheduled 12-round journey. The previous time the pair had met, back in March 1911, Dillon had his way with Berger in a six-round no-decision contest. Although both pugilists were to weigh in at three o'clock in the afternoon at 158 pounds, Berger refused to make weight. Dillon, who was entitled to the weight forfeit, declined. Thus, the show went on; incidentally, situations like this were often an indication of a sizable side wager. As predicted by those placing bets, the Hoosier once again outfought the much heavier Berger. It was 12 fast and uneventful rounds in front of a small crowd.[12] Afterwards, Dillon absconded from the venue, as he had to leave early in the morning for Philadelphia.

As a veteran of more than 100 professional fights, Jimmy Gardner won four times as many bouts as he lost. Looking forward to meeting Jack Dillon at the National Athletic Club on February 3, he knew what to expect; it was the third time the pair had met. Sadly, neither party delivered for attendees. Dillon, who could have ended the fight at any time—he was that dominant—failed to do so.[13] Gardner, who was a large shadow of his former self, was there to last the six rounds. Uppermost in his mind was survival and a paycheck. Struck by an accurate and powerful right hand in the third round, Gardner dropped to the canvas but refused to stay. Perhaps he should have, as his performance was painful to watch; consequently, many fight fans left before the conclusion of the battle.

Since his match against Walter Coffey in New York was postponed, Dillon traveled to Buffalo, where he met Paddy Lavin on February 8. Having gone 10 no-decision rounds against the boxer the previous summer in Indianapolis, Dillon knew he would have his hands full on the fighter's home turf. The contest, held at Convention Hall, had western New York fight circles excited. It was framed as Lavin, a talented welter, meeting Dillon, an adroit middleweight. As the *Buffalo News* saw it:

> Paddy Lavin went gamely to defeat last night at the hands of Jack Dillon in Convention Hall, but thereby lost no friends. Paddy lasted the scheduled ten rounds, but twice the gong made a difference which allowed him to come back when it seemed that the battle was all but over. The ringside weights gave Paddy 154 and Dillon 157½, and it seemed as if Lavin was carrying a little "loose flesh" which did him no good. Paddy's ring generalship made the husky Hoosier lad look rather foolish at times, but it was a fact that Paddy's clever defense was not strong enough to withstand the sledge-hammer swats which Dillon let fly in his direction.[14]

Winning two rounds at best, Lavin took the worst beating of his career. His survival was courtesy of outstanding footwork and superb defensive movement such as ducking and dodging. Dillon, relentless in the pursuit of his adversary, constantly opted for infighting. Dillon's closing remark to the press? "I'm going after Ketchel's title, and any of the boys who think I am not fit to take Stanley's place can try me out."[15]

From Buffalo, Dillon headed southwest to Pittsburgh. There he would meet George Chip, for the fifth time, in a journey scheduled for six rounds. Victorious, Dillon appeared to be guarding a "cauliflowered ear" for a majority of the contest—an injury he suffered during his battle with Frank Klaus the previous year.[16] However, it didn't stop him from boring in on Chip while delivering solid combinations. As the fight progressed, Chip began firing haymakers out of sheer desperation. It was clear by the conclusion who was the better fighter.

As the month ended, Jack Dillon found himself in Columbus, Ohio, going the 10-round journey against local pug Grant "Kid" Clarke. Never in trouble during the battle, he was also never in a position—his timing was off—to dispose of his neophyte adversary.[17] Not thrilled but satisfied with the victory, Dillon received good news the following day: The *Akron Beacon Journal* announced, "Frank Klaus, the Pittsburg[h] middleweight, who defeated 'Sailor' Petrosky in a 20-round contest yesterday has been matched by James Coffroth to box Jack Dillon of Indianapolis here [San Francisco] next month."[18] At last, it was time to battle Klaus over a long journey.[19]

Heading West

Following assorted transportation setbacks, Jack Dillon eventually made it to the West Coast. It wasn't long before he was jettisoning sparring partners at Millett's training camp in Colma, California. However, before he could deal with

Frank Klaus, Dillon had to dispose of Walter Coffey, on March 7, in a contest to be held before the Oakland Wheelmen's Club in the Piedmont Pavilion. Yep, Coffroth wanted to inspect the Hoosier—or goods if you will—before putting him in the ring with Klaus.[20] Coffey was training over at Al White's place, where Frank Klaus happened to be training. If successful against Coffey, Dillon would meet Klaus on March 23, across the bay in San Francisco.

Whether it was the time difference or a sore knuckle on his right hand, Jack Dillon fought cautiously against Walter Coffey. As the *Indianapolis News* noted, "The fight was just ordinary in character ... there was not a time during the short bout [10 rounds] when Coffey seemed to have a chance of gaining the decision."[21] Outclassed, Coffey's performance was debilitating and surprised many of the spectators. The following day, Jack Dillon confirmed he would second for Abe Attell when the former champion battled Harlem Tommy Murphy on March 9 in San Francisco.[22]

By the second week in March, training was getting redundant for Jack Dillon. He decided to contact everyone from club managers to newspaper editors, with hopes of matching with local talent before his contest with Klaus. The action, a sign of inexperience, was indecorous and considered insulting to Coffroth. Not surprisingly, he found no takers.

Speaking of having a difficult time, Dillon's silence was aggravating to beat writers. They couldn't squeeze an opinion out of the reticent pugilist. They even began calling him "Silent Dillon." One San Francisco writer penned the few items he could extract from the pugilist, burdensome to interview:

> Jack Dillon says that he beat Klaus in a six-round affair in Pittsburg[h], and he thinks he will beat him in the 20-round affair, which starts at Daly City at 3 o'clock next Saturday afternoon [March 23]. Dillon also admits that he considers Eddie McGoorty the bear cat of the middleweights, but he hopes to beat him too, if he is fortunate enough to beat Klaus and get the McGoorty match.... Dillon appears to be the one middleweight in the world who would rather fight than talk.[23]

In reference to Dillon's silence, the *San Francisco Chronicle* reported:

> From the time he entered the gym until he was through with his last boxing Dillon had not a word to say, even to his sparring partners or the fellow who was keeping time for him ... a chap who attends strictly to his own business, who is so serious about it that he doesn't even smile, James J. Jeffries never had anything on this fellow.[24]

Frank Klaus versus Jack Dillon— Middleweight Championship of the World

Three days out, fans were offering 5 to 4 that Jack Dillon would get the decision over Frank Klaus. Furthermore, the Klaus money was easy to find at those odds. One day out, Klaus was made a 10 to 9 favorite, but the betting was light. Gamblers predicted it would be even money when the elite pugilists entered the ring.

Two images of Francis "Frank" Klaus (December 30, 1887–February 8, 1948), a talented middleweight boxer from 1904 to 1918. The elite boxer claimed the vacant world middleweight championship in 1913 by defeating Billy Papke (left: Library of Congress, LC-DIG-ggbain-12186, digital file from original negative; insert: Library of Congress, LC-DIG-ggbain-08658, digital file from original negative).

Equally as confident as his opponent, Klaus quipped, "Dillon is a good tough fighter all right, but he isn't quite good enough to bring home the bacon Saturday afternoon."[25]

But let's get the details straight. The place was Coffroth's Mission Street Arena; the day was March 23, 1912. The fight program was as follows: Both participants weighed in at Corbett's, 271 Stevenson Street, San Francisco, at 10 o'clock. Doors opened at 12:30 p.m. A half hour later the reserved section doors opened. The first preliminary, Joe Acheson versus Barney Richter, started at 2 p.m. Both fighters weighed 135 pounds, and their contest was scheduled for six rounds. The second preliminary, Walter Scott versus Babe Picato, started at 2:30

p.m. Both fighters scaled at 127 pounds, and they were scheduled for 10 rounds. The main event, for the middleweight championship, Frank Klaus of Pittsburg(h) versus Jack Dillon of Indianapolis, started at 3:15 p.m. Both fighters tipped at 158 pounds. The referee was Jack Welsh.[26]

Jack Dillon immediately ignited, landing with his left and dancing away. Mesmerizing the crowd with his alacrity and accuracy, the Hoosier instantly impressed. By the time Frank Klaus awoke, three rounds had passed. Taking command, Klaus pounded Dillon's body with combinations. The strain began to show on Dillon's face, and the damage impacted his judgment of distance and punch selection. As Klaus accumulated rounds, Dillon was running out of time.

In the 10th, Abe Attell, who was in Dillon's corner, begged him to open his stance and make a stand. And it made a difference. However, the journey was drawing to a conclusion quicker than Dillon could deliver his volleys. By the 20th and final round, a bloodied and exhausted Jack Dillon resembled a person who had been hit by a truck. Resorting to their bag of tricks, both fighters were warned multiple times for headbutting.

The *Indianapolis Star* noted a key point:

> Dillon, in fact, would have shown far better ring generalship had he stayed out of the clinches and done his fighting in the open. Of the two, he was the boxer and his straight left, which was the best punch he has in his repertoire and practically the only one, landed in the face of the Pittsburgher when he stood off at long range and shot in the glove. Why he abandoned that scheme, which gave him a lead in the first three rounds, and took to clinching that gave Klaus the very opportunity to send in his short arm jolts to the body is a mystery and the answer to the victory of the far–Easterner.[27]

The newspaper continued:

> It might have been called a draw, perhaps, by a timorous referee, but if you care taking into consideration the blows that count the most, the fact that Klaus had Dillon bucking away from him most of the time with the middle-westerner fairly swamped with body punches in the twentieth round and weak from the blows that were struck, you could not but concede that Klaus was entitled to the honors that came his way.[28]

Was it a ring classic? No. Nor was it a memorable event, much to do with the wrestling that occupied a majority of the bout, not to mention the frequency of clinching. In retrospect: Klaus took advantage of his strength, which was infighting, while Dillon couldn't find his and resorted to holding.

Jack Dillon's succinct reaction to the 20-round contest: "He's the referee and I suppose that he knew more about what I was doing than I could tell."[29]

Jack Dillon Opens Up

Jack Dillon arrived back home, accompanied by Tommy Dillon, Nate Farb, and Mrs. Jack Dillon, during the final weekend of March.[30] The sight of a large and ebullient crowd awaiting their arrival at the train station appeared to entice the pugilist to say a few words. It caught many by surprise when he claimed that he received a raw deal—courtesy of referee Jack Welsh—in his 20-round battle against Frank Klaus. The level of detail provided appeared to substantiate the pugilist's claim. Dillon professed:

Klaus had been contractually guaranteed $3,000. Since the battle did not draw as much money as was anticipated by the promoters, a new agreement was necessary. An agreement was made: If Klaus would consent to have his guarantee split, then Referee Welsh would guarantee him the decision. But only if he was on his feet at the end of the 20th round. The betting was all in favor of Klaus and wise gamblers, headed by the controlling gambler, Jim Coffroth, had the cards stacked against him.[31]

Bitter? Without question, as Dillon was convinced that the fight was his entering the final round. However, Klaus, as boxers are prone to do, turned up the heat—increased his punch frequency, movement, and even feinting—in the final term to impress the person responsible for making the decision.[32] Dillon also confirmed that at no time was he hurt by his opponent's weak punches. Members of his entourage stated that the gamblers were so convinced Dillon won the bout that many left the arena before the final round.

Shocked by the verdict, plenty of spectators screamed their dissatisfaction with referee Welsh. One spectator was even knocked out during the near riot at the conclusion of the battle.

Regarding the butting, Dillon explained:

Klaus started it and did most of the butting. He is so short that I could not help putting my head down and I did that when we were in a clinch for, I was trying to make him slug with me. If I had not put my head down, I could not have swapped punches with him. There was not as much butting as the reports made it appear.[33]

The Dillons returned with an exotic bird, a South African cockatoo named Duffy. Mrs. Dillon, whom some of the press had no idea existed, was intent on giving it a dependable home. The pugilist, who had been handling many of his own affairs, claimed it was now time for him to get a competent manager.[34]

Needing to heal an injured knuckle, Dillon hoped to take time off from the ring. Frank Cantwell, who was now looking after his interests, would sort through his offers. Undeterred by the event, Dillon intended to fight Klaus again.

Sure enough, Jack Dillon learned he would meet Frank Klaus once again; moreover, this time it would be over a shorter distance, at Madison Square Garden in New York, on May 3. It would be the pair's third meeting.[35] Prior to his departure, Jack Dillon met Billy Schuster, of Ohio, in Frankfort, Indiana, on April 23. Although the bout was scheduled for 10 rounds, Dillon required a mere two to defeat Schuster.[36] At little risk of injury—Dillon wanted to test his mitts (injured knuckle) before meeting Frank Klaus—the Hoosier boxer was satisfied with the results.

A Klaus Call

Ten tame rounds, at "The Garden," saw Frank Klaus, of Pittsburgh, outpoint Jack Dillon of Indianapolis.[37] Far from what anyone anticipated, the short distance affair favored Klaus and, for some, confirmed his position as heir to Ketchel's title.

Taking a closer look: Dillon took the first two rounds, while Klaus focused on combinations to his opponent's body. Infighting took center stage in the third, as both boxers traded solid right uppercuts. Noticeably slowed in the fourth, Dillon was dropping his guard and allowing Klaus to score with shots to the head.

Klaus picked up the pace in the fourth. Two targeted lefts began the flow of blood from Dillon's muzzle, as Klaus worked sedulously to debilitate his adversary. The pair traded solid blows in the fifth, as if to take a breath while not giving ground. The sixth round was close to a mirror of the fourth. In the seventh, both participants went at hammer and tongs, as they fired wild haymakers in hopes of an ending blow. Dillon's straight lefts were landing to the face of Klaus in the eighth, and his infighting allowed him to take the round.

The *Evansville Courier and Press* detailed the final two rounds:

> Klaus put two rights to the head in the ninth and three very hard body blows, while Dillon got in short-arm rights and a couple of hard uppercuts on the body and chest. The tenth round was full of stiff infighting in which Klaus did the more damage. Neither man exhibited much fatigue at the finish. Klaus had outpointed his man and won clearly on his general forcing of the fight.[38]

The *Indianapolis News* stated it best:

> Great things were expected of Dillon, as he was making his debut before a New York audience, and the bugs looked to see him acquit himself in fine style. Statements made by Dillon some time ago about the alleged injustice done him in the awarding of the decision to Klaus in their fight in San Francisco caused the bugs to expect all there was in Jack to come to the surface. It was a golden opportunity for him, as he was given a chance to shine in Madison Square Garden, which is now considered the greatest of all places for scraps.[39]

Dillon's excuse for his substandard showing: an injured left hand that occurred early in the evening. Did his performance call for an excuse? Not to someone like "Bat" Masterson, gambler, saloonkeeper, lawman, and newspaperman who not only made a reputation in the old American West but also was a respected New York fight critic. Wyatt Earp's former coworker saw the battle as a draw. Despite Masterson's opinion, Dillon made no claim to the title.

In one of those say-it-ain't-so moments, the *Palladium-Item* reported on May 14:

> Bond to the amount of $1,000 has been furnished by Frank Cantwell, manager of Jack Dillon, the Indianapolis fighter, who was arrested May 7 on charges of grand larceny and assault and battery with intent to commit robbery. Henry Wyles and John Willis, the other two men arrested with Cantwell on the day in which Ringling circus visited Richmond [Indiana] and who have two charges against them, are still confined to jail.[40]

It appeared as though the never-ending saga of Dillon's fight management would continue.

For two nights, preceding the Indianapolis 500, city residents looked to the ring and not to the track, as a fistic carnival took place. Jack Dillon took on Hugo Kelly (Kelley) of Chicago for a scheduled 10 rounds on May 28 inside the Empire Theatre.

Born in Florence, Italy, in 1883, Hugo Kelly, a.k.a. Ugo Micheli, fought out of Chicago. Kelly was a talented middleweight who made claims to the title for close to a decade, and his fight with Dillon would conclude an impressive career. Having been in the ring with the likes of "Philadelphia" Jack O'Brien, Tommy Burns, Tommy Ryan, Billy Papke, and Stanley Ketchel, Kelly wasn't afraid to exchange blows with any elite fighter.

Desperate to turn his luck around, Dillon was successful. As a man on a mission, Dillon refused to give his adversary a decent target. The *Anderson Herald* elaborated:

> Kelly's defeat was complete as he went down for the count of five after a half minute of the third round had progressed and when he came up Dillon was at him like a flash, sending him into dreamland with a left swing to the jaw and Kelly went down like a shot. When he again hit the mat, he made a desperate effort to get to his feet but was completely out, and had to be assisted from the ring after the fatal ten had been tolled off by the referee.[41]

Two contrasting challenges—Sullivan with more than 100 bouts under his belt, followed by Brown with just over 20 contests—confronted Jack Dillon in June. He faced Jack "Twin" Sullivan, a talented veteran, over 10 rounds in Buffalo on June 12, and less than a week later he was up against the consistently formidable George "K.O." Brown over the 12-round journey in Winnipeg, Manitoba, Canada.

Was it a question of youth versus maturity? Jack Dillon was born in 1891, while Jack "Twin" Sullivan was born in 1878. Or was it a question of weight? Sullivan could scale about 178, while Dillon could tip about 158. Regardless of perspective, it made for a fascinating pairing.

To the surprise of few, Jack Sullivan made the 10-round distance, but age had taken a toll on the big man.[42] As Dillon bored into his opponent, blasted his midsection, and all but closed his left eye, it was clear who was in command. Covered with red welts at the conclusion of the battle, Sullivan looked relieved. Relying on a quality left jab to keep Dillon at bay, Sullivan failed. The no-decision bout was in favor of Dillon.

On to Winnipeg, Manitoba, Canada, where Jack Dillon met George "Knockout" Brown for the third time. While the Fighting Greek habitually had a claim to make or a story to tell, Jack Dillon ignored him. Since one of his assertions was that he never hit the canvas, Dillon quickly put an end to that declaration. Granted, Brown survived all 12 rounds, but he not once led during the fight. In a nostalgic twist, the bout was refereed by Battling Nelson.

Staying closer to home in July, Jack Dillon faced Joe Thomas in Terre Haute on July 4; Joe "Kid" Gorman in Memphis, Tennessee, on July 22; and George Chip in Indianapolis on July 25. Honestly, with the exception of Chip, not much was expected from these opponents.

A successful California middleweight, Joe Thomas planned on making Jack Dillon earn every cent of the loser's purse. Having been in the ring with Stanley Ketchel (four times), Frank Klaus, and Billy Papke, he wasn't intimidated by anyone. He was, however, coming to the end of a career that began in 1904. For the first two rounds, Thomas resembled a solid opponent. Nonetheless, Dillon landed a series of body punches in the third that had the veteran on shaky ground. The *Indianapolis Star* detailed the end:

> Thomas was knocked out of the ring in the seventh and was groggy when the gong sounded. In the eighth repeated swings to the jaw put the former middleweight champion down for the count of nine, and two seconds later he was floored again, the referee stopping the bout at this point.[43]

Joe "Kid" Gorman, who had fewer than 30 professional bouts, didn't desire one more defeat to even his record to 11–11 (plus no decisions), but Jack Dillon delivered it to him courtesy of a sixth-round knockout. Having toyed with Gorman during the first four rounds, Dillon dropped him in the fifth prior to putting him out in the sixth.

Meeting George Chip for the sixth time removed any thought of it being an early evening for Jack Dillon. Counting on the Pennsylvania boxer to deliver his quintessential competitive fight, it appeared as a useful confrontation for both pugilists. And for the first five rounds, Chip was aggressive. Weakened by Dillon's body blows and punished during the later rounds, amazingly, he managed to make distance. The 10-round no decision belonged to Dillon.

With summer drawing to a conclusion, Dillon wanted to stay close to home in August. In a scene that preceded Bernard Malamud's classic *The Natural*, Jack Dillon hit a baseball so forcefully that he tore the cover off the league ball. It happened during a game between the Dillon Champions and the Nig Shank Stars. The blast, which produced a home run and tied the score, was like something out of a fairy tale. If the middleweight championship contender ever became bored with the ring, he could turn to the diamond.[44]

In an attempt to revive the fight game in Richmond, Indiana, Sam Murbarger, a well-known Indianapolis promoter, signed Jack Dillon to meet Billy Donovan, of upstate New York, in a 10-round main event to be held in the Coliseum on August 12.[45] In the past, Dillon's Richmond bookings were declared off by the authorities. He hoped this time it would be different. Regardless, Dillon planned to continue his training at his open-air Riverside bathing beach.

In front of several hundred spectators at the Richmond Coliseum, Jack Dillon conducted a short and sharp contest that ended with a clean knockout of Billy Donovan. Immediately placing his adversary in a defensive mode, Dillon delivered a merciless beating. The *Indianapolis News* reported, "In the fourth round the Indianapolis fighter rained blows on his adversary's face and jaw and Donovan went down three times, the third time for the count."[46] As an initial promotion, Sam Murbarger's event was a success and conducted without police intervention.

Following an exhibition, on August 15, Jack Dillon suffered an undisclosed illness that required him to cancel a number of matches.

Sam Murbarger

On September 23, 1912, Jack Dillon signed a contract with Sam Murbarger to act as his manager. As a former wrestler, baseball manager, and bicycle racer, Murbarger appeared to be the right person for the job. The *Indianapolis News* noted his initial remarks:

George "Knockout" Brown striking another pose for the camera. His third meeting with Jack Dillon went 12 rounds to a no decision in Canada (circa 1915) (Library of Congress, 1915-LC-DIG-ggbain-12861, digital file from original negative).

> Dillon has as much right to claim the middleweight championship as any of the alleged champions. We will start east as soon as Dillon is in condition, and we will make every effort to get matches with all the best middleweights in the country. No dubs need apply. Jack is the best legitimate middleweight in the country today and he should not have much trouble in demonstrating this fact. We want a fight with Eddie McGoorty [a former Murbarger client] or any of the other fighters who have any claims to make on the title. Dillon is young, as strong as an ox, and he has developed a punch that will make all of them take notice. We will claim the championship and defend it. All the topnotchers are welcome to a fight.[47]

Samuel L. Murbarger was born in Harrison, Ohio, in 1875. He came to Indianapolis with his parents as a child and attended Benjamin Harrison School (No. 2). Proficient at athletics, Murbarger was a world's professional welterweight wrestling champion by the age of 21. He, along with Ed Steinmetz and Dan McCloud, took Indiana wrestling to a whole new level.

Murbarger's gymnasium, located downtown on the site of the old bus station, served as training quarters for the finest pugilists, including Jim Corbett and Bob Fitzsimmons, to visit the city. Athletics were in Murbarger's blood, and he initially appeared to have the respect of Jack Dillon. Understanding from the onset that the pugilist was difficult to manage, Murbarger remained committed to the task.[48]

In their first battle as a team, Murbarger and Dillon headed north to Hamilton, Ontario, Canada, where they greeted Tom McCune at the Butler County Athletic Club. Scheduled for 10 rounds, Dillon decided to make it a short night. Fighting as if his life depended on it, Dillon dropped McCune like a cement block in the second frame.[49]

Following the battle, Murbarger, a talented orator, spewed accolades to the press about his fighter. Dissimilar to anyone who previously represented the fighter, Murbarger was a man fiercely determined to get what he wanted. And, when you listened to him, you were convinced he could. The pair were off to Philadelphia, where Dillon would meet Harry Ramsey over six rounds on October 11. Having an advantage of both height and reach, Jack Dillon had the best of Harry Ramsey during the windup bout at the Nonpareil Athletic Club. Ramsey, with about 25 battles' worth of experience, fought intensely and even managed to bloody Dillon's nose. It was a short and relatively harmless no decision.

Less than a week later, Jack Dillon found himself in Johnstown, Pennsylvania, meeting novice pugilist Emmet "Kid" Wagner inside the Auditorium. For 10 rounds, Wagner sprinted over the canvas and, if caught, clinched for as long as possible. Outclassed, Wagner at least made distance. The no decision belonged to Dillon.[50]

Two days later, Dillon met George Chip for the seventh time. The pair danced six no-decision rounds at Old City Hall in Pittsburgh, with Dillon grabbing the first five rounds. As earnestly as he tried, Chip could not avoid Dillon's straight left. Dominating the infighting, Dillon blasted Chip's gut with machine gun combinations. Yet, Chip remained vertical—in the sixth round, he was close to dropping but was saved by the bell.

Continuing his fast-paced and prolific fight schedule, Jack Dillon traveled to Dayton, Ohio, on October 23 to meet Gus Christie of Milwaukee. Christie, who was the same age as Dillon, grew up on the same street as Bob Moha. Similar to other regional fighters, he started his amateur career at the Milwaukee Athletic Club. To Dillon, he would become a familiar and dependable adversary.

As talented middleweight, Christie, who had more than 20 victories against fewer than a handful of losses, was looking forward to the 15-round contest. On paper, it appeared as a solid match, and the paper didn't lie. Both participants assiduously fought, with Dillon taking the victory. Once again, the Indy boy was unmatched at close quarters. Dillon outfought his adversary and even had Christie's nose bleeding from the second round on. Both men clashed under 158 pounds.

Two days later, and back home in Indianapolis, Jack Dillon met Battling Connors, of Pittsburgh, at the Empire Theatre. The former policeman, who had a losing record as a professional, absorbed punishment like a sponge absorbed water. His secret? He protected his jaw. It wasn't until the seventh round that Dillon locked on it with a commanding left hook. Lights out. The knockout victory was Dillon's final bout of the month.

After his first half dozen fights under Murbarger and his trainer Bob Stolkin, folks noticed Dillon's improved skills. Tom Jones, a *genuine* boxing critic, had this to say:

> It's [the middleweight crown] a badly mixed-up mess now, but there's a coming champion in Indianapolis who is going to straighten it all out, and that comer's name is Jack Dillon. Believe me, he's the most improved fighter I have ever seen. A year ago, I saw him and was not greatly impressed. A few nights ago, I saw him in action, and to say I was surprised is putting it mildly. Dillon has everything now that a champion should have. He hits like a pair of mules kicking at the same time, and is awfully clever with it. I have seen them all, and I know a fighter when I see one, too, but I am willing to go on record that in a year's time this Dillon will be the cock of the 158-pound roost.[51]

On November 4, the *Times* reported, "In the fourth round of a scheduled ten-round contest with Jack Flynn, the 'white hope' of Streator, Illinois, the Indianapolis boxer [Jack Dillon] floored his opponent for keeps after having lifted him from his feet twice in the preceding rounds of the fight."[52] Flynn was even knocked through the ropes in the third round. There wasn't a soul in the Wabash, Indiana, audience that retained any skepticism regarding Dillon's ring prowess.

Four days later, Jack Dillon was in a Memphis, Tennessee, boxing ring facing Jimmy Howard, of Chicago, during an eight-round distance. Despite having a losing professional record, Howard managed to put up a game defense at the Southern Athletic Club. Yet, Dillon dominated most sessions on his way to an eight-round victory.

A few days later, on November 11, Jack Dillon met the familiar face of George Chip in Columbus, Ohio. In their eighth meeting, the pair would travel 10 rounds to a draw. When a slipping incident becomes a highlight, it doesn't say a whole lot about the bout's action. Yet, such was the case. However, from a skills standpoint, the pair also enjoyed pushing each other. It was a yawner, a.k.a. tedious encounter.

Eleven days later, in Columbus, Ohio, Jack Dillon greeted Grant "Kid" Clark inside the Empire Theatre. For one round, and one round only, Clark looked as if he could provide Dillon with a challenge. As the *Fort Wayne Journal-Gazette* reported: "Jack Dillon defeated Kid Clark, of Columbus tonight, the police stopping the bout at the second round. Dillon floored his man twice and the last time it was plainly seen that Clark was in no condition to continue."[53] For Dillon it was retribution. The Columbus fighter bragged about his skills and taunted Dillon prior to their confrontation. Afterwards, Clark had the gall to accuse Jack Dillon of being in cahoots with the police, thus the stoppage. Seriously? It was Clark's hometown.

In his final two battles of the year, Jack Dillon met Gus Christie in Indianapolis on December 11 and Harry Ramsey in Cincinnati on December 19. He had successfully met both fighters earlier in the year. Of the two, Christie, who won more than four times as many bouts as he lost, was the better fighter.

Dillon told the *Indianapolis Star*:

> Christie is one of the strong young fellows who have not had much boosting. But I met him, and I am frank in saying he gave me the hardest battle I ever had. There are few middleweights I would not rather tackle and, believe me, I am going to be in shape when I meet this fellow next week.[54]

Dillon was serious, and it was a testament how serious that he was working out with Young Peter Jackson, a heavyweight.

The *Evansville Journal* summarized the 10-round no decision this way:

> Newspapermen gave Jack Dillon a shade in his battle here [Indianapolis] last night with Gus Christie, of Milwaukee. The fight was fast and furious throughout and early in the battle Dillon sustained a split nose. This was a target for Christie all through the bout. Dillon was the aggressor and pushed the Milwaukee lad at all times. In the 10th round the Indianapolis pug sent Christie to the canvas for the only knockdown of the bout.[55]

Christie had a left jab, along with a straight left, that most pugilists would die for. Plus, he had strong defensive skills. Working to Dillon's advantage was his strength. And it was a targeted right hook to the jaw that dropped Christie in the final session.

In his final battle, Jack Dillon met Harry Ramsey. While Ramsey wasn't as good on paper as Christie, he could be dangerous. On December 19 in Cincinnati, the pair fought to what most considered a draw. Ramsey, who drew size comparisons to Bob Fitzsimmons, targeted Dillon's nose with his left jab until there was little recognizable skin remaining. Though it appeared as though Ramsey was fading early, he finished strong and evened up the battle. Understanding the danger of Dillon's infighting, Ramsey utilized long-range artillery to score. Not a soul inside Jimmy Widmeyer's Queen City Club, at Reichrath's Park, felt that they didn't get their money's worth.

More than 30 bouts with one loss, along with a new manager and trainer, produced a near indestructible Jack Dillon. Having never fought better, he was in tremendous condition and confident of his skills. Working with brother Tommy in the gym, the pair, following their January 17 exhibition, appeared on numerous boxing cards together.[56]

Jack Dillon faced two fighters with more than 60 career victories, Jimmy Gardner and Frank Klaus, and four boxers with losing records. Fighting in California for the first time, he turned heads, including those of influential promoters. Coming out of his shell—much to do with Sam Murbarger—Jack Dillon was slowly engaging with the press. Yet, he still kept his personal life, which included a wife, to himself.

Chapter Five

Never Better, 1913

"If we do not have the depths, how do we have the heights?"
—C.G. Jung, *The Red Book: Liber Novus*

A Great Start

Starting off the year in spectacular fashion, particularly over a challenging opponent, was what kept the heart of a champion beating, as the *Times* reported:

> Jack Dillon of Indianapolis won a hard-fought battle from Gus Christie at the Auditorium yesterday afternoon. The fight was about an even break until the ninth round, when Dillon waded into Christie in a terrific manner. For a minute it appeared that Christie would be knocked out and his manager, Jimmy Murphy, arose to toss the towel into the ring and save his protégé. Christie rallied, however, and was able to weather the storm.[1]

Christie's best punch came early in the New Year's Day bout when he caught Dillon with a sweeping left hook that landed squarely on the boxer's chin, and while it staggered Dillon, it managed to do little else. Astounded that the punch didn't drop his opponent, Christie realized it was going to be a long afternoon. Having taken a beating from Dillon, Christie's survival was courtesy of an impressive defense. Protecting himself from Dillon's powerful "body blows by leaning forward and protecting his face with his gloves and his body with his elbows" enabled the fighter to live another round.[2] Using his height advantage, Christie applied pressure on Dillon during clinches with his hands to slow the fighter; consequently, the action incensed the Hoosier pugilist. In the 10th, Dillon cut loose in hopes of a knockout, and nearly succeeded.

A Northeast Swing

Afterwards, Dillon headed east for what would be a five-fight campaign. Sandwiched between two dates—January 9 and February 10—in Thornton, Rhode Island, were a contest in Pittsburgh and two bouts in Philadelphia.

With his chiseled physique, Frank Mantell was an intimidating and ambitious middleweight. Successfully boxing out of Pawtucket, Rhode Island, the

German-born pugilist held victories over Billy Papke, Battling Levinsky, and Jack "Twin" Sullivan. Having lost to Jack Dillon the previous April, he was conscious of his adversary yet unaware of his refined skills. It would be a lesson learned for the New England pugilist. Disposing of Mantell's ring aspirations, Dillon gave the fighter a terrible lacing that concluded in the 15th round when the referee stopped the fight with a mere 35 seconds left. The action saved Mantell from a humiliating knockout.[3]

Back in Old City Hall in Pittsburgh, Jack Dillon faced Al Rogers of Buffalo over the six-round length on January 18. Initially, Dillon was going to meet Tommy Gavigan, but that match fell through. With more than 50 fights' worth of knowledge, Rogers hoped his strong defensive skills would overwhelm his adversary. They did not. In a tedious bout, Dillon outclassed his opponent in the majority of the rounds. Rogers got a second wind in the sixth and final round, but it was too little too late. It was Dillon's no decision.

On to Philadelphia, where Jack Dillon met Leo Houck at the Olympia Club on January 22. The six-round fight, or the hottest ticket in town, attracted considerable attention: Special trains ran from Lancaster to Philadelphia with a round-trip ticket costing a fan $2.50. Since Dillon had sent Houck home with two broken ribs the last time the pair met, the supposition of many was that the Red Rose boy sought revenge. Would it be Houck's retribution? No, it was too short a distance. While both pugilists vigilantly engaged, Houck behind his left jab and Dillon protected by his straight right, the no decision was seen as a draw. Damage was limited to Houck having a cut on his right cheek and Dillon suffering a sliced lip.[4]

Two days later, Jack Dillon, having remained in Philadelphia, fought a taxing six-round bout against hometown pugilist Frankie Logan at the Nonpareil Athletic Club. Forcing the battle at all possible opportunities, Dillon pounded the former military man's body like a battlefield howitzer. Logan, for no apparent reason, decided to mix it up inside with Dillon. Obviously, the local pug had a death wish. As the *Indianapolis Star* detailed the final round, "The sixth was fast, with Dillon increasing the lead all the time. He bored in and put over his rib-breaking drives with little mercy, and Logan all but out."[5]

Closing out his five-fight out-of-town campaign, Jack Dillon met Bill MacKinnon (McKinnon) of Roxbury, Massachusetts, over 15 rounds in Thornton, Rhode Island. The bout, held at the Rhode Island Athletic Club, saw the pair battle to a draw. The unpopular verdict caused an uproar with fans as many felt Dillon should have been the winner. Having dominated the first four rounds, Dillon was stupefied when MacKinnon chose to avoid him the remainder of the bout. The "awkwardly clever" MacKinnon, bloodied from the second round onward, was lucky he wasn't put out with one of Dillon's uppercuts.[6]

Returning to Indianapolis for about a month, Jack Dillon was thrilled to be home. He was matched for several local ring battles, but only one became a reality: He would meet Jack Denning of New York on February 19 at the Auditorium.

Jack Dillon (left) and Leo Houck (right) met for the second time on January 22, 1913, in Philadelphia. The Olympia Club audience witnessed six fierce no-decision rounds with most believing it was Dillon's fight, even if some newspapers called it a draw.

Having fought no-decision bouts against Mike Gibbons and Billy Papke, the former (1908) national amateur lightweight champion appeared ready to greet Jack Dillon. Even so, appearances can deceive. The *Indianapolis News* noted the conclusion:

> The second round lasted about a minute. Dillon went after Denning like a tiger, and with a succession of body and head blows he sent the visitor down. Denning took the count of five and then got to his feet, Dillon allowing him to get squared away before renewing the attack. Dillon then rushed him across the ring, and with a well-directed blow on the jaw sent him into dreamland. When Denning went down the second time, Dillon turned and walked away, as if confident Denning would not come back. The great crowd was excited for a minute, and about half the fans were standing on their seats.[7]

Understanding he could use a tune-up bout prior to clashing with Willie "K.O." Brennan, Jack Dillon decided to head over to Altoona, Pennsylvania. There

A souvenir button saluting "K.O. Brennan, Buffalo's Champion," a competitive middleweight who fought many top contenders. Brennan, a.k.a. William M. Brenner, served in the army during World War I.

he sparred with Al Rogers of Buffalo in a fast yet uneventful six-round no decision. Although everyone at the Lincoln Athletic Club was hoping for a thriller, they also understood the purpose of the match. A mere two days before Dillon tangled with Brennan, it was time for some target practice.

The show began in the Indianapolis Auditorium at 8:15 p.m. on March 12. Energized by the fight card, boxing fans anticipated an exciting evening of boxing. With the three 10-round bouts—Jack Daly versus Fritz Rudy, Eddie Webber versus Jimmy Burns, and Jack Dillon versus K.O. Brennan—priced at $1.00 or $1.50, it appeared like a bargain. Regarding the main event, the *Evansville Journal* had published this abridgement:

> The Brennan person from Buffalo, he of knockout fame, seemed to be laboring under an impression that he wanted to go to sleep during most of the ten rounds he stepped with Jack Dillon here [Indianapolis] last night and the Indianapolis middleweight won the bout by a big margin. Dillon had Brennan in trouble from the start and the Buffalo pug failed to show any signs of the famous haymaker he is said to possess.[8]

Although he took a beating, Brennan, a.k.a. William Brenner, was cheered at the conclusion. And it put a big smile on the face of the eight-year veteran pugilist.

As a sign of Dillon's ring prowess at this stage, and certainly his confidence: Having run out of sparring partners at 158 pounds, he was advertising for 200-pounders to assist him.[9] It was the first indication that the magic seeds had been planted, and that Jack soon would be climbing the towering beanstalk to the castle of the heavyweight division.

On the Road Again

Leaving town for the month of April, Jack Dillon would meet Albert "Buck" Crouse in Pittsburgh on April 10; George Chip in Youngstown, Ohio, on April 14; Barney Williams in Rochester, New York, on April 17; and Bob Moha in Milwaukee on April 28.

Jack Dillon had intended to meet Albert "Buck" Crouse over the six-round journey in Pittsburgh on March 27, but he only made it as far as Richmond, Indiana, due to flooding.

Rescheduling the matchup for April 10 gave both fighters more time to prepare. And it showed, as the pair fought a slashing six-round contest, with Dillon taking the battle by a shade. As the *Indianapolis Star* noted, "Crouse's cleverness and foot work got him out of harm's way in several of the rounds.... Several times Dillon tried his rushing tactics, but hard left uppercuts straightened him up."[10] It was an entertaining battle with no complaints from the gallery.

Four days later, Jack Dillon met George Chip for the ninth time. Twelve rounds in Youngstown, Ohio, yielded the pair another no decision. Once again, Dillon dominated their battle. Winning 11 of the 12 rounds, the Hoosier boxer was too clever for his adversary. One wonders if Dillon, or his management, used

Barney Lebrowitz, a.k.a. Barney Williams, met Jack Dillon for the first time in 1911, and again in 1913. When "Dumb" Dan Morgan agreed to handle the fighter, however, he changed his moniker to Battling Levinsky (circa 1915) (Library of Congress, LC-DIG-ggbain-15027, digital file from original negative).

the redundant pairing as a way to gage Dillon's skills[11]: a look at Chip's battered countenance typically was a way to see performance improvements.

Proof you can't judge a fighter by his moniker: Barney Lebrowitz, a.k.a. Battling Levinsky, began his professional boxing career under the name of Barney Williams. And it wouldn't be until "Dumb" Dan Morgan took over his guidance that both his name and luck would change. In their first meeting (1911), as you may recall, Dillon grabbed the six-round no decision. This 10-round no decision saw two fighters who had improved greatly since their last meeting. While the contest fell a shade in Dillon's favor, Williams was fast enough on his feet and accurate enough with his left jab to make distance. He had no defense when Dillon bored in, however, and it cost him.

Completing their trilogy, Jack Dillon and Bob Moha met in Milwaukee on April 28. And it didn't take long for most to realize that the popular local fighter was no longer in the same class as Dillon. In front of the Southside Athletic Club, Dillon had his way with Moha for nine of the 10 rounds. Moha gallantly tried to make a stand in the eighth round, but it was not enough.[12] As Moha noted, "I never saw him start a punch, all I saw was the finish, and I felt that."[13]

On to Klaus

As Dillon continued his quest to defeat division contenders, one had to wonder, where did this leave his weight class? As the *Huntington Herald* noted:

> The entire middleweight business is a trifle muddled right now and on dope it is no simple task to figure just who is Dillon's strongest rival. Klaus, by virtue of his wins over Billy Papke, butted higher than ever into the running. But then Klaus has always been whipped by Dillon. Any way you look at it, the records favor Dillon and he will act wisely if he settles down and goes after the honors in earnest.[14]

Speaking of Frank Klaus, the first week of May saw Jack Dillon post forfeits to match with him on May 29, in Indianapolis, also known as the eve before the 500-mile motor race at the speedway (Indianapolis 500). The pair, who had met three times, had been haggling about weight; in the end, Dillon agreed to 160 pounds. Leading up to this battle, Klaus hadn't faced defeat since meeting Hugo Kelly, back on December 20, 1910.

Opening up his training camp at Riverside Park, during the second week of May, Dillon sparred with Jeff Clark of Pittsburgh and entertained the many guests who stopped by, including former heavyweight champion James J. Corbett.[15] To say that fans were thrilled to see such fighters in a personal environment would be an understatement. Klaus held his camp at the Oakley Club, southwest of the city. Dillon understood that he had his hands full, as since he last met Klaus, the fighter had defeated Georges Carpentier (DQ19), Billy Papke (DQ15), and Eddie McGoorty (ND6).[16]

As for the details of the promotion: promoter—Indianapolis Athletic Club;

time—8:15 p.m.; place—Washington Baseball Park; fight card: Kid Fortney versus Teddy Gavin (142 pounds, 10 rounds); Eddie Webber versus Phil Harrison (145 pounds, 10 rounds); and Jack Dillon versus Frank Klaus (160 pounds, 10 rounds); referee—Tommy Dillon (not Jack Dillon's brother); tickets were scaled at $1 general admission, $1.50 and $2.00 for grandstand seats, and $3.00 for box seats.

According to the *Indianapolis Star*:

> It is the biggest fight of the year. It is the biggest middleweight fight that has been pulled off since Stanley Ketchel quit fighting. It is without a doubt the biggest mill that has been staged about Indianapolis in many years.[17]

Under the banner reading "Dillon Can Claim Klaus's Ring Title," the *Indianapolis Star* summed up the battle:

> Eleven thousand fight fans filed out of Washington Park at 11 o'clock last night with the unanimous opinion that Frank Klaus of Pittsburgh should lay claim to something else than the world's middleweight championship. Jack Dillon, pride of Indiana, whipped Klaus in the rounds when there was any fighting at all. Klaus spent most of the 30 minutes in the ring by clinching and blocking blows. Dillon hit him eight times to his one and some of them were solid ones, too. Dillon outfought and outboxed Klaus throughout the last five rounds. The first half of the battle was slow and uninteresting, and Klaus could not be forced into fighting.[18]

By the fourth round, the crowd was screaming for action. Unfortunately, it didn't occur until the sixth. Starting his engines this term, Dillon won the round. In the seventh, he pounded the face and stomach of Klaus, causing him to double over and spit blood. It was Dillon's round again. Unleashing the heavy artillery, the Hoosier sent crushing blows to the countenance of Klaus. Deluged by the assault, Klaus managed few return strikes. The eighth frame belonged to Dillon. Groggy leaving his corner, the Pittsburgher, bloodied from the massacre he was taking, had little choice but to clinch whenever possible. It was Dillon's round by a wide margin, and things didn't look promising for his rival. Desperate in the 10th, Klaus unleashed what artillery he had left, but few reached the target. Firing five solid uppercuts to the jaw of Dillon, Dillon marveled that his adversary remained vertical. And he wasn't alone, as there wasn't a spectator in the park who wasn't impressed by the resiliency of Klaus. Both pugilists fought to the closing bell, but the bout belonged to Jack Dillon. Acknowledged only for his survival, Klaus was a beaten man.

After witnessing this battle, was it fair to deduce that Mr. Dillon's future looked promising? The *Indianapolis Star* deduced:

> If Carpentier is the winner of the European heavyweight title then Jack Dillon can lay claim to it, for he whipped Klaus and Klaus whipped Carpentier. Look out Jack, or you'll have a lot of titles pretty soon.[19]

Will Rogers once quipped, "Too many people spend money they earned ... to buy things they don't want ... to impress people that they don't like." By 1913, Jack Dillon's ring take was estimated at $50,000. Knowing his friend Ray Bronson

It was "America's Greatest Touring Car," and Jack Dillon loved his Premier, made locally at the Premier Motor Manufacturing Company. The pugilist enjoyed gathering up his family members and driving wherever life took them. This is the cover of a handbill created by the Premier Motor Manufacturing Company.

purchased a Pierce-Arrow motor vehicle, Dillon concluded that it was about time he bought a Premier, or "America's Greatest Touring Car." The pugilist favored a number of the motor vehicle's features, including an air reservoir for inflating tires, left side drive, six cylinders, self-starter, electric lights, clean running boards, and concealed hinges. While Murbarger reviewed the daily offers pouring into his office in June, Dillon was out joyriding in his new toy.

Identity Crisis

It was a common misinterpretation among boxing fans that the boxing referee Tommy Dillon was none other than Jack's brother. He was not. Sam Murbarger referenced this with regard to Frank Klaus, "Klaus has tried to make capital of the fact Tom Dillon was the referee, leaving the inference that Tom Dillon is Jack's brother. Now Klaus knows that Jack Dillon's real name is Ernest Cutler [sic] Price. Tom Dillon is a businessman and a politician who has a mighty good reputation in Indianapolis."[20]

Speaking of mistaken identity, Robert McDowell, a 13-year-old runaway from Chicago, had been in Indiana posing as Jack Dillon's half brother. Mrs. Claude McDowell, his mother, was giving chase and came close to finding him in Columbus, Indiana. Young Robert was on the run and heading to Louisville, Kentucky, by that point, however.[21] Admiration for the pugilist came in many forms.

During the final week of June, Jack Dillon began preparing for his July 3 battle against Bill McKinnon at Washington Park. McKinnon had replaced Jimmy Clabby.[22] Training both indoors, in his clubrooms at 39 Illinois Street, and outdoors, at his new summer home northeast of Broad Ripple, gave Dillon considerable flexibility. The latter, located on the White River, allowed him to conveniently include swimming and rowing as part of his training regimen.

Starting out strong, Jack Dillon outclassed Bill McKinnon of Boston before knocking him out in the last minute of their 10-round clash. As the *Star Press* summarized:

> McKinnon was floored 11 times during the fight, twice in the sixth, twice in the seventh, twice in the ninth and five times in the 10th. He came back gamely after each knockdown, but was no match for the local fighter. After the last punch that sent him down, he attempted to rise, but Referee Tommy Dillon had to help him to his corner.[23]

If it sounded as if Dillon was utterly driving over his opponents, it was because he was doing just that. However, his last four adversaries were far from speed bumps, as combined they had more than 150 victories and won three and a half times as many bouts as they lost. And his last eight opponents had more than 340 victories and an even higher winning percentage. At no time had Dillon looked better, and that had much to do with Sam Murbarger. Yet, the young pugilist thought otherwise and split up with his manager. Because there was no written agreement, Dillon saw Murbarger's job description as nothing more than arranging his ring engagements. Did Dillon's confidence in the ring carry over to his life outside it? You betcha! The pugilist would now handle his own calendar.[24] Judging by his inability to turn down challenges, there was speculation that he didn't even own a calendar. Meanwhile, Murbarger began handling the affairs of Gus Christie.

Off to Winnipeg, Manitoba, Canada, where Jack Dillon would meet George "Kid" Ashe, over the 12-round journey. Once Tony Caponi refused to meet Dillon, Ashe, of New York, stepped up to scratch. The pair's bout was part of the entertainment during the popular "Stampede Week." While the referee declared the bout a draw, many spectators considered it an injustice; Dillon had been the aggressor throughout. The highlight of the evening: Ashe sent Dillon to the canvas in the fourth round. While the Hoosier was up quickly, and fought aggressively for the remainder of the contest, the moment was a rarity. Later, Dillon claimed he tripped over Ashe's foot.

The *Indianapolis News* pointed out another factor in the verdict:

[Frank] Cantwell [unofficial spokesman for the pugilist] said Dillon was arrested before the fight and put under bond not to engage in prize fighting. For this reason, he said, Dillon could not afford to knock out Ashe. He said Dillon was discharged from the court on the ground that the exhibition was merely a boxing match and not a prize fight.[25]

Three days later, in Peru, Indiana, Jack Dillon knocked out Jack Kid Williams, a novice Milwaukee middleweight, in the third round. This appeared to be one of those fights where Dillon was paying back a favor rather than seeking a competitive match.

Turning Over a New Car

The *Indianapolis News* carried this report:

Jack Dillon, the pugilist, and a companion [Bob Stolkin] were injured slightly early last evening when Dillon's automobile skidded and turned over on the river road about two miles northeast of Broad Ripple. Dillon and his companion were thrown out, but were only bruised and were able to go on to Dillon's camp, Terrace Beach, for which they were bound when the accident happened. The automobile was demolished. Dr. Mason B. Light of Broad Ripple attended the men. It is said that a muddy spot in the road caused the automobile to skid.[26]

The 3,500-pound automobile flipped over twice on a crossroad from the Alisonville Pike to White River, about two miles above Broad Ripple. Both men were found unconscious and feared hurt. A machine behind them observed the incident. The mishap was not a surprise to those who had witnessed the frequency, not to mention speed, of travel by the pugilist. Later, Dillon claimed his time as an automobile driver had come to an end. Reaffirming his position were chest injuries, followed shortly afterwards by a broken rib.

Ever since his split with Murbarger, Dillon hasn't been able to put a cost-effective fight schedule together. One minute he was headed to California, and the next minute he was off to Winnipeg, Manitoba. The pugilist, along with Bob Stolkin and Tommy Dillon, left for the latter destination on September 8, with hopes of meeting Tony Caponi on September 17. Scheduled for 12 rounds, Dillon would need eight to send the Chicago fighter to dreamland. As the *Fort-Wayne Journal-Gazette* detailed: "After putting Caponi to the floor in the seventh with a hard blow to the head, the Indianapolis boxer early in the next round finished the Chicago man with a short right to the point of the jaw which sent Caponi down and out. He had to be carried to his corner."[27]

Off to beautiful Lancaster, Pennsylvania, to meet Leo Houck for the third time. Battling Houck in his hometown, even during a six-round contest, would be no easy task. And that proved precisely the case, as the consensus of opinion: Houck took the close contest. The *Indianapolis* Star reported:

Houck was the aggressor all through the six rounds, and he had his left jab working to perfection.... The first round was easily Houck's.... Dillon came back strong in the second....

> The third round was an even break.... In the fourth, Houck landed a number of good hard blows on the body and jaw and the round was Houck's.... Both men slugged in the fifth and there was no decided advantage.... But Dillon came back, and they were fighting close in at the finish.[28]

Houck performed brilliantly, in what would be the final time the pair would meet.[29] As an elite boxer, Leo Florian Houck held victories over the best in boxing history, including Jack Britton, Jack Dillon, Frank Klaus, Battling Levinsky, Harry Lewis, Billy Papke, and Jeff Smith. A consistent force in his division, his presence would be missed.[30]

For Jack Dillon, there was little time to react, as he was off to Akron, Ohio. There he battled Walter Monaghan, of Pittsburgh, on October 14. The latter's aspirations to the middleweight championship were presumptuous considering his break-even record, but a paycheck was a paycheck. Four rounds with the Hoosier Bearcat quickly altered Monaghan's career path. Outmaneuvered, his seconds threw up the sponge just prior to the end of the fourth round. It was clear after the first round that the bout would not last the scheduled 12 sessions. As the *Indianapolis News* noted, "About the only clean blow which Monaghan landed was in the first round, when he sent a left to the jaw of referee Walter Kelly."[31] While Dillon was happy with the victory, he was even happier when he later learned Frank Klaus was knocked out by George Chip. In Dillon's mind, this left Jimmy Clabby and Eddie McGoorty as the only contenders left to challenge his claim to the middleweight title. Dillon planned to address the latter on November 3, in Milwaukee.

Jack Dillon would not meet Eddie McGoorty in November, or ever again. McGoorty was off to Australia, where his success would include the middleweight championship of the country. Gus Christie took McGoorty's place; consequently, the Wisconsin Boxing Commission suspended him (McGoorty) for six months.[32] Dillon's bout with Christie would be at catchweights, as the fighter didn't have time to work down. Naturally, having Sam Murbarger in Christie's corner added intrigue to the Auditorium bout.

It was the pair's fourth meeting. They had met twice in 1912, with Dillon taking the honors in each bout, and they met on New Year's Day of 1913. Though Christie's defense had improved in that bout, he took an awful beating. The *Palladium-Item* encapsulated it this way:

> Jack Dillon found an easy mark in Gus Christie last night [November 3], knocking him down once, jolting him severely at intervals, and having him on the defensive throughout the entire ten rounds. Christie went down under almost the very first blow that Dillon landed. The set-to was a real fight throughout.... Dillon carried far more than his customary weight, but still displayed surprising speed.[33]

Hugh McIntosh, the renowned boxing promoter, attended the fight and praised Jack Dillon for his boxing prowess. It was no secret Jack Dillon was negotiating with McIntosh for a possible trip to Paris to meet Georges Carpentier, the

Five. Never Better, 1913

French middleweight champion. Afterwards, McIntosh, a.k.a. Huge Deal, wanted time to think it through.[34] As for Murbarger, he had no comment.

Meanwhile Dillon departed for Butte, Montana, where he battled "Sailor" Petrosky (Petroskey) over 12 rounds on Thanksgiving Day. The latter was a well-known western middleweight, whose losing record didn't reflect his ring proficiency—in 1912 he fought a 20-round draw with Frank Klaus. A week before the battle Dillon was a 7-to-10 favorite. The *Indianapolis Star* gave this synopsis:

> Battered and beaten, his body aching from the terrific punishment inflicted by his opponent, outfought, outboxed, but not out gamed, Sailor Ed Petrosky of San Francisco lost the decision to Jack Dillon of Indianapolis at the Holland Arena this afternoon in one of the grandest contests ever witnessed in the city, and incidentally brought to light, as far as local opinions goes [sic], a man who is certainly entitled to the middleweight championship—Jack Dillon.[35]

The 12 rounds passed quickly, much to do with Dillon's impressive celerity, accuracy, cleverness, and defensive skills. He was rarely in any danger. Petrosky hit the deck for a nine-count courtesy of a crashing right to the jaw. Postponing his December 5 bout against Vic Hansen and having the police stop his contest against Jack Jeffries gave Dillon a much-needed break.

Matched with Gus Christie for a battle at the Delaware Street Arena in Indianapolis on the afternoon of New Year's Day, Dillon's focus turned to the holidays and his family.

Battling 22 times in 1913, Jack Dillon fought well. While he encountered no clear-cut losses, his six-round no decision against Leo Houck on October 9 favored the Lancaster pugilist. Dillon's victory over Frank Klaus left little, if any, question regarding his claim to the middleweight title. Dillon craved a decisive victory, over a long journey, to silence the critics. To do so could mean sailing to Europe or making the long trek to the West Coast—that is, if he or a manager could negotiate the proper deal. The reason for Dillon's split with Murbarger wasn't explained and didn't make sense from an observer's viewpoint as the pugilist had never looked better. Jimmy Walters would now assume the role. Brother Tommy was still working with Jack when and where he could. The pair conducted a four-round exhibition together in Frankfort, Indiana, back in March, and Tommy made the trip north to Winnipeg in September, where he also appeared on the fight card. As usual, the Price boys were tight-lipped regarding their personal lives.

Chapter Six

Indestructible, 1914

> *"In almost all other professions a man must be able to observe carefully and report accurately what he has seen. Those qualifications are unnecessary for journalists, however, since their job is to write sensational stories that sell newspapers."*—Robert Anton Wilson, *Masks of the Illuminati*

Battling Levinsky, one of Dumb Dan Morgan's numerous fistic protégés, was quickly making a name for himself at 168 pounds. He seemingly came out of nowhere, but it was revealed that Barney Williams, whom Jack Dillon fought on October 23, 1911, and on April 17, 1913, was actually Battling Levinsky. It was Morgan, the pugilist's new manager, who convinced the pugilist not to deny his Jewish parentage but to embrace it. Accepting Morgan's advice and his religion, Levinsky became a contender in his weight class.[1]

Speaking of forces in his weight class, Jack Dillon picked up right where he left off in 1913, and decisively defeated Gus Christie over 10 rounds on New Year's Day. Dominating his opponent, the Hoosier pugilist won every round but one, the sixth. As the *Times* detailed:

> In the last four rounds Christie was in bad shape from the terrific punishment and could do little but hang on. However, Dillon did not seem to be able at the close to land a finishing punch, due largely to Christie's hugging tactics. At the end both Christie's eyes were almost closed, and he was battered and beaten.[2]

On January 13, Dillon, along with his manager, Jimmy Walters, left for Denver, Colorado, where the pugilist was scheduled to meet Vic Hansen (Hanson) on January 20. Following this bout, they hoped to head to the West Coast to arrange a bout against Jimmy Clabby. Desire was one thing, however, and reality another.

The news out of Denver on the morning of January 21 was both good and bad. The *Indianapolis Star* reported:

> Jack Dillon of Indianapolis got the decision over Vic Hanson of Salt Lake City in a 12-round bout before the Colorado Athletic Club here tonight. Dillon easily outboxed his opponent and had him on the floor twice for the count of nine. Dillon asserts that when he hit Hanson with his right in the second round, he broke a bone in his hand. During the remainder of the fight Dillon simply feinted with his right and used his left to guard. Hanson did his best to outbox his opponent, but was forced continually to back up. His leads were easily blocked by the Hoosier. During the latter rounds Hanson was hanging on most

of the time. He received vicious punishment about the body. Dillon did not, however, appear to be in the best condition.³

Afterward, Dillon didn't elaborate on his injury. Ten days later, he was healthy enough to drop Harry Baker in the very first round of an exhibition bout, held at Tomlinson Hall, for the United Mine Workers of America.

A Three-Month Tour

Jack Dillon would begin a three-month tour in February, during which he would travel 12 thousand miles and survive nine bouts. He would return to Indianapolis on May 6.

When Jack Dillon signed to meet "Fireman" Jim Flynn, a.k.a. Andrew Chiariglione, the popular heavyweight, for a 10-round battle, many were certain it wasn't Dillon's hand that was injured, but his head.⁴ Standing five feet, nine and a half inches, Flynn, a brawny fireplug, could scale anywhere between 165 and 188 pounds. And like Dillon, he feared no man; incidentally, he had been in the ring with George Gardiner (1904, 1907), Tommy Burns (1906), Jack Johnson (1907, 1912), Sam Langford (1908, 1910), and Billy Papke (1909), to name a few. Fighting best at about 178 pounds, Flynn hoped to be on or near that weight entering the Kansas City ring against Dillon.

Tending to current matters, Jack Dillon was in Windsor, Ontario, Canada where he "deliberately permitted Freddie Hicks to stay the limit of eight rounds, when it appeared that he could stop him almost at will."⁵ Or, at least that was how the promoters saw it. As a result, Dillon was barred from further ring battles. Unhappy with the performance, spectators hissed and screamed at the Hoosier as he exited the ring. Suffice it to say, the fighter was relieved to return to the United States.

Three days later, Jack Dillon, along with manager Jimmy Walters, headed to Memphis, Tennessee, to greet Tommy Danforth, of St. Louis, over a scheduled eight round journey on February 9. The fatuous match was ridiculous on paper, and even more absurd in the ring, as Danforth, a novice pugilist, was dropped four times in less than a round and a half. It was a short blast to the stomach that floored Danforth for the last time. The referee didn't bother with a count.

In his last bout of the month, Jack Dillon faced neophyte Marshall Claiborne in Hot Springs, Arkansas, on February 17. Scheduled for 10 rounds at Whittington Park, the Indianapolis boxer took the victory in three. In the second round, Claiborne made an enormous mistake when he decided to go toe to toe with his opponent. Locked and loaded, Dillon fired an accurate uppercut to the jaw of Claiborne that sent him across the ring and virtually out of it. Managing to right the ship, the local pug courageously stepped out in the third for his execution. Following some significant inside punishment, Dillon, paying no attention to the fans pleading with the referee to stop the fight, unloaded a right-hand smash to his opponent's chin, sending Claiborne horizontal to the canvas.[6]

With the announcement that Jack Dillon would be fighting "Fireman" Jim Flynn—and in, of all places, Kansas City—Indiana boxing fans were upset. And with good reason. First the mayor of Indianapolis barred prizefighting—with other Indiana cities taking the same action—and now in order to see the Hoosier phenom, who happened to be a world champion contender, they had to travel out of state. Over 500 miles away, Kansas City, Missouri, wasn't a simple commute.

"Fireman" Jim Flynn

A former railroad fireman turned pugilist, Jim Flynn likely began his professional boxing career in 1893. Indirectly working his way east from California to Montana and from Utah to Colorado, he managed to pick up a few state titles along the way but didn't step into the limelight until he fought for the world heavyweight title against Tommy Burns (1906). Although knocked out by Burns in the 15th round, Flynn was thrust into the spotlight. Victories over Jack Twin Sullivan, George Gardiner, and Billy Papke kept him relevant. And a newspaper victory over Sam Langford in 1910 carried him into a new decade. His vulnerability began to show in 1912, however, with losses to Jack Johnson and Luther McCarty (twice back-to-back, 1912–3). Three straight knockout victories brought him to Jack Dillon. At age 34, Flynn remained dangerous; his occasional moments of greatness confirmed it. He was, as they say, a "big name" fighter, and Jack Dillon knew it.

Was Jack Dillon the New White Hope?

Jack Johnson became the first Black world heavyweight boxing champion (1908–15), at the height of the Jim Crow era. Once white pugilist James J. Jeffries, the former heavyweight champion, failed to defeat Johnson in 1910, racists were convinced it was time to find a new "white hope." The first world white heavyweight champion was Luther McCarty, a fighter who lost back-to-back bouts to Jim Flynn. McCarty died on May 24, 1913, while defending his title, and it passed to Arthur Pelkey, followed by Gunboat Smith (January 1, 1914).

Setting aside the weight discrepancy (about 20 pounds), Jack Dillon, scaling at about 160, decided to fight "Fireman" Jim Flynn because he was tired of having the first-class middleweights sidestep him. While that was the reason, it didn't stop others from believing he had other motives. The *Indianapolis News* noted:

> Flynn is a bruiser, who has fought all of them from the Big Smoke [Jack Johnson] down, and, while he has gone back as a fighter, he is still a dangerous competitor for any of the big fellows. It is seldom that a little man can hold his own with a big one. Dillon will appear like a boy in the ring with Flynn, and if he escapes a bad beating many of his friends will be surprised. If Dillon defeats the big scrapper—look out. He is apt to challenge Jack Johnson.

Andrew Chiariglione (December 24, 1879–April 12, 1935), a.k.a. Fireman Jim Flynn (top), was a competitive heavyweight boxer who twice attempted to take the world heavyweight title without success. His second title attempt, against Jack Johnson, on July 4, 1912, appears at the bottom (Library of Congress, top: LC-DIG-ggbain-09696, digital file from original negative; bottom: LC-DIG-ggbain-11306, digital file from original negative).

> Dillon has lost battles by a shade, but he has never been hurt. In fact, in his hundreds of battles no one has ever knocked him off his feet, a record, perhaps, that no other fighter in the country can boast. If he wins decisively, it means challenges for Levinsky, Gunboat Smith, Jess Willard, and other white hopes. Next week Dillon is scheduled to fight Jack Lester in Denver. Lester is also a heavyweight with a good record.[7]

While some viewed the newspaper perspective as thought-provoking, others regarded it as racist. To be clear, Jack Dillon never mentioned the world white heavyweight champion as an ulterior motive, nor was he reluctant to fight anyone of any race. And fight he did against "Fireman" Jim Flynn. As the *Indianapolis Star* reported:

Jim Flynn, the "white hope crusher" from Pueblo, and Jack Dillon of Indianapolis fought ten terrific rounds to a draw before five thousand members of the Grand Avenue Athletic Club tonight. Dillon should have been given the decision because of the fact that he floored Flynn three times in the second round, each time for the count of nine. That was the only round that was decisively in favor of either of the fighters.[8]

A right cross and a right uppercut were the power punches responsible for dropping Flynn. Surprising was Flynn's infighting, which appeared to get the better of Dillon. The bout, leaning in favor of the Hoosier pugilist and corroborated by a crowd furious at the verdict, was deemed a draw.

For Jack Dillon it was off to Denver to encounter another Jack, as in Lester, over a scheduled 15 rounds at the Colorado Athletic Club. At a 25-pound disadvantage, Jack Dillon used his skills to counter each move by Lester. Undeniable was the authority in his punches. Brimming with confidence, Dillon appeared to amuse himself with his opponent for the first four rounds. As the *Indianapolis News* outlined:

Jack Dillon, of Indianapolis, made a chopping block of Jack Lester, a white hope from Seattle, in their go at the Colorado Athletic Club here [Denver] last night and forced Lester's second to throw up the sponge in the 10th round of a scheduled 15-round bout. Dillon, who recently whipped Vic Hanson before the same club here, was the aggressor all the way, but the ease of which he pounded and pummeled the giant Lester was a revelation to Denver fans.[9]

Dillon floored his opponent in the seventh, twice in the eighth, and twice in the 10th round. An airborne towel over the ropes concluded Lester's humiliation.

Jack Dillon arrived at Hot Springs, Arkansas, from Denver, on March 15. Two days later, he was scheduled for a 10-round battle with tomato can "Fighting" Dick Gilbert, of Denver. The event was part of a St. Patrick's Day celebration. While Gilbert's best chance for survival was to stay in his corner, he ventured out and lost nine of 10 rounds to Jack Dillon. The bout took place at the Hot Springs Athletic Club. Gilbert, overweight and out of shape, should get credit for making distance. Dillon, who hoped to head home following this bout, instead traveled to Memphis, where he was scheduled to go eight rounds against George K.O. Brown.

Not extending himself, because it wasn't required, Jack Dillon won his fight with Knockout Brown, of Chicago, on March 23. Opting for infighting, thanks to a weight advantage, Dillon picked up the rounds necessary to guarantee victory. Though his wary assaults were evident, there was a reason: Dillon was scheduled to meet Battling Levinsky for what many saw as the world light heavyweight title. The bout was to take place at Holland Arena in Butte, Montana, on April 14.

The *Star Press* suggested what it would mean were Jack Dillon victorious:

The match is advertised as being for the light heavyweight championship of America and should Dillon win, there seems to be no reason why he should not claim the middleweight, light heavyweight, and heavyweight titles of America for white pugs, as there seems to be no one in the country at the present time who could successfully dispute the claim.[10]

Jack Dillon versus Battling Levinsky— Light Heavyweight Championship of America

Jack Dillon arrived in Butte, Montana, on April 3. Planning to intensely train, he hoped to enter the ring against Battling Levinsky, of Brooklyn, at 166 pounds; incidentally, the latter would scale about six pounds heavier. Dillon, along with Jimmy Walters, his manager, quartered at the Finlen Hotel. The charged atmosphere had the vibe of a championship fight, but was it? It sure looked that way as a dedicated five-thousand-seat arena was constructed for the event. The *Miles City Star* reported:

> Not in the history of boxing in Montana has there been such a demand for seats and with the exception of 600 choice seats which have been set aside for the accommodation of out-of-Butte fans every $5 seat in the house has been sold. The big Holland Arena, in which the battle is to be staged, will seat a $10,000 house and it is freely predicted there will not be an empty seat.[11]

As for the pre-fight comments:

> Jack Dillon: I feel confident I will be returned the winner tonight, and will try to win by knockout. I know Levinsky's style of fighting now and have planned my battle accordingly. The Battler is a good man, but has not got a knockout wallop, and since I am satisfied on that point, I'll fight him instead of trying to outbox him, and feel certain victory will be mine when all is said and done tonight. I am thoroughly acclimated and mentally at ease, and I'll give the fans everything that is mine.

> Battling Levinsky: Jack Dillon is a tougher man than most people imagine. I think I won the last time we met, but will try and make it so decisive this time that no one can question the decision. It is my ambition to prove that I have got a knockout punch, despite stories to the contrary. I have been relying largely on speed and boxing ability to carry me against the class of men I have been meeting. It will be the right-cross "poppy punch" for Mr. Dillon tonight if the opportunity comes.[12]

Noted San Francisco glovemaker Sol Levinson was given the honor of producing a made-to-order set of six-ounce gloves for the bout. Both fighters weighed in on April 13 at catchweights: Dillon tipped at 163½, while Levinsky scaled at 170½. As far as betting was concerned, Dillon was the favorite at 10 to 8. Harry Stout, of Milwaukee, was selected to referee the 12-round contest. The preliminary six-round bout featured Young Luther McCarty versus Ray Brown. The semifinal saw Kid Brunell battle Dick Trounce over eight rounds.[13] Jack Dillon brought to the bout more than 100 victories against a handful of losses, while Levinsky, who won more than three times as many bouts as he lost, had about 100 fights' worth of experience.

The *Bozeman Courier* summarized the battle:

> Leading the fight all the way Jack Dillon of Indianapolis won easily from Battling Levinsky at Butte last night before a $9,000 house: Only the clever dodging and footwork of Levinsky saved him from terrific punishment, for Dillon started boring right in at the start and kept up the pace throughout. Practically every round was Dillon's according to reports from ringside, though Levinsky had an even break in the fifth, seventh and ninth.[14]

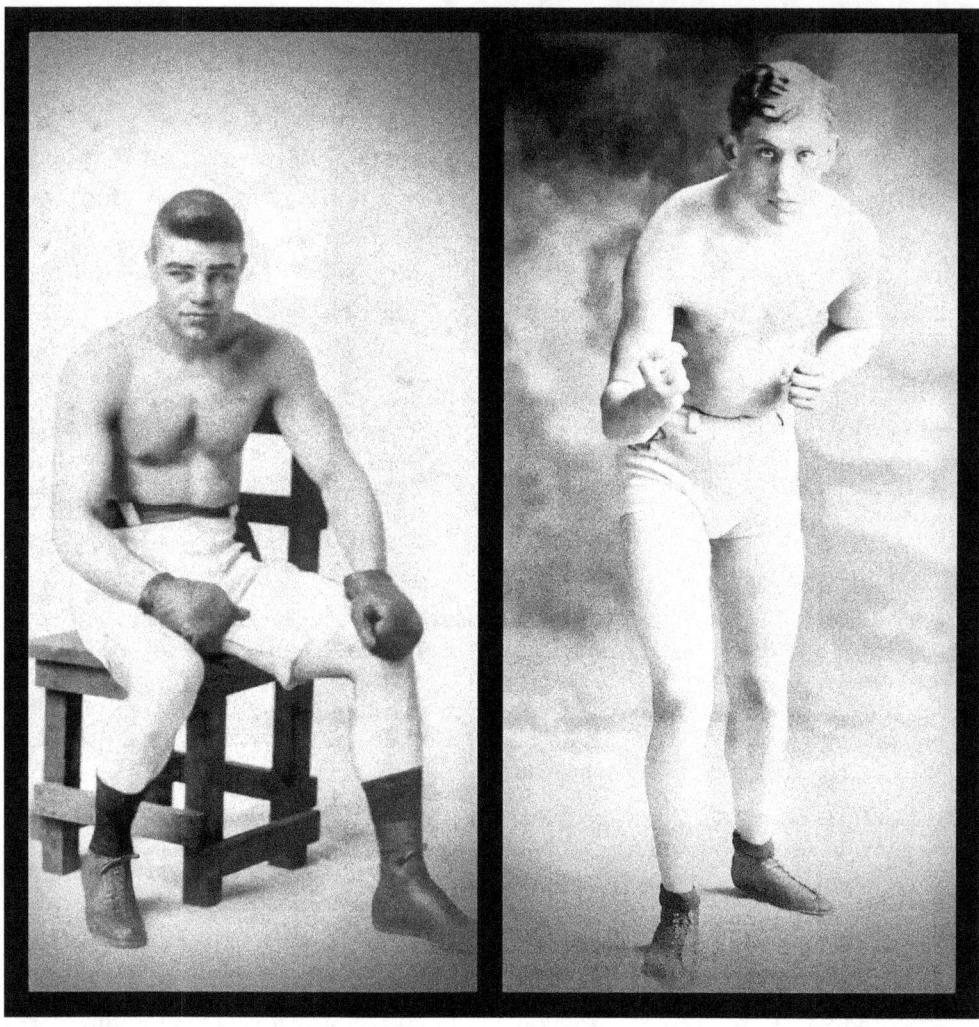

Jack Dillon (left) fought Battling Levinsky (right) 10 times during his career. After defeating Levinsky in their third meeting on April 14, 1914, Jack Dillon claimed the light heavyweight championship of America (left: author's collection; right: Library of Congress, LC-DIG-ggbain-15073, digital file from original negative).

It was a popular decision. The receipts were $8,221, of which Levinsky would receive $2,100 and Dillon about $2,000. By accounts, it was the largest gathering ever recorded in Butte.[15] Dillon stated afterward:

> The only chance I had was to keep after him. Levinsky is a good boxer—fine for his weight. It came out as I figured and I would have finished him if I had taken a chance after the seventh round, when I saw that the body punches had weakened him. He struck me one telling blow. It is hard to fight when you have to chase a clever boxer.[16]

Jack Dillon also declared he would go after Gunboat Smith—who held the world white heavyweight championship of the United States—but he did not specify the title by name. Admitting interest in the heavyweight championship of the world, Dillon did not mention Jack Johnson, who held that title. Both versions of the heavyweight title appeared under consideration.

Confusion surrounded Dillon's following bout. He was scheduled to meet Al Norton, a California heavyweight, on April 28, before veteran Al Kaufman reportedly replaced Norton 10 days prior to the bout. However, Al Norton returned to the fight picture when he convinced Kaufman to reconsider. Was there more behind the switch? Likely. Norton, who was the West Coast's "white hope," was a sparring partner for the deceased Luther McCarty.[17]

The *South Bend Tribune* published:

> Jack Dillon of Indianapolis defended his self-styled light heavyweight title last night when he won a decision over Al Norton of Los Angeles after ten terrific rounds of fighting here. At long range the inexperienced Norton was master of the situation and at infighting Dillon excelled. Referee Bates drew a close line in awarding the fight to the Hoosier.[18]

Returning to Indianapolis on May 14, Jack Dillon felt good and, decked out in a tailored suit, white shirt, and complementary tie, looked like a titleholder. Topped off with a bowler hat, Jack Dillon's new look even had him sporting a cane. The light heavyweight champion of America—and claimant to the middleweight crown—had much to be proud of.

Wedding Bells

On May 14, 1914, the rites of matrimony were legally solemnized, by the Reverend N.H. Carlisle at Covington in the county of Kenton, Kentucky, between Ernest C. Price of Indianapolis and Grace Reed of Indianapolis. Nate Farb acted as Dillon's best man in the private ceremony.

Grace had an eight-year-old son, Ralph Reed, from her previous marriage. Her son was cared for by Grace Schwartzman (Grace's mother). According to census records, Ralph Reed would later be identified as Ralph Price.[19]

No other details regarding the event were given, and rarely would facts surface regarding the couple's relationship.

Indianapolis on Four Wheels

Since May 30, 1911, Memorial Day weekend in Indianapolis has typically included a 500-mile race. And the event continued to grow in popularity. Because it drew thousands of spectators—an estimated 110 thousand fans in 1914—it was a prime opportunity for other forms of entertainment, including boxing. During the second week of the month, Jack Dillon agreed to meet Battling Levinsky over a 10-round journey at Federal League Park on May 29. Levinsky balked, however, and was replaced by Gus Christie. Unsatisfied, the promoters pulled Christie and successfully renegotiated with Levinsky. Such was the glorified life of a fight promoter.

On May 18, Jack Dillon had an appointment in downtown Indianapolis. He hopped inside his large green machine, which resembled a race car, and drove off. Finding a parking spot along the curb on North Illinois Street, he parked and took his appointment. When Dillon returned to the vehicle, a small crowd had gathered. When they noticed he appeared to be the driver, a conversation ensued. The *Indianapolis News* detailed the conversation:

> "Whose car is that?" asked an inquisitive stranger.
> "It is my car," replied Dillon.
> "Who are you?" was the next question.
> "My name is Ernest Price."
> "Are you entered in the race?"
> "No, that is not my line," was Dillon's parting reply.
> The bystander would not have been disappointed had they known that Ernest Price was the right name for Jack Dillon.[20]

Prior to his bout against Battling Levinsky, Jack Dillon told the *Huntington Herald* he had his heart set on a battle against Jack Johnson, heavyweight champion:

> I sincerely believe that I can whip "big smoke." I know that he will have a big advantage in height, weight, and reach, but I don't believe he has the courage necessary to win when he is crowded. And believe me, I'll crowd him if I ever get a chance at him in the ring.[21]

Based on Dillon's previous victories, nobody doubted that a battle with a heavyweight contender, such as Gunboat Smith, could be imminent. Johnson, on the other hand, well, that remained to be seen. Time to once again address Levinsky.

In their fourth meeting, Jack Dillon and Battling Levinsky fought to what entered the books as a 10-round no decision. Not everyone saw it that way, however: headlines included "Dillon Earns the Decision Over Levinsky" (*Indianapolis Star*), "Dillon Is Given a Licking" (*Fort Wayne News*), "Dillon Shades Levinsky" (*Anderson Herald*), and "Battling Levinsky Earns Draw Bout" (*Palladium-Item*).[22] The latter conclusion was given by Edward Smith, referee of the fight. The *Palladium-Item* printed his assessment:

> Battling Levinsky, New York's great battling pugilist, surely made good in the ring last night with Jack Dillon. The battler put up such a rattling finish in the eighth, ninth and 10th rounds of the struggle with the almost unbeaten local star, that he easily earned a draw, to say nothing of the wild applause of thousands of strangers who watched his work. The battle was a corker all the way, with both men in grand shape. Dillon weighed 162 and Levinsky 169. The contest was decided in the new Federal League Park and drew $9,000 at the gate.[23]

Jack Dillon left for the West Coast on June 3. Scheduled for a 12-round battle with Bob Moha on June 13 in Butte, Montana, he wanted to get acclimated to his surroundings before the battle.[24] And as it proved, he arrived in Butte during a hostile miners' strike that caused the battle to be postponed for two days. The *Indianapolis Star* noted:

> Four hundred seceding miners late tonight [June 14] seized the safe of the Western Federation from 20 policemen on a large truck and are carting it to the flat below the city, where it will be dynamited.[25]

Dillon, who witnessed firsthand the temper of the miners, didn't argue with the police when they decided to postpone the fight. It was the correct decision. Old West attitudes surfaced on occasion; incidentally, the last recorded stagecoach robbery in American history wouldn't take place until December 5, 1916.

Jack Dillon was awarded the 12-round decision over Bob Moha in the pair's fourth meeting, but it proved to be a disappointment. In his usual aggressive style, Dillon outclassed an opponent who refused to participate. Repeatedly hissed for his failure to engage, Moha covered similar to a turtle being attacked by a tiger shark. As the *Indianapolis Star* outlined:

> Dillon tried to keep his man at long range and jabbed him repeatedly through his guard. One clinch would follow another and at close quarters Moha tried to inflict damage, but Dillon met him halfway. If any shade existed at the end of infighting, the honors belonged to Moha, but he did no damage, and his close style was displeasing. Dillon outfought, out gamed, and outslugged his man. He was the aggressor in the majority of the rounds.[26]

The Montana Boxing Commission, furious with Moha, ordered the Cooper City Athletic Club not to pay the fighter his purse and ordered an investigation. Dillon, who performed well, was paid his portion for the fight. The event forced the Indianapolis pugilist to cancel a number of scheduled bouts. Frustrated, Dillon returned home on June 21.

Quickly acting to make up for lost time and revenue, Dillon was matched with "Sailor" Ed Petrosky over 10 rounds in Kansas City. The bout was to be held during the Fourth of July weekend at the American Association baseball park. While making his travel arrangements, Dillon learned he had been suspended for a period of six months by the Montana Boxing Commission as a result of his fight with Moha. As for his Milwaukee-based adversary, he lost his $1,500 purse.

By taking eight of the 10 rounds of their July 3 battle, Jack Dillon comfortably defeated "Sailor" Ed Petrosky. Dillon scored the only knockdown of the evening when he dropped Petrosky with a left uppercut in the seventh round. The Indiana pugilist drew criticism, however, for not putting away his California adversary during the journey. Hey, it's boxing.

Confident of his success, Jack Dillon purchased a new Hupmobile prior to his contest with Petrosky. The new four-passenger vehicle was purchased from H.T. Hearsey of the Hearsey-Willis Company, a local distributor. Viewing the vehicle on the showroom floor enticed Dillon to take it for a quick test drive. Sold.

When he wasn't spotted driving or training, Jack Dillon was booking bouts at a record pace. Accepting most challenges created confusion and left Jimmy Walters with the job of cleaning up the mess. Of the ones that came to fruition before the end of the month: Dillon met George "K.O." Brown in Terre Haute over 10 rounds on July 21, followed by Joe Mace three days later in Muncie, Indiana.

Billed as a fight for the middleweight championship of the world, Jack Dillon's bout against George "Knockout" Brown of Chicago was far from it. Dillon appeared uninspired and overweight—he tipped at 168, while Brown scaled at 157—during the sloppy contest. When things appeared to be getting out of hand in the third frame, Brown's manager stepped in and claimed a foul. This ignited a near riot that didn't subside until the police intervened. When order was finally restored, nobody was certain about what they saw. The contest, which entered the books as a 10-round no decision, was viewed either as a draw or Dillon's by a small margin. The fiasco that erupted in the third round was detailed in the *Indianapolis Star*:

On June 15, 1914, Jack Dillon defended his claim to the world light heavyweight title by defeating Bob Moha (pictured here). The latter saw himself as holding the NYSAC light heavyweight crown (Library of Congress, LC-DIG-ggbain-10605, digital file from original negative).

The fighting was fast and brought the crowd to its feet. Suddenly Brown stopped and grabbed Dillon around the legs, forcing him backwards over the ropes. In going down Dillon swung his right and landed solidly on Brown's back. Referee [Tommy] Dillon started to help the fighters to their feet and as he did so Tommy Walsh, Brown's manager, jumped into the ring and claimed a foul, declaring Dillon had hit Brown while he was down. Referee Dillon disallowed Walsh's claim and immediately there was confusion. Brown and Jack Dillon continued slugging each other until Referee Dillon attempted to part them.[27]

It took the police to jump inside the ring in attempt to control Tommy Walsh. It failed. Officers were ordered to arrest Brown, but not before promoter John Jensen was able to push Brown's manager over the ropes. The *Indianapolis Star* noted: "The crowd cheered, and as if by magic seated itself. The fighters were led to their corners and a moment later the gong clanged for the fourth round."[28] The incident would be recalled for years due to its unbelievability.

Three days later, the much-anticipated bout between Jack Dillon and Howard Morrow turned into an unanticipated contest between Dillon and Joe Mace, of Chicago. Having broken his hand, Morrow sent Mace to fulfill his contractual obligations. Was the substitution legal? It appeared that way as the action was accepted. Mace wasn't Morrow, and that became immediately obvious to fight fans. Down for a nine count in the opening round, Mace barely survived until the third frame. Referee Tommy Dillon, noting that Mace was nothing more than a target, stopped the fight in the third before Jack Dillon could turn Mace's lights out.[29]

Yes, There Really Is a Kalamazoo

Having purchased a new cottage near Broad Ripple, Jack Dillon was hoping to take a vacation before the end of summer. The pugilist was repeatedly prone to an attractive fight offer, however. A match with the *real* Howard Morrow, the Benton Harbor middleweight, at Kalamazoo, Michigan, was an offer he couldn't refuse. Scheduled for August 12, the bout shouldn't be a distraction. Besides, he enjoyed training at the cottage and felt Morrow deserved a good licking. Taking advantage of the nearby White River, Dillon's new love was rowing. He took a three-mile row most mornings, and not only was it a beneficial way to exercise certain muscle groups, but it was also relaxing for the pugilist.[30]

It was a Kalamazoo comedy: Howard Morrow refused to enter the ring for his scheduled 10-round go with Jack Dillon. And because of Morrow's behavior, his bout with Dillon didn't begin until about midnight. Moments before he was to enter the ring, Morrow disappeared. By the time he was found—and persuaded by a reduction of rounds to six to return to the Fuller Theatre—the remaining spectators were furious. The Hoosier Bearcat was so upset at Morrow's behavior that he agreed to do battle for nothing. For the few who stayed until the fight began, they witnessed Dillon unleashing an unmerciful battering to the body of Morrow. The no-decision bout, in Dillon's favor, was insulting to the fans and to the sport.

Having numerous offers in September, Team Dillon took three: "Sailor" Gus Einert over 10 rounds in Terre Haute on September 7; George "K.O." Brown over 10 rounds in Vincennes on September 15; and Frank Mantell over 12 rounds in Columbus, Ohio. By the last week in August, Jack Dillon was back with Sam Murbarger. Scheduling debacles, a majority of which were his own fault, were overwhelming the pugilist. Not to mention he was not conducting the proper due diligence in order to augment his career or bank account.

Jack Dillon coasted to a 10-round no-decision victory over novice Gus Einert. It was a pointless booking that attracted few people. It certainly justified the pugilist's decision to bring back Sam Murbarger, however.

Since George "K.O." Brown consistently gave Jack Dillon a competitive battle, their match made more sense; incidentally, the Indianapolis fighter was signed to meet some power punchers over the next few weeks. Welcome back Sam, a manager who understood his fighter. The pair fought 10 fast rounds to a draw at the Knox County Fairgrounds; it was their seventh meeting. It was an aggressive fight with both boxers enduring considerable body punishment. As the *Times* noted, "First one would have an advantage, and then the other would do the forcing, but when it was all over, with both men on their feet and fighting hard, there was practically nothing to choose between them."[31]

The battle with Brown appeared to be the proper prelude to Dillon's scheduled bout against Battling Levinsky. Their September 25 contest was called off, however, so Team Dillon headed to Columbus, Ohio, to meet Frank Mantell. Having met before, both fighters were prepared, even if the execution was weak. The Rhode Island pugilist, having improved his defensive skills, was able to make distance, but he accomplished little else. It was Dillon's 12-round newspaper decision.

In an attempt to call out division contenders, Sam Murbarger posted a certified check for $1,000, signed by Jack Dillon, with the sporting editor of *The Star* as a forfeit for a match with George Chip, Jimmy Clabby, Mike Gibbons, or Eddie McGoorty. The check was a guarantee that his fighter could make 158 pounds, the middleweight limit. Because Dillon at no time hesitated to tackle a heavier opponent, he thought folks had forgotten that he was a middleweight.

By the time the dust settled on his fight offers, Jack Dillon would find himself battling twice in October. Both involved replacements: Substituting for Carl Morris would be "Fireman" Jim Flynn, who would meet Dillon at Kansas City on October 5, and replacing Battling Levinsky was George "K.O." Brown, who would battle the Hoosier at St. Louis on October 14. Both events had considerable drawing power.

Delivering a solid performance, Jack Dillon captured nine of 10 rounds in a solid 10-round victory over "Fireman" Jim Flynn. Although there were no knockdowns, the Pueblo heavyweight's knees repeatedly buckled from the terrific punching he endured. Dillon's speed allowed him to evade damage while punching at will. With little choice, Flynn went to his bag of tricks. If it meant his survival, and a couple of times it did, he had little choice but to hold for dear life.

Up next, the familiar figure of "Knockout" Brown. The pair was meeting for the eighth time. The *Indianapolis Star* reported:

> Dillon realizes that meeting Brown again is not adding anything to his popularity, but at the same time he was forced to fill the date in the Mound City, as he was originally scheduled to meet Levinsky. Jack is in fine shape and will weigh in at about 159 pounds for the Chicago Greek.[32]

Sam Murbarger was asked about Dillon's headhunting for heavyweight "Gunboat" Smith, and the fight manager responded, "We'll fight Smith and beat him—any distance suits us."

It was while working as a railroad fireman in Pueblo, Colorado, before the turn of the century that Jim Flynn turned to pugilism (Library of Congress, LC-DIG-ggbain-09568, digital file from original negative).

Under Arrest for Faking Fight

The *Fort Wayne Journal-Gazette* delivered the shocking news:

> Jack Dillon, claimant of the middleweight championship, his manager, Sam Murbarger, and his second, Robert Stolkin, of Indianapolis, were arrested here [St. Louis] tonight after a bout between Dillon and George "Knockout" Brown was stopped in the fourth round by Referee Eddie Randall, who declared the fighters were merely feigning. The bout was scheduled for 10 rounds. The trio from Indianapolis was arrested at the request of the manager of the club at which the fight was staged. The police declared they would hold Dillon and his manager and second for investigation by the chief of police tomorrow. Throughout the bout the fighters were hissed by the crowd for their lack of aggressiveness.[33]

The charge was obtaining money under false pretense. Evidently, Sam Murbarger, on behalf of Dillon, accepted a $750 advance for the bout. Brown was not arrested because he did not receive an advance. On October 15, the assistant prosecuting attorney refused to issue warrants against the gentlemen, and the three were released. Countering, Dillon began threatening to bring suit against the host club alleging false imprisonment.[34] Team Dillon closed the books for the month following this no contest and not once returned to St. Louis, Missouri.

On November 9, Jack Dillon met Young Charley Weinert, a promising light heavyweight, in Philadelphia. Though still a teenager (19), the East Coast boxer already weighed 178 pounds. While the youngster had a slight advantage in height and reach, that was as far as it went. As the *Indianapolis Star* reported:

> Dillon had knocked Weinert down for a count of nine, near the end of the second round by a right-hand jab which landed flush on the jaw. Weinert was in distress. In fact, he was dazed when he arose. While he was trying to get his bearings, Dillon rushed at him like an infuriated bull, and driving him halfway around the ring, sent him down with a rain of blows. This time Weinert fell way through the ropes. The club physician saw that Weinert was unable to breathe and jumping into the ring rolled him over on his back. The bell rang with Weinert staggering to his feet. Dillon had won the battle.[35]

Weinert recovered and returned to the ring in February 1915.[36]

When Dillon's Madison Square Garden bout against Young Ahearn was called off, his team headed home.

Jack Dillon met Dick Gilbert before the Colorado Athletic Club in Denver on November 24. Originally scheduled for 20 rounds, it was trimmed to 15. Toying with his prey for the first 10 rounds, Dillon looked comfortable. Gilbert ignited in the 11th, however, and forced the Hoosier Bearcat into action. Each blow reaching Dillon cost Gilbert three or four in return. And that punch ratio was rarely a good sign. Dillon was awarded the decision.

By the middle of December, Dillon's schedule wasn't panning out. Part of the ambiguity was due to personal issues. Dillon, a.k.a. Ernest Price, who was seldom one to share anything about his personal life, was in superior court on December 21. He was being questioned by Frank Smith, trustee of the Premier Motor Car Manufacturing Company, which obtained a judgment of $283.55 against Price for automobile repairs. The *Indianapolis News* reported:

> Price had filed a schedule with Sheriff Portteus, alleging that he was worth $40, and that he could not pay the judgement. (He then answered a series of questions.)
>
> Q. *What is the least you ever fought for?*
> A. Ninety cents. That was five years ago in Indiana.... The highest I ever received was $2,100. The lowest I received during the last year outside the St. Louis fight was $70. I didn't get anything out of the St. Louis fight.
>
> Price said his expenses amounted to from $400 to $600 a month. He said he had given his automobile to his wife for a birthday present, although he could not remember the date of her birthday. He told the court he listed everything he had on his schedule except his clothes.
>
> Q. *How many clothes have you got?*
> A. Five suits, along with silk shirts, etc.
>
> The court then ordered Price either to settle the bill or be ready to give up his clothes by Thursday.
>
> A. I don't care what they take away from me, so long as they don't get my boxing gloves.[37]

As a married man, Price was entitled to a $600 exemption, so he could have listed his clothes on his schedule and escaped paying the judgment.

Six. Indestructible, 1914

Jack Dillon took 24 bouts in 1914, and did not face a decisive defeat. Unrivaled, he continued to claim the middleweight championship of America and added to his résumé the light heavyweight championship of America, following his victory over Battling Levinsky. Once again under the wing of Sam Murbarger, his future at no time looked brighter. Tommy Dillon joined his brother on two popular fight cards, the trip out to Hot Springs, Arkansas, on St. Patrick's Day and the Labor Day Boxing Show on September 7 in Terre Haute, Indiana. On May 14, 1914, Ernest C. Price of Indianapolis married Grace Reed of Indianapolis. Not only was he now a husband, but a stepfather as well. Maintaining their privacy, they were rarely a topic of discussion. And that was what Jack Dillon demanded.

Chapter Seven

Head East, 1915

"He looked at me as if I was a side dish he hadn't ordered."
—Ring Lardner

As the recession of 1913–4 slowed, Americans, who had faced a near 10 percent unemployment rate, gradually returned to work. Ironically, much of the economic optimism was due to supplying a world war the country was hoping to avoid.

Establishing an East Coast Reputation

Can you say terrifying? Looking across the ring and viewing the lethal figure of Jack Dillon made opponents quiver and question their sanity. It was indeed similar to looking at a side dish you had mixed feelings about consuming. On top of his game, the Hoosier Bearcat was intimidation personified.

"Don't Cool Out" was the headline that greeted fight fans reading the *Fort Wayne News* on New Year's Day. The article out of Chicago stated:

> For the first time in a number of years not one big pugilistic battle is booked for New Year's, past records proving that there are too many late sleepers on the first day of the incoming year to bank on record houses. What looks like the best battle will be staged over the six-round route at Philadelphia between Jack Dillon and Young Ahearn.[1]

The analysis proved correct, even if the battle verdict was unclear. The reviews of the encounter varied and caused confusion among fight fans. In a random survey of 10 newspapers, the majority saw the six-round no decision in Philadelphia as a draw. The following concluded the contest was even: *Evansville Journal, Gazette, Altoona Tribune, News-Journal, Morning Herald, Pittston Gazette*, and *Pittsburgh Post-Gazette*. But other papers—*Wilkes-Barre Times Leader, Reading Times, Times,* and *Indianapolis News*—concluded that Jack Dillon lost. Not one daily claimed that Dillon had won.

Young Ahearn, of Brooklyn, who won four times as many bouts as he lost, was far better than anticipated. And every observer agreed. His opponent, on the other hand, was a different story. Waiting until the fourth round—which made little sense in a close six-round contest—to ignite, Dillon was strong during the final two rounds, while Ahearn, by staying the limit, prevented a loss.

Jacob K. Woodward (circa 1895–1979), a.k.a. Young Ahearn, a.k.a. The Brooklyn Dancing Master, began his career in 1909 and fought until 1924 (circa 1915) (Library of Congress, left: LC-DIG-ggbain-17687, digital file from original negative; right: LC-DIG-ggbain-17686, digital file from original negative).

Bright Lights, Big City

Lack of East Coast exposure was hurting his fighter, and Sam Murbarger knew it. Jack Dillon's success—and reputation as an unbeatable power puncher—in the Midwest didn't translate well to markets like New York. And that had to change. If Dillon was going to get the respect he deserved—and big money fights—he had to showcase his skills in major markets. Also, Sam Murbarger needed to establish the necessary contacts to guarantee his fighter's success.[2]

Off to New York, where Jack Dillon met Dan "Porky" Flynn of Boston at the Broadway Sporting Club in Brooklyn on January 16. Located at 944 Halsey Street, "The Broadway" was a popular fight club—you know, a smoke-filled joint that attracted gamblers and every street punk or kid who wanted to be somebody—in the Bushwick section of Brooklyn. Every local pug who was worth his salt fought at the venue. Flynn, who turned pro in 1906, had been in the ring with elite fighters such as Frank Klaus, Stanley Ketchel, Joe Jeannette, Battling Levinsky, and Sam Langford. The *Indianapolis News* previewed:

> In meeting Flynn, the Hoosier will take on another heavyweight, but since he himself has all but outgrown his middleweight togs he will not face any particular handicap in the matter of weight. Flynn has been making considerable headway in the fistic arena of late, his most recent achievement being to gain a decision over Battling Levinsky in a 10-round bout before the Broadway A.C., New York, on Christmas day.[3]

Flynn stood six feet, two inches and scaled at about 195 pounds. A mountain of a man, he wasn't intimidated by Jack Dillon, purely defenseless against him. Decisively beaten by the Hoosier Bearcat, Flynn was dropped in the fourth round. Shaken, he was saved by the bell from being counted out. Stumbling through the final rounds, Flynn was able to make distance.

Nothing short of a commanding performance, Dillon impressed. Outweighed by at least 20 pounds, the Hoosier pugilist negated each perceived advantage of his rival.[4] For most observers, that the Hub fighter remained standing at the conclusion of the 10 rounds was a miracle.

Having briefly returned home, Team Dillon left Indianapolis on the evening of January 22. The *Star Press* noted:

> Dillon meets Larry English at Memphis Monday night in an eight-round bout. Before his encounter with English, Jack and his manager will stop off at Christopher, Illinois, for a short boxing exhibition. Frank Hoe, a local middleweight, has been performing in Christopher.[5]

Scheduled for eight rounds, Jack Dillon preferred only four in advance of an unconditional surrender. Flooring Larry English twice in the fourth round, Dillon left the Brooklyn fighter's seconds little choice but to throw up the sponge. Dillon took a vicious head butt in the fourth that split his lip, however. Thankfully, his corner, with assistance of the ring physician, took control of their fighter's bleeding after the bout.

Traveling to Cincinnati on February 1, Jack Dillon attended the 10-round no-decision bout between Ed "Gunboat" Smith and Jim Flynn. As part of his visit, he challenged the winner of the contest. Having won a trifecta over Flynn, Smith was his prime target. And, as fate might have it, Smith was viewed as the victor. Dillon also expressed interest in battling Mike Gibbons, at 158 pounds. Since Gibbons bested Jimmy Clabby, on January 21, in Milwaukee, he had been claiming the middleweight crown. As anticipated, such a declaration didn't sit well with Dillon.

Returning to New York City in February, Jack Dillon toyed with Frank Mantell over the 10-round no-decision route. The adversaries, who had met the previous September, were hoping the city exposure would work to their benefit. Having injured his right arm in the third, Dillon was forced to rely on his left for the remainder of the rounds. The *Indianapolis Star* detailed:

> In the seventh round Dillon managed to land one on Mantell's mouth, which drew blood. As the ninth opened Dillon rushed from his corner and for a few seconds it looked as if he would put his man out. He landed short body punches, which made Mantell fight hard. Both men were fresh when the bout ended.[6]

Three days after this lackluster engagement, Dillon was back in the ring.

Finishing the month in Brooklyn, at the Sporting Club, Jack Dillon met Johnny Howard over 10 rounds. Dillon, who scaled at 175, used his seven-and-a-half-pound advantage to outscore his opponent. In the seventh, in what was the highlight of the bout, Dillon fired a targeted right to the jaw of Howard that briefly dropped the Bayonne, New Jersey, pugilist. Howard, who was bleeding profusely from the nose and mouth, struggled to stand by the end of the battle.

March was shaping up nicely for Team Dillon, which would meet Tom McCarty in Brooklyn on March 2 (this was the postponed February battle) and Ed "Gunboat" Smith in Milwaukee on March 16.

Likely a draw, Jack Dillon went 10 no-decision rounds with Tom McCarty, of Lewistown, Montana. Since the first five rounds were close to even, the last rounds would determine, or in this case confirm, the verdict. Dillon, at a 10-pound deficit, picked up the pace in the sixth term. Rather than long-range artillery, his shorter combinations proved more efficacious. In retrospect, he should have begun his assault a round earlier. Opinions on the fight varied: The *Times* saw McCarty with "a hairline victory," while the *Muncie Evening Press* stated that Dillon "trounced Cowboy Tom McCarty." One wonders where these reporters were sitting.

Edward "Gunboat" Smith

Standing a tall six feet, two inches, Edward "Gunboat" Smith, following a challenging childhood, ultimately found consistency in his life serving in the U.S. Navy. And it was there he began boxing and even won the heavyweight championship of the Pacific Fleet. Establishing himself as a competent sparring partner on the West Coast, he worked with Jack Johnson and Stanley Ketchel, two men who required no introduction. Impressed by what he saw in the youngster, author Jack London helped fund his training.

In 1913, Smith defeated Bombardier Billy Wells, Jess Willard, "Fireman" Jim Flynn, and Sam Langford. In 1914 he posted victories over Arthur Pelkey and Tom McCarty. By defeating Arthur Pelkey, he claimed the controversial White heavyweight title.

In 1915, Smith took a 20-round points decision over Battling Levinsky and a 10-round newspaper decision over "Fireman" Jim Flynn. Understanding that Jack

Dillon, in the spirit of Bob Fitzsimmons, was collecting titles, Smith, a full-fledged heavyweight, was training hard. According to the *Star Press*, "Dillon expects to win and if he does, he will claim the White heavyweight title on the grounds that Smith has a decision over Jess Willard."[7] It was a tactical comment, if you read between the lines.

Attracting considerable attention, the event spurred a special coach operating between Indianapolis and Milwaukee. The Special (train) departed Union Station and arrived at its destination by noon. Everyone was excited, still finding it difficult to fathom that the man who had made a name for himself as a middleweight was in the ring with such a talented heavyweight. The *Star Press* summarized it this way:

> Dillon was too fast for Smith on the infighting, using rights and lefts to the body with good advantage. Smith depended almost entirely upon his left, trying hard wide swings to the head which seldom found their mark. The fight was marred by considerable clinching, Referee Stout being kept busy separating the men.[8]

In the end, Dillon had a shade better of Smith, according to a majority of sporting writers at ringside. George Coogan, former Evansville middleweight, witnessed the no-decision bout and published his view in the *Evansville Journal*:

> Have just returned with about 250 fans from Milwaukee. Dillon won all the way from Gunboat Smith. He started with his head in and kept close to the Gunner all the way. Once Gunboat uppercut a vicious right to the chin, but Dillon came back with two rights to the body. The fight throughout was Dillon's by a wide margin. Dillon today is undoubtedly the best White man in the right at his weight.[9]

Jack Dillon and Sam Murbarger departed to St. Paul on April 1, before heading to Hudson, Wisconsin, to meet "Fighting" Billy Murray on April 6. Dillon had hoped to meet Mike Gibbons, however that match still eluded him. Perhaps disappointment played into Dillon's lifeless 10-round display with Billy Murray, which was about as exciting as watching grass grow. More time spent clinching than fighting had spectators restless—screams for more action could be heard from throughout the arena. In spite of the bellowing, Dillon grabbed a slight edge.

On to Lexington, Kentucky, where Jack Dillon met Marty Cutler of Chicago. As a promising heavyweight, Cutler was a former sparring partner of Jess Willard and Jack Johnson. Dillon was quick to dampen Cutler's spirits, however, by transforming him into a veritable punching bag over six rounds. Forgetting how to defend himself, Cutler was struck at will until his body could handle no more. His seconds agreed, and in went the sponge. As the *Indianapolis News* noted, "At the conclusion of the fourth round he [Cutler] returned to his corner groggy and sick as a result of the body pummeling."[10]

Staying in Lexington, Kentucky—likely as a favor to the promoter, and to Dillon who wanted to make a clear statement with his actions—Jack Dillon met wrestler-turned-boxer Andre Anderson on May 5 at the Lexington Athletic Association's Arena.

Frederick Boeseneilers, a.k.a. Andre Anderson, stood six feet, five inches and routinely tipped over 225 pounds. Naturally, his size alone caught the eyes of many influential individuals in the boxing world, including James J. Johnston. But when folks learned that he was also a decorated military veteran with athletic prowess, many felt they could mold—okay, market or take advantage of—the sportsman into a marketable boxing star. His first professional test: none other than Jack Dillon.

Outweighed by over 30 pounds, Dillon knocked out novice Anderson in the fifth round of a scheduled 10-round bout. Dominant throughout, Dillon didn't erupt until the fifth term, when his blows had the behemoth on thin ice. As the *Indianapolis Star* reported, "Dillon got busy at the beginning of the fifth round, and landing a hard right cross to Anderson's jaw, ended the battle."[11]

Obvious to every heavyweight contender: a Hoosier Bearcat was on the loose. And nothing—not size, not speed, not skill—was going to save his victims.

As for Anderson, he would later be recalled for a brutal battle against Jack Dempsey in 1916, and as a possible influence for Ernest Hemingway's short story "The Killers."

Trying to stay sharp for a possible title bout at the Indianapolis Motor Speedway, Jack Dillon headed to Joplin, Missouri, on May 20, where he met Jack Lester, of Seattle, over 15 rounds. With 50 bouts of experience, Lester was an average fighter who was forced to utilize survival tactics to make distance. Dillon pounded him like a spike over a railroad tie. Although the first eight rounds were slow, Dillon finished strong. As the *Indianapolis Star* reported, "In the thirteenth round a shower of quick jabs to the stomach more or less had him out when Lester dropped to his knees and took a count of nine, the gong saving him."[12]

Ever since big Jess Willard devoured Jack Johnson in Havana, Jack Dillon has been hurling unanswered challenges to the big man. And he wasn't alone. All the offers were neglected because the Pottawatomie Giant, who stood six feet, six inches and weighed as much as he wanted, was enjoying the benefits of the title and in no rush to defend it. Outside the ring, Willard was never more popular. Lucrative offers—from motion pictures and vaudeville to Buffalo Bill's Wild West show—poured in daily from all over the world. For Dillon, whose challenges would continue, it was now a question of patience and perseverance.

When a number of matches failed to pan out, Dillon headed to Rochester, New York, where he engaged with Tom "Bearcat" McMahon over 10 rounds on June 7. McMahon was a veteran heavyweight fighting out of Newcastle, Pennsylvania. Having entered the ring with George Chip, Battling Levinsky, Ed "Gunboat" Smith, Dan "Porky" Flynn, Jess Willard, and Sam Langford, meeting Jack Dillon was just another day at the office.

Anticipating some firepower during the fray, spectators were soon disappointed. The slow 10-round no decision was a lackluster performance. Dillon appeared lethargic. His punch frequency and the steam behind the blows were

Jack Jubeck (1891–1916), a.k.a. Jack "Kid" Lester, was a solid heavyweight who fought out of Washington and Canada early in his career. Thanks to Tommy Burns, he honed his skills in Australia before returning to the United States (Library of Congress, LC-DIG-ggbain-15151, digital file from original negative).

unimpressive. Still, to many it gave him a slight advantage in the battle. Not everyone agreed, as the local newspapers granted the edge to McMahon.[13]

Frustrated by the fight scene in Indianapolis, Sam Murbarger mentioned to the press that they—Team Dillon—were thinking about shifting their headquarters to New York. As a major market, it had far more to offer from a number of perspectives—proximity, a factor in profitability, would no longer be a negotiation issue. It sounded like the right call. The decision awaited the response from Team Dillon's friends and family.

In another sluggardly 10-round no decision, Jack Dillon tangled with Frank Mantell at Redland Field in Cincinnati, Ohio, on June 11. While Dillon opted for infighting, Mantell favored long-range artillery. The Hoosier Bearcat's timing was off the majority of the evening, and if it wasn't for his body assaults against Mantell, he wouldn't have taken the newspaper victory. In a surprise action, the *Indianapolis News* reported:

> In the eighth round of the main bout Jack Dillon was served with attachment papers for his share of the gate money. The Premier Motor Company, of Indianapolis, brought the

suit on a judgment of $285. The show was a loser for Bobby Bower, the promoter, despite the fact that popular prices prevailed.[14]

Not commenting on his legal woes, Jack Dillon headed to Kansas City to do battle against George Chip for the 10th time. Mirroring Oscar Wilde's sentiment that "consistency is the last refuge of the unimaginative," the pair fought to a 10-round draw. In truth, nine out of the 10 bouts between them ended in a draw. As the *South Bend News-Times* noted, "The crowd was displeased with the bout and during the hooting that greeted the boxers in the eighth round, a deep bass voice called out: 'Now kiss.'"[15] As for the Bearcat's excuse, he was feeling weak from trimming to 158 before the bout.[16]

Jack Dillon had planned to meet Gunner Moir near Evansville on July 7, but Mayor Benjamin Bosse announced on July 5 that all matches scheduled to be staged in town had been canceled. On that note, Team Dillon traveled to New York City, or Rockaway, Queens, to be specific. Jack Dillon was scheduled for two 10-round bouts at Brown's Gym, the first against Johnny Howard on July 12, followed four days later by Zulu Kid.

Knocked Down for First Time?

A right-hand smash by Johnny Howard floored Jack Dillon in the eighth round of the pair's 10-round no-decision battle. As the *Indianapolis News* detailed:

> If this is true, it marks the first time in Dillon's long career, covering almost 200 fights, that he has been knocked off his feet. It is evident, judging from all reports, that Dillon gave Howard a hellacious beating, flooring him three times, each time for the count of nine. It is hard to understand how a man, after being floored and beaten, as reports say Howard was, should have sufficient strength remaining to accomplish something no other fighter has ever been able to do.[17]

While the prominence of the knockdown would be debated, the no-decision verdict in Dillon's favor was not.

Waltzing around his opponent as if he was stuck in cement, Jack Dillon took all 10 rounds of his bout against the Zulu Kid, of Brooklyn, at Brown's Far Rockaway Club on July 16. As the *Indianapolis Star* described: "At times the Zulu Kid was backed into a corner, unable to stop the shower of blows poured on him. In the last two rounds, the Brooklyn boxer was in dire distress but by clinching and marathoning about the ring he was able to last until the final bell."[18]

A New Resident

Mr. and Mrs. Jack Dillon would now reside in Muncie, Indiana (on North Elm Street, just north of Main Street). Since Mrs. Dillon's family resided in the city, it would make her husband's long absences easier to handle. The *Indianapolis News* ran some of Jack Dillon's comments:

Mrs. Dillon resided in Muncie previous to our marriage, and she has relatives and many personal friends here. That is one reason why we have given up our cottage just outside of Indianapolis along Fall Creek. I will make my boxing headquarters in New York, but will spend as much of my time as possible at home.[19]

Jack Dillon later commented, "Muncie's got the best schools of any place around here. I want my son to stay here and go to school."[20] Jack's 10-year-old son was a student in the Muncie City Schools. Dillon was rarely one to comment about his home life, so the remarks were a surprise; on the other hand, most knew that Ernest Coulter Price had married Grace Reed the previous year.

Heading west to Lewistown, Montana, Jack Dillon fought 10 competitive rounds to a draw against Tom McCarty, of Montana, on August 17. The latter, who scaled at 181, was aggressive enough to make distance but not quick enough to catch his adversary, who tipped at 169. The *Indianapolis News* noted, "Referee McIntosh said after the fight that if he had given a decision, it would have been in favor of Dillon."[21] However, the victory margin was slight. Returning home, five consecutive battles—two in Pennsylvania, one in Ohio, and two in New York—east of the Mississippi River would make travel easier.

It was six easy no-decision rounds at the Olympia Athletic Club in Philadelphia on August 30 as Jack Dillon, after the opening round, controlled the action against adversary Charles "Sailor" Grande, of California. Afterwards, Dillon was hoping to meet Yankee Gilbert, of New York, in Lima, Ohio, but the sheriff of Allen County, who planned to uphold the state law prohibiting prize fighting, thought differently.

Under the headline "Militia Is Called Out to Stop Jack Dillon," the *Indianapolis News*, on September 7, noted:

> Five thousand persons, at least half of whom came from a distance, some as far as Illinois and Philadelphia, were chased off the Murphy Street baseball park yesterday afternoon [September 6] before the time for the boxing bout between Jack Dillon, of Indianapolis, and Yankee Gilbert, of New York, was scheduled to come off. Company C, Second regiment, Ohio National Guard, participated in the work.... The boxers and not all of the promoters even were on the grounds when the militia arrived.... The mob did not threaten violence, but all Lima was wild with excitement over the event.[22]

Promoter Ed W. Harter planned to file a suit against the sheriff for $20,000, as, in his view, no law was violated.

Hoping to leave his troubles behind, Jack Dillon returned to his training. Heading to Pittsburgh, on September 25 he met Tom McMahon, a local heavyweight, over six no-decision rounds. Smart enough to handle his adversary, the Pittsburgh battler stuck with long-range firepower, while holding Dillon off with a solid left jab. Detailing the sixth and final round, the *New Castle News* stated:

> The sixth was all McMahon's. Shifting so as to bring his right foot and arm forward [southpaw, or an unorthodox stance], he kept pumping his left into Dillon's midriff. Jack was at a loss for a defense against this style of attack, and did little but lock up his man as

soon as he could get close enough to do so. Once or twice the Indianapolis fighter tried to cut loose with a series of hard blows to the body, but these didn't last long.[23]

Even the typically biased newspaper sources varied as to the verdict—a draw was an accurate assessment.

Jack Dillon was scheduled to meet Jim Savage of Orange, New Jersey, at Ebbets Field in Brooklyn on October 1, but rain forced a postponement. The 10-round fight was rescheduled for October 5, at the Broadway Sporting Club. Dillon went right to work and pounded his adversary into submission. As the *Indianapolis News* saw it:

> Savage gave a remarkable exhibition of gameness. After being floored twice in the fifth round and once in the sixth for the count of nine, his nose broken, and bleeding from numerous cuts, he stuck out the ten rounds and had the crowd with him at the bell for his sheer courage.[24]

For the record, Dillon scaled at 174¾, while Savage tipped at 190¼.

In Ketchel's Shadow—The Fifth Anniversary

How good was Stanley Ketchel? Five years later, boxing fans were still digesting his loss. Frank Klaus was acknowledged as holding Ketchel's old title in 1913, followed by George Chip (October 11, 1913–April 7, 1914) and Al McCoy (April 7, 1914–present), but the ground wasn't solid, and they knew it. In between these reigns, if one could call them that, there were claims by Billy Papke, Eddie McGoorty, and Jack Dillon, and you could stir in Leo Houck, Mike Gibbons, Jimmy Clabby, Young Ahearn, and others.

The *Evansville Journal* did a quick comparison of the four leading middleweight contenders by knockout percentage. As they saw it: Jack Dillon was at 36 percent, Mike Gibbons was at 34 percent, and Jimmy Clabby and Eddie McGoorty were tied at 30 percent. Since Dillon was primarily fighting above the middleweight limit, it appeared Mike Gibbons was the heir apparent to Stanley Ketchel's crown.

But appearances, like knockout percentages, seldom told the whole story. For example, Jimmy Clabby had more knockouts than Gibbons. (Obviously, exceeding Ketchel's knockout percentage of 93.88 percent was beyond feasibility.[25]) And of the contenders, Dillon, who tipped at 158 pounds against Chip on July 5, could never be counted out, if you pardon the expression.

Of the first six—Frank Klaus, George Chip, Al McCoy, Mike O'Dowd, Johnny Wilson, and Harry Greb—recognized as holding the middleweight title after Ketchel, Jack Dillon would fight four and defeat three of them.

The attention of Jack Dillon after defeating Battling Levinsky and Bob Moha in 1914 had shifted to the light heavyweights and heavyweights, but if a tempting carrot was dangled in front of his nose, you can bet he would make 158 pounds.

Was Dillon's shift in training quarters working? Sam Murbarger certainly thought it was, as quality offers were pouring in like morning commuters at Grand Central Station. However, Dillon wanted to meet the winner of the battle between Jim Coffey (208 pounds) and Frank Moran (206 pounds), scheduled for October 19, because that victor was promised a crack at Jess Willard. Disposing of either of them would make Dillon the logical opponent. Even the area beat writers were pushing the Hoosier Bearcat to meet Jess Willard, the giant who floored Jack Johnson and took his heavyweight title. But was a match realistic? The *Rushville Republican*'s opinion:

> Jack has a fighting heart, the most valuable asset a fighter can have. And that he could practically put away a man of the size and cleverness of Savage make it not only possible but entirely probable that he could give either Coffey or Moran one awful battle. His bout with Savage proved that a good little man can whip a mediocre big man.[26]

Although fight offers were received daily, many of the heavyweights were running out on the matches as soon as they were being made. As Murbarger wrote to the *Indianapolis Star*, "everything is not gold and glitter in the metropolis."[27]

For Jack Dillon, the month opened appropriately on November 1, as he met Charley Weinert in a 10-round no decision contest inside Madison Square Garden. It was his chance to turn the boxing world upside down, and to his credit he did. As the *Indianapolis News* proclaimed:

Charley Weinert of Newark, New Jersey, billed himself as "world's cleverest heavyweight." The Newark Adonis was twice defeated by Jack Dillon (1914, KO2 and 1915, ND10).

> Before Frank Moran, Gunboat Smith, or any of our other leading heavyweight lights can hope to be considered the foremost contender for Willard's crown they must dispose of Jack Dillon, of Indianapolis. The Bearcat proved conclusively to a crowd that packed Madison Square Garden last night that he is one of the best if not the best light heavyweight in the country by administering a terrific lacing into Young Charley Weinert, who was being groomed to meet the champion.[28]

Madison Square Garden as it appeared in 1916, on its way to becoming the mecca of boxing. Here the venue is being prepared for the fight between Frank Moran and Jess Willard on March 25, 1916 (Library of Congress, LC-DIG-ggbain-21330, digital file from original negative).

The article summarized the bout:

> Outweighed by 15 pounds, outreached by six inches, Dillon pumped right jabs to Weinert's stomach until he pulled his head down within reach. Then he came near to knocking it off. In the fifth and ninth rounds the bell saved the Jersey man from going to sleep. It was a rip-slashing fight throughout between a fighter who can box and a boxer who can fight.[29]

And the article noted the reality:

> The winner of last night's mix is supposed to get a match with Moran. Today there was real speculation among newspaper sport writers as to what chance the Hoosier would have against the giant Willard. One thing they were all agreed on. That was Moran cannot call himself a runner-up to the champion until he has met and licked Dillon. And that is a man-sized job.[30]

When Jess Willard at long last signed articles, on November 3, to defend his title, Frank Moran appeared to be the opponent of choice. Although the selection wasn't firm, it was disappointing to Team Dillon.

No time for disenchantment: the Hoosier Bearcat was off to Oshkosh, Wisconsin, to meet Frank Farmer over 10 rounds on November 18. With victories over Jimmy Ahearn, George Chip, Gus Christie, and Jimmy Clabby, Farmer, at 165 pounds, was more than an impediment. Yet, Jack Dillon was more than *just* another fighter. Noting the encounter, the *Anderson Herald* delivered only two sentences:

> Jack Dillon broke a lower left rib for Frank Farmer in the fourth round of their scheduled 10-round bout here tonight, the defeated aspirant to heavyweight honors remaining on the

mat for fully two minutes. Farmer had taken the count of nine in the second round with a blow flush on the left jaw, but showed great gameness in staying through the round as well as the third.[31]

Can you imagine printing that Frank Farmer exhibited great gameness by making it three rounds in a bout against Jack Dillon? Yet, that was the profound impact Jack Dillon was having on the sweet science.

In his last two New York battles of the year, both taking place at the Broadway Sporting Club and over 10 rounds, Dillon chose to meet "Fireman" Jim Flynn on November 30 and Dan "Porky" Flynn on December 10. (Despite sharing a surname, the two fighters were not related.) Outweighed by about 20 pounds, Dillon pounded Jim Flynn like a sledgehammer over a six-penny nail. Taking a four count in the ninth round, Flynn managed to make distance.

In between bouts, Jack Dillon headed back to Muncie, where his family, who resided on North Mulberry Street, had a new member. The pugilist, who loved hunting, had a new rabbit hound waiting for him. It was a short trip, as Dillon had to head back to the city to greet Dan "Porky" Flynn.

Dillon, outweighed by 22 pounds, fought shoulder to shoulder with his adversary over the first six rounds. From this time forth, Flynn's stamina melted like an ice cube on a summer sidewalk. Opting for survival tactics, Flynn miraculously managed to make distance but not much more.

A Fast Finish

Off to Dayton, Ohio, where Jack Dillon met Yankee Gilbert on December 17. The fight was scheduled to last 15 rounds, but it appeared right from the start that it was going to be a short evening for both fighters. Twice in the second round Gilbert took the count of nine. But when he dropped again in the fourth, it was the point of no return, and the fight was wisely stopped.

A mere three days later, Jack Dillon was in a Memphis ring battling Al Norton, the Los Angeles heavyweight. Similar to his previous bout, the Hoosier Bearcat was unstoppable. Dropping Norton three times, each for a count of nine, in the opening round, Dillon's arsenal was timely and accurate. The matchup was scheduled for eight rounds, but when a helpless Norton went horizontal for nine seconds in the fourth, his seconds threw in the sponge.

As the year drew to a conclusion, here was how the sportswriters viewed the boxers atop their divisions: Jess Willard—heavyweight; Jack Dillon—light heavyweight; vacant (although some viewed Al McCoy)—middleweight; vacant (although some viewed Ted Kid Lewis)— welterweight; Freddie Welsh—lightweight; Johnny Kilbane—featherweight; and Kid Williams—bantamweight. Obviously, those contending in each division had mixed feelings regarding the assessment.

Twenty-six successful bouts saw Jack Dillon, a versatile pugilist capable of battling in multiple divisions, fighting better than ever in 1915.[32] On June 12, he suffered what many believed to be his first bona fide knockdown against Johnny Howard. Thankfully, it was not harmful. At the end of July, the Dillon family moved to Muncie, Indiana, to better accommodate Jack Dillon's career while meeting the needs of Mrs. Dillon. In a wise career move, Team Dillon set up camp in New York City. Meanwhile, Tommy Dillon remained in Indiana, attended occasional exhibitions with his brother, and assisted Team Dillon when he could. On November 15, the newly formed American Boxing Association recognized Jack Dillon as the light heavyweight champion. Getting a heavyweight title shot from Jess Willard appeared to be as hard as striking a hummingbird with an arrow from a bow. It wasn't going to happen regardless of where Jack Dillon set up his quarters, and he could sense it, even if he couldn't accept it.

Chapter Eight

Fisticuffs in Flatbush, 1916

"I've seen them all come and go since Sullivan, and all things considered, this Jack Dillon is the greatest fighter I ever looked at. I've seen him take punches that would have floored an elephant, and never back a step. He hits as hard or harder than Fitzsimmons."—Bat Masterson[1]

Denounced for his talent and desire, Jack Dillon stood alone. Mirroring a starving caged lion searching for his next meal, he was hungry and his appetite unsatisfied.

Jack Dillon's Plight

As the *South Bend News-Times* reported:

Dillon occupies a peculiar position in the prize ring—a fighter who cannot get a fight. He is a legitimate middleweight, but he wants to fight the heavies. He is willing to "spot" them from 40 to 80 pounds and from three inches to a foot in height—but even at that they don't want his stuff. Dillon is truly a marvelous fighter; one of those rarities—the man with the fighting heart. Tom Sharkey had such a heart; so, did John L. and Bob Fitzsimmons. But they passed out of the pugilistic limelight, fighting hearts became extinct among the heavies until Dillon dove into view. "I'll fight any man in the game today—and I won't quibble over weights, heights or terms," asserts Dillon.[2]

Hoping to satisfy his fighter's hunger at least temporarily, Sam Murbarger inked Dillon to meet Dan "Porky" Flynn over eight rounds in Memphis on January 10. Having picked up a decision over Flynn the previous December, the Hoosier Bearcat was enthusiastic. Working out at the Muncie Athletic Club, located as 411½ South Walnut Street, Dillon was anxious and prepared to get his year underway.

Picking up right where he left off the previous year, Dillon took command of all eight rounds against Flynn, without a backward glance. Although there were no knockdowns, he had Flynn weaving against the ropes on numerous occasions. As a catchweight battle, a few extra pounds weren't a concern; still, Flynn looked to have at least a 20-pound advantage. When the final gong sounded, the decision belonged to Jack Dillon.

Tom Cowler, a.k.a. the Cumberland Giant, was Jim Corbett's protégé. An Englishman who stood six feet, two inches and weighed over 200 pounds, he was

Eight. Fisticuffs in Flatbush, 1916

a powerful pugilist who saw himself as a contender. Having been in the ring with Frank Moran, "Battling" Jim Johnson, "Denver" Ed Martin, Ed "Gunboat" Smith, and "Battling" Levinsky, when he was matched with Jack Dillon, he had little, if any, concern. Due to his schedule, however, the contest was postponed. Moving to a slightly smaller opponent, Dillon was scheduled for a 10-round contest at Superior, Wisconsin, against Billy Miske, a promising light heavyweight.

Born in St. Paul, Minnesota (1894), William Arthur Miske turned to professional boxing in 1913. Fighting initially out of the Midwest (Wisconsin), he showed promise and even fought a 10-round no decision against Tommy Gibbons. To further his career he began looking out of state, to Philadelphia, Pennsylvania. After dueling with Harry Greb, Mike O'Dowd, Tommy Gibbons, and Jack Lester in 1915, he decided to up his game in 1916. Opening his year against a force of Jack Dillon's caliber could spell either opportunity or disaster, and it would be the former. The *Times* summarized the encounter:

> Jack Dillon, light heavyweight champion of Indianapolis, found Billy Miske an unexpectedly tough nut to crack last night and the best he could claim in a fiercely contested 10-round go was a draw. Dillon carried the fighting to Miske all the way. In the eighth, Dillon was dazed by a rain of blows to the face and the bell came as a life saver. Dillon's aggressiveness and Miske's holding was all that gained the champion as much as a draw.[3]

Both fighters held their ground. Dillon was impressed by what he saw in Miske—the youngster had power behind both his left and right crosses, along with a snappy left jab. As Murbarger had hoped, the bout proved an excellent prelude to Dillon's bout with Tom Cowler on February 1 at the Broadway Sporting Club.

Tom Cowler was born on March 2, 1892, in Hensingham,

Dan "Porky" Flynn began his career in 1907 and ended it in 1922. Of his estimated 64 career bouts, he won twice as many as he lost. In 1918, he suffered a pair of loses, both via first-round knockouts, against Jack Dempsey (Library of Congress, LC-DIG-ggbain-15322, digital file from original negative).

Whitehaven, England. He began fighting professionally in England in 1910 and quickly impressed the boxing community. Since coming to the United States the previous summer, he had heard stories about Jack Dillon. Tales of him being a giant killer, in Cowler's view, were aggrandized. And it was time to prove it.

Newspapers with limited space used three sentences:

> Jack Dillon proved to be a veritable "Hoosier Bearcat" when he toppled Tom Cowler near the end of the second round in their scheduled 10-round bout here [New York] Tuesday night. Dillon took quite a beating because of the longer reach of the Britisher, Jim Corbett's protégé. Two terrific wallops from Dillon's right put Cowler in slumberland.[4]

It was a breathtaking—like a bomb being dropped from a German Zeppelin—moment to witness.

Willard versus Dillon— Pugilistic Hyperbole or Verisimilitude

As this news hit the press, so did this astonishing tidbit:

> Jack Dillon of Indianapolis will battle champion Jess Willard for the world's heavyweight title in New York between April 10 and 22. Jack Curley and Harry Pollack, the promoters announced this afternoon that the match has been clinched. Dillon, they said will receive $10,000 guarantee and Willard $32,500. The Indianapolis man was offered the bout when the promoters failed to come to terms with Frank Moran.[5]

Was it true? It was hard to believe. The first bad sign: Jack Curley was already arguing with Tom Jones as to who was Jess Willard's fight manager, the latter even claiming that the report was incorrect and that Jess Willard intended on matching with Frank Moran. As for what Jess Willard thought, the *South Bend Tribune* quoted him as follows: "I don't want to be accused of being the man who killed boxing. That is just what would happen if I met Dillon. He weighs 170 pounds, and I weigh 240, so you can imagine what a joke affair it would be." As for Jack Dillon's thoughts: "I have a lot of respect for Willard, but I do not regard him the wonderful fighter one would naturally expect him as a champion to be. He is strong and rugged and takes punishment. He proved he can take punishment when he fought Jack Johnson."[6]

Trying to put the Willard banter behind him, Jack Dillon met Battling Levinsky at the Broadway Sporting Club in New York City on February 8. The 10-round confrontation was the fifth time the pair had met in the squared circle. Delivering a merciless beating for nine rounds, Jack Dillon outfought Battling Levinsky in front of a tremendous crowd who marveled at the presentation. The *Indianapolis News* printed this account:

> Dillon, by his rip-tearing style, managed to win the verdict easily, but Levinsky's awkward defense kept him out of danger of a knockout. Whenever Dillon threatened to put over the finishing punch, Levinsky would run into a clinch and hold on until pried apart by the referee. Dillon showed to best advantage in the third session when he sent his right crashing

against the Battler's jaw three times in succession. If the blows hurt Levinsky he failed to show it and set himself for more punishment. The eighth, ninth, and 10th sessions were hummers with both men slugging at top speed with Dillon having the shade in the eighth and ninth. Levinsky surprised the crowd by a fierce onslaught in the 10th when he pushed the Hoosier.[7]

It's difficult to imagine anyone fighting Battling Levinsky in order to get his mind off of things.

Flooring Vic Hansen of Los Angeles six times garnered Jack Dillon the eight-round victory at Memphis on February 14. Hansen's key to making distance was to hold for the final four rounds. Down for the third time in the fourth round, he was only saved by the bell from being counted out.

A Vaudeville Calling

John D. Rockefeller once quipped, "The secret to success is to do the common things uncommonly well." Being proficient and prolific at defending himself in the prize ring was a common thing for Jack Dillon, and folks noticed. During the second week of February the pugilist secured a vaudeville engagement that would keep him very busy over the next 10 weeks. Opening the third week of the month at the Lyric gave him little time to get acclimated to his new surroundings, yet he felt confident that he could.

The *Indianapolis News* noted the demand:

Challenger Frank Moran (left) poses next to Jess Willard (right), the heavyweight champion of the world. Willard successfully defended his title over 10 no-decision rounds in front of 13,000 New York spectators that included 200 women (Library of Congress, LC-DIG-ggbain-21326, digital file from original negative).

Jack's whirlwind campaign of the last six months, and the fact that he has signed to box Willard, has made him a pugilistic sensation. He will undoubtedly be a big drawing card over the vaudeville circuit. Dillon will give an exhibition of his method of training, and will spar three rounds with a sparring partner who will be selected within the next day or so. It has been several years since local boxing fans have had an opportunity to see Jack in ring costume, and they will undoubtedly welcome the opportunity by turning out in force to attend his debut as a vaudeville headliner.[8]

While an occasion such as this was not rare—past pugilists, such as John L. Sullivan and James J. Corbett, were lured to the stage—Jack Dillon always valued his privacy. It didn't sound like the perfect fit, and it wasn't. Later, Sam Murbarger confirmed the champion's theater run would last for three days. Far more comfortable in a ring than on a stage, it was time to get back to the gym. Besides, March was shaping up to be extremely busy.

The Manhattan Athletic Club celebrated a reopening on March 10. That evening they featured an eagerly anticipated 10-round contest between Jack Dillon and "Fireman" Jim Flynn. It was their fourth meeting, and both pugilists foresaw a slugfest from start to finish—and prepared accordingly. Too big to hide, even in a 24-foot ring, Flynn endured the bulk of the punishment. Dillon, who appeared as if he could deliver his adversary at any moment, did not. Instead, he allowed Flynn time to recuperate from the damage and live another round. As a result, the bout went the distance. Dillon, who was at a 19-pound disadvantage, took the newspaper verdict.

When Charlie Weinert couldn't make his scheduled 10-round bout at the Broadway Sporting Club on March 14 against Ed "Gunboat" Smith, the venue scrambled to find an adequate substitute. Jack Dillon, in town and prepared, was more than happy to fill in. Smith, who hadn't fought since the previous November, was delighted with the selection. Looking better than usual, Smith, who outweighed his rival, fought vigorously but was outpointed over the distance. As noted by the *Logansport Pharos-Tribune*, "The victory was a costly one for Dillon. It cost him one tooth and a slice of his ear. The Indiana wildcat may now go through life with a cauliflower on his port side."[9]

Battling for the third time in a week, Jack Dillon met Whitey Allen, of the Bronx, at the Clermont Athletic Club on March 18. Scheduled for 10 rounds, it was a mismatch from the opening bell. Sensing it was going to be an abbreviated bout, many spectators remained in their seats, with some even imploring Dillon to let the fight last longer. Stalling for three rounds, Dillon ignited in the fourth and dropped Allen. The fourth-round knockout was courtesy of a volley of solid hooks.[10]

Following a much-needed 10-day break, Dillon met Battling Levinsky on March 28. The sixth meeting between the pair took place at the Broadway Sporting Club. As a solid 10-round battle between two rivals, it was fast and action packed. The *Times Union* noted: "Twice Jack had Levinsky in trouble, once in the fourth when he landed both hands to the head and staggered the Hebrew, and again in the seventh when he brought a short-left uppercut to Levinsky's jaw that sent the latter to his knees."[11]

Up instantly, Levinsky continued to take a fierce beating because he could not keep Dillon at a distance. Realizing he was behind in rounds, Levinsky turned on the afterburners over the final rounds. Despite varied opinions, it wasn't enough to keep Dillon from the no-decision verdict. Later, Levinsky claimed he broke two bones in his right hand.

By the end of a busy March, Jack Dillon was matched against Billy Miske for a 10-round bout to be held in St. Paul on April 14. It was the pair's second meeting. And for fighting in Miske's home state of Minnesota, Dillon would pocket a guaranteed $3,000.[12]

The Rub on Willard

Big Jess Willard won the heavyweight championship of the world on April 5, 1915. Yet, he didn't defend the title until March 25, 1916, close to a year later—or to be exact, 11 months, 20 days.[13] Since Frank Moran was given a 10-round failed attempt at dethroning the Pottawatomie Giant, many, including Sam Murbarger, were convinced that Jack Dillon, the light heavyweight champion, had earned an opportunity. Dillon's fight manager even sent a letter to sporting editors all around the country to guarantee the clarity of the challenge, as the *Buffalo Commercial* noted:

> Jack Dillon, despite the great disparity in weight and size, challenges the champion to a long or short bout, and promises to make it considerably more interesting for the champion than Moran did. In fact, Jack Dillon, without boastfulness, believes that he will do something that Moran utterly failed to accomplish—take the title from Willard.[14]

Noting that Dillon fought many men over 200 pounds and acknowledging Willard's schedule commitments with his current employer, the circus, Murbarger asked for the champion's consent to a match the following fall. He promised that his fighter would remain competitive by even entering the ring and defeating Frank Moran. The letter ended in this manner: "In conclusion, Jack Dillon feels that he is entitled to action with Willard, and while waiting to hear from the champion insists on a contest with Moran."[15]

It appeared no matter how big a door Sam Murbarger built, Jess Willard would not walk through it.

Returning home to Muncie on April 5, Jack Dillon had serious training in front of him at the Business Men's Gym, located at New York and Alabama Streets in Indianapolis.[16] Following his 10-round second meeting with Billy Miske, he was inked for a 15-round duel against Battling Levinsky in Kansas City, Missouri, on April 25. Granted they were both familiar opponents, but their skills were far from diminished. Neither had yet to hit the pinnacle of their proficiency.

Jack Dillon's fight with Billy Miske earned him a newspaper verdict at the end of an unimpressive 10-round no decision. From the beginning it was clear Miske was neither going to take any chances nor planning to be the aggressor. Consequently, this didn't sit well with the many local fans, who hissed at him for his lack of forcefulness and frequent holding. The St. Paul Thunderbolt, guided by his defensive skills, pursued the art of avoidance. Worth noting: Dillon's punching celerity was not quick enough to overcome Miske's footwork.[17]

Jack Dillon, accompanied by Sam Murbarger, departed for Kansas City on April 18. While Dillon had a huge obstacle in front of him in the form of Battling Levinsky, whom he would meet in a Kansas City ring in a week, he was obsessed with meeting Frank Moran. *Evansville Journal* opined: "The longer Moran delays the inevitable—which is a knockout at his hands, according to Dillon—the less chance the Indianapolis catamount has for a meeting with a certain Mr. Jess Willard."[18] And thankfully, the deal was getting close to completion as New York promoters offered Moran $17,500 for his share, and Dillon $7,500.[19]

Jack Dillon versus Battling Levinsky— Light Heavyweight Championship of America

Any thoughts of someone other than Jack Dillon being the light heavyweight champion were dismissed on April 25, when he sailed to an easy victory over Battling Levinsky in a 15-round contest held at Convention Hall in Kansas City, Missouri. As for the redundancy of the pairing—it was their seventh meeting, yet their first meeting over 15 rounds—it was not even a consideration. Worth repeating: Both men were approaching the pinnacle of their careers, with skills reflective of elite pugilists. On this day, the triumph belonged to Jack Dillon; moreover, the margin of victory was so large, it could not be disputed. The *Indianapolis News* reported:

> Levinsky claimed today he hurt his hand in the fifth round and was unable to make a good showing. One thing is certain, and that is, hand or not, Dillon gave the Hebrew an awful beating and won as he pleased. Dillon did all the fighting over the entire route. He had Levinsky backing away and running all over the ring in order to avoid that steady rain of punches. The last two rounds, the 14th and 15th, were Levinsky's by a shade. He won them with his left hand entirely. Dillon won 10 rounds, Levinsky three, and two were even, with Dillon the aggressor the entire way.[20]

A man on a mission, Jack Dillon could not be denied. And that type of opponent, as Levinsky could attest to, was the type of adversary nobody wanted to encounter.

By the first week of May, Sam Murbarger had charted Jack Dillon's course over the following two months: On May 23, Dillon would meet Bob Devere, a knowledgeable and competitive heavyweight, over a 10-round journey in Buffalo, and on June 29, Dillon would face Frank Moran, in New York City, in a 10-round duel. The deal with the latter opponent, as claimed by Murbarger, was $10,000 or 20 percent of the entire gross receipts.[21] Of the numerous daily offers for Dillon's services, these were the two that piqued the fighter's interest. And offers came from across the globe, including Sydney, Australia, where a promoter offered Dillon $10,000 to go 20 rounds with Les Darcy.[22]

As Murbarger handled the administrative duties, Jack Dillon had his nose to the grindstone at the Business Men's Gym in Indianapolis. Knowing Bob Devere gave "Gunboat" Smith an impressive pounding on April 28, the Hoosier Bearcat couldn't afford to take the bout lightly.

Boxing fans in Buffalo, forever a great fight town, welcomed Jack Dillon by turning out in droves to the Broadway Auditorium. For 10 rounds they watched Dillon play a game of cat-and-mouse with Bob Devere. It was a classic example of Dillon being Dillon, as the *Indianapolis Star* noted:

> For a few rounds Jack went at the task leisurely, thoroughly tamed his man, gave him a breathing spell, and then started the heavy work. He had Devere on the floor for a count in the fourth round after sending a wicked smash to the New Yorker's jaw. Devere carried from the scene of the conflict a couple black eyes, a bruised and bleeding nose, while his mouth was puffed, and the crimson trickled from his lips. Dillon weighed in at 175 pounds and Devere 192.[23]

Quickly returning back to Indiana, Jack Dillon was slated to meet Ed "Gunboat" Smith at Federal Park on May 29. The event was part of the most anticipated weekend in the state: 6th International 300-Mile Sweepstakes Race—which was a shortened version of the sixth running of the Indianapolis 500, held at the Indianapolis Motor Speedway on May 30. The reduced mileage of the race wasn't the only modification, however. A prosecutor obtained a restraining order on May 25 directed against the promoters of the bout. Done at the urging of Indiana Governor Samuel M. Ralston, the fight was off.[24]

With his fight canceled, Jack Dillon was given extra time to prepare for Frank Moran. He didn't plan to head to New York City until June 19, or 10 days before his scheduled battle.

On to Moran

According to the *Indianapolis Star*:

> It is said that the bout [Dillon versus Moran] will be staged at Washington Park, Brooklyn, on June 24 [changed to 29] and that Dillon will receive $10,000 [later changed to $15,000 and an option for 25 percent of gate] with a privilege of 25 percent of the gross receipts, a share of the "movie" profits and also training expenses. Moran will receive a flat guarantee of $20,000 [later changed to $25,000 and an option for 40 percent of gate] it is said.[25]

Heading to New York via Chicago, Jack Dillon departed from Indianapolis on June 12, accompanied by Sam Murbarger, his manager, and Gus Christie, who was acting as his trainer. They planned to begin training, at Washington Park in New York, on June 15. What they weren't prepared for was what they were about to witness. New York City fight fans were ecstatic about the contest: On Sunday, June 18, Jack Dillon attracted close to eight thousand visitors just to watch his workouts. The intense publicity for the promotion was beyond their expectation. As for Moran, he and his sparring partner Willie Lewis chose to train further north in Saratoga, New York. And they too were attracting large crowds for their workouts.

Fight fans couldn't get enough of the "David and Goliath" comparison, wherein a smaller, weaker opponent faces a much bigger, stronger adversary. The *Fort Wayne Daily News* noted an appropriate historical example:

> Now, can Dillon repeat ring history? Turn over the pages of record to February 23, 1900, and you will find Joe Wolcott, age 28, five feet one and a half inches tall, weighing 147 pounds, beat Joe Choynski, age 32, five feet eleven and three-fourths inches in height, weighing 170 pounds, in seven rounds. It was one of the most sensational contests in ring history. Wolcott just waded into the Californian's body and in less than three rounds he had brought those five feet eleven and three-fourths inches in height down to five feet one and one-half inches. The ten and one-quarter inches of handicap in height and the twenty-three pounds of weight had been completely wiped out. Can Dillon emulate Wolcott? His admirers say yes; Moran and his following say the Pittsburgh heavyweight will jolt him into a state of insensibility.[26]

The *Palladium-Item* noted:

> Many ring experts believe that Frank Moran will win over Jack Dillon in their 10-round bout in Brooklyn tomorrow night, the weather permitting. Betting today [June 28] is 5 to 4 on Moran to win. Moranites have offered 1 to 3 that the Pittsburgher will knock out Dillon, but there isn't any superfluity of Dillon takers. Odds of 5 to 1 that Dillon won't knockout Moran are going begging. Dillon is faster than Moran and shiftier, but Moran's physical advantages are so great that even the staunchest Dillon supporters are not confident that the "giant killer" can overcome them sufficiently to win the verdict.[27]

On to the "Tale of the Tape," and the picture it paints: Frank Moran was older than Jack Dillon by one year, 10 months, and 15 days.[28] Frank Moran, at 202 pounds, outweighed Jack Dillon by well over 30 pounds, and he was taller by over five inches.[29] With a 6½-inch reach advantage, Frank Moran could fire long-range artillery the entire evening with little chance of a successful counter. Moran had a larger chest, neck, and waistline, and his biceps were bigger. Dillon had larger thighs and calves, a.k.a. a bigger support system. The fighters had equal size wrists and ankles.

Frank Moran

Francis Charles Moran was born on March 18, 1887, in Cleveland, Ohio. His parents, who emigrated from County Mayo, Ireland, settled in the Midwest and encouraged Frank to pursue an education. It was while studying dentistry at the University of Pittsburgh that he also excelled in athletics, especially football. He even played professional football for the Pittsburgh Lyceums. It was while serving in the Navy, in 1908, that he found his passion for the sweet science. By 1913, he had turned heads by battling Al Palzer, Tom Cowler, Ed "Gunboat" Smith, and Luther McCarty. Although he lost to Jack Johnson the following year during a heavyweight championship fight, he did manage to survive 20 rounds. Having knocked out Jim Coffey in January and fought 10 no-decision rounds against Jess Willard during their heavyweight championship battle in March, Moran was ready to greet Jack Dillon on June 29.

The Fight

For a review of the fight, we turn to New York columnist Bob Edgren at the *Evening World*:

> Frank Moran stayed 10 rounds with little Jack Dillon last night. That's all that can be said for Moran. Dillon whipped him as thoroughly as a man can be whipped without being counted out. He whipped Moran in the first round, the second—every round right up to and including the 10th. There wasn't a single round in which Moran had a Chinaman's chance. Moran was outclassed so far that the affair was a joke. The only thing Moran showed at all was a vast capacity for taking punishment.[30]

As far as a fighter damage assessment, the account continued:

> There wasn't a mark on him [Dillon]. But Moran—the sorrel-topped terror who knocked big Jim Coffey out twice and fought back when Jess Willard hurled 259 pounds of beef and bone at him through 10 rounds—Moran was a sorry sight. From battered eyes and nose and mouth streamed the red banners of defeat. His forced grin was gone. He had entered the ring filled with a conceit that made him laugh—at first—when he was hit. He left it grim, silent, a hopelessly beaten man.[31]

As far as a financial damage assessment, the account continued: "Financially the fight was not a success. The promoters said that in spite of the large attendance the gate receipts failed to cover the guarantees of the fighters and the expenses."[32]

As far as some round assessments, the account continued:

> Dillon immediately walked into Moran and began hitting him.... It was evident that Frank took himself very seriously as a popular favorite.... But Dillon wasn't doing foolish things.... Moran's body, by the way, hung over his tight belt in a greasy fold. He was "hog fat," as the saying goes. And he smiled an unctuous, superior smile.... After the [third] round, Sam Murbarger asked anxiously: "Can he hurt you, Jack?" "Naw," said Dillon.... [In the fourth round] the crowd was beginning to laugh at Moran and cheer the little fellow.... In the fifth Moran was beginning to look like a punching bag.... [In the sixth round] Dillon danced around him like a Comanche dancing around a prisoner at the stake.... [In the eighth round] he [Moran] tried to fight, but he was weak, wild, winded, and outclassed. As a fighter he was a joke.... There was only one man in the fight and that was Dillon.[33]

The victory eliminated any excuse as to why Jess Willard should not do battle against Jack Dillon. On this day, Jack Dillon was the greatest boxer in the world.

Before leaving New York, Dillon had an obligation to fulfill. He was a witness to the July 1 marriage of Samuel Leroy Murbarger, 38, to Ellen Grubb, 35, of West Michigan Avenue in Indianapolis, in a New York City chapel.[34] Having turned down numerous offers from New York theatrical agents, Dillon wanted to leave the city, fulfill his obligation to meet "Fireman" Jim Flynn in Oklahoma, and return to Indiana to be with his family.

Dewey, Oklahoma, was a long train ride to make for 10 minutes and 47 seconds of serious work, yet Jack Dillon was a man of his word. Granted, pulling down $5,000 for his troubles eased his pain. Scheduled for 15 rounds, the Hoosier Bearcat utilized four to knock out "Fireman" Jim Flynn. It was the fifth time the pair had met. As the *Fort Wayne Journal-Gazette* summarized:

> A left hook to the jaw, followed by a hard right cross, sent Dillon's opponent to the floor for the final count. The first two rounds were even, while Flynn led the third. In the fourth the fireman went to the canvas twice for a count of eight before Dillon sent home the blows that won the fight.[35]

Keeping with the theme of familiar adversaries, Jack Dillon agreed to meet Battling Levinsky over the 15-round journey in Baltimore on July 13—it was the pair's eighth meeting. The reason was simple: Dillon was guaranteed $5,000, Levinsky $2,500. As the fight time (5:00 p.m.) approached, it was clear to the promoter that it was going to be a weak house, estimated at $3,000. Negotiations at this stage of an event were seldom easy, nor were all parties going to be satisfied. The result was a reduction in rounds, from 15 to 10, and salary: Dillon received $2,500, while Levinsky grabbed $1,500. Following an hour and a half delay, the two uninspired battlers entered the ring at Oriole Park. The question was: Which fighter was the least inspired? It proved to be Jack Dillon, who took the newspaper loss in the 10-round affair.[36]

You Can't Be Serious

During his return home, Jack Dillon picked up a speeding violation in, of all places, Frankfort, Indiana. Going before the mayor, who even knew Dillon's parents, he was fined 11 dollars. The pugilist was in Frankfort to referee a few boxing matches. As if that weren't enough trouble, Jack Dillon was arrested in Muncie on August 21 and charged with assault and battery on Robert B. Crabbs. The boxer accused Mr. Crabbs of attempting to force his attentions on Mrs. Dillon. The *South Bend News-Times* described the event:

> Crabbs was walking on the street when Dillon, riding in his automobile and accompanied by Jimmy Watts, Mike Hanahan and John Tracey, stopped the machine and one of the men struck Crabbs. The latter ran into a nearby store, while Dillon and his friends fled in the car. They were arrested and Dillon put up $100 cash bond for the appearance of himself and companions in city court. Crabbs was the chief witness for the state in the prosecution of Mayor Bunch and Gene Williams, former deputy prosecutor on charges of conspiracy to solicit and accept bribes.[37]

Later, it was learned that no attempt would be made to prosecute Jack Dillon for the incident. However, Jimmy Watts (a lightweight pugilist), Mike Hanahan, and John Tracey pleaded guilty to charges of assault and battery and were fined $1 and costs. It was a very peculiar event—a form of reciprocity, perhaps—and had many folks confused.

Having had time to think about a few things, including his last fight with Battling Levinsky, Jack Dillon indicated to Sam Murbarger a desire for a rematch. There wasn't a whole lot to prove by meeting Levinsky for the ninth time, but Dillon felt his prestige had been damaged by the previous affair and wanted to set things right. A match was made, and the pair would meet in Memphis on September 12.

Although the results weren't interpreted as vindication of the fighter's last performance, he was able to get his message across to Levinsky loud and clear. The eight-round duel started out in the usual prudent manner, each warrior cleverly handling himself while measuring his punches. The *Fort Wayne Journal-Gazette* saw it this way: "Dillon forced the fighting in the early stages of the bout and knocked his opponent through the ropes in the second round, but Levinsky came back strong toward the end of the fight and assumed the aggressor. Dillon weighed 169 pounds and Levinsky 175."[38] It was deemed a draw.

Having not had four bouts in a single month since March, Jack Dillon decided to pick up the pace in October. With world affairs uncertain, many boxers were doing the same. On October 10, Jack Dillon knocked out Sailor Grande, of Philadelphia, in the second round of a bout scheduled for 10 rounds at the Broadway Sporting Club. Grande, far from a tomato can, took a targeted right on the jaw, and it was off to dreamland. Unconscious for close to 10 minutes, he had onlookers concerned. A week later, in what appeared to be a favor, Dillon met tomato can Tim O'Neil, a newcomer from Chicago. The scheduled 10-round affair was held at the Broadway Sporting Club. Not much was anticipated from the bout, yet O'Neil made distance. The mundane 10-round no decision favored Dillon.[39] As if O'Neil wasn't enough target practice, Jack Dillon went six no-decision rounds against Larry Williams at the Olympia Athletic Club in Philadelphia, one day before a *believed* major bout. Yep, it was a poor choice. Unless Dillon personally requested the match, it didn't make sense, not when you are meeting a fighter as dangerous as Battling Levinsky the following evening. And in what some recognized as a title fight?

Battling Levinsky versus Jack Dillon, X— Light Heavyweight Championship of America

Meeting for the 10th time, there was no hype. No lengthy articles in the sports section of the major dailies analyzing elements of the bout. The news was, however, like a shot to the gut of most serious fight fans, as the *Indianapolis Star* reported:

> Battling Levinsky of Bridgeport, Connecticut, claimed the light heavyweight championship of America tonight [October 24] after gaining the referee's decision over Jack Dillon of Indianapolis in a 12-round bout. Levinsky's left-hand jab earned him the honors. At the start of the bout the smaller, shorter reaching Dillon, hustled the tall Easterner here, there,

and everywhere and for three rounds there was little to choose between the two, with the shade favoring Dillon. But thereafter Levinsky found himself and outboxed Dillon to the finish. He kept leading with his left and looking for the occasional chance to cross with a right. Dillon tried to land with a heavy right swing, but failed.[40]

The shocking article, describing a performance so uncharacteristic of the Hoosier Bearcat, continued. It even tried to answer the question: What was wrong with Jack Dillon?

> The crowd was the biggest of the year in this year of Boston boxing, and seemed highly pleased with the mill, albeit the fans all knew that Dillon's stamina might be just a mite off standard for the very good reason that he won a battle against Larry Williams over the six-round distance in Philadelphia last night. The fans here [Boston, Massachusetts] are of the opinion that Dillon was not in good shape when he started the fight. He looked thin and a mite drawn, the usual appearance of the athlete who is down too fine, the result of too much work. The comment here, as well as in expert New York fistic circles, is that the "'Giant Killer' has been going at too rapid a pace even for such a physical wonder, or even for such a gamester as is Ernest Cutler [sic] Price."[41]

Jack Dillon ran out of gas. While he may have been able to pull off such a fight with some other contender, Battling Levinsky was an elite fighter. It was an enormous mistake, and a costly one. The day before the contest, the *Boston Post* reported: "Tex Rickard, the fight promoter, who staged the Jim Jeffries–Jack Johnson bout, and a number of big battles, is expected to arrive here today [October 23] to make arrangements for the winner of tomorrow's bout to meet Willard before his New York club on Thanksgiving."[42]

And outside of the ring, things were getting a tad confusing as well. The *Logansport Pharos-Tribune* noted:

> The Jack Dillon–Mike Gibbons bout, which is scheduled for November 27 [rescheduled for November 10] at St. Paul is doing another of its on-again-off-again stunts. This time it is the New York Boxing Commission which is responsible. It seems that Dillon signed to meet Al McCoy in Brooklyn next week. It also seems he put up a $1,000 forfeit guarantee to not engage in any bout for two weeks before the Gibbons bout.[43]

If Dillon battled McCoy, he might be barred and lose his $1,000 forfeit. Where in the world was Sam Murbarger? Something was wrong. Did somebody lose their calendar?

Contract Confusion

Mike Gibbons was next on the menu and Dillon's only fight for the month of November, but he already had Dillon behind the eight ball. He was forcing Dillon to make 163 pounds at six o'clock. No simple task for a fighter who would have to trim at least five pounds. And Gibbons, taking no chances on the Hoosier being overweight, posted a $2,500 weight forfeit. Again, how does a fighter such as Jack Dillon find himself in circumstances like this?

Team Dillon, Jack, and his entourage, consisting of manager Sam Murbarger

Oscar Wilde once quipped, "You can never be overdressed or overeducated." Certainly Mike Gibbons (left) and Jack Dillon (right) would agree. The pair squared off on November 10, 1916, in St. Paul, Minnesota.

and trainers Jack Fisher and Earl Meyers, left for St. Paul, via Chicago, on November 4. They met up with Gus Christie, Dillon's chief sparring partner, in Minnesota. Christie added value by having met Gibbons. Despite the stream of invective in the press regarding Dillon's prolific schedule, Murbarger—although it was probably Dillon—continued to schedule bouts; moreover, he was matching his fighter with Al McCoy and was again considering Levinsky. The primary reason, or excuse, was the looming cloud of World War I. Since Dillon would pocket $7,500 for the Gibbons fight, it's difficult to believe it wasn't about the coin.

Mike Gibbons, of St. Paul, outpointed Jack Dillon, of Indianapolis, in a 10-round no-decision contest held inside the Auditorium. Taking six rounds, Gibbons, who scaled at 153½, effortlessly danced around Dillon, who tipped at 162, and scored courtesy of an accurate left jab. Looking like himself for a mere three rounds, Dillon failed to capture his adversary and implement any type of strategy. At a time when Dillon needed to paint a pretty picture, he couldn't find any brushes. Or maybe he was out of paint.

One week later, the articles started hitting the press. On November 17, the *Times* noted: "Dillon Slipping, Critics Believe." They continued, "Dillon is a hard man to handle, as Sam Murbarger has remarked. He is one of the sorts who listens and then does as he pleases when his manager makes a suggestion."[44]

Thankfully, Dillon's match with Al McCoy was postponed, and his fight terms were not met by Battling Levinsky. This gave the fighter time to celebrate the opening of Jack Dillon's Bar and Café, located at 120 West Ohio Street, in Indianapolis.[45]

Word hit the Evansville press on December 7 that Jack Dillon had quit the ring. At least that was the rumor flying around downtown Indianapolis, as the fighter's new café opened for business. Although the gossip wasn't true, it did manage to create considerable publicity for the fighter's new venture. Mission accomplished.

After his business opened, Jack Dillon headed to New York City. The fighter met Billy Miske at the Broadway Sporting Club on December 19. It was the pair's third meeting. The *Indianapolis Star* delivered the news:

The brothers Gibbons—Mike (left) and Tommy (right)—turned to pugilism as a career. Mike was considered an elite middleweight with exceptional defensive skills, while his younger brother Tommy contended in the heavyweight division (Library of Congress, LC-DIG-ggbain-11026, digital file from original negative).

Billy Miske, the St. Paul light heavyweight, earned a slight shade of the honors over Jack Dillon, of Indianapolis in 10 sizzling rounds before four thousand persons at the Broadway Sporting Club, Brooklyn, tonight [December 19]. While on the losing end, Dillon battled bravely, proving that his nom de guerre of the "Hoosier Bearcat" was well earned.[46]

Eight. Fisticuffs in Flatbush, 1916

Miske chose to beat Dillon at his own game: infighting. Pounding Dillon's stomach like a blacksmith over an anvil, Miske's erudite assaults took five rounds, while Dillon grabbed three and the rest were even. Tipping at 173¾, Dillon was one pound lighter than his rival. It wasn't a good way to end the year, but ever since the loss to Levinsky, things had been sliding downward for the Hoosier Bearcat.

Although folks viewed it differently, here is how the *Indianapolis News* saw the "Winners in Sports in 1916": Boxing: Jess Willard (heavyweight), Jack Dillon (light heavyweight), Al McCoy/Jack Dillon (middleweight), Freddie Welsh (lightweight), Johnny Kilbane (featherweight), Kid Williams (bantamweight), and Jimmy Wilde (flyweight).

Twenty-two bouts—which included one loss, one draw, and nine bouts against elite pugilists—constituted a prolific year for Jack Dillon. As an indisputable force in multiple weight divisions—clearly, the light heavyweight champion until October 24, 1916—opportunity prevented him from the Holy Grail, or the heavyweight championship of the world. Following his fight against Frank Moran, on June 29, Jack Dillon was undeniable—it was his magnum opus. Arguably, he was the best boxer in America. He was overworked by October 24—taking five fights in 42 days, including two against elite pugilist Battling Levinsky—and his final performance against Levinsky was not indicative of his work. And it didn't appear that a title transfer had transpired. The year also witnessed the departure of Sam Murbarger. Filling his role would be Steve Harter. As for Tommy Dillon, he stayed in Indianapolis and battled about a half-dozen times in the area. As an instructor at the Business Men's Gym, he also participated in a few exhibitions.

Chapter Nine

World War I, 1917

> *"We shall fight for the things which we have always carried nearest to our hearts for democracy, for the right of those who submit to authority to have a voice in their own governments, for the rights and liberties of small nations, for a universal dominion of right by such a concert of free peoples as shall bring peace and safety to all nations and make the world itself at last free. To such a task we can dedicate our lives and our fortunes, everything that we are and everything that we have, with the pride of those who know that the day has come when America is privileged to spend her blood and her might for the principles that gave her birth and happiness and the peace which she has treasured. God helping her, she can do no other."*—Woodrow Wilson, "War Message" delivered to Congress, April 2, 1917

As a major supplier of war matériel to the Allies, the United States remained neutral in 1914, predominantly due to domestic opposition. Four days after President Wilson delivered his "War Message," Congress, on April 6, 1917, declared war on Germany as an "Associated Power" of the Allies. It was inevitable; many felt it in their hearts even if they did not want to accept it. Naturally, the war would impact all things, the question was to what extent.

Jack Dillon spent New Year's Day in Dayton, Ohio, over one hundred miles from Indianapolis. Meeting Bob Moha, "the Milwaukee Caveman," was scarcely ever easy, even if it was for the fifth time. Plus, this journey was scheduled for 15 rounds, a distance Moha, incidentally, had traveled only once. Since they last met, back on June 15, 1914, Moha was on a downward slide toward what he thought was retirement. His last battle was against Harry Greb—an adversary who could make retirement appear attractive—back in December of 1915.

The previous day, the final day of 1916, two special Pullman cars filled with fight fans accompanied Team Dillon to Dayton. The *Indianapolis News* noted: "The fight is under the auspices of the Miami Athletic Club, and the advance sale of seats, according to [reports,] indicates a record-breaking attendance. Dillon is a great favorite in Dayton, and the fans of the city are pulling for Jack to get the first crack at Les Darcy."[1]

Embroiled in the politics of conscription during World War I, James Leslie Darcy left Australia for the United States to avoid persecution and establish himself as a force to be reckoned with in professional boxing. Meeting the winner of

World War I began in 1914, with U.S. entry into the war occurring in 1917. Initially, nobody was certain as to just how it would affect professional sports (top: Library of Congress, 1914 LC-DIG-ppmsca-51077, digital file from original; bottom: Library of Congress, 1918 LC-DIG-ppmsca-54676, digital file from original).

this New Year's Day contest, he maintained, would be the quintessential first battle on American soil. However, Mike Gibbons, Battling Levinsky, Al McCoy, and Billy Miske were also under consideration to greet the victor. A rumor afloat had Dillon removing any thought of his retirement in favor of a possible big money bout against Darcy.[2] True or not, the idea excited boxing fans.

In a powerful afternoon of pugilism, Jack Dillon grabbed the newspaper verdict in his 15-round no-decision conflict against Bob Moha. Although Dillon took five rounds, Moha three, and the rest were even, it was a chess match. Each aggressive action by Dillon received an adequate reaction from Moha, exactly what was needed to satisfy spectators. As the *Star Press* reported:

> Dillon's work was a revelation. His punching, jabbing, swinging, and footwork were [sic] superb. Time and again he would land on Moha's face blows that would floor the ordinary man, but Moha merely shook the hair out of his eyes and came back for more. He showed wonderful stamina, and it was only once or twice throughout the entire mill that Dillon was able to crock him.... The crowd was the largest ever attending a fight in this section and yelled its approval at the end of each round, and the decision of Referee Bauman was received with general satisfaction.[3]

With the Moha bout behind him, Jack Dillon was ready to meet Billy Miske at the Broadway Sporting Club in Brooklyn on January 16. Aware that both participants were being considered for a bout with Darcy, fans flocked to the event. Yep, Darcy was creating considerable excitement and interest. As anticipated, both Dillon and Miske delivered a stellar performance. The *Indianapolis Star* noted:

> Billy Miske, of St. Paul, outfought Jack Dillon, of Indianapolis, in a 10-round bout in Brooklyn tonight [January 16]. Miske had the better of every round except the seventh, in which Dillon held him even. Miske weighed 175½ pounds, and Dillon 172. Dillon started with a rush, but his opponent was too fast for him, Miske frequently beating him to the punch. At infighting, Miske was the superior. Dillon held in the ninth after receiving a hard right to the jaw.[4]

A majority of the press saw Miske taking nine of the 10 rounds. Would a longer distance have yielded a better evaluation of both boxers? The *South Bend News-Times* noted, "Ten rounds is too short a distance for this pair of gladiators to prove anything to anybody."[5]

The day after the fight, promoter Tex Rickard signed Jack Dillon to meet Les Darcy, the Australian champion, on February 16. Promoter Tom O'Rourke countered by signing both Dillon and Al McCoy to meet Darcy. The pugilistic chess match had begun. There was no comment, nor were there contract signatures, from Darcy.

By the end of January, Jack Dillon was off to Hot Springs, Arkansas, to rest before heading to New Orleans to meet Battling Levinsky. That contest was scheduled for 20 rounds on February 9. Suddenly it was discovered Dillon had signed to meet Ed "Gunboat" Smith on February 7. Once again, the slipshod scheduling looked to be an issue. And the person responsible was Dillon himself, who could neither ignore challenges nor keep track of them. It took a Dillon eye injury to postpone both bouts.

Hot Springs, Arkansas

As "America's First Resort," there was no place like Hot Springs. More than 40 thermal springs flow on the southwestern slope of Hot Springs Mountain, located in the beautiful Ouachita Mountains. The water, which reaches temperatures over 140 degrees, has been popularly believed for centuries to possess healing properties and was a subject of legend among several Native American tribes. Thus, it was no surprise when the springs and adjoining mountains were set aside

Elite fighter James Leslie Darcy (left), with promoter Tex Rickard (center) and fight manager Tim O'Sullivan (right). Embroiled in the politics of conscription during World War I, Darcy left Australia for the United States to avoid dealing with the issue (Library of Congress, LC-DIG-ggbain-23473, digital file from original negative).

to become the oldest national park. Incorporated on January 10, 1851, the city quickly became a tourist attraction. It also drew numerous other entities such as Major League Baseball spring training, illegal gambling, speakeasies, gangsters, and horse racing.

Professional athletes fell in love with the work-hard-play-hard ethic. They also enjoyed bonding with other athletes. For example, Jack Dillon met numerous members—including Babe Ruth—of the Boston Red Sox, which conducted spring training in Hot Springs. Could the moral principles that govern a person's behavior be altered? Certainly, as a discreet hedonistic existence—brothels as easy to find as moonshine—was also available for those who deviated from the norm.

Jack Dillon's 20-round battle against Ed "Gunboat" Smith was rescheduled for February 16 at the Louisiana Auditorium in New Orleans.[6] The city was hungry for a lengthy battle between the two popular and talented pugilists. Twenty rounds of furious fighting took place before the referee's decision was awarded to Jack Dillon. Despite being outweighed by about 20 pounds, the Hoosier constantly attacked Smith to capture three times as many rounds; to be precise, Dillon was credited with nine rounds, the Gunner three, and the rest were even.

Although there were no knockdowns, both fighters slipped to the canvas. Dillon's go-to punch was a targeted left hook that gradually dismantled the Boston fighter.[7]

Heading home after the fight, Team Dillon planned a short rest before traveling to New York and forcing a fight out of Les Darcy or Fred Fulton. Before facing the Australian, Dillon preferred to tackle Al McCoy. And it appeared there was a chance. The reason was promises, politics, and proximity. Not to mention, McCoy was thought to hold the middleweight title ever since he defeated George Chip back on April 7, 1914. Hey, it's boxing.[8]

The 10-round duel between Al McCoy and Les Darcy, scheduled for March 5 at Madison Square Garden, was prohibited by the New York State Athletic Commission. The organization stated that Al McCoy must first fulfill an oral contract made with the Broadway Sporting Club to meet Jack Dillon on February 27.[9] Let the legal battle begin.

You Can't Be Serious, Can You?

Jack Dillon received the newspaper verdict in his 10-round no-decision bout against Al McCoy. Despite being outweighed by 12 pounds, Dillon was the

Al McCoy (October 23, 1894–August 22, 1966), a.k.a. Alexander Rudolph, was a talented southpaw pugilist who fought from 1910 until 1924. By the time he met Dillon in 1917, he had fought George Chip, Jimmy Clabby, Willie Lewis, and Mike Gibbons (Library of Congress, LC-DIG-ggbain-16398, digital file from original negative).

aggressor throughout and refused to let up. However—and this was one of those "you can't be serious" situations indicative of various markets—since McCoy neither hit the canvas nor was even in danger of a knockout, the Indianapolis fighter was ostracized by New York fight fans and the media. The *Fort Wayne Daily News* reported:

> Criticism is being heaped on the head of Jack Dillon. "He isn't fast. He can't hit. He's slipping." Think of anything derogatory to a high-class boxer and apply it to Dillon and you will have the general New York opinion. Dillon whipped McCoy and he did it with just as much of a flourish as anyone could have expected. The fact that he didn't knockout the alleged champion must be put down as a good mark for McCoy and not as a drawback to Dillon's record.[10]

It took a decision, handed down by the Deputy Attorney General Leonard J. Obermeier, to uphold the substitution of Jack Dillon for Al McCoy in the latter's bout against Les Darcy on March 5. Elated, Dillon trained even harder knowing that he would be meeting the Australian.

Enter Charles Seymour Whitman, the 41st governor of New York, who directed the state athletic commission to prohibit Les Darcy from entering the ring in Madison Square Garden for a bout with Jack Dillon. The *Rushville Republican* noted the executive's remarks:

> "Darcy, so far as I am informed," Whitman said, "is a runaway from his own country." In disguise he left his native land because he was afraid to fight in the cause for which his fellow countrymen are sacrificing their lives. He prefers to give a brutal exhibition at some personal risk for a purse of $30,000.[11]

Not thrilled by the cancellation, Team Dillon countered by looking elsewhere for a host. Solid offers poured in, such as one from Denver promoter Jack Kanner, but the terms required Darcy's acceptance. And yet, the bout could still face legal issues.

Letting the dust settle on the Darcy dilemma, Jack Dillon headed to Memphis to face Jack Moran over eight rounds. Not much was expected from tomato can Moran, yet it was a paycheck. When Moran proved battered and unable to defend himself, the referee stopped the battle in the sixth round. Back to Hot Springs, Arkansas, where Dillon would combine relaxation with business. In his last fight of the month, on March 30, he fought a pugilist who was using the name Jack or Jim Berry (Barry)—nobody was certain of his true identity. The question was: How long would Dillon let him live? The *Daily Arkansas Gazette* detailed:

> Dillon made a punching bag of the Dayton man and before the bell rang in the third Barry took the count of nine. Dillon sailed in to finish him, and a wallop in the middle section sent Barry to the floor the second time. Barry's seconds threw the towel into the ring and ended the bout.[12]

Later, it was confirmed that Jim Barry was Howard Wiggam, an exhibition partner of Tommy Dillon.[13]

As far as Dillon knew, he was headed to Toledo on April 9 to meet Jack

McCarron, Ray Bronson's fighter. Regrettably, the bout was canceled due to illness: Jack Dillon was stricken with an attack of appendicitis and would be bedridden for a time. His convalescence took priority over his scheduling.

Thankfully, Dillon recovered quickly and resumed training on April 26. Optimistic about regaining the weight he lost, he hoped to meet Tom "Bearcat" McMahon in Dayton on May 14. It would be more of a challenge than it sounded because Dillon would be outweighed in the contest and it was scheduled for 15 rounds. Adding to the obstacles of daily life, Dillon had three diamonds worth $1,350, along with $50 in currency, stolen from him. They were taken from the safe of a Turkish bath he frequented in the basement of the Knights of Pythias Building in Indianapolis. It was a period of time when if Dillon didn't have bad luck, he wouldn't have any luck at all.

Five days before his next bout, Jack Dillon and his team headed to Dayton to complete the fighter's training. As for his adversary, with decisions over Battling Levinsky, Ed "Gunboat" Smith, and Bob Moha to his credit, McMahon was ready to dispose of Dillon. The question was: How prepared was Dillon for McMahon? The *Anderson Herald* ran a short summary:

> Tom McMahon and Jack Dillon fought 15 rounds to a draw here [Dayton] tonight. Dillon contented himself throughout with defensive fighting much to the crowd's displeasure. Referee Bauman warned McMahon against holding several times during the bout. Dillon never once opened on McMahon and during the last three rounds permitted the latter to punch him around the ring at will, taking care, however, to ward off blows.[14]

It was a bit of a dance, and a disappointment.

On to Toledo—since the fights were a week apart there was no time to waste—where Jack Dillon had a 10-round appointment with Jack McCarron at the Coliseum on May 21. This was the rescheduled April bout. Before he could think about McCarron, however, he, along with Ray Bronson, received some terrible news. As the *Indianapolis Star* reported:

> Walter Owens, 33 years old, who was known throughout the country among pugilists as a trainer, manager, and general ring man, died last night at the City Hospital from a bullet wound in the left groin, suffered March 26, when he was shot at Jack Dillon's saloon, 118–120 West Ohio Street [Indianapolis], while attempting to catch two automobile thieves.... Owens was employed by Dillon as a bartender.... Owens made his home with an aunt at 655 South Delaware Street. He made the trip around the world with Ray Bronson, acting as assistant manager.[15]

Obviously, the incident caught both Dillon and Bronson by surprise. Neither made any public comments, however. And Dillon easily outpointed McCarron, who was working with Ray Bronson, in their 10-round no-decision bout. The *Indianapolis News* reported:

> The contest was nothing more than a workout for Dillon, who appeared to be pulling his punches in several of the rounds. McCarron had one punch, but it didn't worry Dillon. It was a short-left jab that seldom reached its mark. Dillon forced the fighting all the way, and when McCarron would show any ambition to mix Dillon would give him a sound

beating.... McCarron was outclassed.... His judgement of distance was poor.... Every round went to Dillon, who weighed 163½ pounds. McCarron tipped the scales at 159½.[16]

Did Dillon *really* pull a few punches? Likely, out of respect for Bronson. However, no elite fighter would ever admit to such an insulting action.

It has been speculated bad news surfaces as a trilogy. A few days later, Dillon was beginning to think it was true.

The Death of Les Darcy

On May 24, 1917, James Leslie Darcy, 21, died from pneumonia contracted after septicemia, along with medical complications thought to be from dental work he received to replace teeth that had been knocked out during a bout.

The Maitland Wonder, born in Stradbroke Island, Queensland, Australia, began his professional career in 1910. Battling in more than 500 rounds, Darcy compiled more than 45 victories against only four defeats—Bob Whitelaw (Australian), back-to-back against Fritz Holland (American), and Jeff Smith (American). His final professional battle was a knockout victory over George Chip on September 30, 1916, at Sydney Stadium in Sydney, Australia. With a knockout percentage above 60 percent, he was an intimidating opponent.

A controversy over his enlistment, along with being denied a passport, led to him being stowed away aboard a Standard Oil tanker. Although his hope of reaping his ring riches in America never came to fruition, he attracted intense media coverage that made him a boxing household name. Branded with the term "slacker," his image proved difficult to overcome. Applying for naturalization as a United States citizen, he joined the United States Flying Corps.

After his death, Darcy's embalmed body was returned to his parents in West Maitland, Australia, where an estimated half-million people paid their respects.

In his final battle for the month of May, Jack Dillon met George Chip at Redland Field in Cincinnati, Ohio, on May 29. For 10 rounds, the two rivals, who had met 11 times, pounded each other to a draw. Or that was the way the ringside media saw it. Not everyone agreed, as the *Cincinnati Post* saw it advantage Dillon. The *Fort Wayne Daily News* reported: "Jack Dillon, of Indianapolis, shaded George Chip, of Newcastle, Pennsylvania, in a hard 10-round bout before a big crowd at the local ballpark last night [May 29]. There were no knockdowns, but Dillon rocked Chip several times with right-handers to the jaw."[17]

As far as a damage assessment: Chip was bleeding from the nose over a sliced lip at the conclusion of the battle, while Dillon had a bruised left eye.[18]

A Visit with Uncle Sam

On June 5, Ernest Coulter Price, a gentleman of medium build, brown hair, and blue eyes, walked into the registrar's office of James M. Brafford and dictated a typed registration card. The 26-year-old professional athlete, known to most as Jack Dillon, resided with his mother, wife, and child at 522 Highland Drive in Indianapolis, Indiana. He claimed exemption from the draft because he was the sole support for his family.

Back on May 14, the *Evansville Courier and Press* noted:

> Probably the heaviest [Indianapolis] recruiting was done by Company I, the new outfit at 5 North Meridian Street, when 35 men joined within three days. The company is commanded by Captain Nathan A. Morris with Stewart Jackson as First Lieutenant and Ed C. Ball, second lieutenant. Lieutenant Jackson's position in civil life as sporting editor of an Indianapolis daily brought him in touch with the boxing fraternity of the city and he has enlisted practically every pugilist in Indianapolis, including Stewart Donnelly, Jimmy Dalton, Jack Riley, Joey Farb, and others.[19]

When called upon, the boxing community was more than willing to serve the needs of the country.

On June 10, Jack Dillon enlisted in the United States Navy. Having filed a registration card a few days earlier, he could have waited to be called. He did not. The *Indianapolis Star* reported his remarks:

> "I just thought it would be the best thing to do," said Dillon after signing the application and taking the eye test at the recruiting station, 12 West Ohio Street, yesterday afternoon. "I would be drafted into something anyhow, and I figured it would be better to go into the navy than the army, because if a fellow gets into them trenches over there, he's liable to have rheumatism the rest of his life. I haven't taken all the examination yet; just that eyesight thing; I'll finish up tomorrow."[20]

Dillon was encouraged to join the Navy by Robert Dennis, a good friend who was in charge of a recruiting station. Identical to all naval recruits, Dillon returned home with instructions to remain there until notified for duty. In the meantime, the government allowed pay. The pugilist hoped to continue his busy schedule until called.

Jack Dillon, who scaled at 172, was scheduled to meet Fred Fulton, who typically tipped at 230, at Toledo on July 4. Fulton was the only man standing between Dillon and heavyweight champion Jess Willard. To stay sharp, yet put considerable coin in his pocket while it was possible, Dillon met Len Rowlands, of Milwaukee, in Memphis on June 25. The *Indianapolis Star* detailed:

> In the second round it looked like the end of the night for Rowlands, and that it was not was probably no one's fault but Dillon's. Dillon followed a ripping left to the body with a right cross to the jaw and Rowlands crumpled to the floor. Steadying himself on one hand and knee he came up and after another right to the head clinched the round out. Rowlands took the fifth round, when he spurted and outboxed Dillon, landing several right crosses to the face. The sixth and eighth were about even. Dillon showed little desire to fight in these rounds.[21]

For Dillon, it was smooth sailing, despite a ripple or two, over eight rounds.

When a couple of his matches fell through, including the bout with Fulton, Jack Dillon ended up meeting "Sergeant" Ray Smith on July 4 in Terre Haute,

Indiana. It was not expected to be a competitive match, and it wasn't, as Smith was flattened in the opening round. As the *Anderson Herald* reported, "In breaking from a clinch near the close of the [opening] round Dillon landed a right that sent Smith to the floor. The soldier was floored again, and the gong saved him from a knockout. His seconds threw up the sponge."[22]

Six days later, Jack Dillon defeated Jack Clifford over 10 fast rounds at the Broadway Sporting Club in New York. Like a heavy bag, the Brooklyn boy could take punishment. As the *Indianapolis Star* reported:

> Dillon dropped Clifford with a right in the sixth round and almost sent him through the ropes, but the Brooklynite bounded to his feet without taking a count. In the seventh and eighth, Clifford appeared weary from body punching, but in the last two rounds was fighting back, trying to down Dillon with a punch.[23]

On to Harry Greb

Nicknamed the Pittsburgh Windmill, the Smoke City Wildcat, and the Pittsburgh Bearcat, Edward Henry Greb was born on June 6, 1894, in Pittsburgh, Pennsylvania. Of German descent, Greb was raised in a working-class household. Boxing locally, he began a professional career in 1913. Similar to many, Greb took his lumps and was even knocked out in the second round of a six-round contest by a fighter named Joe Chip.

He improved at an accelerated pace, and a brief shift to the Philadelphia market in late 1914 brought him greater opportunities and increased exposure. More than 25 fights into his career by January 1915, he was facing world-class opposition, and while not invariably taking the newspaper verdict, he was quickly improving. By the

Edward Henry Greb (June 6, 1894–October 22, 1926) successfully fought his way from welterweight to heavyweight, beginning in 1913 and ending in 1926. Widely regarded by many boxing historians as one of the best pound-for-pound boxers of all time, he was an aggressive and unrelenting opponent.

spring of 1917, Greb had won seven of eight bouts—he took a six-round newspaper loss to Mike Gibbons. Twelve bouts later, and not far from 90 contests into his career, he found himself greeting Jack Dillon having disposed (via newspaper verdicts) of Al McCoy, Jeff Smith, and George Chip along the way.

As the first boxing show ever held at Forbes Field, the atmosphere was electric, as the *Pittsburgh Post* detailed:

> Automobiles lined the streets and parking spaces in great numbers in the vicinity of the park and the gathering seemed more like a gay football throng than a fistic assemblage. All in all, the crowd was a big boost to the pastime. Probably eight thousand wended their way through the turnstiles before the main bout was put on. The ring was pitched between home plate and the screen behind home plate and had been constructed following yesterday's baseball game between the Pirates and Giants. The crowd was early in arriving and for a time there was a jam at the gates. It was cleared up before 8:30, however, and once inside, the spectators were seated without any difficulty. Sufficient lights were turned on in the stands to facilitate the handling of the patrons, but they were dim compared with the eight very strong white lights above the ring, which made everything out of their reach look dark. They threw a bright glow on the ring and afforded everybody a fine view of all the battles.[24]

The first two paragraphs of the *Pittsburgh Post-Gazette* provided a perspective:

> Jack Dillon of Indianapolis was outclassed by Harry Greb of this city, in their 10-round bout last night in Forbes Field. It was the first meeting between these middleweights, and seven thousand fight fans from all sections of Western Pennsylvania attended. The big crowd was certain of a few things at the conclusion of the bout, chief of which is that Greb was the complete master of the Hoosier and that Dillon's star has set.
>
> Dillon is not the fighter of yesteryear. He does not possess the punching power that once characterized his work in the ring. Neither is he capable of warding off the rushes of a young and determined adversary like Greb. Last night Greb won all the way, and never was Dillon able to keep him away. Greb waded through the barrier and hit the once terrible Hoosier when and where he liked.[25]

A biased account in favor of Greb? Unreservedly, but the catchweight battle—both fighters weighed below 163 pounds—was an eye-opener. Greb's quickness was undeniable and efficacious: He used it to pin Dillon to the ropes before pounding him with combinations that effectively negated his rival's power punches (Dillon could not set them up quickly enough).

Heading home after the bout, Jack Dillon had a lot to think about. And there was plenty of time for the loss to set in: Most of August was spent at his camp in Broad Ripple. Since he wasn't scheduled for another battle until September 3—he would meet Mike Gibbons over 10 rounds in Terre Haute—he could heal, relax, and referee. Although he made no comments, there was speculation that the fighter was troubled.

Having met Mike Gibbons before, he knew the St. Paul fighter wasn't going to roll over against him. Yet, Dillon did not take his fight preparation seriously, and he should have. Pounded like a rug on a line during spring cleaning, Jack Dillon's performance was pathetic. From start to finish the St. Paul Phantom took the fight to Dillon and by the fifth round was his master. The *Richmond Item* noted:

> In the fifth round Gibbons rocked Dillon's head with a left jab and delivered repeated blows to the face drawing blood and inflicting punishments.... He closed in with a straight left as the gong sounded. Dillon showed signs of stress in the remaining rounds but displayed remarkable grit which kept him on his feet even after blows that staggered him. Gibbons made a cautious fight during the ninth and tenth rounds but showered rights and lefts at the finish, Dillon staggering to his corner.[26]

Back-to-back beatings, by two elite boxers, was something Jack Dillon had never faced; moreover, exhibiting his vulnerability to any pugilist was a nightmare realized. A few days passed before an alibi surfaced, as the *South Bend Tribune* reported:

> Jack Dillon knew he had surrendered vitality in getting down to 162 pounds, but did not realize how much until the second round with Mike Gibbons. "I am going to rest for six weeks," he said, "and not run a hand. My vitality is gone after jumping around the country and fighting for 10 years. It was foolish to get down to weight to fight Gibbons. I don't detract from Gibbons, for he is a wonderful fighter, the master boxer of them all. He can hit from any angle and hit clean, too. There is no one who can beat him at his weight." Gibbons says he realized in the first round that it was not the Dillon he fought in St. Paul last fall.[27]

Hardly ever turning down a fight opportunity, Dillon had to rely on Steve Harter, his current manager, to assemble a reasonable schedule and, more importantly, disregard challenges under 165 pounds.

In a tame 10-round no-decision battle, Jack Dillon met Hugh Walker out at Fort Riley, Kansas. More of a favor than anything else, Dillon sailed through the battle. The *Manhattan Mercury* reported:

> However, their exhibition was good and had it not been for the fact that Walker slipped and fell to the platform in the third round, spraining his left wrist, would have been much better. Considering the pain, he felt each time he used his left hand during the seven remaining rounds, no one would have blamed him if he had left the ring immediately after the accident. However, he stuck it out and deserves credit for the showing he made against the champion.[28]

Clearly, Dillon understood the situation and performed appropriately.

Heading east for a few weeks, Dillon was optimistic about landing some competitive bouts. First up was a six-round no-decision battle against Willie Meehan, at the Olympia Athletic Club in Philadelphia on October 15. The California heavyweight, unintimidated by Dillon, used a roundhouse left hook to the Hoosier's midsection, forcing him to break ground. The *Indianapolis Star* noted:

> Meehan fought on a worked-out plan. He knew that Dillon was a terrific puncher, and he never permitted the man from the middle West to get set. Once in the first round and twice in the second Dillon clipped Meehan with a long right to the jaw that hurt Willie, but they were too high to do any serious damage. After that Willie fought in an awkwardly clever manner and time after time made Jack miss long right-hand leads.[29]

Outpointed, Dillon took the loss in stride.

In hope an alteration of surroundings might transform his luck, Jack Dillon headed across the border to Montréal, Québec, Canada. There he met Zulu Kid over 10 rounds at Sohmer Park on October 17. Yep, a mere two days later and he was back in the ring. Under the title, "Zulu Kid Gets Decision," the *Star-Phoenix* reported:

> The Zulu Kid, of New York, outpointed Jack Dillon, the Indianapolis "Man Killer," in a 10-round bout here [Montreal] tonight [October 17]. The Zulu Kid was on the aggressive from the first gong until the finish of the bout and kept after Dillon continually. He earned the decision. It was a clever exhibition of infighting, and neither man gave the other many openings. The Zulu Kid weighed 163 pounds and Dillon 168.[30]

Dillon's Prestige Wanes

Reaching the end of the line was seldom pretty, but was Jack Dillon there? It was painful to read the headline, yet the *Palladium-Item* ran it with some choice words:

> A year ago, Dillon was the ring sensation of the day. After he had flattened Charlie Weinert and the giant Tom Cowler and made a punching bag of Frank Moran, Dillon was looked upon as the leading heavyweight contender and there were not a few good judges who thought he might bring down Jess Willard if he got a chance to meet him in the ring. But of late Dillon has gone far back. Last spring, he barely held his own in a bout with Al McCoy and later he was the easiest kind of mark for Mike Gibbons. Since then, he has shown little of his old ability, and it will be no surprise to hear that some second rater has put him down for the count.[31]

Spending hours thinking about how to end the year, Jack Dillon took a benefit bout on November 3. Knocking out novice Joe Stanley in the second round at the Empire Theatre in Indianapolis appeared to be a promising first step. Yet, his confidence was waning and the waning perceptible. His decision not to end his year at this point was one of the worst of his career. Granted, there was a world war going on—the Frawley Act was also concluding the following day—but where was Steve Harter?

Team Dillon arrived in New York City on November 12. The following evening Jack Dillon met Billy Miske, of St. Paul, over 10 no-decision rounds at the Broadway Arena. It was the fifth time the pair had met, and everyone in attendance anticipated a war.

Over 10 rounds, Jack Dillon received the severest thrashing of his career. It wasn't a question as to who would win the battle, only how long the Hoosier could remain vertical. The *Press and Sun Bulletin* reported:

> Only once in the entire 10 rounds was Dillon on the floor, and that was at the beginning of the ninth session. A stiff right hander dropped Dillon on his side, but he sprang to his feet before the referee even counted one. It was one of the last bouts of importance before the passing of the Frawley law.[32]

During the early twentieth century, Hot Springs, Arkansas, was known not only for baseball training camps but also as a sanctuary for professional boxers. This is a view of "Bathouse Row" (Library of Congress, LC-DIG-det-4a17945, digital file from original).

In an attempt to regain his old form, Jack Dillon, along with his manager Steve Harter, headed to Hot Springs, Arkansas, on November 22. If anyplace could revitalize the fighter, it was this facility. Although Dillon planned to stay for three weeks, he also understood that he had an obligation fulfill. Dillon was scheduled to meet Hugh Walker, of Kansas City, in Little Rock on Thanksgiving Day. The *Indianapolis Star* reported:

> Dillon injured his right hand in the second round of his bout with Billy Miske recently, but it is about completely healed now. In the second round of that contest, according to Harter, Dillon nearly hung a knockout on his opponent. Dillon was beaten in points, being tired at the finish. It was because of this that he decided to try the baths in an effort to regain his form.[33]

On November 29, Jack Dillon and Hugh Walker fought 10 fast and even rounds to a draw at the Army Athletic Association in Little Rock, Arkansas. As primarily an exhibition of infighting, the final rounds told the story, as the first five rounds were even. The *Daily Arkansas Gazette* detailed:

> About the middle of the [ninth] round, however, Dillon caught Walker off balance and sent a short right cross to the back of his neck, sending him to the floor, but only for an instant.

The Kansas City boy was up again and going for his man. The 10th was the fastest final round ever staged here. The men came right in, exchanging punches and jabs to all parts of the body, but both took the punishment well.[34]

In a wise move, Jack Dillon called off his December 17 battle against Harry Greb. It's worth stating again: It was an astute decision not to take another no-decision bout against Greb. Though a handful of beat writers concluded the action was an indication that Dillon was through with the fight game, he was not. Meanwhile, in a rare occurrence, Mrs. Jack Dillon spoke about diet to the *Indianapolis Star*: "Jack likes his steaks, but he thinks the meatless and wheatless days are fine. We always have lots of cornbread on Wednesday and many other days of the week. Jack is very fond of cornbread and milk."[35]

Perhaps a strict diet of cornbread and milk was in order.

Twenty bouts—which included no formal losses but at least six defeats via newspaper verdicts—composed an erratic year for Jack Dillon. Although he remained in the pugilistic spotlight, his image was dimming. Any thoughts of battling for the heavyweight championship of the world were gone. Overworked once again, he would not listen to his manager—it was the reason for the departure of Sam Murbarger, and would likely lead to the dismissal of others. Dillon abhorred criticism, especially by the few who surrounded him. Unfortunately, his worst enemy was himself, no better exemplified than by his scheduling of bouts. Suffering two back-to-back no-decision loses, granted to two elite boxers, took a toll on his confidence: he lost half of his remaining battles. Was Jack Dillon through? It was hard to say. Looming overhead: World War I.

Chapter Ten

A Bearcat Redux, 1918

"And now we come to boxing, of which there has been but little in Indianapolis for nearly four years. Jack Dillon, Indianapolis's best pugilist, after getting away to a great start, attempted to take on too many contenders for the light heavyweight championship and became so stale and off form that he was outpointed on several occasions by men whom he had previously beaten."—Indianapolis Star, January 1, 1918[1]

Redundant, or Essential

Corroborating part of the newspaper's analysis, Jack Dillon's first three fights of 1918—George Chip on January 25, Hugh Walker on February 22, and Harry Greb on March 4—were with familiar opponents whom, with the exception of Greb, he had beaten. Familiarity with an opponent typically worked to the advantage of the Hoosier pugilist, not to mention that it wasn't easy finding competitive opponents. As Jack Dillon marked his 10th year as a professional pugilist, experience, which equated to more than 200 ring battles, had taught him much about the fight game. Comfortable scaling at 163, he understood his body and hoped to schedule his fights with greater efficiency over the months ahead.

Having spent the last few weeks relaxing and training in Hot Springs, Arkansas, the pugilist felt invigorated and hoped to reestablish himself as contender in multiple divisions. Manager Steve Harter, along with Patsy McMahon and One Round Riley, had the fighter's back and were prepared to escort him up the championship ladder.

At Duluth, Minnesota, the confidence expressed by Team Dillon gradually eroded as its fighter was outpointed over 10 no-decision rounds by George Chip. The pair's 12th meeting was dominated by the Newcastle, Pennsylvania, native, who even had Dillon's right eye bleeding profusely by the eighth round. Afterwards, the loss was blamed on Dillon's holiday weight reduction; consequently, he was not at his strongest and had to fight cautiously.[2] It was a poor excuse, as nobody forced Dillon to take the bout.

Meanwhile, outside the ring, the fighter faced a distraction. As the *Indianapolis News* reported:

George Chip (left) and Jack Dillon (right) met a dozen times in the ring. Their final contest took place on January 25, 1918, in Duluth, Minnesota.

> Thomas Dillon and Mike Hanrahan, who were employed in the Jack Dillon saloon, 128 West Ohio Street, last March at the time Walter Owens, barkeeper there, was fatally shot, both testified in criminal court today that Joseph Benson shot Owens after drawing a revolver and ordering the men in the saloon to hold up their hands. Benson is charged with murder in the second degree.[3]

Benson's defense was a plea of self-defense on the rationale that Owens attacked him before the shot was fired. His defense failed, and he was sentenced to state prison for life.

On Saturday, February 2, 1918, Jack Dillon spent his 27th birthday training, along with Patsy McMahon, Don Curley, and Solly Epstein, at his headquarters in downtown Indianapolis. Afterwards, it was home for a birthday celebration with the family.

Bear Tracks—Dillon Puts Pen to Paper

The Hoosier Bearcat, outside of character, agreed to pen a few boxing articles exclusively for the *Indianapolis Star*.

Regarding his thoughts about an opponent's size:

Followers of boxing often have said that a good big man could beat a good little man, and in most instances this statement has been true. Personally, however, I am of the opinion that a good little man, if he possesses the iron nerve, strength, and speed, has an advantage over a larger opponent. I always have found it so.... Regarding Moran: I believe I could have stopped him in a few more rounds, for he was mighty glad when the final bell rang.... Outweighed: He [Andre Anderson] weighed 230 pounds. I raised the beam at 160 pounds when I took him on. [An opponent's size always grew with time.] He was extremely confident at the start, for I looked like a pygmy opposing him. I took the heart out of him, however, by not flinching under his hardest blows—when he landed them—in the sixth round caught him with a terrific right to the jaw. He was out for 15 minutes.[4]

Regarding the hardest blow of his career:

It was in the third round [November 1, 1911, at the old Auditorium] that [Eddie] McGoorty gave me the hardest punch I ever have stopped. We had breezed along for two stanzas, with neither man having an apparent advantage. Then in the third I thought I saw an opening and started a right-hand punch to his jaw. The Oshkosh boy, however, beat me to it and caught me flush on the jaw with a terrific left hook. I seemed to be soaring in the air, being lifted clear off the floor. The punch carried such force that it literally shook the rafters of the building. I was not put down for the count—no man has ever done that—but was what is known among followers of boxing as being out on my feet. Intuition carried me through the round.... My head did not clear until the seventh round.[5]

Regarding the succeeding heavyweight champion:

[Jack] Dempsey, in my estimation, is one of the fastest two-handed heavyweights developed since Jeffries's time. He can both box and fight, and this combination is practically unbeatable. If he ever gets Willard in the ring my money will be placed on the youngster. The champion has been inactive too long, and his lack of training will tell on him when he decides to re-enter the ring, and against a fellow like Dempsey I would not be surprised if he was decisively defeated, provided the bout goes over 10 rounds.[6]

Regarding the succeeding middleweight champion:

Harry Greb, the Pittsburgh boxer, in my opinion, will be the next middleweight champion of the world if he can get down to 158 pounds. He has the speed of a lightweight and the aggressiveness of a McGovern and, best of all, he always is in splendid condition. Greb's only weakness is in inability to hit hard.... Greb appears to be at the zenith of his career right now and I do not look for anyone to stop him in 1918.[7]

Jack Dillon agreed to meet Harry Greb in a 12-round bout in Toledo on March 4, 1918. Those who witnessed the Hoosier's previous performance against the Pittsburgh Windmill were convinced the report was a mistake. It wasn't. Dillon believed he could defeat Greb at a longer distance. Having requested a 15-round contest, he compromised at 12. Emphatic that he would not meet Greb over a short distance, or under 10 rounds, he was confident with the terms.

In what ended up being a solid warm-up match, Jack Dillon outpointed Hugh Walker, of Kansas City, during a fierce 12-round battle on February 22. The *Indianapolis Star* reported: "Dillon's terrific punches carried Walker off his feet, and he continually backed away from the Hoosier's fierce attacks. Dillon shook Walker up several times, but was unable to drop him." Tipping at 164, Dillon was outweighed by nine pounds. Inside the Southwest Athletic Club, the capacity crowd was thrilled with the presentation. It appeared the perfect prelude to his next battle.

The Rematch with Harry Greb

Training at his headquarters, at 223 North Illinois Street in downtown Indianapolis, Jack Dillon felt competitive. Coming off the Walker victory, he was confident in his skills. In addition to Patsy McMahon, both Don Curley and Solly Epstein joined him for some fine-tuning, as did Gus Christie. As anticipated, interest in the battle grew daily; moreover, approaching three thousand Coliseum seats sold, it appeared a sellout was inevitable.

It took Harry Greb to uncover the secret to success against Jack Dillon. And it was called timing. The *Indianapolis News*, under the title "Jack Dillon Is Walloped by Pittsburgh Scrapper," along with the detailed subtitle "Harry Greb Uses Wicked Left Without Giving Hoosier Bearcat Chance to Get Set—Outpoints Local Lad All the Way, Who Waits for Chance to Slip Over Haymaker," summarized the event:

Harry Greb met Jack Dillon for the second and final time on March 4, 1918. Since they had last met, Greb had defeated Battling Levinsky, Jeff Smith, George K.O. Brown, George Chip, and Bob Moha, to name only a few.

The speedy youngster from the Smoky City bobbed in and out repeatedly for points, Dillon biding his time for an opportunity to end the mill with one punch.... Greb opened in his usual fast style and took the first round by a shade.... Greb shook the Hoosier Bearcat in the second and third rounds. In the fourth, he was breezing along in great fashion until the Indianapolis man caught him with a hard left to the stomach. The fifth and sixth stanzas were repetitions of the preceding rounds, Dillon being cautious and watching for the opening that never came. In the seventh Greb showed to splendid advantage, using his speed to give him a big edge... [Dillon switched tactics in the 10th, allowing Greb to hit him, so to draw him inside.] The eleventh and final rounds were fast.... Dillon was not even hot, having done little but defend himself. He was willing at all times to make a fight of it, but found Greb unwilling to swing with him. The principals fought at catch weights. Dillon weighed 160 pounds and Greb 162 several hours before the fight.[8]

Greb's acute performance was impressive and flawlessly executed. Although Dillon fans were screaming at their fighter to "come out of his shell," the effort failed. The opening the Hoosier desperately sought never surfaced. It was nothing short of an utter failure by Team Dillon.

Aftereffects

In defeat, Dillon questioned his perception. Did he miss an opportunity? And it also triggered his emotions, exposed his vulnerability, and, similar to any defeat, created a psychological speed bump he would have to overcome. Losing, which Dillon was unaccustomed to, prompted many feelings, including anger, blame, and depression. These additional feelings could prompt actions, not all of them good. And actions bred consequences, few of which were positive.[9]

Jack Dillon detested revealing a weakness. Exposing his vulnerability, like a baseball prospect who can't hit a particular pitch, could have an enormous impact on his career. He witnessed it when his adversaries began targeting his nose to draw blood and slow his assaults. As a power puncher, Dillon would now have to alter his punch delivery by reducing his setup time.

Did his fight strategy against Greb fail? Yes. The analysis and comments he wrote about Greb for the *Indianapolis Star* support the existence of a psychological element. Was Dillon beaten before he even entered the ring? Yes. It was a lot to think about.

Matched for a plethora of battles—a common occurrence for Jack Dillon—something had to give. Manager Harter, sensing his fighter's condition, moved the events he could and conscientiously tried to save each offer, but he wasn't Harry Houdini. Stating he could not get into shape, which nobody understood, Dillon withdrew from his contest with Homer Smith on March 18—one day prior to the bout. Naturally, he was accused of running out on the battle. As a favor, "Steamboat" Bill Scott, of Toledo, filled in for Dillon. In retrospect, the changes worked to Dillon's advantage.

Jack Dillon met "Steamboat" Bill Scott on March 22, at Campbell's Auditorium in Muncie—reciprocation for Scott's service. As a veteran of more than

60 bouts, the Toledo pugilist was a competitive middleweight before stepping up to heavyweight. And it was as a member of the lower class that he defeated Billy Miske. Having the advantage of weight (30 pounds), reach, and strength, Scott—a boxing partner and trainer for Jess Willard during his bout with Jack Johnson—was ready to deal with Jack Dillon.

A large crowd watched as Jack Dillon, who forced the fighting, fought 10 rounds to a draw with Bill Scott, who put up a fabulous defense. Unhesitant, Dillon waded into shallow waters and exchanged blows with his larger adversary. Afterwards nobody was talking about the draw, however—only about Jack Dillon being knocked to the canvas in 10th frame. Pounded off his feet, the Hoosier Bearcat at least knew enough to bounce right back up. The final gong sounded before Dillon could avenge the action. Despite the drop, Dillon looked impressive earlier in the battle, as the *Star Press* noted:

> The fight as early as the fourth round gave promise of furnishing a knockout, with Scott on the "out" end. It appeared at times that he was on his last legs, figuratively speaking. But he invariably came through—and gave and took.... His [Dillon] hammering on Scott's wind had telling effect and he hung the Panama champion up against the ropes three times within the period [sixth round], watching for a chance to uppercut him on the point of the jaw.[10]

Afterwards, Dillon's manager, Steve Harter—who was also the matchmaker at the Muncie Athletic Club—denied reports that his fighter hit the canvas. According to Harter, and reported to the *Indianapolis News*: "Because of the loose canvas Dillon slipped to one hand after coming out of a clinch in the final round. He was up like a rubber ball and, according to reports, all but had Scott down and out as the bell ended the fight. Jack still holds the record of never having been knocked down."[11] To modify a line from Tolstoy, "It is amazing how complete is the delusion that a knockdown was really an accident."

Convalescing at home, Jack Dillon was filling his gaps of time by refereeing.[12] Not letting his role as arbiter interfere with his training, he was well aware he was scheduled to meet Hugh Walker over eight rounds in Memphis on April 15.

Walker, who was coming off a 12-round draw against Eddie McGoorty on April 12, was confident of his chances to beat Dillon. But confidence, like a tank of gas, could only take you so far. Would it prove enough? As the *Indianapolis Star* reported:

> Dillon had six rounds and two—the fourth and eighth—were even. But for the fact that Dillon hurt his right hand in the third round, Walker might have taken a worse beating. It was the case of the pupil in the hands of the master. Dillon's victory was due principally to his ability to dictate the style of battle. He dictated it by continually backing Walker to the ropes, where several times Dillon staggered Hugh with hard right crosses to the face. There were no knockdowns, but Dillon landed the only staggering punches. Walker's only offensive weapon—and a good one it would have been had he possessed a punch—was his left.[13]

Classroom training for national army men began in Indianapolis schools on April 18. The curriculum included auto mechanics, iron repair, and firearms, to name but a few subjects. Dillon, having offered to instruct classes in boxing, would do precisely that.[14] In addition, Edwin W. (Steve) Harter, Dillon's boxing manager—who had handled Harlem Tommy Murphy, Frank Mantell, and Patsy McMahon—reported to Camp Taylor on April 26.[15]

The end of April found Jack Dillon heading west to the state of Washington. Once there he would face Frank Farmer of Kapowsin, Washington, at Eagles Hall in Tacoma on May 7. Farmer, a popular fighter, was the Pacific Coast heavyweight champion. Other possible matches were being considered, but nothing was set. Dillon was excited about his first appearance this far west. He planned on training at St. Leo's Gym for his six-round catchweight bout.

Anticipation was high, as Jack Dillon's reputation preceded him. The *Seattle Star* noted:

> Jack Dillon, much-lauded Hoosier bearcat, failed to materialize over at Tacoma Tuesday night. Contrary to schedule, he did not knockout Farmer. Instead, by dint of hard hitting and long arms, Farmer fought his way to victory. He got the decision. Today the pride of Tacoma is more proud than ever, and the light heavyweight championship of the coast adorns his rugged brow like a triumphant laurel. Chet McIntyre, trainer, is "strutting a little hour over the board," Farmer smiles seraphically, and Tacoma is exultant.[16]

Canceling his plans (an additional two fights), a dejected Jack Dillon headed home on the first train leaving the city. The behavior was uncharacteristic of the pugilist, and the *Tacoma Daily Ledger* accused him of "Running Away." Ironically, the *Indianapolis News* reported he defeated Farmer.[17] With the weather improving, it was time for a transformation, so Dillon moved his headquarters to his summer home in Broad Ripple.[18]

In his last battle of the month, on May 29, Jack Dillon knocked out Joe Walters, of Columbus, Indiana, in the third round of a scheduled 10-round battle. The bout was part of a boxing carnival held under the auspices of Company B of the Connersville Liberty Guards. All the proceeds were used to purchase uniforms for the guards.[19] In keeping with the military theme, Jack Dillon fought three exhibition rounds to a draw against Private Hoe, a member of the Sixty-First Engineers.

It was out to Tulsa, Oklahoma, on June 17, where Jack Dillon met Hugh Walker over 12 rounds at the Grand Opera House. As the opening show for the Mid–Continent Athletic Club, the Monday evening event included 30 rounds of quality boxing. Seat prices were scaled at $1, $2, $3, and $4. Dillon's stablemate and traveling companion, Patsy McMahon, was also on the boxing card. It was the fifth meeting between Dillon and Walker, the latter now carrying the moniker "Most Perfect Man," due to his chiseled physique.

Having the better of the first 10 rounds, Jack Dillon was Hugh Walker's master. The latter ignited in the final two rounds with hope of gaining a draw, but it was too little, too late. As the *Tulsa World* noted: "Dillon's infighting and ring generalship was far superior to that of Walker, but the latter used his left to better advantage.... The fight was slow up until the seventh round. From that time on both men opened up, Dillon drawing blood from Walker in the seventh and again in the ninth."[20]

Jack Dillon arrived back home on June 19. Learning that some of the fight reports had him losing the contest disappointed the pugilist.[21] The press also hinted that Dillon, stationed at Camp Bowie, might be headed to France soon. Trying to set the war aside to focus on his boxing wasn't as easy as it sounded for any pugilist.

Leaving for Charleston, West Virginia, on July 2, Jack Dillon was scheduled to swap punches with Al McCoy over 10 rounds. The close 10-round holiday (4th of July) decision had mixed reviews. The *New York Herald* noted, "The general opinion of sports writers at the ringside was that the bout was a draw, but some gave Dillon a slight shade."[22] Upon his arrival back in Indianapolis, the fighter complained of illness. No details were given, but the fighter took a few weeks off.

In July, Bill Reddy, the manager of Billy Miske, spoke to the *Brooklyn Citizen*: "Jack Dillon, who was supposed to be well fixed financially, is in reality a poor man. Precisely where Jack's money went Reddy says is a mystery." It was a rare insight into the life of a private man.

Willing to do their part, Jack Dillon and Patsy McMahon donated their services for an exhibition bout at the Speedway Boxing Carnival on August 2. And the three-round exhibition delighted the troops. According to the *Indianapolis Star*, "His [Dillon's] next act of patriotism will be to show his prowess at Valparaiso, Indiana, for the benefit of the athletic fund at that camp. Before being approached by any of the officers at this camp Jack volunteered his services."[23] The *Indianapolis Star* reported:

> Jack Dillon, of Indianapolis, light heavyweight champion, and Jack Dailey, of Indianapolis, fought a tame six-round draw tonight in the open-air arena at the local military training camp before an audience estimated at two thousand persons. Each round was two minutes' duration. Dailey had two, Dillon two, and two even. Ed Smith of Chicago refereed. Dillon never really tried, but contented himself with a clever defense.[24]

Al McCoy

Alexander Rudolph, born on October 23, 1894, didn't appear destined for the ring until he moved with his family from New Jersey to New York City. It was in the Brownsville section of Brooklyn that the teenager quickly learned the art of self-defense. Picking up bouts for preliminary fighters who failed to show at local boxing clubs, the southpaw appeared to have a natural aptitude for the ring. Turning professional in 1910, he primarily fought out of New England (Boston, Massachusetts, and Bangor, Maine) and New York City. And, probably on the advice of famed boxing trainer Charley Goldman, he changed his name to Al McCoy. Although he had met some *names*—Young Otto, Young Erne,

Al McCoy (1894–1989), middleweight contender (left), and Israel "Charley" Goldman (1887–1968), his trainer, pose for the photographers (Library of Congress, LC-DIG-gg-bain-17870, digital file from original negative).

and Mike Gibbons—in the ring, it wasn't until he stunned the boxing world by knocking out George Chip, for the middleweight title, on April 7, 1914, that folks took notice. Inconsistent during the years that followed, McCoy was still considered dangerous. He held the title until November 14, 1917, when he was knocked out in the sixth round by Mike O'Dowd. That loss took the wind out of his sails, as Dillon noticed when he met him on July 4. Still, McCoy was a savage southpaw. The pair would meet on August 21, at Campbell's Auditorium in Muncie.

Pulling no adjectives, the *Star Press* reviewed the performance:

Rotten! Ro-o-otten! As the finale of a good card at Campbell brothers' auditorium last evening, Al McCoy and Jack Dillon stalled the entire 10 two-minute rounds. McCoy was wearing a green skirt for tights and Dillon was dressed in white silk tights and the kind of "hugging stuff" they put on is usually of a class confined to a front or rear porch swing rather than a roped arena. McCoy started stalling with the tap of the bell in the first round, hugging Jack for all he was worth and kept clinching until the last round when the two men went over the ropes with Dillon on the bottom. From then until the bell sounded the end of the fight, 45 seconds later, Dillon was out for blood. It was Dillon's fight. In fact, Dillon was the only man, besides Coonie Checkaye, the referee, who tried to fight.[25]

Taking the review in stride, Dillon participated in a couple of exhibitions before heading to Charleston, West Virginia. Meeting Billy Ryan, a Cincinnati welterweight with about 25 bouts of experience, didn't present an enormous challenge over 10 rounds for Dillon, yet the bout went the distance. Many ringside saw it to Dillon's advantage. The biased *Cincinnati Post*, however, credited Ryan with a draw.

Traveling to Cedar Rapids, Iowa, Jack Dillon met novice Jack Duffy, a hard-hitting heavyweight from Chicago, over a 10-round journey on October 4. It proved more of a challenge than he expected; in other words, Duffy appeared to gain strength with each passing round. Nevertheless, Dillon took nine out of 10 fast rounds and delivered considerable damage: Duffy slightly injured his leg when he fell through the ropes in the fifth term and was bleeding from his nose and a cut above his eye from the seventh round onward.

It's Over Over There

On November 11, 1918, an armistice was signed between the Germans and the Allies, ending World War I. Fighting continued in several places during and after that time, however, including on the Western Front, which meant that supplies were still needed. Following a series of Indiana exhibitions for the United War Fund Campaign, Jack Dillon headed to Chillicothe, Ohio. The *Indianapolis Star* detailed his visit:

> Jack Dillon of Indianapolis showed old-time form and gave Harry Krohn, Akron, Ohio, light heavyweight, a terrible lacing in one of the best fights ever witnessed in Ohio. Jack showed he is still the best light heavyweight in the country today [November 16]… 3,500 soldiers [witnessed the battle].[26]

Continuing his easy money tour, Jack Dillon met tomato can Bob York (Yorke) on November 21 at Rock Island, Illinois. This was the rescheduled bout from October 17, and the Empire skating rink was packed. Dillon swept a majority of the 10 no-decision rounds. The *Dispatch* noted late highlights: "The seventh round was a draw, but in the eighth, ninth, and last rounds Dillon did the fighting and gave Bob some hard blows to the face along with the usual uppercuts which he can so ably execute."[27]

In his last Indiana contest of the year, Jack Dillon met the familiar face of Gus Christie. As the *Indianapolis Star* reported: "Jack looked as though he had been through an illness and fought listlessly. Yet he still holds his old-time perfect defense and Christie was unable to do Jack any harm."[28]

Don't yawn, the boys weren't home yet, and Dillon had one more engagement. In his final bout of the year, Jack Dillon defeated novice Ted Block over 10 no-decision rounds at the Loyal Moose Show in Detroit, Michigan. Matchmaker Charley Best, along with spectators, appeared satisfied with the December 13 event.

Seventeen bouts—which included one official loss (Frank Farmer) and one clear loss via no decision (Harry Greb)—composed a satisfactory but far from stellar year for Jack Dillon. Given his previous standings in multiple weight

Ten. A Bearcat Redux, 1918

divisions, the caliber of his current opponents was embarrassing. The combined records of his last five opponents: 34–26–11. Granted, many competitive fighters were now serving their country in World War I, affecting the talent pool, yet the quality level of some of Dillon's matches was unsatisfactory.

Speaking of serving his country, Jack Dillon took numerous exhibitions to raise awareness and money for the war effort. While he came out of his shell a bit to put pen to paper in a series of newspaper articles, he continued to shroud his personal life. One family tidbit surfaced: Tommy Dillon and his family, along with his mother, were planning to move to the St. Petersburg, Florida, area. They remained uncertain of the timing, however.

Ever since Jack Dillon's newspaper loss to Harry Greb on July 30, 1917, he struggled. It was clear following his second meeting with Greb, and supported by his comments, that he had mentally surrendered his middleweight dominance to the fighter. Jack Dillon had gone from fighting in Madison Square Garden (November 1, 1915) to dueling in the Empire skating rink (November 21, 1918) in three years and 20 days. Regardless of the conditions, it was food for thought for the fighter.

Chapter Eleven

Bearcat Blues, 1919

> *"In the light heavyweight class Battling Levinsky has been recognized as the best, but he gave way to Clay Turner. Jack Dillon has passed almost into oblivion. Poor Jack was a wonderful fighter when he was right, but his decline the last two years has been gradual and now he is nothing but a shadow of his former self, from a fighting standpoint."*—Jersey Observer and Jersey Journal, January 3, 1919[1]

Where's Jack?

Was Dillon's obituary presumptuous? Nobody was certain. Having last fought Ted Block to a draw on December 13, 1918, Jack Dillon was missing in action. Stating to his friends that he hadn't been feeling well, he did not disclose the reason.

Following a hunting trip in Wisconsin during the second week in January, he returned home and expressed to the media that he didn't anticipate boxing until February. Although he hoped to gradually work himself into shape, there was a sense of uncertainty in his remarks.[2] The behavior was peculiar, even for Jack Dillon, who was a person who kept his cards close to his chest.

Feeling a bit better, Jack Dillon traveled to Toronto, Canada, in January to referee the second monthly smoker at the D'Arcy Athletic Club. Easing into his training while attempting to regain his confidence, he appeared confident. Yet again, he provided no details.

Celebrating his 28th birthday on February 2, 1919, he delighted in hearing that many folks, including the sportswriters at local newspapers, hadn't forgotten about him. The *Indianapolis Star* reported, "Jack Dillon senses he has a great comeback coming this year and that before his next birthday rolls around, he will be mixing things with all the best light heavies in the game."[3]

Meanwhile, boxing was booming in Hot Springs. Promoter Eddie Barnsback, who handled events at numerous local clubs and even at the Auditorium theater, was working overtime trying to find talent. And that included Jack Dillon. The pugilist had "sent word to friends in the Spa that he was headed Southward and would hit the baths and get into condition for an active campaign," but nothing had been heard from him since.[4] Barnsback was hoping to match Dillon against Al

McCoy. Later, the Arkansas promoter received word that Dillon was "sick with the flu in an Indianapolis hospital."[5] Following his release, the pugilist sent word he would arrive in Hot Springs the third week of February, and that he would presumably require a month's training to prepare for Al McCoy.[6] Dillon failed to show up.

Dillon's protégé and friend, Patsy McMahon, was trying to lure his mentor from seclusion and join him in Battle Creek, Michigan, for a few rounds in front of the returning troops. Although not immediately successful, he did manage to convince Dillon to participate in a couple of exhibitions. Yet, little information surfaced regarding Dillon's involvement.

The World's Greatest Boxers—Memphis Centennial Celebration

It was a creative way to commemorate the Memphis Centennial Celebration Week, May 19–22: take four outstanding pugilists—Jack Britton, Jack Dillon, Mike Gibbons, and "Peerless Pal" Moore—and match them with challenging competitors. And thus far, it looked as if those challengers, "K.O." Brown, Johnny Griffiths, and Phil Harrison, were far from tomato cans. Billy Haack, a local boxing promoter, was behind the event. Dillon was scheduled to meet Phil Harrison over eight rounds at the Lyric Theatre on May 24. Similar to Dillon, Phil Harrison was a seasoned light heavyweight. As a powerful puncher, he loved to go toe to toe with an opponent. The *Commercial Appeal* noted: "One of Harrison's most notable accomplishments was a near-knockout victory over Eddie McGoorty ... he floored McGoorty for a count of nine.... He [Harrison] is short and stocky of build, but with an exceptionally long reach and a terrific right-handed puncher."[7]

Jack Dillon hoped this bout would begin his comeback campaign, but it wasn't to be, as the *Tulsa Tribune* noted:

> Jack Dillon's pugilistic star has set. The "giant killer" has ceased to exist pugilistically. He was knocked out in the second round here [Memphis] tonight by Phil Harrison of Chicago. The end was pitiful. A right dazed Dillon in the first round when Harrison could probably have finished him. Dillon made a few futile efforts to swing in the second and then staggered backward and to the floor from a stiff right in the mouth. Harrison handled the crushed fighter as carefully as possible, apparently delaying the finishing punch, for it was evident that Dillon was helpless.[8]

Referee Billy Haack, sensing the sensitivity of the situation, grabbed Harrison's hand and lifted it in victory without starting a count. For Dillon, the performance was humiliating.

Billy Haack, A Class Act

Later, Billy Haack, referee and fight promoter, commented about the event to Ed W. Smith, who reported it to the *Fort Worth Star-Telegram*:

Dillon was only a shell of his former great self and if it had been anybody else in the world but Dillon, I never would have paid him a cent for the exhibition. He fought like a man grogged up to the limit, but I happen to know he wasn't. Harrison punched him around for a couple minutes. And then when I saw Dillon couldn't hold his hands up, I told Harrison to go in and finish the job. This he did with one punch. I started to count the poor fellow and got up to "three" when I realized he used to be one of the greatest fighting machines they ever produced. As he never had taken the count, I didn't have the heart to continue and merely called the thing off then and there, giving the fight to Harrison. Dillon did me a lot of favors when he was good, and I wanted to do something for him when he is bad. If he takes my advice he will never put on another glove. I don't want to take any credit away from Harrison, who is a good strong boxer and a whale of a hitter. He can beat a lot of them.[9]

No sooner had the fight ended when critics began penning another round of Jack Dillon eulogies. Another presumptuous assessment? Nobody was certain. Of all the observations, this brief printed by the *Times Union* appeared to hit the target:

The boxing world realized what it had expected when Jack Dillon was knocked out. But instead of some well-known fistic [lightweight,] the punch soporific on his jaw … had to be [from] an ordinary pug called Phil Harrison, of Chicago, whom not one in 10 fans around here ever heard of. This knockout was coming to Dillon a long while. It was not long after he cut Frank Moran into ribbons at Washington Park, the monument in Brooklyn to the folly of the lamented Federal League, that Dillon suddenly began to go back. First his decline was slow, but he gained in speed as he slid down the toboggan, the end being reached in Memphis. Dillon was reputed to be a wealthy man at one time. He had a business in Indianapolis that was prospering, but Jack did not know how to husband his financial resources any more than his health and the wind-up was the Harrison wallop. His story differs not in the slightest degree from that of many before him.[10]

The piece spoke to what many in the fight scene were thinking but were afraid to express in a public forum.

The Summer of 1919—Dempsey versus Willard

By June all eyes shifted to Toledo, Ohio, even those of Jack Dillon. The *Buffalo Courier* announced:

Speaking of the Willard–Dempsey shindig next, July 4. The *Courier* sure has arranged a great staff of special writers to keep its readers informed. If there's any angle of the bout that won't be covered by Jess Willard, Jim Corbett, Jack Dillon, Damon Runyon, the Associated Press, and the Universal News, we'd like to see 'em trotted out.[11]

As for a slant, Jack Dillon hoped to go four rounds with both participants, provide his perspective, and predict a winner. It was an honor few would ever have, and when folks thought about it, Jack Dillon was well suited for such an assignment.

Dillon on Dempsey

Never in all my career as a ringman have I ever seen a faster heavyweight than Jack Dempsey, a harder man to hit or a more terrific puncher for his poundage and inches.

Dempsey is something of a ring freak—and certainly a marvel of the pugilistic world. I took him on here this week in a four round affair to see what he's got—and he lacks nothing. Prior to climbing into the ring with him I watched him closely; studied that seemingly wide-open style when attacking. And I said to myself: "This fellow is going to be rather easy to hit, because he doesn't try to cover." But when I tried to hit Dempsey through every one of those four rounds my only reward was a few glancing blows. And I believe that those who have followed my ring career will agree that my timing of punches always has been good; that whenever I shot for a target, I usually hit it—and not with any glancing wallop. Dempsey had the most elusive style [I have] ever faced, crushing force in lightest blows, and short blows that carry tremendous sting.... Jack Dempsey, all things considered, is the "miracle-man" of the prize ring; the greatest natural fighter I have ever seen since I first picked up a boxing glove. And I've seen the greatest of them all.[12]

William Harrison "Jack" Dempsey (June 24, 1895–May 31, 1983), a.k.a. Kid Blackie and The Manassa Mauler, competed from 1914 to 1927 and reigned as the world heavyweight champion from 1919 to 1926. He was a cultural icon of the 1920s, with a style of pugilism often compared to Jack Dillon's (1920) (Library of Congress, LC-DIG-ggbain-32443, digital file from original negative).

Dillon on Willard

Only a super-fighter ever will be able to break through the almost impregnable head defense of Jess Willard for the purpose of landing a knockout punch to the jaw. I tackled the champion in his training camp here, tried with every means at my command to reach his chin, and I failed miserably. A further confession is that Willard really was not exerting his full defensive energies to keep me from hitting him, either. Those long and powerful arms of Willard, his dazzling left hand, his tremendous height, and his natural stance in the ring—these jointly form a barrier for his jaw unlike that of any ring man I have known. Through 1914, 1915, and 1916, I gained a lot of experience fighting giants. I took on fellows that were from five to eight inches taller than myself. The skeptics told me at the outset that I never could reach enough to land on their jaws. But I did—and I was lucky enough to hit most of them hard enough to win the fight for me over the knockout route. I thought because of my success against other big men of the ring that I would not have considerable trouble in whacking Willard just where I wanted to whack him. But my ideas are far different now. Ability to punch with great force, a superb defense for the head, none whatsoever for the body and no speed—that's what I discovered in my workout with Jess Willard.[13]

Jess Myron Willard (December 29, 1881–December 15, 1968), a.k.a. Pottawatomie Giant, won the world heavyweight title in 1915 by knocking out Jack Johnson. Powerfully built, Willard stood just over six feet, six inches and scaled at 245 pounds (Library of Congress, LC-USZ62-28943, b&w film copy negative).

Dillon on the Fight

My Guess is that Jack Dempsey will be the next heavyweight champion of the world, with victory coming to him on July 4 over the decision route. But my conclusion based upon my battling with both of them, is that the shiftiness of the smaller man will in a short time so bewilder Willard that his timing of punches and his judgement of distance will become awry, and he will begin, and then continue, to swing wild. And wild swings, you know, bring home the bacon only one in a hundred fights.[14]

Does Size Matter?

David, a.k.a. William Harrison "Jack" Dempsey, was matched with Goliath, a.k.a. Jess Myron Willard, for a battle on July 4, 1919, a.k.a. Independence Day. Standing six feet, one inch and tipping at 187 pounds, Dempsey was not intimidated by Willard, who stood six feet, six and a half inches and scaled at 245 pounds. The pair were looking forward to the conflict: the heavyweight championship of the world.

Although ring history was replete with matches in which size differences overshadowed boxing prowess, this battle appeared to redefine the meaning: It symbolized an underdog situation, a contest wherein a smaller, weaker opponent confronts a much larger, stronger adversary. It had the potential, from the very instant it was matched, to become the "David and Goliath" moment of the twentieth century, but would it? Or would it be another case of "a good big man, defeating a good little man."

Back in 1916, when Jack Dillon was desperately trying to match with Jess Willard, The *Fort Wayne News* pointed out, "There is plenty of precedent to justify matching [the pair] even though there may be a 75-pound advantage for the champion [Willard]." The newspaper selected 17 random heavyweight fights to prove their point: "Out of the seventeen contests the bigger men won only nine of them, one was a draw and three of them were close decisions." The seven examples where a small man defeated a big man: "Jim Corbett (185 lbs.) over John L. Sullivan (220 lbs.); Bob Fitzsimmons (164 lbs.) over Jim Corbett (190 lbs.); Tommy Burns (165 lbs.) over Marvin Hart (210 lbs.); Joe Walcott (140 lbs.) over Joe Choynski (165 lbs.); Joe Walcott (150 lbs.) over Fred Russell (240 lbs.: largest weight differential); Jim Flynn (185 lbs.) over Carl Morris (230 lbs.); and Jack O'Brien (165 lbs.) over Al Kaufman (215 lbs.)."[15] The point was clear, even if the opportunity never presented itself to Jack Dillon.

By April 1919, the hype for the heavyweight championship of the world was underway. Everyone in and around the fight game had an opinion, and many of those outlooks could be found in print. Jack Dillon, who had seldom been a favorite with press, suddenly was being mentioned in the same breath as Jack Dempsey. The best example, and certainly the most quoted, came from Billy McCarney, one of the biggest boxing promoters in the West:

> Jack Dempsey will knock out Jess Willard in less than five rounds.... He is a combination of chained lightning and fighting skill. He works in the ring like a lightweight, although he weighs almost 200 ponds and stands almost six feet in the air.... Dempsey, in McCarney's estimation, is the neatest piece of fighting machinery that has been thrown into the ring in years. He went as far as to class Jack Dillon and Dempsey in the same form. He said that Jack Dillon was just about three years ahead of a chance to make a young fortune. He explained this by saying that a fight between Dempsey now with Dillon at his apex would have been such a fight that would have been a thriller. When Dillon fought Moran in New York, I thought he was one of the best machines I had glimpsed in some moons, but he didn't last long enough to get a chance at the whirlwind that has sprang up in the last year.[16]

One of the benefits of attending the prestigious battle was walking down the streets of Toledo and running into the great old champions. Not only was Jack Dillon there, but also Jack McAuliffe and even Battling Nelson. Thrilled to be recognized, these champions even took the time to chat with fight fans or sign autographs. The impressions of the fighters varied from one person to the next, or even one newspaper to the next. The *Daily Free Press* printed this view of the Hoosier Bearcat:

There was Jack Dillon—old Bear Cat Jack—who has whipped in his time many a heavyweight who aspired to the throne held by Jess Willard. He's like an old man as he wanders the streets of Toledo, shaking hands with old acquaintances. Jack's legs have gone back on him, and never again will he be able to perform the feats that made him the greatest fighter of the age, even though his weight usually was far less than that of the men he battled. But none ever will forget the masterful licking he administered to Frank Moran—a man considered equal to the task of whipping champions.[17]

Dillon on the Fight Results

Lost the championship sitting down—that's a sorry end to the pugilistic record of Jess Willard. It's probably the first time in ring history that the championship was lost in such a cheap and unsatisfactory way. It showed that Willard, giant that he is, has something the matter with his heart. It's not the kind of heart that stands up under terrific punishment. It's not the kind of heart that will stay to the end, even though the first knockout blow on the jaw is inevitable. It's not the kind of heart a champion ought to have. Money has been the unmaking of Willard as a fighter. Money the last few years has made living easy for him. He has tasted of the luxuries and maybe this weakened his fighting heart more than his fighting body. I felt that Dempsey would win as soon as he had uncovered that tremendous left of his to Willard's jaw in the first round. It showed that Jack had sufficient power to floor the big fellow. That knockdown gave him a world of confidence in himself, even more than he had when he entered the ring, though even then he was complete master of himself. It was the case of the midget David and the giant Goliath all over again.[18]

Jess Willard (left) lost his title to Jack Dempsey (right) on July 4, 1919, in Toledo, Ohio. Dempsey knocked Willard down for the first time in his career with a left hook in the first round. Many believe Jack Dillon should have been matched with Willard in 1916 (Library of Congress, LC-USZ62-41454, b&w film copy negative).

Down seven times in the first round, jaw broken, ribs broken, cheekbone split, Jess Willard miraculously managed to survive three rounds before his corner tossed in the towel. For many at Bay View Park Arena, the third-round technical knockout was proof that size matters only when it comes to the heart.

Honestly, witnessing Jess

"Jack The Giant Killer"

A Dozen Weight Disadvantages

Dillon lbs.	Opponent	Yr.	lbs.	+lbs.
170	Andre Anderson	1915	240 ?	70 ?
168	Frank Moran	1916	204.5	36.5
170	Tom Cowler	1916	205.75	35.75
160	Jack Lester	1914	185	25
173	Porky Flynn	1915	195	22
158	Al Norton	1914	180	22
160	Jim Flynn	1914	180	20
154	Bob Moha	1911	172	18
175	Bob Devere	1916	192	17
174.75	Jim Savage	1915	190.25	15.5
171	Charlie Weinert	1915	185	14
162.5	Johnny Howard	1915	175	12.5

Living up to his moniker as "Jack the Giant Killer," Dillon welcomed opponents far larger than himself. Here are a dozen weight disadvantages he faced. Dillon claimed he was at a 70-pound disadvantage against Andre Anderson on May 5, 1915.

in the ring with Jack made it easy for many fight fans to envisage the latter being Dillon rather than Dempsey. And as heartbreaking as it was for fight fans, one could imagine the thoughts racing through the mind of Jack Dillon. To get so close to a dream that you could almost touch it had to hurt, and hurt bad. By the end of July, it appeared as if Jack Dillon would reenter the ring on Labor Day (September 1, 1919).

Depression

As if Dillon's leg issues—believed to be damaged cartilage, specifically a torn meniscus in his right leg—were not enough, he added to his physical issues some cognitive concerns.[19] For months, Jack Dillon had faced the grasp of mental depression. The *Commercial Appeal* noted a letter they received from the pugilist:

Jack states: "I have been under the care of a physician for more than five months and was unable to condition myself for the fight [Labor Day]. The excitement shattered my nerves and I collapsed." Since the fiasco [Harrison bout] Dillon has been up in the mountains, camping, and fishing, and is again feeling as good as when he was earning the title that he justly deserves "The Giant Killer." Since his return to civilization Dillon has stood a rigid physical examination, and the reports from the physician say that he can again regain the same condition that he once enjoyed.[20]

Training was going to take time, and when Dillon was ready—both mentally and physically—he planned another comeback. This time it would be different, as he hoped to gradually work himself up in competition. Once successful, Dillon planned to return to Memphis—where he lost in embarrassing fashion to Phil Harrison—to redeem himself.[21]

Recovery for Jack Dillon had become a day-to-day struggle. Never anticipating the loss to Harrison—although the depression began with nemesis Harry Greb—would have such a dramatic effect on his life, he turned inward. Could he have suffered an accident of some kind that contributed to his fall from grace? If he was injured, the last thing he wanted made public—especially to promoters, God forbid—was that he was damaged goods. Nobody had any answers, and few appeared to know where he was or what he was doing. During the third week of December, Dillon surfaced in Richmond, Indiana, at the Coliseum. As he refereed an event in front of 600 fight fans, one of his friends yelled out, "Come on back, Jack, and lick Dempsey." Dillon turned to him, and said, "It would be a tough job—a tough job."[22]

Having traveled as a pugilist, Jack Dillon found the warmer weather more conducive to his soul. Since Florida was gradually becoming a second home for his family members, he began spending more and more time there. His mother, Amanda Jane Price, who was living with his brother Paul in Indiana (according to the 1920 census), planned a permanent move to beautiful Sarasota, on the west coast of the state, partly because her oldest son, Russell, had settled nearby—across Tampa Bay to the north—in St. Petersburg.

Chapter Twelve

Comeback, 1920

"The loneliest moment in someone's life is when they are watching their whole world fall apart, and all they can do is stare blankly."—F. Scott Fitzgerald

Boxing fans recall 1920 for three things: The Walker Law (legalized professional boxing in New York, and its code of boxing rules), the Eighteenth Amendment (Prohibition, which saw to it that the country went dry), and Jack Dempsey (heavyweight champion from 1919 until 1926). As an anonymous fan put it, "Not only did you know if Jack won or lost, but you remembered it in the morning."

Out of Hibernation

"It's him, it's him, it's Jack Dillon." Sure enough, Jack Dillon was back in Richmond, Indiana. Nobody would ever understand how difficult it was for him to be there. Secured to referee boxing bouts at the Coliseum on January 26, he felt better than he had in months. And it felt right.

It was just like old times. When Nashville fight fans learned that Jack Dillon, acting in a training capacity, would be in town with his fighter (and friend) Patsy McMahon during the final week of January, they were excited. McMahon was scheduled to meet the winner of the Avera–Herring bout—which would prove to be Herring—and his old friend was assisting him. Since Dillon planned to spar with McMahon each afternoon, fans had the opportunity to witness the workouts. As a glimpse of the past, it was fine, but if it was a view into the future that would be even better. It would be the latter. Dillon was reentering the ring. Announcing he was under the management of Benny Kauff, the Giants outfielder—how the baseball player was going to handle this role was anybody's guess—was proof.[1]

The motivation behind the comeback: Part of the press assumed Dillon was destitute, while others, having witnessed the recent reemergence of a few old stars, held the opinion it was the prospect of boxing becoming legalized in New York. It was both. The Hoosier Bearcat, 29, was growling again.

Naturally, while in Nashville, Dillon got pinned down by the press. Nostalgia—and current affairs—sells. The *Nashville Banner* noted some answers to reporters' questions.

His thoughts on Bob Martin, champion heavyweight boxer of the American Expeditionary Forces (A.E.F.):

> Bob Martin, champion heavyweight boxer of the A.E.F., would have about as much show against Jack Dempsey as the proverbial snowball would have in the heated regions. There are half a dozen good American middleweights today who could rock Martin into the land of nod without straining themselves. Martin beat all the soldier boys in France, but he has never been up against a real ring fighter. Mike O'Dowd, Battling Levinsky, Billy Miske, Mike Gibbons—any number of others I could name, would put Martin to sleep so quick that he would think he was in a cradle with ball-bearing attachments.... Either Dempsey or Carpentier would make him look foolish.[2]

His thoughts on Bob Martin, who was defeated by Ray Smith—the latter a fighter he had knocked out two years prior:

> Even in my present crippled condition, with a bum pair of fighting legs, I will stake my bottom dollar that I can lick Bob Martin in 10 rounds, winner take all, and bet him on the side as well. If I couldn't stop him inside that time I would disappear from the ring for good.[3]

His thoughts on Jack Dempsey being called a slacker (concerning his military service):

> They are certainly handing Jack Dempsey a raw deal. They are trying to call him a slacker and all that sort of thing when he's not any more a slacker than a bunch of those fellows who are bawling loudest. It has been shown that Jack Dempsey never ducked service in the army, and that he was duly classified and ready for the ranks whenever he was called.... My case was somewhat similar to that of Dempsey. I was put in Class 4-A, and was ready to serve when called, although married and supporting my wife. They are not calling me a slacker.... The man in the [heavyweight] saddle is bound to get some jolts, even though he rides a horse which he conquered himself.[4]

After the Herring–McMahon mill ended in a deadlock, the latter, along with Dillon, headed for the train station. Boarding a railcar for Miami, they had a dream to catch.

A Valiant Return and Rematch

Battling Halstead, of Chicago, and Jack Dillon, of Indianapolis, fought eight rounds to a draw at the Miami Sporting Club on February 9. Despite the obvious loss of old-time vigor, Dillon fiercely contested each round. As the *Miami News* noted:

> Only occasionally did he [Dillon] show flashes of the old-time speed and cleverness, but when he did open up his assortment of hooks, crosses, and short-arm jolts, coupled with experience and ring generalship, [there] were things that caused his opponent considerable discomfort and made him exceedingly cautious.[5]

Dillon won the first three rounds, the fourth and fifth were even, and the last three rounds belonged to Halstead. It was an impressive start to his comeback.

While negotiating a battle in Havana, Cuba, Dillon scheduled a rematch with Halstead at the Armory in West Palm Beach, Florida. Besides, rematches were his specialty, or so he hoped. It was a grueling contest over eight action-packed three-minute rounds. The *Palm Beach Post* detailed:

> It was a battle of brains and brawn, in which the younger man shaded Dillon to some extent and is entitled to the decision, which was left to the newspaper men by the referee. Halstead landed, by actual tally, two blows to every one of his opponent's and made Dillon miss time and again in every round. Had not Halstead changed his tactics in the middle of the bout he would not have been entitled to the decision and might have been shaded, for he is not an in-fighter, but a long-range, shifty, powerful fellow built on Corbett's lines, a hard hitter, aggressive and quick as a panther. After the fourth round Halstead stopped swapping punches on the inside route and fought his man at arm's length, asserting at once his mastership of the art of scientific boxing.[6]

Welcome back to the fight game, Mr. Dillon.

From Miami, Jack Dillon headed north to Hot Springs, Arkansas, to visit his old friend Eddie Barnsback and to tackle a fighter called Young Fitzsimmons, a.k.a. Charley Nashert, inside the Auditorium on March 11. While the local press hyped the bout and praised Dillon's return prior to the bout, victory was not in the cards. The 10-round no-decision contest was viewed as a victory for Fitzsimmons. The *Commercial Appeal* reported:

> The Jack Dillon that stumbled his way through the 10 furious rounds with Fitzsimmons was not even the shadow of the Giant Killer that battled his way to the heights of the light heavyweight realm. Slow and sluggish on his feet and off in his judgment of distance Dillon pitted the spirit and frame of the once Indianapolis bearcat against a fair third-rater and was beaten. The punches of the Oklahoman never stung the heart of the former champion, nor did they dampen the spirit of the fighting man. Fitzsimmons used a straight left to the head and a right to the jaw as the instruments with which to carve his way to victory. Opening the bout with a left the westerner kept that member in Jack's face throughout the entire 10 rounds, with Dillon too slow to evade the punch or to get home a counter.[7]

Keeping to himself following the contest, Jack Dillon traveled to Dallas, Texas, where he met Paul Roman, of Kansas City, on March 18. This two-sentence synopsis was published by the *Seattle Union Record*: "Paul Roman, Kansas City middleweight, won the popular verdict from Jack Dillon in 10 rounds before the Soldiers' and Sailors' Athletic Club here [Dallas] last night. In the fifth Dillon took the count of eight and covered successfully until the gong."[8]

Fight accounts varied, even in the same newspaper: The *San Francisco Bulletin* noted, in their March 19, 1920 (page 23), even printed (side-by-side) two different rounds—the fifth and sixth rounds—in which Dillon was thought to be knocked down.[9] Both articles claimed he was knocked down once. Nobody noted two knockdowns, until the *Cincinnati Enquirer* confirmed both knockdowns.[10] This was correct. The *Star Press* claimed it was a draw.[11] It was incorrect. Those who viewed the no-decision bout supported the newspaper verdict in favor of Roman.

After the bout Jack Dillon, along with Patsy McMahon and Edwin W. (Steve) Harter, headed back to Hot Springs, Arkansas. Despite the circumstances,

McMahon had faith in his friend, and—more importantly—Dillon believed in himself. While Jack Dillon remained in Hot Springs under the care of an expert physician, McMahon and Harter headed back to Indianapolis. Catching up with the returning pair, the *Indianapolis Star* noted:

> Latest word from Dillon's camp indicates that his ailment, which has held him down for the past two years, was caused by torn ligaments in the legs. In this debilitated condition the pride of Hoosierdom met his first knockdown two years ago at the hands of Phil Harrison at Memphis, Tennessee. It was the last real fight which Dillon participated. Since, he has been resting but not until recently was it definitely determined what caused his weakness in foot work.[12]

Harter, who managed both boxers, remained optimistic about the future:

> If those ligaments heal properly, you want to watch out for the greatest comeback ever staged in the history of the ring. Word of Dillon's "comeback" has already reached the East. Dillon received an offer last week from promoters in Newark, New Jersey, of $5,000 for a bout with Al Weinert. The offer was turned down to permit Dillon to gain more care under his expert physician. Dillon will go East in about two weeks, for a series of engagements.[13]

Nothing Left but a Reputation?

Feeling better, Jack Dillon was off to Wichita Falls, Texas, on May 3. There he met the familiar face of Young Fitzsimmons, at the Camel Athletic Club. Scheduled for 10 no-decision rounds, Dillon took a beating. Yet, he managed to make distance. Firing at will, the Oklahoma City pugilist was prolific with his punches but could not drop the former champion. As the *Wichita Falls Times* reported:

> Dillon's greater weight and his uncanny ability to absorb punishment was all that saved him from a terrific beating. He had at least 10 pounds on Fitz. In the final frames Dillon uncorked several haymakers that might have put Fitz to sleep, had they indeed landed, but the latter was too nimble and avoided his swings with ease. The exhibition was a clean affair throughout but was much tamer than the bouts staged at the club's former quarters.[14]

Yes, he was beaten. However, he had his moments, such as the fifth round where he took control of his opponent and muscled him around the ring firing telling blows. While it was easy for the newspaper to conclude, "Jack Dillon showed last night … that he has nothing left but a reputation," it was clear that Dillon felt differently.[15]

Back in Indiana, the published results were different, "The opinion at ringside was that the bout was a draw." Did Steve Harter get to the Hoosier press? Likely, but you can't blame him for not wanting to crush his fighter's confidence. Besides, the title of the article was optimistic: "Jack Dillon Is Coming Back."[16] Speaking of confidence, Harter claimed Dillon would meet either Tom Cowler or Gene Tunney at Philadelphia on June 17. Cowler, whom Dillon defeated back in 1916, was winding down his career, while Tunney was less than two years from picking up the light heavyweight championship of America. Thankfully, neither bout would take place.[17]

Toward the end of May, Jack Dillon decided to take a ride north to Kokomo, Indiana, to see his old friend Nate Farb. Handling local heavyweight Jack Riley, who had recently returned from France, Farb was enjoying his role. Having participated in the popular A.E.F. tournament, Riley exhibited significant skills. Although Dillon sparred with Riley, it was an informal event.

On June 3, Jack Dillon met veteran K.O. Sweeney, of St. Louis, at the Sipe Theatre in Kokomo. Scheduled for 10 rounds, Dillon decided to take less than half to defeat his adversary. Noting the lacing their fighter was being given by the Hoosier Bearcat, Sweeney's seconds threw in the sponge in the fourth round. It was a respectful showing for Dillon.[18]

Struggling with his health at the end of the month, Jack Dillon sought a break. It appeared as if the pace of his comeback was too much. If money became an issue, he knew he could pick up refereeing assignments. For example, he acted as arbiter for three bouts that were part of the boxing card at the Speedway during the second week of July.

To entice Jack Dillon to meet him in Gary, Indiana, on July 14, Nate Farb promised a 10-round no-decision bout against his fighter, Jack Riley, a.k.a. "Solider" Jack Riley—hey, patriotism sells. The *Star Press* described the event: "Jack Dillon, of Indianapolis, got credit last night [July 14] for a knockout in the eighth round over Solider Jack Riley, in a scheduled 10-round bout that had a bad odor. The fans saw a good exhibition, that's all."[19]

Did the fight have questionable underpinnings? Yes. Yet, it was possible Farb's very good friend required a confidence builder. And it worked. Nine days later, Jack Dillon was in El Reno, Oklahoma, taking on "Battling" Pat Weiss over 10 no-decision rounds at the Derry Airdome. To some in attendance, the Hoosier Bearcat looked like his old self. The *Indianapolis Star* noted: "Dillon scored two knockdowns, one in the fourth and another in the seventh. Dillon decisively defeated his opponent in every round. The Hoosier battler impressed ringsiders of his fitness and ability to step around the ring in old-time form."[20]

Columnist Charles J. Brill, who was at the battle, penned a sanguine perspective:

> Dillon may be down and out for the time being so far as the big show is concerned, but he does not believe he has shot his bolt. Gradually he is regaining the use of his legs which gave out on him a couple years ago because of excessive road work, and he hopefully declared early yesterday morning while in Oklahoma City that he believed the doctors' prediction that he could go East again in September with underpinning good enough to enable him to get back into the scramble. He says his legs are infinitely stronger today than they were two months ago.[21]

Three days later, Jack Dillon was in Scammon, Kansas, meeting Young Fitzsimmons for the third time in 1920. Unfortunately, he lost the 10-round no decision. A trilogy of losses was enough to conclude that this would be the final time the pair would meet. But would it be? Aggressive and unrelenting, Fitzsimmons

A handbill/advertisement for Jack Dillon's bout against Bud Clancy on September 4, 1920. Clancy, a.k.a. the St. Louis Wild Cat, bested the Hoosier Bearcat on this occasion.

took command from the opening bell and did not let up once. Surprisingly, Dillon stood up to the violent punishment.[22]

Fatigued and frustrated, the Hoosier Bearcat yearned for a break, as the *Indianapolis Star* detailed:

> Jack Dillon, local light heavyweight boxer, arrived home last night from the West, where he had two bouts, one with Pat Weiss, and the other with Young Fitzsimmons. Dillon won the newspaper decision over Weiss, and the bearcat says he held Fitzsimmons even. Dillon will rest up for a while and then start out on a busy boxing campaign. Dillon says that he is feeling as good as ever and is confident that he can step with the best of them yet.[23]

Jack Dillon enjoyed the time off. Accepting an occasional refereeing gig kept him close to the ring. He still found it difficult to decline the fight offers, but his aches and pains were playing a greater role in his decision-making. For example, a Speedway boxing card was being constructed and the promoters wanted Dillon to meet Milburn Saylor. Local bouts were logically difficult to ignore, yet Dillon turned it down.

The pugilist agreed to substitute for Jake Ahearn and meet novice Bud Clancy, of Detroit, in Cedar Rapids, Iowa, on September 4. It would be over the 10-round journey at the opening show of the Athletic Club. Clancy was thrilled at the opportunity to meet the Hoosier Bearcat. Fighting an elite fighter such as Dillon added instant credibility to any pugilist's résumé, and Clancy knew it. The *Gazette* noted:

In a letter received from Dillon, today [August 28, 1920], he says he is living at his cottage, about 12 miles from Indianapolis, and is training every day. He claims to be in better condition than any time during the past year, stating his stay at Hot Springs worked wonders for him, and that he is now ready to take on the best men in his class.[24]

Dillon arrived at Cedar Rapids early to put the final touches on his fight preparation. Daily workouts, he hoped, would give fight fans an opportunity to see that his claims were correct.

Charles Dodgson, a.k.a. Lewis Carroll, once said, "Imagination is the only weapon in the war against reality." Reality was that Bud Clancy earned a newspaper verdict over Jack Dillon. The *Des Moines Register* reported:

Bud Clancy of Detroit shaded Jack Dillon in 10 rounds here [Cedar Rapids] tonight. The fight was a tame affair from start to finish. Dillon was the aggressor, but could not get by Clancy's long left. Clancy used a left jab throughout the fight and Dillon could not find a defense for it. Dillon swung wild, but caught Clancy with a right swing in the sixth which shook him up, but he recovered quickly.[25]

One Moment in Time

Afterwards, Jack Dillon was off to Benton Harbor, Michigan, where Jack Dempsey was defending his heavyweight championship of the world against Billy Miske. Prior to what would be a successful defense via third round kayo, Johnny Coulon, Jack Dillon, and Charlie White were introduced to a loud and impatient crowd. The *Commercial Appeal* noted the event that included this priceless announcement:

Now, ladies and gentleman, I want to introduce to you one of the greatest men the ring game ever had; a man whose work was an honor to himself and the sport that he represented; a fighter from the ground up, and one who probably was robbed of the honor of being the champion of them all when fate ruled him "through" just when he was ready and could have beaten the best man in the world at any weight. I take great pleasure in introducing to you Jack Dillon, the scrappiest ring bearcat that ever lived.[26]

Everybody arose to their feet and wildly cheered. Dillon, who was sitting several rows back from the ring, was led to the ring. Receiving the largest ovation of the evening, he was assisted back to his seat to screams of "We want Dillon."[27] It was the most poignant ring introduction many had ever witnessed.

A Final Push

Returning home, he had a short break before heading to Springfield, Missouri, where he was scheduled to meet Battling Halstead on October 4. Reality again struck, as Dillon was outpointed by Halstead over the 10-round journey. The first eight lackluster rounds seemed like an eternity as both fighters conducted a defensive dance. The *Springfield News–Leader* noted the conclusion:

In the last two rounds both boxers fought for a knockout. Each received and gave punishment. Dillon showed that he packed the necessary punch, but when that vulnerable spot a short distance south of the mouth was in view he could not hit as quickly as Halstead could dodge. Dillon showed that he had come back a long way, but not yet good enough to tackle the present champion. His bout with Halstead was the third with that youngster and is the third decision for Halstead.[28]

Not winning a single round was devastating to the former champion. Later, Jack Dillon would assist Patsy McMahon in his training.

Tentatively scheduled for a bout on October 13 in Springfield, Ohio, a suitable opponent for Dillon was yet to be found. Scheduling issues plagued the pugilist at the beginning of November, before a bout against Jack Moran was scheduled for Thanksgiving Day, at the arena of the Victory Athletic Club in Shreveport, Louisiana. Having lost three times as many battles as he won, Moran was still finding his land legs. According to the *Times*: "Moran is determined to put a kink in the Giant Killer's aspirations. During the war he gained recognition as an aviator and held a commission as second lieutenant. He proposes to make Dillon feel a bomb had landed on him out of the clouds."[29]

No bomb came out of the clouds, but Jack Dillon hit Jack Moran's arm so solidly it sounded like a bolt of lightning hit a tree. Dillon was awarded a second-round technical knockout when Moran could no longer go on. Any victory, over anyone named Moran, was a good moment for the elite Hoosier fighter.

The Indianapolis Mauling Brigade, a.k.a. Patsy McMahon and Jack Dillon, arrived in Hot Springs, Arkansas, on December 21. McMahon, a lightweight, was battling Red Herring, of Little Rock, in the main event at the Auditorium the following night. In an uncommon event, Dillon agreed to conduct a four-round exhibition against Harry Foley, of Seattle, as a preliminary. It was a wonderful holiday gift for fight fans. By the way, McMahon lost his bout.

Ernest Hemingway once quipped, "Don't you ever get the feeling that all your life is going by and you're not taking advantage of it?"(*The Sun Also Rises*). Jack Dillon had no intention of feeling that way, not if he could help it.

Twelve. Comeback, 1920

Scheduled to meet—who else?—Young Fitzsimmons in San Antonio on December 28, Dillon once again felt healthy leaving Hot Springs. Unfortunately, it would not be enough. Although it was over 12 rounds this time, Young Fitzsimmons easily defeated Jack Dillon. As the *Fort Worth Star-Telegram* summarized: "Fitzsimmons was the aggressor in every round, and it was a shame the way he pounded the Indianapolis boy.... Dillon seemed to have lost all of his old-time class and his inability to move around was the chief cause of his unmerciful beating."[30]

Thirteen bouts and two exhibitions—which did not include an official loss, though a majority of the 10 no-decision bouts were not in his favor—made for a mediocre year for Jack Dillon. And combining the results with his physical ailments, one could surmise it was a miserable experience as well. It was not the comeback he envisioned. Occasional signs of brilliance, along with paychecks, were enough to keep Dillon from retirement, but for how long? As he was a living legend, his attendance at an event was a crowd-pleaser—ask anyone who witnessed Dillon's ring introduction prior to Dempsey's successful title defense against Billy Miske in Benton Harbor, Michigan. Dillon was determined to squeeze every last opportunity out of the ring, so the gloves remained on.

Chapter Thirteen

The Roaring Twenties Begin, 1921–1922

"The worst loneliness is to not be comfortable with yourself."—Mark Twain

Jack Dillon and Patsy McMahon enjoyed the comforts of a new year in Hot Springs, Arkansas. Optimistic about their future, both pugilists were working out daily and assisting others in their training. For example, Jack Dillon was working with James Bryan "Red" Herring. As a sergeant in the U.S. Army during World War I, the latter was stationed at both Camp Pike, Arkansas, and Camp Shelby, Mississippi, where he served as a boxing instructor. Herring, well aware of Dillon's résumé, was thrilled at the opportunity to work with the elite pugilist. And what better place, as the *Tulsa World* confirmed:

> Beginning of the new year has brought to Hot Springs the greatest invasion of pugilists that this resort has ever experienced, and although the hot baths and water located here, as well as the ideal facilities for training of the boxer, is undoubtedly the major reason for the invasion, the activity of the Vapor City Athletic Club, under the management of the local promoter Ed Barnsback, has been a great drawing card for some of the most prominent figures in Fistiana.[1]

During the second week in January, the *Commercial Appeal* ran a buoyant column about Jack Dillon:

> Just about a year ago we received a letter from Dillon out of Florida stating he was going to make a final effort to regain his place in the pugilistic sun. There was a tone of sincerity in Dillon's statement.... Jack had been out of the game for nearly a year and had spent most of that time practically an invalid in a rolling chair.... [Last year, 1920] Jack met no fighter of any prominence. He announced at the start that he intended starting at the bottom and working his way back to the top if it was within his power.... There was never a more honest ring workman nor a more popular fighter than Jack Dillon.[2]

With a plethora of boxers at Hot Springs, impromptu exhibitions were common. Going a few rounds with Harry Foley, Jack Dillon felt rejuvenated.

A Rocky Road

For his first and only contest of the month, Jack Dillon met "Frisco" Pete Brown at the Jefferson Theater in Louisville, Kentucky, on January 25. Those who received the condensed version of the battle in their morning newspaper learned that the bout between the pair ended with a typical technical knockout verdict for Jack Dillon. The longer version, published by the *Indiana Daily Times*, gave a bit different perspective:

> Jack Dillon, veteran fighter of Indianapolis, and "Frisco" Brown of San Francisco, principals in the feature event at a show given Tuesday by the Phoenix Athletic Club, were booed throughout their engagement for showing a disinclination to put action into their contest. The bout ended in the seventh round when Brown's seconds tossed a towel into the ring. Brown was getting the best of Dillon by a wide margin on points in the seventh round when, to the astonishment of spectators, his seconds tossed in the towel. The Phoenix Athletic Club announced to the State athletic board of control its intention of bringing suit against both fighters for the money it was forced to pay for the match.[3]

On February 1, the *Star Press* reported: "The Kentucky state boxing commission has suspended, pending trial, Jack Dillon, of Indianapolis, and 'Frisco' Pete Brown on charges of stalling in their recent fight before the Phoenix Athletic Club."[4] Let it suffice to say that a one-year suspension wasn't the 30th birthday gift Jack Dillon expected.

From Louisville, Kentucky, Jack Dillon headed south to Alexandria, Louisiana, to meet neophyte Billy Edwards, a local heavyweight, at the Alexandria Auditorium on February 11. The bout was scheduled for 15 rounds.

Did someone bury the kryptonite? Jack Dillon, labeled superman—37 years before the DC Comic character was even created—of the ring, demonstrated conclusively that he was on top of his game by knocking out Billy Edwards in the third round. The *Town Talk* elaborated:

> Dillon exhibited class and power, for which he is noted, and more than lived up to advance notices. He won the match by sheer fighting ability, which is almost as matchless today as of yesteryear, when he dropped his opponents as rapidly as they appeared. Time seems to have dealt kindly with this ring marvel, for his youth is as apparent as ever, his movements in the ring are as fast, and his method of attack is just as furious.[5]

Was this the performance everyone was waiting for? It appeared that way. Game the entire abbreviated journey, Edwards had no solutions. He was indolent, confused, and defenseless. The newspaper continued:

> Then came the third. The men met in the center of the ring and Dillon quickly placed a short arm blow to the stomach; quick as a flash, and before Edwards realized it, a right uppercut caught him on the jaw, and he dropped to the canvas for a count of seven. Dillon allowed him to fully regain his feet, then he sent him reeling upon the ropes with a left hook to the chin. As he left the ropes a right cross was sent to the jaw and Edwards was down again. The bell sounded on the count of eight and, as Billy was regaining his feet, his seconds tossed in the towel in token of defeat, and Referee Ben Levy raised Dillon's hand. It was an exhibition of gameness on Edwards part.[6]

With little time to appreciate his victory, Dillon boarded a train to Atlanta, Georgia. Scheduled to meet novice Jack Denham over 10 rounds at the Auditorium on February 15, Dillon's Saturday afternoon arrival was noted by the press.

Not commenting about his opponent yet still being baited by many questions, Dillon simply confirmed he was ready to do battle.

Nervous—who wouldn't be staring across the ring at the Giant Killer?—Jack Denham handled himself cautiously over the first few rounds. The *Atlanta Journal* noted the closing rounds:

> Then in the fifth round Denham came out with a furious volley of punches and actually drove Dillon to the ropes then knocked him head-first out of the ring. At least I suppose it was head-first. The upset took place exactly across from where I sat and the last thing I saw was Dillon's feet, which were pointing at the ceiling. Dillon clambered back into the ring, a wicked grin on his square face, and resumed his chase of the flying Denham, who at this stage of the battle had a good lead. In points and despite his runaway tactics—which were precisely what he should have followed—he looked like a winner if he could keep it up.[7]

The newspaper made a size comparison between the two, stating that "it was reminiscent of Corbett versus Sullivan."[8]

Clear to observers was Dillon's weak foundation. The article continued:

> So, Dillon resumed the game of tag with a beautiful glitter in his eyes, and right away he tagged Denham—a vicious short right jolt to the stomach—and Denham went down, badly hurt. He had been down a couple of times before, and had coolly taken all the count he could, getting up in fair shape. But this time he was hurt and weakened. That stomach punch was the one that beat him. His flash was over; and in the next round Dillon had little trouble reaching him and driving in the short-arm jabs that seemed to be the only blows that carried a sting. Denham fought back gamely but without effect, until it was plain that he was out on his feet—I saw Dillon jab three times to Denham's face without Jack even raising his gloves to protect himself. The towel came out in a good time.[9]

Only occasional signs of brilliance—and a paycheck—kept Dillon from calling it a day. The athletic foundation he once had—specifically his legs—was failing him.

Thirteen. The Roaring Twenties Begin, 1921–1922

For those who followed the fight game, the symbolism was staring them in the face: The vigor of youth versus the knowledge of age. Jack Denham, a high school boy, faced Jack Dillon, the best there ever was. Even if he was not at the pinnacle of his art, it was easy to imagine him that way. To be toppled by a man who had floored the biggest and best of his day was a scrapbook memory.

Symbolism or not, Jack Dillon was off to Helena, Arkansas, to do battle with neophyte Ed Warner at the Grand Opera House on February 18. Unavoidable delays meant the Hoosier pugilist would not arrive in town until the night before the contest. Promoter Walk Miller, to his credit, didn't overpromote the show. Instead, he made it clear to spectators that they were viewing a ring legend who was fighting Father Time, not Warner.

Jack Dillon, making a respectable showing, was outboxed by Ed Warner over 10 no-decision rounds. The *Commercial Appeal* noted: "Warner, faster a foot than Dillon, danced in and out and landed often and effectively, although there were no knockdowns. Dillon was slow on his feet and missed often with rights and lefts."[10]

The day after the bout, Jack Dillon was informed:

> The National Boxing Association of the United States tonight [February 18] announced that it had upheld the one-year suspension imposed upon Jack Dillon, of Indianapolis, and ["Frisco" Pete] K.O. Brown of San Francisco, by the Kentucky state board of athletic control. The two fighters, who were charged with "stalling" in their contest in Louisville, will be barred from participating in bouts in all [17] states holding membership in the association, it was stated.[11]

Without comment, Jack Dillon returned to Hot Springs, Arkansas. There he met up with Patsy McMahon before the pair headed back to Indiana. Following a brief stay, Jack Dillon, along with Patsy McMahon, departed for New York on April 5. The latter had a cottage in Rockaway Beach, New York, and planned to stay all summer. Dillon joined him there. The pugilist did return to Louisville, Kentucky, on April 8, to appear before the boxing board and plead for reinstatement, but he was denied.

On May 13, New York State Boxing Commission granted a boxing license to Jack Dillon. Wasting no time, the *Standard Union* reported:

> Jack Dillon, the "Hoosier Bearcat" is training strenuously at the Brighton Beach Music Hall, home of the Brighton Beach Sporting Club, for his bout with Tommy Thompson, the light heavyweight champion of the U.S. Navy, on Thursday Night [May 19]. Dillon is working with Joe Cox, the big heavyweight, and boxed several interesting rounds before a gathering of fans yesterday afternoon.[12]

Everything appeared ready to go until the New York State Boxing Commission barred Dillon for being out of condition; subsequently, Billy Bush acted as a substitute for the fighter.

Surfacing, as a result of the incident, the *St. Louis Dispatch* noted, "Up to a short time ago John Barleycorn [alcoholic beverage] was the only fighter that ever put down Jack Dillon; the last time he floored Jack the fighter apparently stayed down."[13] Could that have contributed to Dillon's past problems? And had Barleycorn returned?

Dillon was frustrated by the commission's control, but his contacts were strong enough to land him bootleg battles to line his pockets and to stay in shape, if he desired.[14] But as long as he was content staying close to the fight game—through assisting other boxers and refereeing—or maintaining his business investments, there would be no need.

Keeping up with the former champion, the *Lincoln Journal Star* reported:

> Jack Dillon, former middleweight boxer of Indianapolis, now engaged in the ice business, denies the rumor that he was going to return to the mitt sport this winter. Dillon ... now tips the beam at close to 190. He formerly fought at 160. Dillon is only just passed 30 years old.[15]

The longer the pugilist was away from the fight game, the harder it would be to reenter the ranks. Knowing this, he continued assisting a few fighters—Chuck Wiggins, for example. Dillon would look after his corner on October 3, when Wiggins squared off against Harry Foley in New Orleans. Whenever Dillon was in a city the media would flock to ask him questions. His answer to the comeback questions this time was affirmative: a comeback was possible.

In the meantime, Jack Dillon continued refereeing numerous regional bouts to stay in shape. On December 29, the *Elwood Call-Leader* noted: "The American Legion has a good boxing card scheduled for Saturday night.... Jack Dillon of Indianapolis, better known as the Hoosier Bearcat, will battle Joe Walters of Columbus in a 10-round go as the final bout of the evening."[16] It had the markings of a discreet undertaking, but was it? On January 2, the *Elwood Call-Leader* noted:

> The boxing bout at the Harting Hall Saturday [December 31, 1921] evening under the auspices of the American Legion was all that its promoters had promised and a large crowd of followers of the sport were well pleased with the offering. To prevent a knockout, the second of Joe Walter, of Columbus, Ohio, threw up in the sponge in the four-round bout with Jack Dillon of Indianapolis and he was awarded the match [a four-round technical knockout]. Other bouts between local talent were interesting preliminaries.[17]

Participating in only five battles for the entire year—not to mention a license suspension, and the inability to meet conditioning requirements—painted a picture of a fighter unable to accept the inevitable, or retirement. Was it a nostalgic presentation? Yes. But it was also difficult to watch. Granted, Dillon's symbolic victory over Jack Denham was a glimmer of hope for the future. But similar to a former major league baseball pitching star returning to the minor leagues to throw a shutout, it was more of a sentimental undertaking than anything else.

1922

"To go for a drink is one thing. To be driven to it is another."
—Michael Collins, 1922, Irish revolutionary, soldier, and politician

Prohibition, which brought hundreds of thousands of arrests, was a failure. Illegal stills flourished in remote rural areas and created wealth beyond the imagination of many. The Great Depression needed a remedy, and repealing the Twenty-First Amendment was it (Library of Congress, LC-USZ62-123257, b&w film copy negative).

Jack Dillon, staying in the Indianapolis region, was off to Terre Haute to referee what would be a short battle between "Bud" Taylor, a local flyweight, and Solly Epstein, an Indianapolis bantam. At one minute and 51 seconds of the opening round, Epstein was lying helpless against the ropes. The *Indianapolis Star* noted, "Nearly 200 boxing fans, businessmen and city officials of Indianapolis were in the delegation which came to Terre Haute in special cars for the contest."[18] Regarding Dillon's stance on his career at this point, he was introduced as "the next heavyweight champion."[19]

In 1917, James F. Hanley composed a song with lyrics by Ballard MacDonald titled "(Back Home Again in) Indiana." It became extraordinarily popular and would exemplify the spirit of Indiana residents: A person may leave the state of Indiana, but his heart will forever be there. Jack Dillon was delighted to learn that his old friend Ray Bronson was back in town. The prospect of revitalizing the Indiana fight game, thanks to legislation (The Walker Law, 1920), was what brought him home. Since 1922 was part of the infancy of the so-called roaring twenties, or a period of economic prosperity with a distinctive cultural edge, reestablishing legal boxing was welcome. Other aspects of life were not, however. Prohibition, which began in the United States in 1920, was a nationwide constitutional law (Eighteenth Amendment) prohibiting the production, importation, transportation, and sale of alcoholic beverages. While the legal alcohol industry hit a brick wall, the production of illegal alcohol flourished; incidentally, the latter would create more millionaires—Al Capone, Joseph Kennedy, Arnold Rothstein, and Bugsy Siegel, to name a few—than the former.

The *Indianapolis Star* noted an event that took place on January 28:

> Jack Dillon, ex-pugilist, is being sought by Sheriff Snider and Motor Policemen Schley and Englebright on charges of violating the prohibition law. The official went to Dillon's cottage on Liberty Beach Drive, northeast of the city last night, and say they found a 16-gallon keg containing about three gallons of beer. A woman at the camp said the beer came Friday night from Hamilton, O, and the keg bore the name of a Hamilton Brewing Company. She told the police; however, Dillon did not have it there for sale but there had been a big party at the place. She said Dillon came to the city yesterday morning, but the officers were unable to locate him. In addition to the beer, officers said they found a half pint of White Mule whisky, a box containing 25 new half pint whiskey bottles, 11 empty quart whiskey bottles. Thirteen five-gallon jugs and four 16-gallon kegs, all empty.[20]

Jack Dillon was caught and charged. Pleading guilty to the charge, Ernest Price was fined $50 and costs in city court. He did not testify.[21] Before you think less of the pugilist, understand Prohibition was a miserable failure from numerous perspectives. And Dillon was neither the first nor the last pugilist involved with some violation of the Prohibition law.

On February 15, Lou Davis, a local promoter, held an all-star boxing carnival at the Gayety Theatre, located at 411 East Washington Street in Indianapolis. The card included many of Indy's finest fighters. The highlight of the evening was Jack Dillon—who was given a great introduction by Abe Nathonson, followed by a warm reception—sparring three rounds in an exhibition with Patsy McMahon.

In addition to local refereeing gigs, Jack Dillon signed on as an instructor at the Hoosier Athletic Club, succeeding Jimmy Dalton. The *Indiana Daily Times* noted: "Working with all the boxers at the athletic club and doing plenty of work there himself, he hopes to regain some of his former excellence at the boxing trade."[22] Patsy McMahon, in his 11th year in the ring, would be training with his old friend Jack Dillon again. McMahon would meet Tommy Phillips on April 3 in Indianapolis.

The Jack Dillon Benefit, May 10, 1922

For months, talk of a Jack Dillon Benefit filtered through the boxing fraternity. Prompted by Steve Harter, the pugilist's former manager, and in conjunction with a number of prominent individuals in the Indianapolis business community, an idea was transformed into reality. Acknowledging the fighter was but a shell of the pugilist he once was, and that he had fallen on unfortunate times in recent years, they hoped the event would assist Dillon in rebuilding his life. After selecting May 10 as the date, Washington Park baseball field was secured as the location.

The dynamic scheduling called for 12 exhibitions, featuring some of the greatest boxers in history, along with four 10-round bouts and five six-round bouts. The event was a testament to the popularity and contributions of Jack Dillon.

The Original Card

For a variety of reasons, not every fighter could make the event. Substitutions were made.

Exhibitions (two rounds, two minutes each):
Jack Dillon, "Hoosier Bearcat," versus Mike Gibbons, "St. Paul Phantom"
Chuck Wiggins, Indianapolis, versus Harry Greb, Pittsburg(h); (Greek Brown replaced Greb.)
Battling Nelson, ex-lightweight champion, versus Stewart Donnelly
Ray Bronson, ex-welterweight champion, versus Jack Britton, world's champion; (Mayor Shank acted as referee; Bobby Lee replaced Britton.)
Harvey Thorpe, Kansas City, versus Bobby Lee, Indianapolis
Sammy Mandell, Rockford, Illinois, versus Bud Taylor, Terre Haute; (Sidney Glick replaced Mandell.)
Ritchie Mitchell, Milwaukee, versus Bud Purrell, Terre Haute
Tommy Gibbons, St. Paul, versus K.O. Brown, San Francisco; (Gibbons acted only as referee.)
Johnny Buff, bantamweight champion, versus George Teague, Terre Haute; (Johnny Buff couldn't attend.)
Arlis Fanning, Kansas City, versus Jimmy Dalton, Indianapolis
Jimmy Katz, Toledo, versus Don Carson, Indianapolis
Sailor Dalton, Indianapolis, versus Jack Curley, Indianapolis
Jack Johnson, former heavyweight champion, versus Jack Leslie, Indianapolis; (Substitute bout)
Jimmy Dalton, Indianapolis, versus Willie Doyle, Detroit; (Substitute bout)

Ten-Round Fights (W=winner, Results listed for KO bouts only)
Bob Martin, champion A.E.F. (W), versus Soldier Jack Dorrell, Pacific Coast champion (heavyweights), (Result: KO1)
Jeff Smith, Bayonne (W), versus Otto Hughes, Philadelphia (middleweights), (Result: KO4)

Patsy McMahon, Indianapolis, versus Willie Doyle, Detroit (lightweights)
Tut Jackson, Courthouse (W), versus Battling Gross, Roanoke (Result: KO2)

Six-Round Fights:
Eddie Ketchell, New York, versus Tommy McDuff, Indianapolis (126 pounds)
Freddie Boorde, Indianapolis, versus K.O. Jeakle, Toledo (185 pounds)
Maxie Epstein, Indianapolis, versus Quincy Quigley, Dayton (118 pounds)
Sidney Glick, Indianapolis, versus Kid Burch, Indianapolis (135 pounds)
Bobby Bridges, Indianapolis, versus Leo Roberts, Terre Haute (142 pounds)

Four-Round Fights:
Tommy McDuff, Indianapolis, versus Eddie Ketchell, Toledo

Referees:
Ed. W. Smith, Mike Collins, Billy McCarney, Tom Andrews, Billy Haack, Al Libbey, Heze Clarke, Tommy Dillon, Frank Harry, Howdy Wilcox, Oren Chillson, Louis Chevrolet, and Chick Johnson. Also, announcers, Ed Chappell, Simmy Henderson, Blaine Patton, Biddy Bishop, and Abe Nathonson.

Notable guests: Mayor Shank, Chief of Police Rikhoff, and the new boxing commission.

The *Indiana Daily Times* noted:

> Big boxers, trim boxers, fat boxers and little boxers turned out last night to do their respective turns at the Jack Dillon testimonial fisticuff card at Washington Park and the fans in attendance were given a complete variety of glove entertainment. Some of it was serious, some of the exhibition brand and some comical.[23]

The weather was picture perfect. From where most were sitting, they had an excellent view of the ring, which was erected over the pitcher's mound. Sixteen events were conducted, and three knockouts—all of which took place in 10-round contests—occurred. The newspaper continued:

> Jack Dillon, the former light heavyweight champion, and for whom the big event was staged, made his appearance before the fans in a two-round sparring exhibition with Mike Gibbons, the St. Paul Phantom. The spectators gave Dillon and Gibbons a great hand. Tommy Gibbons, brother of Mike, also attended the show and acted as referee in one of the early bouts. Mike Gibbons is a contender for the middleweight title and Tommy Gibbons for the light heavyweight and heavyweight championships.[24]

Of the highlights, and there were many, the newspaper detailed:

> The appearance of Battling Nelson, former lightweight champion, drew a big hand. He had his trick boxing dummy with him, and he demonstrated a few punches for the spectators. A flock of "shines" [a racist term for a Black person] then put on a roughhouse with the dummy and drew plenty of laughs. Stewart Donnelly sparred with Nelson and the crowd was kept in an uproar. Both Stew and the battler swung so hard they became unbalanced and flopped on the canvas, Donnelly nearly cracking the boards when he hit the floor....
> Jack Johnson, former heavyweight champion who is doing a vaudeville turn in the city

this week, sparred two rounds with Jack Leslie of this city. Johnson was given a hand by the fans. Jack seems to be a little fat, but he demonstrated he still could box in an effective manner.... Jack Britton, Harry Greb, Johnny Buff and Johnny Wilson, who were scheduled to appear but didn't, sent their respects to Dillon by wire. There were enough prominents [*sic*] present without them.... The crowd was estimated at about six thousand.[25]

The benefit for Jack Dillon hoped to raise between $2,000 and $3,000.[26] Later, it was learned that it exceeded the projection. If Jack Dillon had family present, they were not acknowledged or identified—nor were Dillon's friends outside of work.

It was announced the first week of June that Jack Dillon would appear in person at the Rialto. He would be an extra added attraction to the venue's "Musical Extravaganza, The Only Show of the Kind in Town, Girls! Girls! Plenty of Speed, 2 shows in 1, Special Feature Picture Program." Jack Dillon, along with San Francisco Greek K.O. Brown, conducted "An Exhibition of the Dempsey–Carpentier Fight, as fought blow for blow." He wasn't the first pugilist to engage in this form of activity, nor would he be the last. Meanwhile, Battling Nelson was up the road in Anderson appearing with his famous boxing dummy. Hey, it had been a hit at Dillon's benefit.

Since Dillon was turning heads with his actions, why not turn more? Agreeing to manage boxer Jack Leslie—described as a "colored heavyweight of this city," rather than by his weight class or athletic prowess—he looked forward to the challenge.[27] If anyone had an issue with it, they could reach Dillon, at "P.O. Box 520, Indianapolis, Indiana."[28]

And turning even more heads, the *Indianapolis Times* reported in August:

There was a party at Jack Dillon's camp on White River, about 10 miles north of the city, Sunday night [July 30]. Patsy [McMahon] was there, and Jimmie Watts, a local featherweight, and Cecil Williams, a taxi man, and Joe Shea, Tommy McDuff, Tom Breen, Charlie McMahon, Paul Crosby, Denny Griffin, Frankie Martin, and Jack Dillon—all names that mean something, if you are a follower of local fight activities. About midnight there was a fight. Fists, clubs, a gun, blackjack, and broom were said to have been wielded with impartial hands. Patsy McMahon, who is no slouch in a battle, seems to have got the worst of it, maybe because he was hit while he was asleep.[29]

McMahon, who was working with Dillon, was forced to cancel his upcoming bout. It appeared to be a story with legs, as details were surfacing daily. And, even when Dillon wasn't there, things could go wrong. The camp, leased at the time to William Sullivan, was raided by authorities on September 13. The *Indianapolis News* wasn't shy reporting:

Jack Dillon's summer camp at Liberty Beach, on White River, north of Broad Ripple, which has been the scene of numerous orgies during the summer months, was raided Wednesday night [September 13] by George Snider, sheriff and a squad of federal agents and deputy constables. Two men were arrested on "blind tiger" [an illegal bar] charges and several bottles of White Mule were confiscated.[30]

The raided camp, located between Seventy-Eighth Street and White River, east of the Liberty Beach Hotel, had a beer keg that tested 3.5 percent alcohol, so Jack Dillon became a wanted man. Upon learning this, the pugilist surrendered and was released on bond. (He was arrested on a similar charge some months prior.)[31]

As Jack Dillon was working through his issues, word came on October 23 that another member of the family had issues of his own. The *Princeton Daily Clarion* reported:

> Ralph Dillon [Price], 16, son of Jack Dillon, of Indianapolis, was arrested here [Princeton, Indiana] yesterday afternoon by Chief Fettinger and placed in city lock-up. He is charged with taking money from rooms in the Princeton Hotel. One report was that the boy took sums estimated in the aggregate at more than $60. Jack Dillon, the father, is said to have made the money good with the guests of the hotel. He left here at noon today. Young Dillon will be arraigned in the circuit court tomorrow on a charge of petit larceny, it was said.[32]

Naturally, the matters were tough for the champion to ignore. The *Evansville Journal* noted, "Ralph had been sent to the St. Meinrad School at Jasper, Indiana, by his parents, but had not attended his classes for about a week it is said."[33] The Price family—Ernest, Grace, and Ralph—were renting a place at 832 Washington Street, in Marion, Indiana.[34]

To get his mind off his problems, Jack Dillon did what he has continuously done: He looked to the ring and assumed his refereeing duties.

As a living legend, he drew fans by his attendance and not only at boxing events. The roaring twenties were roaring, and at times so was the pugilist. The escapades at the summer cottage were a black eye, while his troubles with his son were part of being a parent; consequently, both would be forgiven and forgotten with time. What wouldn't be forgotten, it was hoped, was his ring legacy. The Jack Dillon Benefit, which should have been called The Jack Dillon Salute, was a well-deserved celebration of an elite career.

CHAPTER FOURTEEN

From Boxing to Breadlines, 1923–1942

"When Mike Gibbons was in Butte [Montana] recently he stated that Jack Dillon was the hardest hitting middleweight of them all and Jack could, in addition, give anyone in his class a masterful boxing lesson."
—*Anaconda Standard*[1]

The Twenties Conclude

Jack Dillon faced Joe Walters in his first ring battle of 1923. Yep, The Hoosier Bearcat was back in the ring. The *Palladium-Item* noted:

> Jack Dillon, former light heavyweight boxing champion, defeated Joe Walters, of Columbus, in a 10-round bout here [Bicknell, Indiana, January 11, 1923]. Dillon scored two knockdowns in the seventh round and had his opponent in a bad way in the final round. Last night's bout was the first of a campaign mapped out by the former champion in an attempt at a comeback.[2]

If a comeback plan was designed over the holiday, nobody spoke about it. Meanwhile, the elite pugilist continued his refereeing duties in Indianapolis.

The *Oakland Tribune* reported the impetus behind Dillon's comeback:

> Frank Klaus, former middleweight champion, has a soft drink place on a quiet street in Pittsburgh; Billy Papke is farming in southern California; Jack Dillon needs the money and wants to fight again; Sam Langford is boxing occasionally; Gunboat Smith is a stevedore [loading and unloading cargo ships] in New York.[3]

Dillon, who turned 32 on February 2, 1923, was being deemed "ancient" by periodicals such as *The Fresno Morning Republican*.[4] Despite the tag, he felt far different. Staying sharp meant keeping busy. The former champion likely picked up a few bootleg battles during this period, as he was spotted at a number of locations looking for contests.

On March 21, Dillon went eight no-decision rounds with Johnny Mack, Cincinnati middleweight, in Greensburg, Indiana. Decisively defeated, Dillon afterwards neither gave a response nor provided any indication of retirement.

In May, the *Indianapolis Star* reported:

> Ku Klux Klan investigators visited a roadhouse and dancing pavilion in the Melrose addition, near Liberty Beach, last night and a few moments later Sheriff Snider and Capt. Claude M. Worley, special investigator for the Criminal court, raided the place, arresting Ernest Price, otherwise known as Jack Dillon, an ex–prize fighter, on a bootlegging charge. Scotch, Irish, and Canadian whisky was seized in the place, the officers said. Price, who has been operating the roadhouse, was held under $1,500 bail.[5]

Was Jack Dillon reliving the previous year? It certainly appeared that way. The *Indianapolis Times* noted:

> Officers said there were six couples in the house when the raiders arrived.... The sheriff said Dillon claimed the liquor [a detailed list was provided] and declared "he did not handle Mule." Dillon has been arrested twice before on charges of operating a blind tiger. He was convicted once.[6]

On June 6, Ernest Price, a.k.a. Jack Dillon, was fined $100, plus costs, and sentenced to 30 days in jail on a blind tiger (illegal bar) charge by Judge Delbert O. Wilmeth in city court. The case was appealed in criminal court. The testimony didn't bode well for the pugilist.[7] It appeared as if too many liberties were being taken at Liberty Beach.

Jack Dillon agreed to participate in the July 4 boxing and wrestling carnival being conducted by the American Legion, Post No. 89, in Seymour, Indiana. Greeting the familiar face of Joe Walters, of Columbus, the pair engaged in 10 rounds. The *Tribune* noted:

> In the Jack Dillon–Joe Walters bout there was considerable action as well as clinching, Dillon for the most part being on the receiving end of the punching. Walters couldn't knock him out, though Dillon is but a shadow of the Dillon that used to be. He still retains some power of assimilation of punches, and keeps wading in.[8]

Since this action-packed bout went 10 rounds and utilized the services of a skilled referee (Howard Wiggam), its legitimacy wasn't questioned; moreover, it was never advertised as an exhibition, nor did it appear as such.

In somewhat of a surprise move, Ernest Price, a.k.a. Jack Dillon, withdrew an appeal to the criminal court from a city court conviction on a charge of operating a "blind tiger." The *Indianapolis News* noted:

> The city court fine of $100 and costs and a sentence of 30 days at the State Farm will stand. Price was arrested after a small quantity of liquor was found at his summer cottage on the bank of the White River, north of Broad Ripple. It is expected he will appear in court Monday to withdraw the appeal and be put in the custody of Sheriff George Snider, who will take him to the Indiana State Farm.[9]

Jack Dillon began serving his sentence on Monday, October 1, 1923. Upon his release, the pugilist maintained a low profile.

In 1924, Jack Dillon and Jimmy Watts took over the Hub Athletic Club, located at 400 East Louisiana Street in Indianapolis. The pugilists enjoyed each other's company and were friends. The club had a strong membership base and gave both pugilist owners an opportunity to work with not only promising local boxers but also those in town participating in events.[10]

Battles with Barleycorn

Jack Dillon couldn't escape the lure of alcohol, specifically the laws pertaining to Prohibition. A series of arrests for operating an illegal bar struck hard on his wallet and reputation. The *Indianapolis Times* reported, "Ernest Price, alias Jack Dillon, 33, Liberty Beach, former light heavyweight prize fight champion, was arrested [a small quantity, April 2, 1924] on blind tiger charges by Deputy Sheriffs Roland Snider and H. Clausen."[11]

Having been apprehended on February 8, 1922, and June 6, 1923, Mr. Price had his hands full. On June 14, 1924, the iconoclastic pugilist was arrested on the same charge. This, the fourth arrest, grew out of a serious motorcycle accident, where both individuals involved admitted obtaining liquor from Dillon. The pugilist was released under $1,500 bond.[12] The judge discharged Dillon for the latter case. The police in charge of enforcement of Prohibition continued to watch Jack Dillon's resort near Liberty Beach as if Al Capone were using it as his headquarters.

For the third arrest in June, Jack Dillon was sentenced to 60 days imprisonment and fined $200 by criminal judge James A. Collins. The pugilist denied selling the half pint of White Mule whiskey. Dillon, whose obstinate determination had been a strength and a downfall, sarcastically remarked that he sold only authentic whiskey.

On November 3, things at the Hub Athletic Club were about to change. Jack Dillon and Jimmy Watts were taken into custody on charges of violating the national Prohibition laws and maintaining a nuisance. They were bound over to the federal grand jury under a bond of $1,000 each.[13] Dillon and Watts entered pleas of not guilty to charges of violating the liquor laws.

The humiliation felt by Jack Dillon was worse than anything he ever felt in the ring. Three days into 1925, he was mentioned in the newspapers not for being in a ring but for being behind bars. The *Indianapolis Times* ran an article about the new sheriff. In the piece, the officer pointed to his pugilist prisoner in a shaming manner. While it was hurtful, it was also a dose of reality for those considering breaking the law.[14]

Regarding the fourth arrest on November 3, 1924: On March 16, 1925, Jack Dillon was sentenced to 90 days in jail and fined $200 and cost. Jimmy Watts received a similar sentence.[15] When the immutable behavior would end was anybody's guess.

What was happening at Liberty Beach? According to the officers who raided the hedonistic location, it had become an all-night party hub for young people. Alcohol was available for consumption at a reduced price.[16] Jack Dillon was discharged from Marion County jail on July 13, 1925. It was time to look elsewhere for accommodations.

(Top) A popular auto repair shop in Hialeah, Florida. (Bottom) The Hialeah Park Race Track was opened in 1922. (Both images [phf155, rc07636] courtesy Florida Memory, State Library and Archive of Florida).

Hialeah, Florida

During the summer, Jack Dillon began looking south for a residence. It wasn't a surprise considering everything he had been through. As he had family in Florida, that state became an option. An area—and that was what it was at the time—that caught his interest was Hialeah, Florida. Incorporated as a city on September 10, 1925, it was located west-northwest of Miami; the "high prairie" was between Biscayne Bay and the Everglades. It catered to some of Dillon's interests: hunting, fishing, gambling (the Hialeah Park Racetrack opened in 1925), and entertainment (Miami Movie Studios). Although the State of Florida legally went dry in 1919, a year before nationwide alcohol prohibition, many areas were so isolated, especially west and southwest of Miami (Monroe, Miami-Dade Counties), that enforcement of Prohibition laws was a rare.

Jack Dillon opened a restaurant in Hialeah in 1925. Serving a population estimated at about two thousand, it did well. It was an excellent way to meet area residents. And everyone Dillon greeted was thrilled to come face to face with the elite pugilist.

As 1925 drew to a close, the former champion was back in the news—and back home again in Indiana—for an automobile incident in which he was not hurt. Dillon's automobile ran off a road and down an embankment east of Anderson, Indiana. Alcohol was not involved in the mishap. It was ironic that Dillon, perhaps as part of a rehabilitation, was conducting health lectures.[17]

The second half of the decade began with Jack Dillon once again in the news. There were many with the intimidating moniker, but the one making headlines wasn't Ernest Price. It was Cincinnati welterweight Young Jack Dillon—no relation—who was garnering attention for his ring prowess.

Sadly, the restaurant he had opened in 1925 caught fire on February 21, 1926. The fire began at a nearby office building and spread quickly, taking Dillon's restaurant with it. In June 1926, Jack "the Giant Killer" Dillon announced plans for opening a café in Hialeah, on Palm Avenue, near Thirteenth Street.[18] While in the area Dillon wasn't bashful about attending regional boxing matches wherever they happened to be, whether in Miami or next door.

In an age where you built a venue to fit the entertainment, promoter Jesse O. Baugh planned to conduct an event, Gene Tunney versus Young Stribling, at the Hialeah Fight Stadium. It was an aggressive move considering the level of talent mentioned. The first of many problems was that the Hialeah Fight Stadium didn't exist. It needed to be built. Since there was a residence that adjoined the proposed stadium site on Palm Avenue, the promoter talked to the homeowner, Jack Dillon. Soon, construction on a wooden stadium began. When rumors flew that the fight promoter, who was already selling tickets, had financial issues, a writ was obtained from a supplier. When the deputy sheriff, doing his duty, sought the stadium to attach a notice, what existed of it was gone. The gossip had prompted many suppliers to disassemble the stadium piece by piece.[19]

Demon Alcohol

Alcohol addiction, during Prohibition, came in two forms: those who drank it and those who produced it. While ingesting alcohol could cost you money, producing it could make you money—okay, it could make you rich. There were ramifications associated with both.

For Jack Dillon, additional alcohol-related incidents—a pattern of malfeasance, or perhaps addictive behavior—took place during the second half of the decade.

When they mopped up Hialeah on Labor Day 1926, the liquor raids made the front page of the *Miami News*. Sad to relate, one of the places—Kentucky Bluebird, Twenty-First Street and Palm Avenue—owned by Jack Dillon was featured. Upon arrest, the pugilist decided not to produce bond, opting instead for the comforts of a jail cell.[20]

On March 15, 1927, Jack Dillon was detained by federal Prohibition agents conducting raids in the northwest section of Hialeah. He was released on $100 bail.[21] Dillon had been operating a poolroom at Hialeah Racetrack.

In July 1928, Jack Dillon was apprehended in Miami on warrants based on sales made to Prohibition agents. He was released on $100 bond.

On February 13, 1929, Jack Dillon was fined $100 and costs in the Miami Court of Crimes for illegal possession of liquor.

On June 27, 1929, Jack Dillon was sentenced to 10 days in the county jail and fined $250 in the Dade County Court of Crimes as a second offender for illegal possession of liquor. The incident took place at his café in Hialeah.

On December 8, 1929, Jack Dillon was arrested on charges of liquor possession at his Hialeah café. With him was his brother Paul Price, held on a similar charge. Both individuals made $100 bond.

The unlawful—bear in mind, he was warned numerous times prior to his arrests—and habitual behavior of the former champion was difficult to witness for his friends and family. Whether driven by a disease such as alcoholism, or avarice such as bootlegging, these egocentric actions were dominating his life. Clearly, the measures taken to counter the problem—from fines to incarceration—had so far failed.

Particularly sad: The frequency of the arrests dulled the shine on Jack Dillon's brilliant boxing career. For those who loved the sport, and even grew up admiring the deftness of the pugilist, it was heartbreaking.

It also countered his altruistic acts, which he performed unobtrusively. For example, Thanksgiving was a holiday that challenged everyone, even pugilists, to reach out to their brothers and sisters in need. Knowing that in his neighborhood there were dozens of less fortunate individuals who were homeless, Jack Dillon decided to act. He provided everyone he could round up with a Thanksgiving meal. From turkey to pumpkin pie, Jack Dillon's generosity filled the hearts and stomachs of his forlorn neighbors. Another unselfish act, which was witnessed by his Hialeah neighbors, was his love for animals, especially feral cats and dogs. Even in his declining state of health, the former pugilist would walk long distances to purchase food for the animals. As he was a person who cherished his privacy, his compassionate actions were largely unknown. But as his close friends could verify, it was a part of who he was.

Death of Grace M. Dillon

The 41-year-old wife of Ernest C. Price, Grace M. Dillon, of Palm Avenue and Twenty-First Street in Hialeah, died at a local hospital on Saturday, July 27, 1929. She left behind her husband, Jack; a son, Ralph; two brothers, George and Jake Swartzman (Schwartzman), of Ohio; and two sisters, Agnes and Theresa Swartzman (Schwartzman), of Indiana.[22]

Grace Dillon's funeral was conducted on Monday, July 29, 1929, by the W.L. Philbrick Funeral Home, on 660 West Flagler Street in Miami, Florida.[23] Not much was publicly known about Mrs. Jack Dillon, as the couple valued their privacy. Tommy Dillon would accompany her on occasion to Jack's bouts, such as he did during his brother's bout with Moran in 1916, but he refused to comment about the couple.

French-born American diarist Anaïs Nin quipped, "Love never dies a natural death. It dies because we don't know how to replenish its source. It dies of blindness and errors and betrayals. It dies of illness and wounds; it dies of weariness, of witherings, of tarnishings."[24] Although nobody was certain, the couple's relationship appeared complex. Yet, Grace Price made the move to Hialeah, Florida. Such a commitment, under complex circumstances, speaks volumes.

The Great Crash, a.k.a. the Crash of '29, or Black Thursday, was a major American stock market crash occurring in the autumn of 1929. There were early signs, during the months of September and October, when share prices on the New York Stock Exchange (NYSE) collapsed. Many were ignored, however. The high-flying bull market of the 1920s concluded with a catastrophic collapse of the NYSE in late 1929. Many, including a plethora of pugilists, lost their fortunes during the maelstrom. The result was a ubiquitous Great Depression.

The Thirties

It would be a decade defined by a global economic and political crisis that culminated in the Second World War. The collapse of the international financial system, beginning with the Wall Street Crash of 1929, the largest stock market crash in American history, was working its way through society, or income levels, if you will. It wasn't a question if you would be impacted, only when.

The subsequent economic downfall, called the Great Depression, had traumatic social effects worldwide, leading to widespread poverty and unemployment. For the average family, it was a scary time. For Ernest C. Price, the decade would prove a challenge.

In January of 1930, Jack Dillon was hit with a $100 fine from his last alcohol-related arrest. In April, Dillon headed back to Indianapolis to assist in the training of Walter Pickerd, a local heavyweight. The stop was part of a trip Dillon was taking to California. He looked healthy—he was far from overweight, his muscles were well-defined, and he was wearing his hair—sprinkled with gray—longer. The only giveaway to his maturity showed in his face; the skin, once taut, was now sinking in the usual places (chin, neck, etc.), and there were wrinkles around his eyes.[25]

In February 1930, Jack Dillon was given a suspended sentence on a liquor law violation on the condition that he leave the county. He picked up another violation when he returned to Hialeah on June 11, 1930. The incident found him back in county jail.

Jack Dillon celebrated his 40th birthday on February 2, 1931. On the occasion, newspapers nationwide published tributes to "Jack the Giant Killer." Damon Runyon, who was fond of hanging a label on a character, even penned a syndicated column in tribute of "the Indianapolis Man Mauler." For Dillon's name to be used in the same breath as the great Jack Dempsey, and by a such preeminent wordsmith as Runyon, was beyond imagination. Dillon was Dempsey before Jack, and that was how many felt.

Death of Amanda Jane Price

Amanda Jane Price, 70, of Sarasota, Florida, died on May 8, 1931. She passed on while visiting her son Ernest in Hialeah. As a member of the Methodist Church, she told stories to her friends of her native Indiana, and leaving for the state for Florida over a dozen years prior. Of her four sons, three were surviving, Russell C. of St. Petersburg, along with Ernest and Paul of Hialeah. Her private funeral was held at the same funeral home as that of Ernest's wife, Grace.[26]

Legally Jack Dillon

Ernest Coulter Price, born in Frankfort, Indiana, on February 2, 1891, legally changed his name to Jack Dillon on June 24, 1931. The action was conducted by Price's attorney Gordon R. Broome and granted by circuit court judge Uly O. Thompson. Dillon gave his residence as Hialeah, Florida. The timing of the event, following closely after the death of his mother, seemed a bit peculiar, even if the action was not.

In March, Jack Dillon was serving a 60-day sentence in Dade County Jail for liquor possession. He was sentenced to hard labor, but Dr. E.C. Thomas, county physician, deemed it impossible because Dillon was "punch drunk." Thus, the former champion was removed to the county hospital.

When a pugilist takes a punch to the head, the brain moves inside the skull. If the punch is powerful enough, it can damage communication pathways to the brain. This causes confusion to the recipient and memory loss. Temporary unconsciousness or confusion caused by a punch to the head is called a concussion. The damage caused by extensive exposure to concussions, a form of neurotrauma, led to participants in early twentieth-century medicine to label it "punch drunk syndrome." Later, the term was referred to as "dementia pugilistica." Those who suffer from the illness can face behavioral or psychiatric symptoms, diminished cognition, and physical damage; they may have trouble walking. The serious and damaging condition can be heartbreaking to witness. Since the progression of the illness, not to mention the intensity, varies with those suffering from the disorder, it was a risk every pugilist took. Jack Dillon understood this was an occupational hazard but hoped he could avoid it. He could not.

Adding to the complexities associated with dementia pugilistica was Jack Dillon's depression. His world was getting smaller. Daily activities, even the simple ones such as eating and sleeping, were a challenge. The desire for food was gone, and forcing it down his throat didn't work. Aspirations felt similar to memories, and Dillon didn't know why. Impulses were scary, even confusing. When he was tired, Dillon understood he had to sleep, but he couldn't shut his mind down because the thoughts wouldn't go away. His surroundings could be enigmatic. With no one qualified to assist him, Dillon found solace with traditional means, turning to friends and family for whatever support they could provide or through self-medication. During the early part of the twentieth century, depression was poorly understood.

A Case of Fake Identity

A reporter for the *Evening Star* in Washington, D.C., caught up with man claiming to be Jack Dillon in September 1932, after the supposed former boxer drove his car to the nation's capital to take part in the "Bonus Expeditionary Forces March." The *Evening Star* detailed Dillon's journey:

> Jack (The Giant Killer) Dillon has no alibis to offer about his last big fight, the one that still punishes after 14 years. Three machine gun bullets killed the punch in his right arm and a trench infection took eight toes off his nimble feet, but was Jack glad to fight with the Marines? ... He was glad in 1917 and in 1932 he's still glad, for those Marines were "swell guys," and it was a "grand fight," although it finished him as a fighter—the only profession he ever knew. Jack got no compensation for his disability, nor is he crying for any.[27]

The article, with its surprising information, continued:

> The Giant Killer, at the age of 42, was fit all right—fit to help at the hospital in the Salvation Army barracks, for room and board.... He's broke, his post-war savings from the fight game have long since dwindled away—"a couple of health farms, a hotel that didn't go so good." ... Jack came here from Indianapolis with the bonus army, was routed by the soldiers and returned several weeks ago. Jack's automobile—his last wordily possession—burned with the shacks on Anacostia flats. "Right!" said Jack, "but that's O.K., it wasn't much of a car anyhow!"[28]

Once news of the article, which included a photograph, reached various members of the media, it was deemed a "fake." The charade was over. Admiration comes in many forms, from using the name "Jack Dillon" in the ring, which many had the world over, to even faking an identity for a national newspaper.[29]

Death of Paul W. Price

Paul W. Price, of 2310 Palm Avenue, in Hialeah, Florida, died on October 17, 1933. He had suffered from an unnamed illness for months. Having come to the area from Daytona Beach about a year and a half prior, he enjoyed the region and what it had to offer. He was survived by his brothers Jack Dillon, of Hialeah, and Russell C. Price, of St. Petersburg. The W.L. Philbrick Funeral Home, of Miami, Florida, handled the arrangements.

During the prior 1,543 days, Jack Dillon had endured the loss of his wife, his mother, and his youngest brother. Living through such bereavement was something you wouldn't wish upon your worst enemy, yet Jack Dillon persevered. Pain had always been part of his life. He accepted it even though he couldn't contain it.

Conclusion of Prohibition

On December 5, 1933, Prohibition ended when Amendment Twenty-One to the Constitution was ratified. It repealed the previous Eighteenth Amendment, which had established a nationwide ban on the manufacture, sale, and transportation of alcohol. The reason was greed. The Great Depression left the government strapped for cash. The solution to the problem was tax. Grab the potential tax revenue from alcohol sales. While the millionaires created by Prohibition were not forgotten, its victims were.

Jack Dillon, a.k.a. "Jack the Giant Killer," remained in Hialeah and in a less than flattering conditions; frankly, his impecunious state was difficult for visitors to understand or ignore. Turning 43 in 1934, he loved to tell guests that three great men were born in February, and the other two were Washington and Lincoln. He used the line ad nauseam and even included it in his schtick to the media. Operating his small refreshment stand near the Hialeah Racetrack, he was content. Admitting that times were tough, he knew others had it even harder.

A lunacy petition was filed in Miami County Court on September 28, 1934, against Jack Dillon. The petition was signed by five individuals. A commission of three was assigned to investigate Dillon's mental condition. Meanwhile, he resided in the county jail. Handicapped by a number of noticeable issues, including problems with his eyesight, Dillon was struggling to survive.[30]

Briefly comprehending what he might be facing, Jack Dillon put himself back together with the help of friends. He continued to operate a small saloon in a building he rented. It wasn't much, but it was affordable. The three-room building even had sleeping quarters in the back that he shared with his old friend Jimmy

Watts.³¹ Operating it as long as he could, Dillon was ultimately forced to close its doors in June 1937.

That month, in an attempt to stabilize his condition and perhaps rekindle some past memories, Jack Dillon—tanned, clean-shaven, and with a full head of hair—returned to Indianapolis. Walking and talking slower, the former champion did his best to recall his life in the Hoosier State, but at times he drifted. In other words, it was easy for him to lose his train of thought or get confused. Yet, when he was asked specific questions about his career, he occasionally responded with coherent answers. Of his immediate plans, he had none. However, he hoped to catch the heavyweight championship fight between Joe Louis and James J. Braddock in Chicago on June 22, 1937. And he managed to do that; he was even introduced at the event.

While in Indy, Dillon stayed at the home of J.J. Canning at Terrace Beach, his old training camp. Naturally, he was a welcome guest at area boxing events, and he attended many. Not wanting to wear out his welcome, Jack Dillon did not take long to realize it was time to return to Hialeah.

On January 28, 1939, Jack Dillon, 47, was taken into custody at First Avenue and Twenty-First Street, in Hialeah, Florida, for selling untaxed liquor. Bond was set at $500. In one of those say-it-ain't-so moments, Jack Dillon was released, following a guilty plea, to the custody of Jess Willard, former heavyweight champion.³² If you would have told him years earlier that the next place he would meet Willard face to face was a courtroom, he never would have believed you. Big Jess was convinced he could find employment for Dillon. And to Willard's credit, he assisted Jack Dillon where he could and for as long as possible.³³

The Forties

Renting at house number 23, on Twenty-First Street in Hialeah, Jack Dillon, unable to care for himself, faced institutionalization. He was brought to the State Hospital at Chattahoochee by Miami attorney George Pitts in April 1942; it was the only way to guarantee his safety and well-being. The living conditions at the facility were reprehensible, yet reflective of the times. Critically ill with bronchial pneumonia for several months, Jack Dillon, 51, died on August 7, 1942. Three days later, his funeral was conducted at the State Hospital at Chattahoochee, where he was buried in the institution's cemetery.³⁴

As in the fairy tale, Jack Dillon outwitted his giant adversaries. And rather than by yielding an ax, he sealed their fate with his fists. As a defensive craftsman, he possessed extraordinary speed allowing him to avoid damage. As an offensive terror, he was adroit at finding angles and delivering powerful assaults. His cunning infighting enabled him to deliver deadly short-range jabs and combinations, enhanced by violent uppercuts. Not once exhibiting any form of emotion,

Aerial view of the Florida State Hospital—a hospital and psychiatric hospital—in Chattahoochee, Florida. Established in 1876, it was Florida's only state mental institution until 1947 (Image [lc357aerial] courtesy Florida Memory, State Library and Archive of Florida).

his stare cut through a rival like a hot knife through butter. From the opening gong, it was clear to every opponent, regardless of size or skill, that they were destined for destruction.

The Ring magazine founder Nat Fleischer ranked Dillon as the #3 light heavyweight of all time, while boxing promoter Charley Rose placed him at #2. The International Boxing Research Organization rated Dillon as the 16th best light heavyweight ever. He was inducted into *The Ring* magazine hall of fame in 1959 and the International Boxing Hall of Fame in 1995.

In 1919, a letter to columnist Thomas Aloysius "Tad" Dorgan provided a fight fan's perspective regarding the greatest pugilist ever. The *Pomona Progress* published it:

> I've been reading your articles on the "greatest fighter that ever lived," and it seems strange to me that not one of your correspondents has named the man who in my opinion, was the daddy of them all. My choice is Jack Dillon, nicknamed by the sporting writers "Jack the Giant Killer," and they didn't peg him wrong. Can you name a big boy that Dillon ever

Fourteen. From Boxing to Breadlines, 1923–1942

Inside of the Florida State Hospital—a hospital and psychiatric hospital—in Chattahoochee, Florida. (top) The dining hall and dormitory of the facility (both images [47c43791-6a6c, n028779] courtesy Florida Memory, State Library and Archive of Florida).

sidestepped? They don't build them big enough for Jack. Do you remember over in Brooklyn when he socked Tom Cowler on the chin and sent Jim Corbett into the movie business? Do you remember the pasting he handed to big Frank Moran at Ebbets Field when they thought it a crime to let Jack fight? Do you remember what he did to Charlie Weinert, the Adonis of the ring when they met in Philly? When he was in his prime Dillon was unbeatable. Tom Bigger, boxing commissioner for the State of Michigan, is with me in this pick and Tom was never on a dead one. I don't think Dillon's equal has ever been seen. He was a real fighter, and I am for real things.[35]

"Jack the Giant Killer" was real.

Appendix A: Ernest Coulter Price, a.k.a. Jack Dillon—Boxing Record

Name: Ernest Coulter Price; He legally changed his name to Jack Dillon on June 24, 1931.

Born: February 2, 1891, in Frankfort, Indiana

Nationality: Scotch/Irish/American

Education: First year of high school

Spouse(s): Admitted being married in 1910 (unconfirmed); Married Grace Reed on May 14, 1914.

Died: August 7, 1942, in Chattahoochee, Florida

Siblings: Three brothers: *Chester B. Price, four years older than Ernest, September 25, 1887–May 28, 1905, died boxing, used moniker Kid Austin; *Russell Clay Price, a.k.a. Tommy Dillon, two years older than Ernest, February 15, 1889–September 24, 1967, eventually moved to St. Petersburg; *Paul W. Price, six years younger than Ernest, September 6, 1896–October 17, 1933, moved to Daytona Beach, Florida, in 1931, before heading to Hialeah, Florida. Believed to be shorter than all of his brothers, Paul especially admired Ernest.

Aliases: Hoosier Bearcat, Hoosier Hurricane, Jack the Giant Killer, Hoosier Mankiller, White Sam Langford

Alias Origin (Jack Dillon): Famous racehorse Sidney Lou Dillon

Stance: Orthodox, and like many, struggled with southpaws

Measurements (1916): Height: 5' 7½"; Reach: 71" (reported at 72½" in 1911); Chest: 42"; Neck: 16½"; Wrist: 8½"; Biceps: 14½"; Waist: 31"; Thigh: 22"; Calf: 16"; and Ankle: 9½"

Selected Fight Managers: Wick Davidson (1908), Izzy Brill (1908), Cecil Day (1909), Sid Cox (1909), Nate Farb(es) (1909), Clint Truesdale (1910), Jimmy Walters (September 1910), Frank Cantwell (1911), Cantwell and Roy Schooley (1911), Norman Anthony (1911), Buck Carroll (1911), Roy Schooley (1911), Frank Cantwell (1912), Sam Murbarger (1912–3, 1914–6), Jimmy Walters (1913–4), Edwin W. (Steve) Harter (1916/17–8, 1920) and Judge Joe Flanagan (c. 1918), Benny Kauff (1920), Billy Kramer (1920), Eddie Barnsback (1920), and Jack Fisher (1921)

Fighters Managed by Murbarger: Gus Christie (1913), Jack Dillon, Eddie McGoorty, and many others

Trainers/Seconds: George Coogan, Thomas Dillon, Nate Farb, Harry Hart, Willie Parson, Bob Stolkin (first under Murbarger), John Tracey (Tracy), Jimmy Watts, Teddy Hayes, and many others

Sparring Partners: Ray Bronson, Kid Dalton, Harry Donahue, Larry Donovan, Willie Fitzgerald, Bobby Long, Billy Mayfield, Young Neese, Kid Thompson, and many others

Career Span: 1908–25, most sources end in 1923

Acknowledged Championship Span: April 14, 1914–October 24, 1916

Punch Analysis: Powerful uppercuts, great left hand

Trademark Move/Action: Strong opening round, prolific body puncher

Boxing Inspirations: Battling Nelson, Ad Wolgast

Boxing Style: Aggressive, especially early in career; his first wallop was typically a right just below the heart

Superstitions: Brought his own water to Southern bouts; avoided the number 13; said a prayer in his corner prior to each ring battle in which he was engaged

Hardest puncher he faced: Eddie McGoorty

Mascot: A dog named Major

Wardrobe: He typically wore white running pants

Favorite Training Activity: Rowing along the White River in Indiana

Favorite Pastime: He loved animals, especially horses, dogs, and cats.

Fighter earmarked as next Jack Dillon, or having similar qualities: Many, from Jack Dempsey to Solly Epstein. Nat Fleischer, *The Ring* editor, stated that, of all the fighters he had seen, Mickey Walker was the most like Dillon.

First Mention of Being Champion: "Dillon Will Be Welterweight Champion in Year, Says Manager," *Indianapolis Star*, April 4, 1910, page 8. Spoken on April 3, 1910.

First Rivalry: Ray Bronson

Rivalries: Ray Bronson, George Chip, Battling Levinsky, Billy Miske

Toughest fight: Eddie McGoorty (1910)

Largest Gate: Dillon versus Moran: Dillon received $15,000 and an option for 25 percent of gate, a share of the "movie" profits, and also training expenses. The gross receipts for the Dillon–Moran bout totaled $28, 521.

Injury that derailed his career: Torn ligaments in the legs

Notes: *People*—There were many individuals named Jack Dillon. There was a well-known New York welterweight by the name of Jack "the Battleship" Dillon who died in November 1907 at his home in New York. There were a number of boxers named Young Jack Dillon. However, the pugilist who fought out of Denver around 1919 was likely the most talented. As a light heavyweight whose career spanned 1922 to 1934, Young Jack Dillon was born in Louisville, Kentucky, and fought out of Tennessee; Jack Dillon, the boxing referee, emigrated from Ireland

and settled in Pittsburgh, Pennsylvania. He was a gifted athlete (especially in football and boxing) and found a calling as a boxing referee. Popular in Pittsburgh, he also owned and operated a restaurant in the city. A couple of fighters by the name of Jack Dillon emerged out of New York City by 1920. And don't forget John Francis Dillon, who was born in New York City (1884–1934). As a talented director, Jack Dillon's best-known work was likely *Call Her Savage* (1932).

Places—The Dillon Athletic Club was located at 604 East Washington Street in Indianapolis in 1910. (Today, the site is a parking lot.) His open-air quarters were located at Thirty-Third Street and Sutherland Avenue. The Dillon-Bronson Athletic Club was located at South and Illinois Streets in Indianapolis. Later, it was called simply the Dillon Club (1912). His headquarters in 1918 was given as 223 North Illinois Street.

Things—A popular referee by the name of Tommy Dillon, who hailed from Indianapolis, was repeatedly mistaken for Jack Dillon's brother.

Abbreviations: AC=Athletic Club; Aud=Auditorium; Bldg=Building; D=Draw; DV=Date of fight varies; EX=Exhibition; IBHOF= Member of the International Boxing Hall of Fame; KO=Knockout Victory; L=Lost; ME=Main Event; LKO=Lost via KO; MSG=Madison Square Garden; ND=No Decision; NWD=Newspaper Decision; Post=Postponed; RV=rounds vary; SC=Sporting Club; SP=Spelling Variations; Stad=Stadium; Sub=Substitute; TBD=To Be Determined; TK=Technical Knockout; W=Won; WD=Won by disqualification; **=appeared on fight card with his brother Russell Price, a.k.a. Tommy Dillon

To better frame the career of Jack Dillon, assorted tentative bouts that never took place, due to one reason or another, are included. Additional information, such as an illness, injury, suspension, or a significant event in the pugilist's life may also be listed. The no-decision era was prone to subjectivity, thus creating ambiguity as to the victor in certain situations. Many times, terms were not met following a match. Forfeits, often for weight and appearance, were common. All fights have been confirmed by at least three sources; moreover, fights that failed this process appear in italics, as do exhibitions. Rounds were three minutes in length unless otherwise indicated here or in the text.

Professional Bouts

1908

Date	Opponent	Location	Result	Comments
Apr 12	Tommy Dawson	Indianapolis, IN	—	Opening new Apollo AC
Apr 18	Jimmy Kelly	Indianapolis, IN	—	Apollo AC; Scheduled
Apr 18	Fortville Kid Brown	Indianapolis, IN	D6	Marion Club; Dillon's pro debut; paid $7.50
May 28	Fortville Kid Brown	Martinsville, IN	—	Crystal Theater; Stopped by sheriff

Date	Opponent	Location	Result	Comments
Jul 7	*Young Saylor*	*Indianapolis, IN*	*EX4*	*Apollo Athletic Club; same manager*
Jul 20	Joe McAree	Indianapolis, IN	D6	Verified; often reported as W6
Jul	*Fortville Kid Brown*	*Dayton, OH*	*D6*	
Aug 5	*Ben Harper*	*Indiana*	—	*Bootleg battle; refused to fight*
Sep 19	Jack Laffy (Laffey)	Indianapolis, IN	KO4	Marion Club
Oct 5	Lem (Lee) Potter	Indianapolis, IN	KO4	Verified
Oct 27	Tom DeLane	Columbus, IN	KO4	
Nov 3	*Willy Reilly*	*Muskogee, OK*	*EX10*	*Exhibition*
Nov 13	Pat Lark	Indianapolis, IN	KO4	
Nov 20	Teddy Malone	Dayton, OH	D10	Also listed as Tony Mullane
Dec 19	Tommy Clark	Indianapolis, IN	W10	

Notes: Later, Dillon's match with Pat Lark was incorrectly reported as a draw; Ring earnings estimate quoted as $77.50 for the year by the *Indianapolis Star* (See "Dillon's Ring Record for First Two Years," June 11, 1911, 52).

1909

Date	Opponent	Location	Result	Comments
Jan 22	Joe McAree (McCrea)	Indianapolis, IN	WD4	Miners' convention; Auditorium
Feb 3	Kid Simms (Sims)	Indianapolis, IN	KO3	Auditorium; likely TK
Feb 20	Charles Humphries	Indianapolis, IN	KO2	Bowlers Benefit; Marion Club
Feb 24	Grant "Kid" Clark	Columbus, OH	KO6	Verified
Mar 3	Tommy Dawson	Indianapolis, IN	—	Scheduled: 133 lbs.
Mar 3	Pat Lark	Indianapolis, IN	W6	
Mar 4	*Kid Griffin*	*Indianapolis, IN*	*EX4*	*Exhibition for Retail Hardware Association*
Mar 12	Ray Bronson	Hartford City, IN	D6	Gymnasium; 133 lbs.; Edge: Bronson
Mar 31	Willie Riley	Indianapolis, IN	—	
Mar 31	Bobby Long	Indianapolis, IN	ND4	Dillon replaced Lee Patterson: Aud; TK4
Apr 2	Andy Howell	Indianapolis, IN	—	
Apr 2	Young Kid Gray	Indianapolis, IN	TK2	Mitchell Club; Police presence; 10-oz. mitts
Apr 28	Terry Nelson	Indianapolis, IN	—	Scheduled: six-rounds; Canceled
May 10	Young Connors	Indianapolis, IN	W5	Knights of Columbus Hall
May 21	Jimmy Kid Sullivan	Terre Haute, IN	Rescheduled	
May 28	Jimmy Kid Sullivan	Terre Haute, IN	KO3	
Jul 2	Tommy Scanlon	Terre Haute, IN	KO6	Dropped 3X in 6th
Jul 22	Everett Reeves	Anderson, IN	KO5	Grand Opera House
Aug 12	*Ray Bronson*	*Indianapolis, IN*	—	*Likely exhibition*
Sep 8	Joe Perconte	Evansville, IN	—	
Sep 12	Jack Redmond	New Orleans, LA	—	West Side AC

Date	Opponent	Location	Result	Comments
Sep 19	Jack Redmond	New Orleans, LA	—	West Side AC
Sep 19	Kid Sparks	New Orleans, LA	KO2	West Side AC; sub for Redmond

Suffered strain that required an operation

Date	Opponent	Location	Result	Comments
Dec 20	Ford Munger	Saginaw, MI	—	Valley AC; Canceled
Dec 22	Jimmy Cooley	Indianapolis, IN**	W6	Mitchell AC; DV

Notes: The spelling of McAree varied; Ray Bronson was the first fighter Dillon met with more than 40 professional bouts; Although many sources call Dillon's bout against Bronson a draw, the reports indicate Bronson had a slight edge; The September 19 bout was courtesy of Charles Olson, a local Indy wrestler, who was matchmaker for the relatively new club and friends with Izzy Brill; Most sources state KO5, as a result for Dillon's battle against Bobby Long. This was only a four-round preliminary (*Indianapolis News*, April 1, 1909). Officially, the fight was ruled ND4; Ring earnings estimate quoted as $355.00 for the year by the *Indianapolis Star* (See "Dillon's Ring Record for First Two Years," June 11, 1911, 52).

1910

Date	Opponent	Location	Result	Comments
Jan 31	Jap Roberts	Newport, KY	KO2	Clifton AC
Feb 8	Jimmy Cooley	Indianapolis, IN	ND6	Mitchell AC; Draw
Feb 13	Willie Fitzgerald	Anderson, IN	—	Matched
Mar 4	*James J. Corbett*	*Indianapolis, IN*	*EX3*	*One-minute rounds–IBHOF*
Mar 8	Willie Fitzgerald	Anderson, IN	—	Substituted (see below)
Mar 8	Ray Bronson	Anderson, IN	D8	Bronson sub for Fitzgerald; Dillon floored?
Mar 11	*Ike Garfinkle*	*Olean, IN*	—	*Cannot verify*
Mar 22	*Young Donnelly*	*Indianapolis, IN***	*EX4*	*Dillon AC*
Mar 28	Kid Dalton	Indianapolis, IN	—	Scheduled; Canceled
Mar 29	*Ad Wolgast*	*Indianapolis, IN*	—	*Empire Theatre; Replaced*
Apr 2	Rube May	Anderson, IN**	KO5	TKO; fought at 140 lbs.
Apr 21	Dick Fitzpatrick	Anderson, IN	ND10	Grand Opera House; verified 10 rds.
May 30	Howard Morrow	Anderson, IN**	D8	Referee ruled it a draw
Jun 8	Ray Bronson	Evansville, IN	—	Matched; Replaced with Kid Dalton
Jun 20	Freddie Hicks	Newark, OH	W15	Controversial low blow
Jun 30	*Nate Farb*	*Broad Ripple, IN*	*EX4*	
Jul 28	Jack Ryan	Anderson, IN**	KO6	Grand Opera House
Aug 31	Jack Morgan	Indianapolis, IN**	—	Police Intervention; Mitchell AC
Sep 7	Ray Bronson	Richmond, IN	—	Matched; Richmond AC
Sep 16	Battling Juhre	Milwaukee, WI	—	Canceled
Sep 17	Jim Perry	Pittsburgh, PA	D6	Old City Hall; Advantage Perry
Sep 27	Jack Morgan	Muncie, IN	—	Canceled; Negotiations failed
Oct 3	Jack Herrick	Winnipeg, Man, Can	ND12	Advantage: Dillon
Oct 11	Dixie Kid	Pittsburgh, PA	—	Offered
Oct 12	Howard Wiggam	Richmond, IN	—	Canceled
Oct 21	Billy Berger	Pittsburgh, PA	—	Canceled: Old City Hall

Date	Opponent	Location	Result	Comments
Oct 21	George Chip	Pittsburgh, PA	ND6	1st bout of a dozen battles for pair
Oct 25	Jack Morgan	Muncie, IN	—	Canceled; Negotiations failed
Oct 26	Kid Burns	Richmond, IN	—	Canceled
Oct 28	Kid Burns	Richmond, IN	—	Coliseum; Jack replaced by Tommy
Oct 29	Billy Berger	Pittsburgh, PA	ND6	Venue incident; tier of seats collapsed
Nov 1	Jack Morgan	Muncie, IN	—	Canceled; Negotiations failed
Nov 11	Jack Herrick	Winnipeg, Man, Can	ND12	
Nov 26	Young Loughrey	Pittsburgh, PA	—	Matched; Opponent declined
Nov 26	Jack Abbott	Pittsburgh, PA	—	Matched; Opponent declined
Nov 28	George "K.O." Brown	Springfield, OH	W20	Dillon 117 lbs.; 1st meeting; Paid $63

Dillon confirmed that this fight (above) was his first big break.

| Dec 16 | Eddie McGoorty | Fond du Lac, WI | L10 | First loss; 1st bout with McGoorty |

Notes: Admitted to being married in 1910 (See "Sports Gossip of General Interest," *Buffalo Courier*, March 20, 1911, 8), but the name of the woman he married was not given nor was a marriage record found; Also stated the death of a brother within the past year; Stated his big break with Brown in the *Indianapolis Star* (See "Jack Dillon Received $63 for his hardest contest," February 10, 1918); Dillon's September 17 bout, against Perry, marked his debut as a middleweight; Jack Dillon was to box Kid Burns, but his brother Tommy Dillon replaced him. Police reduced the rounds to one-minute and three-quarters (see *Palladium-Item*, October 29, 1910); Stated fight with Eddie McGoorty, on December 16, 1910, was his toughest battle (See "In Corbett's Corner," *Macon Telegraph*, June 25, 1919).

1911

Date	Opponent	Location	Result	Comments
Jan 2	Harry Mansfield	Pittsburgh, PA	ND 6	Adv.: Dillon; Old City Hall
Jan 11	Eddie McGoorty	Winnipeg, Man, Can	D12	158 lbs.; 2nd meeting; Draw by law
Jan 24	George Chip	Dayton, OH	W15	2nd meeting; 154 lbs.
Feb 4	Mike Glover	Pittsburgh, PA**	ND6	Old City Hall; Draw
Feb	*Various*	*Indianapolis, IN*	EX3	*3-round exhibitions at Empire Theatre*
Feb 18	Young Loughrey	Pittsburgh, PA	ND6	Old City Hall
Feb 22	Jimmy Gardner	Indianapolis, IN	ND10	Auditorium; 154 lbs.; Advantage Dillon
Mar 4	Billy Berger	Pittsburgh, PA	ND6	Old City Hall; Advantage Dillon
Mar 7	Leo Houck	Boston, MA	—	Houck canceled battle—IBHOF
Mar 14	Jimmy Mellody	Brazil, IN	KO3	Sourwine Theatre
Mar 15	Young Loughrey	Indianapolis, IN	ND10	Auditorium; Draw
Mar 17	Mike "Twin" Sullivan	Buffalo, NY	ND10	Auditorium; Advantage Dillon
Apr 1	Billy Clark	Pittsburgh, PA	KO4	Old City Hall

Appendix A: Boxing Record

Date	Opponent	Location	Result	Comments
Apr 4	Frank Mantell	Boston, MA	W12	Armory AA; 1st meeting
Apr 10	Billy Mayfield	Crawfordsville, IN	KO1	Phoenix AC
Apr 12	Jack Stevens	Evansville, IN	KO1	Theater
Apr 18	Kid Dalton	Lafayette, IN	—	Police intervention; Stopped prior
Apr 18	George Chip	Buffalo, NY	—	Rescheduled
Apr 19	George Coogan	Evansville, IN	—	Signed articles
Apr 20	Paddy Lavin	Buffalo, NY	—	Matched
Apr 22	Jimmy Gardner	Pittsburgh, PA	D6	Duquesne Garden; Advantage Dillon
Apr 24	Hugo Kelly	Indianapolis, IN	—	Matched
Apr 26	Frank Mantell	Dayton, OH	—	Matched; Dayton Gymnastic Club
Apr 28	George Chip	Terre Haute, IN	ND10	3rd meeting; Fair Grounds Casino
Apr 29	Tony Caponi	Winnipeg, Man, Can	—	Rescheduled then canceled
May 3	Bob Moha	Indianapolis, IN**	ND10	Auditorium; 1st meeting
May 19	Paddy Lavin	Terre Haute, IN	—	Scheduled
May 20	Jack Herrick	Pittsburgh, PA	ND6	Pittsburgh AA Clubhouse; 3rd battle
May 30	Jimmy Clabby	Indianapolis, IN	—	Scheduled; Called off at ballpark
Jun 5	Ralph Young Erne	Muncie, IN**	ND10	Muncie AC; Petty Aud; Advantage Dillon
Jun 12	Tony Caponi	Indianapolis, IN	—	Matched
Jun 21	Paddy Lavin	Indianapolis, IN	ND10	Auditorium
Jul 3	Jimmy Howard	Memphis, TN	—	Matched; Canceled
Jul 3	Bob Moha	Buffalo, NY	ND/D10	International AC; 2nd meeting
Aug 23	Glenn Coakley	Vincennes, IN	ND10	Lakewood Park
Sep 4	Eddie McGoorty	New Orleans, LA	L4	3rd bout; Referee stopped fight
Oct 4	Jack Graham	Vincennes, IN**	TK4	Police stopped bout in 4th round
Oct 20	Jack Herrick	South Bend, IN	ND10	4th battle; Magyar Hall; 158 lbs.
Oct 23	Barney Williams	Philadelphia, PA	ND6	a.k.a. Battling Levinsky; IBHOF; 1st meeting
Oct 24	Leo Houck	Boston, MA	—	Armory; Barney Williams subs—IBHOF
Oct 28	Young Ralph Erne	Pittsburgh, PA	ND6	
Oct 31	George "K.O." Brown	Cleveland, OH	—	Rescheduled
Nov 1	Eddie McGoorty	Indianapolis, IN	ND10	4th meeting
Nov 11	George "K.O." Brown	Pittsburgh, PA	ND6	2nd meeting
Nov 22	George Chip	Youngstown, OH	ND12	4th meeting; Sub for Buck Crouse

Date	Opponent	Location	Result	Comments
Dec 6	Frank Klaus	Pittsburgh, PA	ND6	Likely Draw; IBHOF; 1st meeting
Dec 21	Howard Morrow	New York, NY	—	Scheduled

1912

Date	Opponent	Location	Result	Comments
Jan 1	**Leo Houck**	**Indianapolis, IN**	TK6	158 lbs.; IBHOF; 1st meeting

Claimed middleweight championship of the world
Claimed from this point, until his loss to Frank Klaus (March 23)

Date	Opponent	Location	Result	Comments
Jan 10	Bob Moha	Pittsburgh, PA	—	Moha declared overweight
Jan 17	Tommy Dillon	Frankfort, IN**	EX4	Armory; rare brothers' exhibition
Jan 20	Terry Martin	Pittsburgh, PA	—	Injured hand
Jan 20	Jimmy Howard	Pittsburgh, PA	—	Replaced by Griffiths
Jan 20	Billy Griffith	Pittsburgh, PA**	ND6	Old City Hall
Jan 26	Howard Wiggam	Indianapolis, IN**	KO2	Miners' Convention; Tomlinson Hall
Feb 1	Billy Berger	Youngstown, OH	ND12	Auditorium
Feb 3	Jimmy Gardner	Philadelphia, PA	ND6	National AC
Feb 6	Walter Coffey	New York, NY	—	Matched; Postponed
Feb 8	Paddy Lavin	Buffalo, NY	ND10	Convention Hall
Feb 10	George Chip	Pittsburgh, PA	ND6	5th meeting; Old City Hall
Feb 15	Jack "Twin" Sullivan	Cleveland, OH	—	Canceled; Dillon injured hand
Feb 22	Grant "Kid" Clark(e)	Columbus, OH	ND10	Location often listed incorrectly
Mar 6	Walter Coffey	Oakland, CA	—	Original date
Mar 7	Walter Coffey	Oakland, CA	W10	Wheelmen's Club/Piedmont Pavilion
Mar 13	Walter Coffey	Oakland, CA	—	Optional date
Mar 23	**Frank Klaus**	**San Francisco, CA**	L20	IBHOF; 2nd meeting; Mission Street Arena

Middleweight championship of the world

Apr 23	Billy Schuster	Frankfort, IN	KO2	*Verified through two sources*
May 3	Frank Klaus	New York, NY	ND10	IBHOF; 3rd meeting; MSG; Adv.: Klaus

Bat Masterson saw the bout as a draw.

May 28	Hugo Kelly	Indianapolis, IN	KO3	Empire Theatre
Jun 12	Jack "Twin" Sullivan	Buffalo, NY	ND10	Convention Hall; 20 lb. dis.
Jun 17	George "K.O." Brown	Winnipeg, Man, Can	ND12	3rd meeting
Jul 4	Joe Thomas	Terre Haute, IN**	KO8	White City Park
Jul 22	Joe "Kid" Gorman	Memphis, TN	KO6	
Jul 25	George Chip	Indianapolis, IN	ND10	6th meeting
Aug 12	Billy Donovan	Richmond, IN	KO4	Richmond Coliseum; Murbarger promotion

Date	Opponent	Location	Result	Comments
Aug 15	Nig Shank	Indianapolis, IN	EX3	Riverside Athletic Club; sub for Sammy Trot
Suffered undisclosed illness				
Aug 19	Kid Clark	Columbus, OH	—	Matched; Canceled
Sep 5	Willie Lewis	New York, NY	—	Signed; St. Nicholas Club; Called off
Sep 5	Johnny Thompson	Memphis, TN	—	Signed; Canceled
Sep 10	George "K.O." Brown	Chicago, IL	—	Matched; 158 lbs.; Canceled; 4th meeting
Signed with manager Sam Murbarger				
Oct 2	Tom McCune	Hamilton, Ont, Can**	KO2	Butler County AC
Oct 4	Patsy McMahon	Wabash, IN	EX6	—
Oct 11	Harry Ramsey	Philadelphia, PA	ND6	Nonpareil AC
Oct 17	Emmett "Kid" Wagner	Johnstown, PA	ND10	Auditorium
Oct 19	George Chip	Pittsburgh, PA	ND6	7th meeting; Old City Hall
Oct 23	Gus Christie	Dayton, OH	W15	1st meeting
Oct 25	Battling Conners	Indianapolis, IN	KO7	Empire Theatre
Nov 4	Jack Flynn	Wabash, IN**	KO4	
Nov 8	Jimmy Howard	Memphis, TN	W8	Southern AC
Nov 11	George "K.O." Brown	Memphis, TN	—	Matched; 8 rds.
Nov 11	George Chip	Columbus, OH	D10	8th meeting
Nov 22	Grant "Kid" Clark	Columbus, OH	TK2	Empire Theatre
Dec 9	Howard Morrow	Syracuse, NY	—	Refused
Dec 11	Gus Christie	Indianapolis, IN	ND10	2nd meeting; Dillon by a shade
Dec 13	Frank Mantell	Cincinnati, OH	—	Scheduled
Dec 16	Leo Houck	Providence, RI	—	Scheduled
Dec 19	Harry Ramsey	Cincinnati, OH	ND/D10	2nd meeting this year; Draw

Notes: Dillon's battle against Billy Schuster was confirmed (see "K.O.'s At Frankfurt," *Indianapolis News*, April 24, 1912); Some sources note that Jack Dillon claimed the light heavyweight title following his bout against Hugo Kelly. The title was vacated by Philadelphia Jack O'Brien; Dillon's knockout victory over Tom McCune, a confirmed bout, has not appeared in other resources; Dillon would recall his March 23 battle against Frank Klaus in San Francisco as his toughest battle.

1913

Date	Opponent	Location	Result	Comments
Jan 1	Gus Christie	Indianapolis, IN	ND10	3rd meeting; Auditorium
Jan 9	Frank Mantell	Thornton, RI	TK15	Stopped fight 35 seconds from end
Jan 18	Al Rogers	Pittsburgh, PA	ND6	Old City Hall
Jan 22	Leo Houck	Philadelphia, PA	ND6	IBHOF; 2nd meeting; Olympia Club
Jan 24	Frank Logan	Philadelphia, PA	ND6	Nonpareil AC
Feb 10	Bill MacKinnon	Thornton, RI	D15	Rhode Island AC; Favored Dillon
Feb 12	George Brown	Indianapolis, IN	—	Canceled

Appendix A: Boxing Record

Date	Opponent	Location	Result	Comments
Feb 19	Jimmy Clabby	Indianapolis, IN	—	Scheduled; Offered international bouts
Feb 19	Jack Denning	Indianapolis, IN	KO2	Auditorium
Feb 27	Tommy Connors	Indianapolis, IN	—	Matched
Mar 4	*Tommy Dillon*	*Frankfort, IN***	*EX4*	*Exhibition*
Mar 10	Al Rogers	Altoona, PA	ND6	Lincoln AC
Mar 12	Willie "K.O." Brennan	Indianapolis, IN	ND10	Auditorium
Mar 17	Bob Moha	Milwaukee, WI	—	Canceled; could not make 160 lbs.
Mar 23	*Dave Smith*	*Indianapolis, IN*	*EX*	*Dillon Club, on South Illinois Street*
Mar 27	Albert "Buck" Crouse	Pittsburgh, PA	—	Canceled due to flooding
Apr 10	Albert "Buck" Crouse	Pittsburgh, PA	ND 6	
Apr 14	George Chip	Youngstown, OH	ND12	9th meeting
Apr 17	Barney Williams	Rochester, NY	ND10	a.k.a., Battling Levinsky; IBHOF; 2nd meeting
Apr 28	Bob Moha	Milwaukee, WI	ND10	3rd meeting
May 29	Frank Klaus	Indianapolis, IN	ND10	IBHOF; 4th meeting; Washington Park

Claimed middleweight championship of the world

Date	Opponent	Location	Result	Comments
Jun 16	Tony Caponi	Winnipeg, Man, Can	—	Canceled due to Dillon's sore arm
Jul 3	Jimmy Clabby	Indianapolis, IN	—	See below
Jul 3	Bill MacKinnon	Indianapolis, IN	KO10	Also spelled McKinnon; Sub for above

Brief split with Sam Murbarger

Date	Opponent	Location	Result	Comments
Aug 8	Tony Caponi	Winnipeg, Man, Can	—	Signed; Caponi refused to take bout
Aug 8	George "Kid" Ashe	Winnipeg, Man, Can	ND12	
Aug 11	Jack Williams	Peru, IN	KO3	

Suffered chest injuries in car accident, followed by a broken rib

Date	Opponent	Location	Result	Comments
Aug 26	Frank Klaus	Boston, MA	—	Scheduled; 12 rounds; Called off
Sep 1	Leo Benz	Butte, MT	—	Matched
Sep 17	Tony Caponi	Winnipeg, Man, Can**	KO8	
Oct 9	Leo Houck	Lancaster, PA	ND6	IBHOF; 3rd meeting; Advantage Houck
Oct 14	Walter Monaghan	Akron, OH	TK4	
Oct 15	Dick Gilbert	Cincinnati, OH	—	Queen City AC
Nov 3	Eddie McGoorty	Milwaukee, WI	—	Scheduled; 10 rounds; Called off
Nov 3	Gus Christie	Milwaukee, WI	ND10	4th meeting
Nov 27	"Sailor" Ed Petrosky	Butte, MT	W12	Holland Arena
Dec 5	Vic Hansen	Denver, CO	—	Postponed
Dec 17	Jack Jeffries	Elwood, IN	—	Matched; Sheriff intervention

Notes: Rhode Island Sheriff McCuster stopped the Dillon-versus-Mantell bout to prevent a decision; Dillon's clear-cut victory over Frank Klaus, left little, if any, question regarding his claim to the middleweight title. Unfortunately, he was not given the recognition he deserved. It is quite possible that the injuries he suffered during the automobile accident were far more serious than reported and recurring.

1914

Date	Opponent	Location	Result	Comments
Jan 1	Gus Christie	Indianapolis, IN	ND 10	5th meeting; Claimed as his 131st bout
Jan 20	Vic Hansen	Denver, CO	W12	Also spelled Hanson
Jan 30	*Harry Baker*	*Indianapolis IN*	*EX1*	*United Miners' Exhibition; Tomlinson Hall*
Feb 4	Freddie Hicks	Windsor, Ont, Can	ND8	Windsor AC
Feb 9	Tommy Danforth	Memphis, TN	TK2	Phoenix AC
Feb 17	Marshall Claiborne	Hot Springs, AR	TK3	Whittington Park Theater
Mar 3	"Fireman" Jim Flynn	Kansas City, MO	D10	1st meeting; Grand Ave. AC
Mar 10	Jack Lester	Denver, CO	KO10	Colorado AC; Dillon 25-lb. disadvantage
Mar 17	"Fighting" Dick Gilbert	Hot Springs, AR**	W10	Hot Springs AC
Mar 23	George "K.O." Brown	Memphis, TN	W8	Phoenix AC; 5th meeting
Apr 14	**Battling Levinsky**	**Butte, MT**	W12	IBHOF; 3rd meeting; Holland Arena
Claimed light heavyweight championship of America				
Apr 28	Al Kaufman	Kansas City, MO	—	Grand Avenue AC
Apr 28	Al Norton	Kansas City, MO	W10	

Later, Nat Fleischer's All-Time Ring Record Book, *a.k.a.* The Ring Record Book, *noted that Dillon "won international recognition as light heavyweight title."*

Date	Opponent	Location	Result	Comments
May 29	George Chip	Indianapolis, IN	—	Original opponent
May 29	Gus Christie	Indianapolis, IN	—	Forfeits posted; 158 lbs.
May 29	Battling Levinsky	Indianapolis, IN	ND10	IBHOF; 4th meeting; Likely a draw
Jun 13	Bob Moha	Butte, MT	—	Postponed by police
Jun 15	**Bob Moha**	**Butte, MT**	W12	**4th meeting; Moha failed to engage**
Claimed/defended light heavyweight championship of America				
Jun 23	Charlie Weinert	New York, NY	—	Matched
Jun 25	Jim Murphy	Salt Lake City, UT	—	Matched
Suspended for six months by Montana Boxing Commission				
Jun 29	Jack Herrick	Memphis, TN	—	Matched
Jul 3	"Sailor" Ed Petrosky	Kansas City, MO	W10	Association Park
Jul 4	Al Norton	Kansas City, MO	—	Matched
Jul 19	George "K.O." Brown	Terre Haute, IN	—	Date moved
Jul 21	George "K.O." Brown	Terre Haute, IN	ND10	Baseball Park; Police inter.; 6th meeting
Jul 24	Howard Morrow	Muncie, IN	—	Wysor Grand Opera House; Broke hand

Date	Opponent	Location	Result	Comments
Jul 24	Joe Mace	Muncie, IN	TK 3	Wysor Grand Opera House
Aug 12	Howard Morrow	Kalamazoo, MI	ND6	Fuller Theatre; Controversial

Sam Murbarger returns as Jack Dillon's manager.

Date	Opponent	Location	Result	Comments
Sep 7	"Sailor" Gus Einert	Terre Haute, IN**	ND10	Labor Day Boxing Show
Sep 15	George "K.O." Brown	Vincennes, IN	ND10	7th meeting; Knox Co. Fairgrounds; Draw
Sep 25	Battling Levinsky	St. Louis, MO	—	Signed; Postponed until October 14
Sep 28	Frank Mantell	Columbus, OH	ND12	Goodale Arena; Advantage: Dillon
Oct 1	Leo Houck	Lancaster, PA	—	Signed
Oct 5	Carl Morris	Kansas City, MO	—	Replaced by Flynn (see below)
Oct 5	"Fireman" Jim Flynn	Kansas City, MO	W10	2nd meeting; Sub for Carl Morris
Oct 14	Battling Levinsky	St. Louis, MO	—	Replaced by Brown (see below)
Oct 14	George "K.O." Brown	St. Louis, MO	NC3	8th meeting; Arrested for faking fight
Oct 21	Young Ahearn	New York, NY	—	MSG; Called off
Nov 9	Charley Weinert	Philadelphia, PA	KO2	
Nov	Young Ahearn	New York, NY	—	MSG; Called off
Nov 24	"Fighting" Dick Gilbert	Denver, CO	W15	Colorado AC
Dec 8	Bob Moha	Denver, CO	—	Matched
Dec 14	Mike Gibbons	Philadelphia, PA	—	Matched; Denied match
Dec 14	Young Ahearn	Philadelphia, PA	—	Matched

Notes: Al Kaufman, also spelled Kaufmann, substituted for Al Norton (confirmed on April 18, 1914); Dillon was owed $750 for his battle against Brown, on October 14. The amount was held in a trust for years; Dillon's fight with Brown on October 14 was a disaster, as fans tossed chairs at the arc lights.

1915

Date	Opponent	Location	Result	Comments
Jan 1	Jake "Young" Ahearn	Philadelphia, PA	ND6	Olympia AC; Mixed reviews; Draw
Jan 16	Dan "Porky" Flynn	Brooklyn, NY	ND10	Broadway SC
Jan 23	*Young Halstead*	*Christopher, IL*	*KO3*	*Exhibition; Verified*
Jan 23	*Frank Hoe*	*Christopher, IL*	—	*Exhibition*
Jan 25	Larry English	Memphis, TN	TK4	Scheduled for 8 rds; Lt. Heavyweight
Feb 16	Tom McCarthy	Brooklyn, NY	—	Postponed
Feb 18	Frank Mantell	New York, NY	—	Federal AC; Called off due to attendance
Feb 20	Frank Mantell	New York, NY	ND10	Federal AC; Advantage: Dillon
Feb 23	Tom McCarty	Brooklyn, NY	—	Called off
Feb 23	Johnny Howard	Brooklyn, NY	ND10	Broadway SC; Advantage Dillon
Mar 2	Tom McCarty	Brooklyn, NY	ND10	Broadway SC; likely a draw

Appendix A: Boxing Record

Date	Opponent	Location	Result	Comments
Mar 16	Ed "Gunboat" Smith	Milwaukee, WI	ND10	Auditorium; Advantage Dillon; 1st meeting
Mar 23	*Tommy Dillon*	*Portland, IN** *	*EX6*	*Exhibition*
Apr 6	"Fighting" Billy Murray	Hudson, WI	ND10	Arena
Apr 22	Al Reich	New York, NY	—	Federal Athletic Club
Apr 29	Marty Cutler	Lexington, KY	TK6	Ben Ali Theatre
May 5	Andre Anderson	Lexington, KY	KO5	Lexington AA Arena; outweighed
May 20	Jack Lester	Joplin, MO	W15	Southwest AC
May 28	George Chip	Indianapolis, IN	—	Matched: American Association Ballpark
May 31	Ed "Gunboat" Smith	Brooklyn, NY	—	Ebbets Field
Jun 7	Tom "Bearcat" McMahon	Rochester, NY	ND10	Slow; Advantage varied by source
Jun 11	Frank Mantell	Cincinnati, OH	ND10	Redland Field; Advantage Dillon
Jun 25	Johnny Howard	New York, NY	—	Moved to July 12
Jun 28	Gunner Moir	Evansville, IN	—	Postponed; On barges; 25 rds.
Jul 5	George Chip	Kansas City, MO	D10	10th meeting; Draw; 158 lbs.
Jul 7	Gunner Moir	Evansville, IN	—	All Evansville bouts canceled by mayor
Jul 12	Johnny Howard	Rockaway, NY	ND10	First genuine knockdown of Dillon
Jul 16	Zulu Kid	Rockaway, NY	ND10	Not Young Zulu Kid
Jul 28	*Heck Mannini*	*Muncie, IN** *	*EX4*	*Moose Carnival; T. Dillon show Mgr.*
Aug 17	Tom McCarty	Lewistown, MT	D10	Judith Theatre; Advantage Dillon
Aug 30	Charles "Sailor" Grande	Philadelphia, PA	ND6	Olympia AC
Sep 6	Yankee Gilbert	Lima, OH**	—	Police intervention; American AC
Sep 25	Tom "Bearcat" McMahon	Pittsburgh, PA	ND6	Federal League ballpark (Expo Field); Draw
Oct 1	Jim Savage	Brooklyn, NY	—	Ebbets Field; Postponed due to rain
Oct 5	Jim Savage	Brooklyn, NY	ND10	Broadway SC; Advantage Dillon
Oct 19	Leo Houck	New Haven, CT	—	Postponed; Houck ankle injury
Nov 1	Charley Weinert	New York, NY	ND10	Madison Square Garden; Advantage Dillon

Newly formed American Boxing Association recognized Jack Dillon as the light heavyweight champion on November 15, 1915.

Nov 18	Frank Farmer	Oshkosh, WI	KO4	Broke Farmer's rib
Nov 22	Battling Levinsky	Philadelphia, PA	—	Matched

Date	Opponent	Location	Result	Comments
Nov 30	"Fireman" Jim Flynn	Brooklyn, NY	ND10	3rd meeting; Advantage: Dillon
Dec 7	Dan "Porky" Flynn	Brooklyn, NY	ND10	Advantage: Dillon
Dec 17	Yankee Gilbert	Dayton, OH	TK4	
Dec 20	Al Norton	Memphis, TN	TK4	
Dec 29	George Lewis	Toledo, OH	EX	

Notes: Anderson significantly outweighed Dillon during their May 5 battle. Sources vary from 30 to 70 pounds; The June 7 battle, in Rochester, was the main event of Jake Carey new Airdrome AC.

1916

Date	Opponent	Location	Result	Comments
Jan 10	Dan "Porky" Flynn	Memphis, TN	W8	Memphis Arena
Jan 25	Battling Levinsky	Brooklyn, NY	—	Broadway SC; Moved
Jan 25	Tom Cowler	Brooklyn, NY	—	Broadway SC; Postponed, Dillon ill
Jan 28	Billy Miske	Superior, WI	ND10	1st meeting; IBHOF; Draw
Jan 28	Fred Fulton	New Orleans, LA	—	Matched; Canceled
Feb 1	Tom Cowler	Brooklyn, NY	KO2	Broadway SC
Feb 8	Tom Cowler	Brooklyn, NY	—	Broadway SC
Feb 8	Battling Levinsky	Brooklyn, NY	ND10	IBHOF; 5th meeting; Advantage Dillon
Feb 14	Vic Hansen	Memphis, TN	W8	Phoenix AC; Hansen floored six times
Feb 27	Al McCoy	New York, NY	—	Unconfirmed
Mar 10	"Fireman" Jim Flynn	New York, NY	ND10	4th meeting; Broadway AC; Adv. Dillon
Mar 14	Ed "Gunboat" Smith	Brooklyn, NY	ND10	Sub for Charlie Weinert; Adv. Dillon; 2nd
Mar 17	Jess Willard	New York, NY	—	Sparred with Willard; large gloves
Mar 18	Whitey Allen	Brooklyn, NY	KO4	Clermont AC
Mar 28	Battling Levinsky	Brooklyn, NY	ND10	IBHOF; 6th meeting; Broadway SC
Apr 10	Jess Willard	New York, NY	—	Matched; From this date until April 22
Apr 14	Billy Miske	St. Paul, MN	ND10	2nd meeting; IBHOF; Advantage: Dillon
Apr 25	**Battling Levinsky**	**Kansas City, MO**	**W15**	**IBHOF; 7th meeting**

Dillon defended the light heavyweight championship of the world.

May 18	Dan "Porky" Flynn	Chattanooga, TN	—	Rose AC
May 23	Bob Devere	Buffalo, NY	ND 10	Broadway Auditorium
May 29	Ed "Gunboat" Smith	Indianapolis, IN	—	Federal Park: Speedway Week; Stopped
Jun 29	Frank Moran	Brooklyn, NY	ND10	Washington Park; Advantage Dillon

There was no question after this bout—the pinnacle of his career—that Jack Dillon, light heavyweight champion, was clearly the top contender for Jess Willard's heavyweight crown.

Considered Jack Dillon's magnum opus

Date	Opponent	Location	Result	Comments
Jul 4	"Fireman" Jim Flynn	Dewey, OK	KO4	5th meeting
Jul 13	Battling Levinsky	Baltimore, MD	ND10	IBHOF; 8th meeting; Adv. Levinsky
Aug 8	*Gus Christie*	*Indianapolis, IN*	*EX4*	*Tomlinson Hall; Failed to appear*
Sep 12	Battling Levinsky	Memphis, TN	D8	IBHOF; 9th meeting; Draw
Sep 21	Jim Coffey	Brooklyn, NY	—	Matched
Oct 10	Charles "Sailor" Grande	Brooklyn, NY	KO2	Broadway SC
Oct 17	Tim O'Neil	Brooklyn, NY	ND10	Broadway SC; Adv. Dillon
Oct 23	Larry Williams	Philadelphia, PA	ND6	Olympia AC; Advantage Dillon
Oct 24	**Battling Levinsky**	**Boston, MA**	**L12**	**IBHOF; 10th meeting**

Levinsky claimed the light heavyweight championship of the world.

Date	Opponent	Location	Result	Comments
Nov 10	Mike Gibbons	St. Paul, MN	ND10	IBHOF; Auditorium; Adv. Gibbons; 162 lbs.
Nov 21	Al McCoy	Brooklyn, NY	—	Matched; Postponed
Nov 27	Mike Gibbons	St. Paul, MN	—	IBHOF; Auditorium
Nov 28	Battling Levinsky	Boston, MA	—	Matched; Moved
Dec 5	Battling Levinsky	Boston, MA	—	Matched; Postponed
Dec 12	Battling Levinsky	Boston, MA	—	Matched; Postponed
Dec 19	Billy Miske	Brooklyn, NY	ND10	3rd meeting; IBHOF; Broadway SC

Notes: Levinsky's claim to the light heavyweight championship of the world on October 24, 1916, did not resemble a title transfer yet has been recognized as such by various sources. That said, Jack Dillon's performance was not indicative of a champion.

1917

Date	Opponent	Location	Result	Comments
Jan 1	Bob Moha	Dayton, OH	ND15	5th meeting; Advantage: Dillon
Jan 9	Battling Levinsky	Boston, MA	—	Scheduled
Jan 9	Billy Miske	Brooklyn, NY	—	Moved
Jan 16	Billy Miske	Brooklyn, NY	ND10	4th meeting; IBHOF; Advantage: Miske
Feb 7	Ed "Gunboat" Smith	New Orleans, LA	—	Moved
Feb 9	Battling Levinsky	New Orleans, LA	—	Signed; 20 rounds
Feb 16	Les Darcy	New York, NY	—	Signed
Feb 16	Ed "Gunboat" Smith	New Orleans, LA	W20	3rd meeting; Louisiana Aud.; Adv. Dillon
Feb 27	Al McCoy	Brooklyn, NY	ND10	Broadway SC; Advantage: Dillon; 1st meeting
Mar 5	Les Darcy	New York, NY	—	MSG; NYS governor intervention
Mar 19	Jack Moran	Memphis, TN	TK6	Phoenix AC

Date	Opponent	Location	Result	Comments
Mar 30	Jack Berry	Hot Springs, AR	KO3	Real name Howard Wiggam
Apr 2	Jack McCarron	Toledo, OH	—	Moved
Apr 9	Jack McCarron	Toledo, OH	—	Managed by Ray Bronson; Canceled
Stricken with appendicitis				
Apr 16	Bob Devere	Kansas City, MO	—	Canceled
May 14	Tom "Bearcat" McMahon	Dayton, OH	D15	Highland Ballpark; Advantage Dillon
May 21	Jack McCarron	Toledo, OH	ND10	Coliseum
May 29	George Chip	Cincinnati, OH	ND10	11th meeting; Redland field; Likely a draw
Jun 25	Len Rowlands	Memphis, TN	W8	Phoenix AC; Advantage Dillon
Jul 1	Charlie Weinert	New York, NY	—	Matched; Manhattan AC
Jul 4	Fred Fulton	Toledo, OH	—	American Association Ballpark; Stalled
Jul 4	"Sergeant" Ray Smith	Terre Haute, IN	KO1	Mismatch
Jul 10	Bob McAllister	Brooklyn, NY	—	Scheduled
Jul 10	Jack Clifford	Brooklyn, NY	ND10	Broadway SC
Jul 17	Battling Levinsky	Boston, MA	—	
Jul 30	Harry Greb	Pittsburgh, PA	ND10	1st meeting; IBHOF; Advantage: Greb
Sep 3	Mike Gibbons	Terre Haute, IN	ND10	IBHOF; Fairgrounds; Adv.: Gibbons
Voluntary time off				
Oct 3	*Alex Karnegay*	*Fort Riley, KS*	*EX*	*Scheduled; Exhibition*
Oct 5	Hugh Walker	Fort Riley, KS	ND10	Cavalry Gymnasium; Advantage: Dillon
Oct 8	Charles Weinert	Philadelphia, PA	—	Olympia AC; Signed
Oct 12	Al McCoy	Providence, RI	—	Matched
Oct 15	Willie Meehan	Philadelphia, PA	ND6	Olympia AC: Advantage: Meehan
Oct 16	Jeff Smith	Brooklyn, NY	—	Broadway SC
Oct 17	Zulu Kid	Montreal, Que, Can	ND10	Sohmer Park: Advantage: Kid
Nov 3	Joe Stanley	Indianapolis, IN	KO2	Benefit bout
Nov 9	George Chip	Duluth, MN	—	Signed articles
Nov 13	Billy Miske	Brooklyn, NY	ND10	5th meeting; IBHOF; Advantage: Miske
Nov 29	Hugh Walker	Little Rock, AR	D10	Army AA; 10 rds. At 158; Draw; 2nd meeting
Dec 17	Harry Greb	Cincinnati, OH	—	Called off

Note: Knockout Brennan, of Buffalo, substituted for Dillon against Jack McCarron in Toledo.

1918

Date	Opponent	Location	Result	Comments
Jan 25	George Chip	Duluth, MN	ND10	12th meeting; Civic Auditorium

Appendix A: Boxing Record

Date	Opponent	Location	Result	Comments
Jan 31	Homer Smith	Fort Wayne, IN	—	Michigan heavyweight
Feb 10	"Big" Bob Martin	Hattiesburg, MS	—	Camp Shelby; Called off
Feb 15	Phil Harrison	Racine, WI	—	Matched; Postponed
Feb 22	Hugh Walker	Joplin, MO	D12	3rd meeting; Southwest AC; Adv.: Dillon
Mar 4	Harry Greb	Toledo, OH	ND12	2nd meeting; IBHOF; Advantage: Greb
Mar 15	Homer Smith	Fort Wayne, IN	—	Matched; Moved
Mar 18	"Steamboat" Bill Scott	Muncie, IN	—	Campbell Auditorium; Moved
Mar 19	Homer Smith	Fort Wayne, IN	—	Matched; Scott sub; Dillon withdrew
Mar 22	"Steamboat" Bill Scott	Muncie, IN	D10	Draw
Mar 25	Phil Harrison	Racine, WI	—	Matched
Apr 15	Hugh Walker	Memphis, TN	W8	4th meeting; Phoenix AC
May 7	Frank Farmer	Tacoma, WA	L6	Eagles Hall smoker; Advantage: Farmer
May 29	Joe Gorman	Connersville, IN	—	Boxing benefit program
May 29	Joe Walters	Connersville, IN	KO3	Connersville Auditorium
Jun 11	Private Hoe	Indianapolis, IN	EX3	Fort Benjamin Harrison; Open air arena
Jun 17	Hugh Walker	Tulsa, OK	ND12	5th meeting; Grand Opera House; Adv.: Dillon
Jul 4	Al McCoy	Charleston, WV	ND10	Seen as a draw, or slight shade by Dillon
Aug 2	Patsy McMahon	Indianapolis, IN	EX3	Speedway Boxing Carnival
Aug 8	Jack Daly (Dailey)	Valparaiso, IN	D6	Army Drill Grounds; two-minute rounds
Aug 21	Al McCoy	Muncie, IN	ND10	Campbell's Auditorium; Adv.: Dillon
Sep 13	Hugh Ross	Louisville, KY	EX4	Camp Taylor
Sep 18	Patsy McMahon	Indianapolis, IN	EX4	Arsenal Technical Institute
Sep 25	Billy Ryan	Charleston, WV	ND10	Armory Arena; Advantage: Dillon/Draw
Oct 4	Jack Duffy	Cedar Rapids, IA	ND10	Auditorium; Advantage: Dillon
Oct 10	Packey McFarland	Indianapolis, IN	—	Six rounds; Tomlinson Hall; Called off
Oct 17	Bob York (Yorke)	Cedar Rapids, IA	—	Canceled due to influenza; Rescheduled
Nov 13	Howard Wiggam	Richmond, IN	EX6	United War Fund Campaign; 175 lbs.
Nov 14	Howard Wiggam	Anderson, IN	EX4	United War Fund Cam.; Wiggam injured
Nov 16	Harry Krohn	Chillicothe, OH	W6	Advantage: Dillon
Nov 21	Bob York (Yorke)	Rock Island, IL	ND10	Empire Skating Rink
Nov 23	Gus Christie	Indianapolis, IN	ND4	6th meeting; Fistic Carnival; Adv.: Dillon

Appendix A: Boxing Record

Date	Opponent	Location	Result	Comments
Nov 29	*Gus Christie*	*Indianapolis, IN*	*EX3*	
Dec 13	Ted Block	Detroit, MI	ND10	Loyal Moose

Notes: Dillon's August 8 battle against Jack Daly (Dailey) was likely an exhibition; Dillon's August 21 battle against McCoy has been viewed by some as an exhibition due to the two-minute rounds; Dillon's November 23 match with Gus Christie could be viewed as an exhibition as well. It was part of a fistic carnival where little real fighting actually took place.

1919

Date	Opponent	Location	Result	Comments
Mar 3	*Patsy McMahon*	*Battle Creek, MI*	*EX4*	*2-minute rds.; Camp Custer Boxing Show*
Mar 4	*Patsy McMahon*	*Battle Creek, MI*	*EX4*	*base hospital*
May 20	Phil Harrison	Memphis, TN	—	moved
May 21	Phil Harrison	Memphis, TN	—	moved
May 22	Phil Harrison	Memphis, TN	—	moved
May 24	Phil Harrison	Memphis, TN	LK2	Lyric Theatre; 1st undisputed KO

Suffered a "collapse," in the words of the media

Note: Clearly, Jack Dillon was suffering from some cognitive issues in addition to his physical ailments.

1920

Convalescence in Florida

Date	Opponent	Location	Result	Comments
Jan	*Patsy McMahon*	*Nashville, TN*	—	*Exhibitions*
Feb 9	Battling Halstead	Miami, FL	ND8	Miami Sporting Club; Draw
Feb 20	Battling Halstead	West Palm Beach, FL	ND8	Armory; Advantage: Halstead
Mar 11	Young Fitzsimmons	Hot Springs, AR	ND10	Auditorium; Adv. Fitzsimmons
Mar 18	Paul Roman	Dallas, TX	ND10	Soldiers & Sailors AC; Adv.: Roman
Mar 25	Freddie Edwards	Springfield, MO	—	Convention Hall
Apr 30	Texas Tate	Little Rock, AR	—	Scheduled
May 3	Young Fitzsimmons	Wichita Falls, TX	ND10	Camel AC; Advantage: Fitzsimmons
May 16	*Jack Riley*	*Kokomo, IN*	*EX*	*Exhibition; Riley just returned to U.S.*
Jun 3	Bob "K.O." Sweeney	Kokomo, IN	TK4	Sipe Theatre; technical knockout
Jun 7	Leo Houck	Lancaster, PA	—	Scheduled
Jun 7	Joe Borrell	Philadelphia, PA	—	Proposed
Jul 2	Bryant Porter	Evansville, IN	—	Not in condition to fight
Jul 5	Howard "Kid" Wiggam	Rochester, IN	—	Not in condition to fight
Jul 5	Paul Roman	McAlester, OK	—	Not in condition to fight
Jul 12	Young Fitzsimmons	Fayetteville, AR	—	Not in condition to fight
Jul 14	Jack Riley	Gary, IN	KO8	Questionable legitimacy; A Farb favor

Date	Opponent	Location	Result	Comments
Jul 23	Pat Weiss	El Reno, OK	ND10	Derry Airdome; Advantage: Dillon
Jul 26	Young Fitzsimmons	Scammon, KS	ND10	a.k.a. Charley Nashert; Adv.: Fitzsimmons
Voluntary time off				
Sep 4	Bud Clancy	Cedar Rapids, IA	ND10	Cedar Rapids; Advantage: Clancy
Oct 1	Battling Halstead	Springfield, MO	—	Changed date
Oct 4	Battling Halstead	Springfield, MO	ND10	Advantage: Halstead; Confirmed
Oct 9	*Battling Logan*	*Clarksville, AR*	—	*Unconfirmed*
Oct 9	*Jack Hall*	*Clarksville, AR*	*ND10*	*Unconfirmed*
Oct 13	*TBD*	*Springfield, MO*	—	*Scheduled*
Nov 2	*Battling Halstead*	*Fort Smith, AR*	*ND10*	*Unconfirmed*
Nov 11	Tommy Ridge	Indianapolis, IN	—	Scheduled
Nov 24	Jack Riley	Rockford, IL	—	Scheduled; K.O. Brown sub for Dillon
Nov 25	Jack Moran	Shreveport, LA	TK2	Moran suffered arm injury
Dec 22	*Harry Foley*	*Hot Springs, AR*	*EX 4*	*Exhibition; Verified*
Dec 24	Joe White	Atlanta, GA	—	Matched
Dec 28	Young Fitzsimmons	San Antonio, TX	ND12	a.k.a. Charley Nashert; Adv.: Fitzsimmons

Notes: Dillon's knockout of K.O. Sweeney has been stated in different rounds; Dillon's knockout bout with Jack Riley has been noted by some sources as in June; Dillon's battle with Jack Hall has been noted by some sources, but as occurring on a different date; Dillon's November bout with Battling Halstead has been noted by some sources; At this time, Dillon's recollection was unclear, and some exhibitions may have been confused for real bouts.

1921

Date	Opponent	Location	Result	Comments
Jan	*Harry Foley*	*Hot Springs, AR*	*EX*	*Unsure of rounds*
Jan 25	"Frisco" Pete Brown	Louisville, KY	TK7	Legitimacy of bout and verdict questioned
Suspended for one year by Kentucky State Boxing Commission				
Feb 9	Ed Warner	Helena, AR	—	Scheduled; Opera house; 10 rds.; moved
Feb 11	Billy Edwards	Alexandria, LA	TK3	Alexandria Auditorium; Dillon outstanding
Feb 15	Jack Denham	Atlanta, GA	KO6	Auditorium; Symbolic victory
N.B.A. upheld suspension by Kentucky State Boxing Commission				
Feb 18	Ed Warner	Helena, AR	ND10	Grand Opera house; Advantage: Warner
Feb 18	----------			N.B.A. upheld one-year suspension
May 13	----------			Granted license by New York State Boxing Commission
May 19	Tommy Thompson	Brooklyn, NY	—	Brighton Club; 15 rds.; sub. Billy Bush

Barred by New York State Boxing Commission for lacking condition

Date	Opponent	Location	Result	Comments
Jul 2	Bryant Porter	Evansville, IN	—	Coliseum; out of condition
Sep 5	Jack Riley	Danville, IL	—	Event stopped by governor
Dec 31	Joe Walters	Elwood, IN	TK4	American Legion; Harting Hall

Note: The December 31, 1921, battle against Joe Walter(s) has been incorrectly listed in some resources.

1922

Date	Opponent	Location	Result	Comments
Feb 15	Patsy McMahon	Indianapolis, IN	EX3	Gayety Theatre
May 10	Mike Gibbons	Indianapolis, IN	EX2	Washington Park Baseball Field

The Jack Dillon Benefit

Date	Opponent	Location	Result	Comments
Aug 17	Jack Phillips	Blandinsville, IL	EX10	American Legion Picnic; Advertised

1923

Date	Opponent	Location	Result	Comments
Jan 12	Joe Walters	Bicknell, IN	ND10	Verified; Adv.: Dillon
Mar 21	Johnny Mack	Greensburg, IN	ND8	Verified; Adv. Mack
Jul 4	Joe Walters	Seymour, IN	ND10	Verified; Scheduled; Adv.: Walters

1924

Date	Opponent	Location	Result	Comments
Unsure	Chuck Burns	Asheville, NC	NC6	Noted by Dillon

1925

Date	Opponent	Location	Result	Comments
Unsure	Battling Halstead	West Palm Beach, FL	EX	Noted by Dillon

Note: See "Old Jack Dillon Trains Every Day," *Miami Herald,* June 8, 1926, 11.

Appendix B: Official Records of Associated Members of the International Boxing Hall of Fame

Abbreviations: ND = no decision, NC = no contest.

Note: Many of these fighters battled during the no-decision era, making an accurate assessment of the result of a bout subjective.

Inductee	Ind. Yr.	Bouts	Won	Lost	Drew	KOs	ND	NC
James J. Corbett	1990	19	11	4	3	7	–	1
Les Darcy	1993	49	45	4	0	29	–	–
Jack Dillon	**1995**	**245**	**94**	**7**	**14**	**64**	**129**	**1**
Mike Gibbons	1992	127	62	3	4	38	58	–
Tommy Gibbons	1993	106	57	4	1	47	43	1
Harry Greb	1990	299	105	8	3	48	183	–
Leo Houck	2012	212	158	9	11	21	34	–
Stanley Ketchel	1990	64	52	4	4	49	4	–
Frank Klaus	2008	90	51	4	2	27	33	–
Battling Levinsky	2000	289	77	19	15	34	178	–
Billy Miske	2010	106	48	2	2	35	54	–
Billy Papke	2001	62	37	11	6	30	8	–
Jeff Smith	2013	185	149	31	5	52	–	–
Jess Willard	2003	36	24	6	1	21	5	–

Chapter Notes

Chapter One

1. "Today's Sportorial," *Washington Times*, February 3, 1916.
2. "Today's Sportorial," *Washington Times*, February 3, 1916.
3. John D. Price died in 1871.
4. Sarah Beckhorn Price was born in 1809 and died in 1855.
5. According to the 1860 United States Census.
6. Winfield Scott Price was born in 1854 and died in 1896.
7. Initially assigned a quota of 7,500 soldiers to join the Union Army.
8. Lincoln was more a centrist than a die-hard conservative.
9. Both of Amanda's parents (J. Sigler and Levina Miller) were born in Virginia.
10. Russell C. Price had blue eyes and brown hair. He had a tall, muscular build. In 1917, Russell C. Price was residing at 1145 West Twenty-Seventh Street in Indianapolis, Indiana. In addition to being married with a child, he also took care of his mother. Paul W. Price had blue eyes and black hair. He described himself as having a short, slender frame. In 1918, he was residing at 702 North Alabama in Indianapolis, Indiana, and worked for his brother Jack Dillon.
11. This is a direct distance. Today, it is a driving distance of about 47 miles.
12. Winfield Scott Price was buried in the IOOF Cemetery in Frankfort, Indiana.
13. "Artist Cash Interviews Jack Dillon," *Indianapolis Star*, May 28, 1913.
14. For a better understanding and precise measurements see various studies including Goldin, Claudia. *The Race between Education and Technology*. Harvard University Press, 2008, 195.
15. "Artist Cash Interviews Jack Dillon," *Indianapolis Star*, May 28, 1913.
16. Sterling R. Holt, of Indianapolis, was the owner of Sidney Dillon. The horses typically quartered at the tracks where they were racing.
17. Standing about five-four, he was still growing.
18. "Amateur Pugilist Dies After Practice Bout," *Indianapolis News*, May 29, 1905.
19. "Amateur Pugilist Dies After Practice Bout," *Indianapolis News*, May 29, 1905. Chester Price also fought under the name of Austin Price, of Chicago, along with Kid Austin. Today, the Pathways to Peace Garden is located at 315 North Senate Avenue.
20. Often rendered as Ernest Colter Price, that name is incorrect, as proven with numerous legal documents such as his World War I, 13–3–13–A draft registration card #149, filed on June 5, 1917.
21. "Boxing History Eventful," *South Bend Tribune*, January 1, 1908. Without legitimate organizations, division championships were about challenges, claims, and perception.
22. "Speak Well of Your Own City," *Indianapolis Star*, January 1, 1908.
23. This estimate was calculated using data from "Historical Population Change Data (1910–2020)." Census.gov. United States Census Bureau. Archived from the original on April 29, 2021. Retrieved October 24, 2023.
24. Letter from Theodore Roosevelt to Lincoln Steffens (June 5, 1908). Theodore Roosevelt Collection. MS Am 1454 (39). Harvard College Library.
25. Davidson handled local fighters Tommy Dawson, Kid Gory (Gorey), Kid Underwood, and Kid Brown, to name a few.
26. "Boxing Bouts at Marion Club," April 20, 1908, *Indianapolis News*. Brown was aware that Dillon was going to be a force to contend with in his weight class.
27. "Gossip of the Boxers," *Indianapolis Star*, May 5, 1908.
28. "Sheriff Bain Objected," *Reporter-Times*, May 29, 1908. Handbills were circulated late in the afternoon on Thursday, May 28, 1908.
29. "Gossip of the Boxers," *Indianapolis Star*, July 8, 1908.
30. "Boxing Lid In Danger For minute, But Rests Safely," *Indianapolis Star*, August 6, 1908.
31. It wasn't that Dillon understood this, only that he was convinced by Izzy Brill.
32. "Local Boxer Said To Be Comer," *Indianapolis Star*, August 25, 1908.
33. The victory over Lem Potter could not be verified by three independent sources.

34. "Dillon Gets Decision," *Indianapolis Star*, December 20, 1908.
35. "Strong Demand For Indianapolis Boxers," *Indianapolis News*, January 2, 1909.
36. "Boxing Card Completed," *Indianapolis Star*, January 13, 1909. There was a scheduled 28 rounds of boxing on the card.
37. "Murphy To Meet Dunn," *Indianapolis Star*, January 7, 1909.
38. *Catchweight* was a common term to describe unrestricted weight in a boxing match. While it is true that punching power depends on various factors such as technique, speed, and strength, if weight is properly added it can increase overall strength.
39. "Benson And Dunn Bout Ends with Honors Even," *Indianapolis News*, January 23, 1909.
40. Often forgotten, Indianapolis was not a major fight market like New York City.
41. Popular in eighteenth-century England, the event gradually fell out of favor but continued in America. Ironically, it grew in popularity after the American Civil War—it was used, as many abolitionists and social reformers confirmed, as a social element to suppress slaves. Although states such as New York banned the practice in 1911, it continued for decades in the South and even in the Midwest. Prejudice is, and always will be, the child of ignorance.
42. "Gossip of the Boxers," *Indianapolis Star*, February 23, 1909.
43. Ray Bronson managed to make it 13 rounds before being knocked out by the first elite fighter he faced in his career. Jack Dillon would be the second.
44. "Boxers Hard at Work," *Indianapolis Star*, February 28, 1909.
45. Hartford City is located about 100 miles from Indianapolis International Airport.
46. "Fine Boxing Contests at Hartford City," *Star Press*, March 13, 1909.
47. "Honors Even in Two Auditorium Contests," *Indianapolis News*, April 1, 1909.
48. "Police See Boxing Show," *Indianapolis Star*, April 3, 1909.
49. "Police See Boxing Show," *Indianapolis Star*, April 3, 1909. Some reports saw it as a fourth-round technical knockout.
50. Scotty Brown, the aggressive fight manager out of the Windy City, was handling Nelson.
51. "Cole Loses to Bezenah," *Indianapolis News*, May 29, 1909.
52. "Boxers Were Poorly Matched," *Brazil Daily Times*, July 3, 1909. Dillon had a noticeable weight advantage. Referee Hugh McGann stopped the bout.
53. "Boxers Train For Battles," *Indianapolis Star*, July 16, 1909. Both Farb and Watts would be lifetime friends with Jack and Tommy Dillon.
54. "Jack Dillon Has An Easy Time With Anderson Boxer," *Indianapolis News*, July 23, 1909.
55. "Big Demonstration at Bronson-M'Farland Go," *Indianapolis News*, September 20, 1909.
56. "Dillon Shows High Class, Besting Cooley," *Indianapolis News*, December 23, 1909.
57. "Joins Jack Dillon's Camp," *Indianapolis Star*, December 26, 1909. Marvin Hart (September 16, 1876—September 17, 1931) was the world heavyweight boxing champion from July 3, 1905, to February 23, 1906.

Chapter Two

1. Willie Fitzgerald, from Brooklyn, New York, was an active pugilist and had great praise for Dillon.
2. "Sporting Gossip," *Cincinnati Enquirer*, January 19, 1910.
3. Few historians talk about it, but bandages, or wraps, varied during this time. Some fighters liked them; others did not. Many fighters had their own custom wraps, which included all sorts of adhesives—even electrical tape (used by Benny Leonard).
4. "Dillon Is Winner," *Cincinnati Post*, February 1, 1910. Dillon's punching power was superior to that of many of his opponents.
5. "Cooley And Dillon Meet in Even Bout," *Indianapolis Star*, February 9, 1910.
6. "Corbett To Train Here for Jeffries," *Indianapolis Star*, February 22, 1910. Sure enough, Corbett went three solid exhibition rounds with Jack Dillon on March 4.
7. "Corbett To Train Here for Jeffries," *Indianapolis Star*, February 22, 1910.
8. "Gossip of Boxers," *Indianapolis Star*, March 9, 1910. Team Dillon was indeed thinking about branching out to other fight markets, but that was dependent upon reasonable offers for his services.
9. Bronson was coming off back-to-back battles against Matty Baldwin and felt great. Maybe he replaced Fitzgerald to put Dillon in place. Was Bronson a bit jealous of Dillon's success? Perhaps. Or—and I wouldn't put it past Truesdale—was this a setup to get Bronson in the ring? It was likely the former.
10. "Boxing Bouts Are Seen at Anderson," *Muncie Evening Press*, March 9, 1910.
11. Some believe Bronson took the bout to prove his superiority over his sparring partner, which was likely true.
12. "May's Conqueror Returns," *Indianapolis Star*, April 4, 1910.
13. "Match For Jack Dillon," *Indianapolis News*, April 12, 1910. More and more bouts were being brought off at the Dillon Athletic Club for the benefit of the members, and likely for the promotion skills of the Price boys.
14. "Friends Expect Victory: Dillon to Win in Bout," *Indianapolis Star*, April 16, 1910. *Anderson Herald* ran a two-column photo of Jack Dillon on April 21, 1910, 6.
15. "Dillon Wins All the Way Over Dick Fitzpatrick," *Indianapolis News*, April 22, 1910.

16. "Corking," *Anderson Herald*, April 22, 1910.
17. "Hicks Succumbs to Dillon," *Indianapolis Star*, June 21, 1910. A low blow was an illegal punch that strikes below an opponent's waist. Determined by the referee, it was a very subjective discernment.
18. "Jack Did Not Foul Hicks," *Indianapolis Star*, June 22, 1910.
19. "Would Fight 2 In Same Ring July 4," *Indianapolis Star*, June 26, 1910.
20. "Dillon Fights Best Bout of His Career," *Indianapolis News*, July 29, 1910.
21. The show was conducted under the auspices of the Mitchell Athletic Club. At the end of the nineteenth century, the most prominent athletic clubs were private establishments many times founded by elite businessmen or socialites. Since they were not open to the general public, many of their activities were not monitored by authorities. Germania Hall was a five-story building located at 39 South Delaware Street in Indianapolis.
22. "Gore Shows Police the Line of Demarcation," *Indianapolis News*, September 1, 1910. Was Dillon's muzzle a chink in the pugilist's armor? Only time would tell.
23. "Perry And Dillon in Fast Bout," *Pittsburgh Post-Gazette*, September 18, 1910.
24. The Pittsburgh dailies gave the edge to Perry, a local pugilist.
25. "Want Dillon to Agree," *Indianapolis News*, October 5, 1910.
26. "Indianapolis Fighters Were After the Bacon," *Indianapolis News*, October 4, 1910.
27. New Castle was also home to boxer and manager Jimmy Dunn, who handled Johnny Kilbane.
28. "Ketchel Dies from Murder's Rifle," *Salt Lake Herald-Republican*, October 16, 1910.
29. This excludes the end date.
30. Billy Papke may have held the title upon Ketchel's death, but he would certainly relinquish it to Frank Klaus on March 5, 1913. Papke would fight 14 times during that term, losing half his battles. While he would defeat Ed Williams, Dave Smith, Jim Sullivan, Billy Leitch, Marcel Moreau, Georges Carpentier, and George Bernard, he would lose to Dave Smith, Cyclone Johnny Thompson, Sailor Burke, Bob Moha, Frank Mantell, Jack Denning, and Leo Houck.
31. "Boxing Bouts for Tonight," *Pittsburgh Post*, October 20, 1910.
32. "Jack Dillon Bests Chip," *Indianapolis Star*, October 22, 1910.
33. "Jack Dillon All but Stops Berger," *Indianapolis Star*, October 30, 1910.
34. "Hoosier Middleweight Victor in Boxing Bout," *Indianapolis News*, November 12, 1910.
35. Time off from his training didn't stop him from working with other fighters or refereeing.
36. "M'Goorty Is Victor Over Jack Dillon," *Times*, December 17, 1910.
37. "Jack Dillon After Langford's Scalp," *Pittsburgh Press*, December 30, 1910.

Chapter Three

1. "Promising Brights Lights in Hoosier Pugdom," *Indianapolis News*, January 14, 1911.
2. "Jack Dillon And Harry Mansfield Fight on Monday," *Pittsburgh Press*, January 1, 1911. Ethnicity and religion were forever defining marketing features of the fight game. The fight was at catchweights.
3. News, even in 1911, traveled fast: A prime target for every Dillon adversary was at this point his nose. An opponent needed to start the blood flowing to slow the Hoosier pugilist.
4. "Dillon faced McGoorty at a big disadvantage in experience, was ten pounds lighter, and was shorter in reach and in height," *Indianapolis Star*, January 12, 1911.
5. Five days later, two participants were arrested and charged with being about to engage in a prizefight. This incident likely put a nail in the coffin of Winnipeg boxing. (See "Pinch 'em at Winnipeg," *Indianapolis News*, January 16, 1911.)
6. "Indianapolis Boxer meets George Chip in Second Battle," *Indianapolis Star*, January 25, 1911.
7. "Pittsburg(h) Fighter Escapes Knockout," *Indianapolis Star*, January 26, 1911.
8. "Hypnotic Eyes of Jack Dillon Claim Another Victim in the Ring," *Indianapolis Star*, January 29, 1911.
9. "Jack Dillon Has an Unusual Reach," *Pittsburgh Press*, February 1, 1911.
10. "Jack Dillon and Glover Meet Tonight," *Pittsburgh Press*, February 4, 1911.
11. "Dillon Outpointed by Mike Glover of Boston," *Pittsburgh Post*, February 5, 1911. Opposing viewpoints provide a glimpse into the subjectivity involved during the no-decision era.
12. "Dillon Punishes Loughrey in Ring," *Indianapolis Star*, February 19, 1911.
13. "Gossip of the boxers," *Indianapolis Star*, February 16, 1911.
14. "Fight Pugs Pleased with Dillon's Work," *Indianapolis News*, February 23, 1911. The action was an example of Dillon's sportsmanship.
15. "Father files Affidavits," *Indianapolis Star*, February 25, 1911. Mr. Carroll was an invalid whose wife had died several months prior and was attempting to control his daughter's behavior. Yes, it helped that Farb's father was a bondsman. (See also "Jack Dillon Under Arrest," same issue, page 23.)
16. "Pugilists Are Fined," *Indianapolis Star*, September 29, 1911.
17. "Jack Dillon Is Ready for Hugo Kelly's Game," *Indianapolis Star*, March 6, 1911.
18. "Western Fistic Experts Pick Jack Dillon as Likely Successor to Stanley Ketchel," *Buffalo Courier*, March 12, 1911.

19. The more favors in the back pockets of fight managers, the better their pants fit.
20. "Mike Twin Met More Than His Match," *Buffalo News*, March 18, 1911.
21. "Jack Dillon Knocks Out Billy Clark," *Pittsburgh Post-Gazette*, April 2, 1911.
22. "Prize Fight Just a Rotten Lemon Farce," *Evansville Press*, April 13, 1911. Some members of the press believed Stevens dropped to avoid humiliation and injury.
23. "Jimmy Gardner's Work Displeases Local Fight Fans," *Pittsburgh Press*, April 23, 1911.
24. Gardner split two battles (1–1) with Klaus in 1910, drew him on January 31, 1911, and had the better of him over six rounds on April 11, 1911. Both Hub fighters, they knew each other well.
25. "Jack Dillon Defeats Chip," *Star Press*, April 29, 1911.
26. "Dillon Outboxes Milwaukee Rival," *Indianapolis Star*, May 4, 1911.
27. "Millionaires See Dillon Win Bout," *Indianapolis Star*, May 21, 1911. Following a decade-long pugilism career, Jack Herrick moved to California to become an actor. And he was successful during the mid–1920s and early 1930s.
28. "Buffalo Boy Holds Own for Ten Rounds," *Indianapolis Star*, June 22, 1911.
29. "Dillon in Draw," *Indianapolis News*, July 4, 1911.
30. "Dillon Bests Coakley," *Indianapolis News*, August 24, 1911.
31. "Dillon's Poor Showing Causes Riot at Show," *Indianapolis News*, September 5, 1911.
32. "Opening Fight a Fluke; Half Refund Is Offered," *Times-Democrat*, September 5, 1911.
33. "Police Stop Bout in the Fourth," *Evansville Courier and Press*, October 5, 1911.
34. "Dillon Floors Williams for 24 Seconds in First," *Indianapolis Star*, October 24, 1911.
35. "Pugs Indicted," *Rushville Republican*, October 26, 1911.
36. Dillon would return to the county in 1914.
37. "George Brown Is Beaten by Jack Dillon," *Pittsburgh Post-Gazette*, November 12, 1911.
38. "Klaus and Dillon End Fierce Battle with Honors Even," *Pittsburgh Post*, December 7, 1911.
39. "Dillon Master of Frank Klaus," *Indianapolis Star*, December 7, 1911.

Chapter Four

1. Before formal organizations, recognition came in the form of claims. And claims were subject to interpretation.
2. "Houck Stopped in Sixth Round," *Indianapolis News*, January 2, 1912.
3. An examination by the club physician found no traces of a rib fracture.
4. A fact attested to by Louis H. Durlacher, Houck's manager (see "Jack Dillon Gets Praise," *Evansville Press*, January 4, 1912).
5. "Sport Sidelights and Comment," *Indianapolis Star*, January 2, 1912.
6. McCarey proposed a middleweight championship bout against Mike Gibbons, the St. Paul fighter.
7. The name Billy Griffith also appeared in print as Billy Griffiths. Griffith replaced Jimmy Howard, who had replaced Terry Martin because of an injured hand.
8. "Dillon Has Easy Time Beating Billy Griffith in Six Rounds," *Pittsburgh Post*, January 21, 1912. Dillon scaled at 158½.
9. "Houck No Quitter; Three Ribs Broken," *Times*, January 24, 1912.
10. "Dillon Puts the Kibosh to Wiggam," *Evansville Journal*, January 27, 1912. Note that Hoy is defined by his race rather than his ability.
11. "Fought Jack Dillon and Took a Beating...," *Buffalo Enquirer*, February 6, 1912. As Paul Harvey would often quip, "now you know the rest of the story."
12. Dillon had Berger close to hitting the canvas, but that was as far as he got—not a single knockdown was registered.
13. "Dillon Easily Bests Gardner," *Philadelphia Inquirer*, February 4, 1912. The article also stated, "It was Dillon all the way through, but the latter pulled considerably, which accounted for Gardner being on pins at the end."
14. "Dillon Too Much for Paddy Lavin," *Buffalo News*, February 9, 1912.
15. "He's as Good as Ketchel," *Fort Wayne Daily News*, February 9, 1912.
16. A "cauliflower ear" refers to a deformity of the ear caused by blunt force trauma. It was a common pugilist condition.
17. Dillon had injured his left hand in the first round and did not use it during the remainder of the bout.
18. "Frank Klaus to Meet Dillon," *Akron Beacon Journal*, February 23, 1912.
19. Later, Dillon was also offered a match with Frank Mantell on St. Patrick's Day by fight promoters in Los Angeles.
20. Granted, a little display in front of gamblers could work to the promoter's benefit.
21. "Jack Dillon, with Bum Mitt, Bests Coast Pug," *Indianapolis News*, March 8, 1912.
22. Attell and Murphy met twice in 1912, this was the fight before the famed "bloodbath" photo was taken on August 3.
23. "Dillon Refuses to Talk About His Ring Feats," *San Francisco Bulletin*, March 19, 1912. This interview sounded as if the statements were made by the reporter in the form of questions, and Dillon simply shook his head in agreement or uttered a one-word answer.
24. "Middleweights Do Last Boxing in Gymnasium," *San Francisco Chronicle*, March 22, 1912.
25. "Hoosier Bearcat Is Confident of Victory," *Indianapolis News*, March 22, 1912.
26. On July 19, 1911, the city government agreed and formally returned the "h" to Pittsburgh.

27. "Klaus Is Lucky to Gain Favor of Ring Judge," *Indianapolis Star*, March 24, 1912.
28. "Klaus Is Lucky to Gain Favor of Ring Judge," *Indianapolis Star*, March 24, 1912.
29. "Klaus Is Lucky to Gain Favor of Ring Judge," *Indianapolis Star*, March 24, 1912.
30. "Dillon Says He Was Job Victim," *Indianapolis Star*, March 30, 1912. This was one of the first public references to a Mrs. Jack Dillon, however no marriage license could be found. It may have been Grace Reed traveling with Jack Dillon.
31. "Dillon Says He Was Job Victim," *Indianapolis Star*, March 30, 1912. Dillon also claimed that the referee had a $500 bet on Frank Klaus. An X-ray confirmed he had a slivered bone in his knuckle.
32. Klaus wanted to not only impress the referee making the decision but also the beat writers.
33. "Dillon Says He Was Job Victim," *Indianapolis Star*, March 30, 1912.
34. "Jack Was Trimmed. Says So Himself," *Evansville Journal*, April 2, 1912.
35. "Mandot Arrives for Fight with Saylor," *Indianapolis Star*, April 22, 1912. The pugilist departed Indianapolis for Gotham on April 25.
36. "K.O.'s at Frankfurt," *Indianapolis News*, April 24, 1912.
37. "Claus Outpoints Jack Dillon," *Evening Standard*, May 4, 1912. Note: Klaus was spelled wrong in the title.
38. "Klaus Wins Again from Jack Dillon," *Evansville Courier and Press*, May 4, 1912. The Madison Square Garden scales were not accurate and weighed both fighters as 10 pounds heavier. Estimated weight: Klaus scaled at 158 earlier in the evening, while Dillon tipped two pounds lighter.
39. "Jack Dillon Puts Up Poor Fight with Klaus," *Indianapolis News*, May 4, 1912.
40. "Release Cantwell on a $1,000 Bond," *Palladium-Item*, May 14, 1912.
41. "Hoosier Lad Lands Knockout in Third," *Anderson Herald*, May 29, 1912.
42. Sullivan rarely failed to make distance. Having created a strong fan base in Buffalo, New York, he always wanted to provide a solid performance. *The Buffalo News* reported that Sullivan, who scaled at 167, had only a three-pound advantage (it was likely more). Two fights after his battle against Dillon, he would battle Edward "Gunboat" Smith during a 10-round no decision.
43. "Dillon Is Victor in Thomas Bout," *Indianapolis Star*, July 5, 1912. It is unclear what middleweight championship they were referring to.
44. "Dillon Makes Home Run," *Indianapolis Star*, August 1, 1912.
45. Ticket prices were scaled at 50 cents, 75 cents, and one dollar, for the Richmond Coliseum event.
46. "Referee Sounds toll Over Buffalo Scrapper," *Indianapolis News*, August 13, 1912.
47. "Will Campaign for Championship Title," *Indianapolis News*, September 23, 1912.
48. See obituary: "Sam Murbarger, Athletic Board Secretary, Dies of Seizure," *Indianapolis Star*, December 13, 1944.
49. "Jabs and Counters," *Star Press*, October 4, 1912.
50. There were mixed reviews of the contest. More than 1,200 spectators saw the Dillon-dominated contest. Wagner claimed the $50 weight forfeit as Dillon was overweight.
51. "Jones Asserts That Dillon Will Be...," *Indianapolis Star*, October 30, 1912.
52. "Dillon Administers K.O. in Fourth Rd," *Times*, November 5, 1912.
53. "Dillon Bests Clark," *Fort Wayne Journal-Gazette*, November 23, 1912.
54. "Dillon Begins to Train for Christy," *Indianapolis Star*, December 2, 1912. Dillon respected Christie's perseverance.
55. "Jack Dillon Wins Bout with Christie," *Evansville Journal*, December 12, 1912.
56. For the record, Tommy Dillon lost all four contests where he appeared on the same boxing card as his brother. See the Index for shared bouts.

Chapter Five

1. "Dillon Defeats Gus Christie," *Times*, January 2, 1913.
2. "Gus Christie Defense Baffles Jack Dillon," *Indianapolis News*, January 2, 1913.
3. Sheriff McCuster stopped the bout to prevent a decision.
4. "Leo Houck and Jack Dillon Box a Draw," *Harrisburg Daily Independent*, January 23, 1913.
5. "Dillon Beats Navy Star in Short Bout," *Indianapolis Star*, January 25, 1913.
6. "Dillon Wins Favor in Providence Bout," *Indianapolis Star*, February 11, 1913. The bout concluded in Dillon's favor.
7. "Bearcat Slaughters Much Touted Denning," *Indianapolis News*, February 20, 1913.
8. "Jack Dillon Wins Over K.O. Brennan," *Evansville Journal*, March 13, 1913.
9. "Sport Skimming," *Evansville Journal*, March 23, 1913.
10. "Jack Dillon Scores Victory Over Crouse," *Indianapolis Star*, April 11, 1913.
11. This, according to some of his team, was exactly what was taking place. It was a method of gauging the strengths and weaknesses of Dillon's skills.
12. "Dillon Easily Bests Moha," *Muncie Evening Press*, April 29, 1913.
13. "Moha's Excuse," *Indianapolis News*, April 30, 1913.
14. "Jack Dillon Looks Good for Champ Class," *Huntington Herald*, May 1, 1913.
15. James J. Corbett stopped by Dillon's camp on May 20.
16. Frank Klaus also defeated Marcel Moreau and Pietro Boine while in France in September

1912. The disqualifications were an indication of the ability of Klaus to aggravate his opposition.
17. "Eyes of World on Dillon–Klaus Fight," *Indianapolis Star*, May 28, 1913.
18. "Dillon Can Claim Klaus's Ring Title," *Indianapolis Star*, May 30, 1913.
19. "The Passing Show," *Indianapolis Star*, June 1, 1913.
20. "Jack Dillon Is Ready to Fight," *Fort Wayne Sentinel*, June 19, 1913.
21. "Poses as Dillon's Brother," *Indianapolis Star*, July 1, 1913.
22. Jimmy Clabby was coming off two fights against the hard-hitting Eddie McGoorty and didn't want to head back east from Montana. Also, he was booked for a number of bouts in San Francisco.
23. "Dillon Has M'Kinnon Out in Tenth Round," *Star Press*, July 4, 1913.
24. "Jack Dillon Now Without Manager," *Richmond Item*, July 10, 1913.
25. "Dillon Returns Home," *Indianapolis News*, August 11, 1913.
26. "Dillon Hurt in Car Upset," *Indianapolis Star*, August 16, 1913.
27. "Jack Dillon Outpoints Caponi," *Fort Wayne Journal-Gazette*, September 18, 1913.
28. "Dillon and Houck Fight Fast Battle," *Indianapolis Star*, October 10, 1913.
29. Leonard Florian Houck would compete in each weight division from flyweight to heavyweight. During his 24 years in the ring, he met 12 world champions from several divisions. Houck, with more than 200 bouts to his credit, hung up the gloves in 1926. As the head boxing coach at Penn State for over 25 years, Houck guided 48 boxers to college championships. He was inducted into the International Boxing Hall of Fame in 2012.
30. Houck also faced the likes of Harry Greb, Gene Tunney, and Mike Gibbons.
31. "Monaghan's Swat Gets Referee—Not Dillon," *Indianapolis News*, October 15, 1913.
32. Team Dillon felt Eddie McGoorty ran out on the bout. However, McGoorty had been eyeing a trip to the island in the Southern Hemisphere.
33. "Jack Dillon Finds Gus Christie Easy," *Palladium-Item*, November 4, 1913.
34. Dillon was offered three matches: Jeff Smith, Georges Carpentier, and one yet to be determined. Hugh Donald "Huge Deal" McIntosh (1876–1942) was an Australian theatrical entrepreneur, sporting promoter, and newspaper owner. He staged the 1908 world championship heavyweight title fight between Burns and Jack Johnson.
35. "Indianapolis Boy Is Easy Winner," *Indianapolis Star*, November 28, 1913.

Chapter Six

1. Don't let the name fool you, as Dan Morgan (1873–1955) was one of boxing's great managers and most colorful figures. He was essential to the boxing careers of Battling Levinsky, Jack Britton, Knockout Brown, and Al McCoy.
2. "Jack Dillon Wins over Gus Christie," *Times*, January 2, 1914.
3. "Dillon Victor Over Hanson at Denver," *Indianapolis Star*, January 21, 1914.
4. The fight agreement was signed on February 28, 1914.
5. "Sporting Brevities," *Muncie Evening Press*, February 5, 1914.
6. "Dillon Puts K.O. on Claiborne in Third," *Indianapolis Star*, February 18, 1914.
7. "Dillon Branches Out as New White Hope," *Indianapolis News*, March 3, 1914.
8. "Jack Dillon Has Shade Over Flynn," *Indianapolis Star*, March 4, 1914. At one point fans stormed the doors of the venue and occupied ringside seats, leaving many ticket holders helpless.
9. "Dillon Wipes Up Ring with Jack Lester, White Hope," *Indianapolis News*, March 11, 1914.
10. "Jack Dillon May Claim Three Titles; If He Wins," *Star Press*, April 9, 1914. This said, none of these titles would likely be universally recognized.
11. "Battling Levinsky Arrives at Butte," *Miles City Star*, April 8, 1914. A $20,000 house was also quoted.
12. "Championship Bout for Butte Fistic Devotees," *Butte Daily Post*, April 14, 1914.
13. "Championship Bout for Butte Fistic Devotees," *Butte Daily Post*, April 14, 1914.
14. "Jack Dillon Defeats Levinsky with Ease," *Bozeman Courier*, April 15, 1914.
15. "Dillon Easy Winner in Levinsky Tangle," *Anaconda Standard*, April 15, 1914.
16. "Dillon Easy Winner in Levinsky Tangle," *Anaconda Standard*, April 15, 1914.
17. A chance blow, thrown by Arthur Pelkey, struck just below the heart of McCarty after one minute and 45 seconds of a bout for the World White heavyweight title. The bout took place on May 24, 1913, and McCarty died on this date. The punch, many believe, contributed to his death. By the way, Al Norton was a pugilist who not only fought Dillon twice but also fought Jack Dempsey three times.
18. "Dillon Shades Norton," *South Bend Tribune*, April 29, 1914. Later, *Nat Fleischer's All-Time Ring Record Book*, a.k.a. *The Ring Record Book*, noted that Dillon "won international recognition as light heavyweight title of America." After the battle, Billy McCarney hoped to rematch his fighter with Dillon over 20 rounds.
19. United States Census Records, 1920.
20. "Learns All About It," *Indianapolis News*, May 19, 1914.
21. "Dillon Would Meet Big Smoke," *Huntington Herald*, May 26, 1914.
22. All the article headlines given were from their respective newspapers on May 30, 1914.
23. "Battling Levinsky Earns Draw Bout," *Palladium-Item*, May 30, 1914.

24. Whenever Dillon went West, he was always concerned about adjusting to the conditions.
25. "Dillon–Moha Bout Off," *Indianapolis Star*, June 14, 1914.
26. "Jack Dillon Wins Decision Over Moha," *Indianapolis Star*, June 16, 1914.
27. "Clown Antics in 'Hot' Contest," *Indianapolis Star*, July 22, 1914. Nobody acknowledged the gong or officials, and Walsh had to be chased back to his corner three times. Prosecutor Wernke, sitting ringside, ordered Walsh arrested, stating that he had information that the bout, or the fight if you will, was framed.
28. "Clown Antics in 'Hot' Contest," *Indianapolis Star*, July 22, 1914.
29. Since Howard Morrow sent Joe Mace to fulfill *his* fight contract, one questions the legitimacy of the bout.
30. "Hoosier Battler Rowing to Keep Himself...," *Indianapolis Star*, August 5, 1914. The White River is a two-forked river—the west, or main, fork is about 312 miles long—that flows through central and southern Indiana and is the main tributary to the Wabash River. Indianapolis is located on the river.
31. "Dillon Fights Brown Draw," *Times*, September 16, 1914. Attendance was estimated at four thousand.
32. "J. Dillon After 'Gunboat' Smith," *Indianapolis Star*, October 8, 1914.
33. "Sam Murbarger Is Under Arrest for Faking Fight," *Fort Wayne Journal-Gazette*, October 15, 1914.
34. "Jack Dillon Is Sued," *Indianapolis News*, October 16, 1914. Dillon sought $50,000 in damages.
35. "Dillon Scores K.O. on Weinert," *Indianapolis Star*, November 10, 1914.
36. Charles Weinsachzyowski, a.k.a. Charlie Weinert, fought until 1929 and became a respected pugilist.
37. "Jack Dillon Forgets to Schedule His Clothes," *Indianapolis News*, December 22, 1914.

Chapter Seven

1. "Don't Cool Out," *Fort Wayne Daily News*, January 1, 1915.
2. Yes, the ambiguous nature of the sentence was intentional.
3. "Dillon to Meet Porky Flynn in Gotham Bout," *Indianapolis News*, January 4, 1915. Togs are boxing clothes and accessories.
4. Dillon's weight was also quoted at 173 pounds and at 175½ pounds.
5. "Jabs and Counters," *Star Press*, January 24, 1915.
6. "Both Fresh at End of Scrap," *Indianapolis Star*, February 21, 1915.
7. "Ringside Jottings," *Star Press*, March 12, 1915. This was made before Willard defeated Jack Johnson on April 5, 1915. And Willard expressed little, if any, interest in the white heavyweight championship.
8. "Dillon Gets a Shade Over Gunboat Smith," *Star Press*, March 17, 1915.
9. "George Coogan Says It Was Dillon's Bout," *Evansville Journal*, March 18, 1915.
10. "Scrap News," *Indianapolis News*, April 29, 1915.
11. "Anderson Easy for Jack Dillon," *Indianapolis Star*, May 5, 1915. Anderson, with very little fight experience but an abundance of size, was likely signed by Murbarger as a confidence builder for his fighter. Dillon's weight disadvantage grew over time, as he later quoted at 70 pounds.
12. "Lester No Match for 'Bearcat' Dillon," *Indianapolis Star*, May 21, 1915. The mayor would not grant a permit for a fight at the speedway.
13. *Rochester Democrat and Chronicle* saw the fight in favor of McMahon, who outweighed Dillon by about 20 pounds.
14. "Mantell Easy Picking for Hoosier Bearcat," *Indianapolis News*, June 12, 1915.
15. "News of the Boxers," *South Bend News-Times*, July 6, 1915.
16. "Dillon and Chip in Draw," *Star Press*, July 6, 1915. This bout appeared to be taken more out of frustration or necessity, as Dillon was having difficulty having his matches come to fruition.
17. "Jack Dillon Knocked Down for the First Time," *Indianapolis News*, July 13, 1915.
18. "Beats the Zulu Kid," *Indianapolis Star*, July 17, 1915.
19. "Scrap News," *Indianapolis News*, July 30, 1915.
20. "Scraps," *Muncie Evening Press*, February 4, 1916. The use of the phrase "my son" may indicate Dillon's formal adoption of his stepson.
21. "Jack Dillon in Draw," *Indianapolis News*, August 18, 1915. Only the 10th round was won by a wide margin, and it fell in favor of Dillon.
22. "MILITIA IS CALLED OUT TO STOP JACK DILLON," *Indianapolis News*, September 7, 1915.
23. "M'Mahon in Draw with Jack Dillon," *New Castle News*, September 27, 1915. The attendance was small.
24. "Scrap News," *Indianapolis News*, October 6, 1915.
25. "Jack Dillon Leads Other Middleweights," *Evansville Journal*, January 20, 1915.
26. "Coffey Meets Moran Tuesday," *Rushville Republican*, October 16, 1915.
27. "Boxing Briefs," *Indianapolis Star*, October 28, 1915.
28. "New Champion Looms Up in Hoosier Fighter," *Indianapolis News*, November 2, 1915.
29. "New Champion Looms Up in Hoosier Fighter," *Indianapolis News*, November 2, 1915.
30. "New Champion Looms Up in Hoosier Fighter," *Indianapolis News*, November 2, 1915. Dillon scaled at 171, while Weinert tipped at 185.
31. "Jack Dillon Breaks Frank Farmer's Rib," *Anderson Herald*, November 19, 1915.

32. Twenty-six bouts in a single year, while there are members of the International Boxing Hall of Fame with fewer than 40 professional bouts in their entire career.

Chapter Eight

1. "Thinks Well of Dillon," *Indianapolis News*, December 15, 1915.
2. "Darcy, Champion of Australia, Is Coming Our Way," *South Bend News-Times*, January 3, 1916.
3. "Jack Dillon Held to Draw by Miske," *Times*, January 29, 1916.
4. "Kayo for Cowler by Jack Dillon," *Richmond Item*, February 2, 1916.
5. "Dillon to Meet the World's Champion," *Evansville Press*, February 2, 1916.
6. "Little Dillon Not Afraid of Willard," *Fort Wayne Daily News*, February 12, 1916.
7. "Jack Dillon Outfights Levinsky All the Way," *Indianapolis News*, February 9, 1916.
8. "'Man Killer' Hears Call of Footlights," *Indianapolis News*, February 15, 1916.
9. "Box Fighters," *Logansport Pharos-Tribune*, March 15, 1916. Smith tipped at 180½, while Dillon scaled at 170¼. How often does any division champion substitute for another boxer?
10. Allen scaled at 186, while Dillon tipped at 173. How often does any division champion battle three times in a week?
11. "Jack Dillon Is Easy Winner Over Levinsky in Fast Bout," *Times Union*, March 29, 1916. Levinsky scaled at 177½, while Dillon tipped at 169½. Sources varied on the decision, but eyewitness accounts favored Dillon.
12. "Soft One for Dillon," *Buffalo Times*, March 30, 1916.
13. This total excludes the end date.
14. "Jack Dillon Anxious to Box Either Willard or Moran, Any Time, Any Place," *Buffalo Commercial*, March 31, 1916.
15. "Jack Dillon Anxious to Box Either Willard or Moran, Any Time, Any Place," *Buffalo Commercial*, March 31, 1916.
16. "Boxers IN Workouts," *Indianapolis Star*, April 9, 1916. Tommy Dillon, Jack's brother, was the instructor at the gym.
17. Could this be a chink in Dillon's armor? It was hard to say.
18. "One Goal for Jack Dillon," *Evansville Journal*, April 16, 1916.
19. "Jack Dillon Matched to Meet Moran In New York," *Evansville Journal*, April 18, 1916. Moran would negotiate for more of a guarantee and a take of the gate.
20. "Dillon Hands Levinsky Lacing in 15 Rounds," *Indianapolis News*, April 26, 1916. Dillon scaled at about 168, while Levinsky appeared about 174.
21. "Dillon Practically Is Matched to Box Moran In New York," *Indianapolis Star*, May 1, 1916.
22. "Offers Jack Dillon $10,000 to Box Darcy," *Star Press*, May 5, 1916.
23. "Jack Dillon Plays with New York Man," *Indianapolis Star*, May 24, 1916.
24. "Restraining Order Against Boxing Now," *Republic*, May 25, 1916.
25. "Dillon and Moran Matched," *Indianapolis Star*, May 11, 1916. Later, Tom O'Rourke, promoter, offered Moran $25,000. This was an excellent example of just when you thought a deal was closed, the negotiation had only begun.
26. "Can He Emulate Wolcott?" *Fort Wayne Daily News*, June 22, 1916.
27. "Experts Pick Moran to Win Dillon Scrap," *Palladium-Item*, June 28, 1916.
28. This total excludes the end date.
29. It was believed Moran outweighed Dillon by 36½ pounds entering the ring.
30. "R. Edgren's Column," *Evening World*, June 30, 1916.
31. "R. Edgren's Column," *Evening World*, June 30, 1916.
32. "R. Edgren's Column," *Evening World*, June 30, 1916. The gross receipts for the Dillon–Moran bout totaled $28,521. A ticket account breakdown was printed in the *Indianapolis News* on July 3, 1916. The state took 7½ percent of gross receipts.
33. "R. Edgren's Column," *Evening World*, June 30, 1916.
34. "Short Sport News," *South Bend News-Times*, July 1, 1916.
35. "Dillon Knocks Out Pueblo Fireman," *Fort Wayne Journal-Gazette*, July 5, 1916. In Mrs. Murbarger's 1941 obituary it listed the couple's wedding anniversary as January 30, 1916, rather than July 1, 1916.
36. "Levinsky Victor; Outboxes Dillon," *Star Press*, July 14, 1916. Sources varied regarding the verdict; some called the bout a draw. Of the fighters' payments, some quoted Dillons take a bit higher.
37. "Jack Dillon Arrested on an Assault Charge," *South Bend News-Times*, August 22, 1916. The event, as they used to say, "smelled funny." It had that quid pro quo fragrance.
38. "Jack Dillon and Levinsky Draw," *Fort Wayne Journal-Gazette*, September 13, 1916.
39. Dillon tipped at 173, while O'Neil scaled at 172. The spelling of his opponent's surname varied and included O'Neal and O'Neill.
40. "Referee Decision Against Dillon; Title Goes," *Indianapolis Star*, October 25, 1916.
41. "Referee Decision Against Dillon; Title Goes," *Indianapolis Star*, October 25, 1916. Price's middle name was Coulter not Cutler.
42. "Winner Is to Fight Willard," *Boston Post*, October 23, 1916. Rickard failed to land the bout with Willard.
43. "Dillon in Pickle Over His Fights," *Logansport Pharos-Tribune*, October 27, 1916.
44. "Dillon Slipping, Critics Believe," *Times*, November 17, 1916. There were indications that

Dillon was impulsive, demanding, and recalcitrant with his fight managers.
45. This is where the One America Tower Garage/Skyline Club is today.
46. "Dillon Beaten in Tough Battle with Miske," *Indianapolis Star*, December 20, 1916.

Chapter Nine

1. "Indianapolis Admirers See Dillon Meet Moha," *Indianapolis News*, January 1, 1917. James Leslie Darcy (1895–1917) was an outstanding Australian boxer, who simultaneously held both the middleweight title and the Australian heavyweight championship title.
2. "Sport Snap Shots," *Muncie Evening Press*, January 4, 1917.
3. "Decision to Dillon at Dayton," *Star Press*, January 2, 1917.
4. "Gives Fight to Miske," *Indianapolis Star*, January 17, 1917.
5. "Neither Man Gets Shade in Ten Rounds," *South Bend News-Times*, January 17, 1917.
6. He would train at the famous Young Men's Gymnastic Club.
7. According to the *Muncie Evening Press*, "Dillon was an 8 to 5 favorite, many betting 3 to 2 that Smith would not last fifteen rounds." See "Dillon Beats Gunboat Smith," *Muncie Evening Press*, February 17, 1917.
8. "In the Squared Ring," *Indianapolis Star*, February 20, 1917. Murbarger came close and even had Dillon substituting for Al McCoy, who had inked a deal with Darcy for March 5. The reason? There was big money involved: Dillon would grab $15,000, while Darcy's take would be $25,000.
9. "M'Coy–Darcy Match May Be Prohibited," *Evansville Courier and Press*, February 21, 1917. NYSAC was founded in 1911, when the Frawley Law legalized prizefighting in New York state.
10. "The Boxfight Fans Peeved," *Fort Wayne Daily News*, February 28, 1917.
11. "Whitman Calls Les Darcy a Slacker," *Rushville Republican*, March 2, 1917.
12. "Dillon Wins from Barry," *Daily Arkansas Gazette*, March 31, 1917.
13. Honestly, it appeared like a setup bout to get Jack Dillon to return to Hot Springs. Permission granted to use your imagination regarding the reason.
14. "M'Mahon–Dillon Go Is Flat," *Anderson Herald*, May 15, 1917.
15. "Bandit's Shot Proves Fatal to Well-Known Ring Man," *Indianapolis Star*, May 20, 1917.
16. "M'Carron Easy Target for Dillon's Punches," *Indianapolis News*, May 22, 1917. Some reporters, such as M.E. Donnelly from the *Toledo Times*, saw the fight in favor of McCarron.
17. "Dillon Beats Chip," *Fort Wayne Daily News*, May 30, 1917.
18. "Dillon and Chip in Another Draw," *Richmond Item*, May 30, 1917.
19. "Jack Dillon and Other Pugs to Enlist," *Evansville Courier and Press*, May 14, 1917.
20. "Jack Dillon, Local Pug, Takes on Kaiser by Joining Navy," *Indianapolis Star*, June 11, 1917.
21. "Dillon an Easy Winner over Rowlands at Memphis," *Indianapolis Star*, June 26, 1917.
22. "Dillon Wins in One," *Anderson Herald*, July 5, 1917.
23. "Clifford Is Sent to Mat, but Stays the Limit with Dillon," *Indianapolis Star*, July 11, 1917.
24. "Great Crowd, in Size and Class, Attends Bouts at Forbes Field," *Pittsburgh Post*, July 31, 1917.
25. "Greb Outfights Dillon in Ten Rounds," *Pittsburgh Post-Gazette*, July 31, 1917.
26. "Gibbons Master of Jack Dillon," *Richmond Item*, September 4, 1917. Both fighters to weigh in at 162 pounds at 9 a.m.
27. "Dillon Has Alibi," *South Bend Tribune*, September 7, 1917. I'll ask it for you: Why did Dillon agree to fight him at 162 pounds? His manager, at this time Steve Harter, should have known better.
28. "Champ May Come," *Manhattan Mercury*, October 8, 1917.
29. "Dillon Outpointed by Willie Meehan in Six Fast Rounds," *Indianapolis Star*, October 16, 1917.
30. "Zulu Kid Gets Decision," *Star-Phoenix*, October 18, 1917.
31. "Dillon's Prestige Wanes," *Palladium-Item*, October 30, 1917.
32. "Jack Dillon Is Roundly Beaten," *Press and Sun-Bulletin*, November 14, 1917. The Frawley Act was a piece of New York state legislation permitting boxing exhibitions under strict guidelines (July 26, 1911, to November 14, 1917). For example, it allowed 10-round bouts with eight-ounce gloves. The prohibition of boxing in the state lasted until 1920. The 1920 Walker Law legalized professional boxing in New York state.
33. "Dillon Goes to Springs to Get Into Condition," *Indianapolis Star*, November 22, 1917.
34. "Walker and Dillon Stage Classy Draw," *Daily Arkansas Gazette*, November 30, 1917.
35. "'Meatless' Meals Minus Grumbles," *Indianapolis Star*, November 29, 1917.

Chapter Ten

1. "New Year Has Task to Keep Up 1917's Pace," *Indianapolis Star*, January 1, 1918.
2. "Dillon Under Handicap," *Indianapolis Star*, January 27, 1918. According to the *Star Tribune* (January 26, 1918), Dillon scaled at 161, while Chip tipped at 163. The event drew a gate of $5,000.
3. "Two Witnesses Tell How Owens Was Killed," *Indianapolis News*, January 23, 1918.
4. "Jack Dillon at His Best Against Heavy Boxers," *Indianapolis Star*, February 17, 1918. This was his second article. The first dealt with his big break against George "K.O." Brown.

5. "McGoorty Struck Dillon Hardest Blow Here 1911," *Indianapolis Star*, February 24, 1918.
6. "Dillon Believes Dempsey Will Be Next Champion," *Indianapolis Star*, March 3, 1918.
7. "Dillon Believes Greb Will Lead the Middleweights," *Indianapolis Star*, March 10, 1918.
8. "Jack Dillon Is Walloped by Pittsburgh Scrapper," *Indianapolis Star*, March 5, 1918.
9. Consequences, as most would observe, were seldom considered in Dillon's decision-making.
10. "Dillon–Scott Go Declared a Draw," *Star Press*, March 23, 1918.
11. "Dillon Not Knocked Down," *Indianapolis News*, March 26, 1918. At this point in time, these statements were redundant and seldom accurate.
12. At one point, he was scheduled to be the third man in the ring when Harry Greb met Jack Reed at Muncie on April 8. That fight never took place, however.
13. "Jack Dillon Has Better of Walker," *Indianapolis Star*, April 16, 1918.
14. "Class Work for Selects Starts in Local Schools," *Indianapolis Star*, April 19, 1918.
15. "Watty's Former Bat Boy to Fight for Uncle Sam," *Indianapolis News*, April 22, 1918.
16. "Jack Dillon Fails to Materialize; Frank Farmer Wins Fight," *Seattle Star*, May 8, 1918.
17. "Scrap News and Gossip," *Indianapolis News*, May 22, 1918. Likely an early deadline prompted the report.
18. This, as it would later prove, would become a distraction.
19. "Jack Dillon K.O.'s Walters in Third," *Richmond Item*, May 30, 1918. About 800 persons attended the event.
20. "Jack Dillon Shades Hugh Walker; Otto Wallace...," *Tulsa World*, June 18, 1918.
21. Later versions of *The Ring* record book incorrectly stated a loss for Dillon.
22. "Dillon Boxes a Draw," *New York Herald*, July 5, 1918.
23. "Jack Dillon Is Patriotic; to Box at Valparaiso," *Indianapolis Star*, August 6, 1918.
24. "Jack Dillon and Dailey Box Draw; Butsch Walloped," *Indianapolis Star*, August 9, 1918. Dillon's August 8 battle against Jack Daly (Dailey) was likely an exhibition. Some resources view it as a legitimate bout because of Daly's experience level.
25. "Dillon and M'Coy Stage Poor Bout," *Star Press*, August 22, 1918.
26. "Dillon Whips Krohn," *Indianapolis Star*, November 17, 1918.
27. "Dillon the Victor," *Dispatch*, November 22, 1918.
28. "Fistic Carnival Affords Little Real Scrapping," *Indianapolis Star*, November 24, 1918.

Chapter Eleven

1. "Look for a Revival of Interest in Fistic Sport," *Jersey Observer and Jersey Journal*, January 3, 1919.
2. "Erne Postpones Show Until 20th," *News-Journal*, January 8, 1919.
3. "Jack Dillon Has Birthday," *Indianapolis Star*, February 2, 1919.
4. "Boxing Game Experiencing Great Boom in Hot Springs...," *Arkansas Democrat*, February 5, 1919.
5. "Dillon Has Flu," *Arkansas Democrat*, February 6, 1919.
6. "Nate Jackson to Box Jack Douglas," *Daily Arkansas Gazette*, February 16, 1919. Promoter Jimmy Dime sent a contract to Jack Dillon for a match with George Chip in Hot Springs.
7. "'Junk King' to Box Here IN Centennial Contest," *Commercial Appeal*, May 15, 1919.
8. "Giant Killer Knocked Out in Second Round by Battling Harrison," *Tulsa Tribune*, May 25, 1919.
9. "Jack Dempsey May Be Expected to Resort to His 'Elbow Punch...,'" *Fort Worth Star-Telegram*, June 15, 1919. Bill Haack, a class act, ran one of the Memphis fight clubs. Some claim he worked 10 thousand fights (see *Newport Daily News*, November 15, 1954, 11). Haack was a man of character during an era when the sport had few.
10. "Sport Topics," *Times Union*, June 2, 1919.
11. "Before and After," *Buffalo Courier*, June 2, 1919.
12. "'Giant Killer' Jack Dillon Says Dempsey Is Marvel of Ring," *San Francisco Examiner*, June 20, 1919.
13. "Superfighter Only Can Land on Willard's Jaw with a Knockout," *Washington Post*, June 22, 1919. Willard was guaranteed, and paid by Tex Rickard, the sum of $100,000.
14. "Dempsey Will Get Verdict on Points, Says Jack Dillon," *Commercial Appeal*, June 24, 1919.
15. "Chart," *Fort Wayne Daily News*, February 5, 1916, 9.
16. "Champion Will Not Last with Jack Dempsey," *Indianapolis Star*, April 14, 1919.
17. "Oldtimers Hang Out Around Fight Center," *Daily Free Press*, July 3, 1919. Many other champions arrived the day before, or the day of, the historic heavyweight championship.
18. "First Time IN History," *Cincinnati Enquirer*, July 5, 1919.
19. The meniscus is a thin fibrous cartilage between the surfaces of some joints, in this case the knee. It is extremely painful and very difficult to heal. For Dillon, lateral leg movement was impossible, and he felt as if both leg bones were grinding together.
20. "Jack Dillon May Regain the Title of 'Giant Killer,'" *Commercial Appeal*, September 14, 1919.
21. Redemption, he believed, would cure his depression.
22. "Coliseum. Matches Uninteresting to Big Crowd of Fans," *Palladium-Item*, December 16, 1919.

Chapter Twelve

1. In December 1919, Kauff and his brother were implicated in a car theft. After only 55 games in 1920, the Giants traded Kauff to Toronto of the International League. Later, on March 10, it was announced that Arkansas promoter Billy Kramer would assist Dillon as a matchmaker.
2. "Martin Turns Heads at A.E.F.," *Nashville Banner*, January 27, 1920. (check)
3. "Martin Turns Heads at A.E.F.," *Nashville Banner*, January 27, 1920.
4. "Martin Turns Heads at A.E.F.," *Nashville Banner*, January 27, 1920.
5. "Halstead–Dillon Bout Results in No Decision," *Miami News*, February 10, 1920.
6. "Battling Halstead Outpoints Dillon in Grueling Bout," *Palm Beach Post*, February 21, 1920.
7. "Jack Dillon Loses in Fight with Young Fitzsimmons," *Commercial Appeal*, March 12, 1920.
8. "Jack Dillon Loses in 10-Rounds Fracas," *Seattle Union Record*, March 19, 1920.
9. "Jack Dillon Beaten," *San Francisco Bulletin*, March 19, 1920.
10. "Sporting Gossip," *Cincinnati Enquirer*, April 4, 1920.
11. "Jack Dillon Gets a Draw," *Star Press*, March 20, 1920.
12. "Dillon Prepares for 'Comeback' in Ring," *Indianapolis Star*, April 5, 1920.
13. "Dillon Prepares for 'Comeback' in Ring," *Indianapolis Star*, April 5, 1920.
14. "Young Fitzsimmons Has Clean Win Over Jack Dillon in Ten Round Match at Camel A.C.," *Wichita Falls Times*, May 4, 1920.
15. "Young Fitzsimmons Has Clean Win Over Jack Dillon in Ten Round Match at Camel A.C.," *Wichita Falls Times*, May 4, 1920.
16. "Jack Dillon Is Coming Back," *Anderson Daily Bulletin*, May 5, 1920.
17. "Saxon to Meet Martin at Clarksburg May 20," *Indianapolis Star*, May 12, 1920. The comment was a confidence builder, as Harter knew his fighter was in no condition for such an event.
18. Perhaps Farb had something to do with the results.
19. "Boxing Briefs," *Star Press*, July 16, 1920.
20. "Jack Dillon in Victory Over Battling Wells (Weiss)," *Indianapolis Star*, July 25, 1920. Weiss was down for a count of nine, then eight.
21. "Pacing the Sport World," *Daily Oklahoman*, July 25, 1920.
22. "Jack Dillon Bested," *Topeka Daily Capital*, July 27, 1920.
23. "Jack Dillon Home for Rest from Western Trip," *Indianapolis Star*, July 29, 1920. Dillon's interpretation of the battle differed from most.
24. "Jack Dillon, 'Hoosier Bearcat,'" *Gazette*, August 28, 1920.
25. "Bud Clancy Wins from Jack Dillon," *Des Moines Register*, September 5, 1920. Fight attendance was estimated at two thousand.
26. "When Dillon Was Introduced at Labor Day Title Match," *Commercial Appeal*, September 21, 1920.
27. "When Dillon Was Introduced at Labor Day Title Match," *Commercial Appeal*, September 21, 1920.
28. "Battling Halstead Wins Easy Decision Over Jack Dillon," *Springfield News-Leader*, October 5, 1920.
29. "Giant Killer and Moran to Settle Old Grudge," *Times*, November 21, 1920.
30. "Young Fitzsimmons Beats Jack Dillon," *Fort Worth Star-Telegram*, December 29, 1920.

Chapter Thirteen

1. "Boxing Thrives in Hot Springs," *Tulsa World*, January 9, 1921. Fighters at Hot Springs included Eddie Coulon, Jack Dillon, Joe Donnell, Harry Foley, Bobby Hughes, Patsy McMahon, Joe Nelson, Ray Rivers, and Texas Tate.
2. "Fighting Spirit Yet Burns in Breast of Jack Dillon," *Commercial Appeal*, January 9, 1921.
3. "Farce Bout Staged," *Indiana Daily Times*, January 26, 1921.
4. "Boxing Briefs," *Star Press*, February 1, 1921.
5. "Billy Edwards Is Knocked Out," *Town Talk*, February 12, 1921.
6. "Billy Edwards Is Knocked Out," *Town Talk*, February 12, 1921.
7. "Denham Last Until 6th Round Against Jack Dillon," *Atlanta Journal*, February 16, 1921.
8. "Denham Last Until 6th Round Against Jack Dillon," *Atlanta Journal*, February 16, 1921.
9. "Denham Last Until 6th Round Against Jack Dillon," *Atlanta Journal*, February 16, 1921.
10. "Dillon Is Outpointed," *Commercial Appeal*, February 191, 1921.
11. "Jack Dillon Kicked Out by National Association," *Indianapolis Star*, February 19, 1921.
12. "July 2 Most Interesting Date in Sporting History of France," *Standard Union*, May 17, 1921.
13. "Wray's Column," *St. Louis Dispatch*, May 29, 1921.
14. There were signs that he may have been coerced into taking a few bootleg battles. There were other pugilists fighting under the name of Jack Dillon—such as Young Jack Dillon, who was fighting out of Tennessee at the time, and Jack Dillon, battling out of New Bedford, Massachusetts, to name a couple—but the elite fighter, at this point in his career, knew everybody, especially in Indiana. And he knew how to keep matters quiet.
15. "Short Sport Notes," *Lincoln Journal Star*, September 8, 1921.
16. "Legion's Boxing Card," *Call-Leader*, December 29, 1921. Elwood is a city in Madison and Tipton Counties. The Madison County portion, which is more or less all of the city, is part of

the Indianapolis–Carmel–Anderson metropolitan statistical area.

17. "Boxing Bout Pleased Crowd," *Call-Leader*, January 2, 1922.
18. "Taylor Hangs K.O. on Solly Epstein in Opening Round," *Indianapolis Star*, January 6, 1922.
19. "Fight Decision," *Fort Wayne Sentinel*, January 6, 1922.
20. "Jack Dillon's Cottage Raided by Dry Agents," *Indianapolis Star*, January 29, 1922.
21. "Pugilist Fined $50 and Costs in Tiger Case," *Indiana Daily Times*, February 8, 1922.
22. "Jack Dillon, 'Who Feared No Man,' Becomes Teacher of Boxing at the Hoosier A.C." *Indiana Daily Times*, March 25, 1922.
23. "Boxing Fans Given Plenty of Variety at Huge Fistic Testimonial for Jack Dillon," *Indiana Daily Times*, May 11, 1922.
24. "Boxing Fans Given Plenty of Variety at Huge Fistic Testimonial for Jack Dillon," *Indiana Daily Times*, May 11, 1922.
25. "Boxing Fans Given Plenty of Variety at Huge Fistic Testimonial for Jack Dillon," *Indiana Daily Times*, May 11, 1922.
26. On May 20, 1922, it was reported by the *Wilkes-Barre Times Leader* that Dillon took home $9,300.
27. "Dillon to Manage Leslie," *Indiana Daily Times*, June 24, 1922.
28. "Dillon to Manage Leslie," *Indianapolis Star*, June 24, 1922.
29. "Patsy M'Mahon Takes Count in General Melee," *Indianapolis Times*, August 1, 1922.
30. "Dillon Summer Camp Raided; Two Men Held," *Indianapolis News*, September 14, 1922.
31. "Dillon Is Arrested," *Indianapolis Times*, September 18, 1922.
32. "Young Dillon Is in Trouble," *Princeton Daily Clarion*, October 24, 1922.
33. "Dillon Aiding Son in Trouble," *Evansville Journal*, October 24, 1922. Ralph Dillon was registered at the Princeton Hotel.
34. This was based on the 1920 census data. Ernest listed his occupation as a partner in a taxi line.

Chapter Fourteen

1. "Some Montana Ring Tails," *Anaconda Standard*, January 14, 1923.
2. "Jack Dillon Comes Back in Bout at Columbus," *Palladium-Item*, January 12, 1923.
3. "Frank Klaus Has Gone Through Fortune," *Oakland Tribune*, January 28, 1923.
4. "Ancient Jack Dillon Stages a Comeback," *Fresno Morning Republican*, February 14, 1923.
5. "Jack Dillon Taken by Dry Agents in Roadhouse Raid," *Indianapolis Star*, May 16, 1923.
6. "Raiders Arrest Jack Dillon on Liquor Charges," *Indianapolis Times*, May 16, 1923.
7. "Jack Dillon, Pugilist, Held on Blind Tiger Charge," *Indianapolis Star*, June 7, 1923.
8. "Thousands Come to Spend the Day," *Tribune*, July 5, 1923. Howard Wiggam handled the refereeing duties.
9. "Dillon to Recall Appeal," *Indianapolis News*, September 29, 1923.
10. "Watts and Dillon Owners of Hub A.C.," *Indianapolis Star*, March 11, 1924.
11. "Jack Dillon Arrested," *Indianapolis Times*, April 3, 1924.
12. "Arrest Dillon on Liquor Charge," *Indianapolis Star*, June 15, 1924.
13. "Two Former Pugilists Bound to Federal Jury," *Star Press*, November 4, 1924.
14. "Feed Them Well, Sheriff's Slogan," *Indianapolis Times*, January 3, 1925.
15. "Baltzell Give More Stiff Court Rulings," *Tribune*, March 16, 1925.
16. "Jack Dillon to Serve 90 Days in County Jail," *Indianapolis Times*, March 16, 1925. The property would become Joe Canning's professional football training camp.
17. "Jack Dillon Has Mishap Near Here," *Anderson Herald*, November 11, 1925.
18. "Old Jack Dillon Trains Every Day," *Miami Herald*, June 8, 1926.
19. "Deputy Seeks to Seize Hialeah Fight Stadium but Finds It Gone," *Miami Tribune*, July 14, 1926. The promotion, which never found solid ground, or at least not permanently, had encountered financial issues.
20. "Six Captured in Rum Raids Upon Hialeah," *Miami News*, September 7, 1926.
21. "Five Are Arrested by Liquor Raiders," *Miami Herald*, March 16, 1927.
22. Grace Swartzman married W.J. Reed on January 7, 1906. Mrs. Ellen Grubbs was a close friend of Grace.
23. The funeral home later became the Rivero Funeral Home during the 1960s.
24. Anaïs Nin, "goodreads," goodreads.com, Goodreads Inc., accessed July 15, 2024.
25. There were rumors that Jack Dillon was picking up bootleg battles in armories and at fight clubs.
26. Amanda Jane (Sigler) Price was born on May 3, 1861, in Frankfort, Clinton County, Indiana. Her remains were cremated.
27. "War-Time Boxer in Breadline, but Not Kicking, He Says," *Evening Star*, September 30, 1932.
28. "War-Time Boxer in Breadline, but Not Kicking, He Says," *Evening Star*, September 30, 1932.
29. This charade surfaces periodically to those researching the exploits of the former champion. Many are unaware that it was a farce.
30. "Lunacy Charge Against Dillon," *Miami Herald*, September 29, 1934. Alcoholics Anonymous (AA) dates its founding to Bill Wilson's (Bill W.) and Bob Smith's (Dr. Bob) first commiseration alcoholic-to-alcoholic in 1935. AA

meetings began in 1935 in Akron, Ohio, and the successful program quickly grew. While Jack Dillon's condition and location prohibited him from using the organization, it is never too late for others. To get help call toll free at (800) 934–9518.

31. "Playing the Field of Sports," *Indianapolis Star*, February 8, 1937.

32. "Jess Willard Given Custody of Jack Dillon," *Miami Herald*, February 1, 1939. Judge Ben C. Willard of criminal court ordered the release.

33. The pair sparred with large gloves in New York on March 17, 1916.

34. The Florida State Hospital is a hospital and psychiatric hospital in Chattahoochee, Florida. Established in 1876, it was Florida's only state mental institution until 1947. Existing at a time when many illnesses were misunderstood, the hospital was investigated for allegations of mistreatment of patients. The facility treated some notable patients, including Victor Licata (axe murderer). Dillon's attending physician was Dr. J.B. O'Conner, who confirmed the elite pugilist's illness.

35. "Tad's Tid-Bits," *Pomona Progress*, April 19, 1920. The letter was penned by Jack O'Reilly.

Bibliography

Books

Baker, Mark Allen. *Between the Ropes at Madison Square Garden: The History of an Iconic Boxing Ring, 1925–2007*. McFarland, 2019.
_____. *Title Town USA: Boxing in Upstate New York*. History Press, 2010.
_____. *The World Colored Heavyweight Championship, 1876–1937 (Drawing the Color Line)*. McFarland, 2020.
Goldin, Claudia. *The Race Between Education and Technology*. Harvard University Press, 2008.
Goldman, Herbert G., ed. *The Ring Record Book and Boxing Encyclopedia*. The Ring, 1985.
Sugar, Bert Randolph. *Boxing's Greatest Fighters*. Lyons Press, 2006.
_____. *The Ultimate Book of Boxing Lists*. Running Press, 2010.

Archival Sources

Library and Archives Canada
The Library of Congress

Internet Sites

ancestry.com
boxingtreasures.com
boxrec.com
case.edu
chronicalingamerica.loc.gov
ctboxinghof.com
cyberboxingzone.com
ebay.com
findagrave.com
fl.gov
floridamemory.com
heavyweightcollectibles.com
history.com
ibhof.com
ibroresearch.com
josportsinc.com
newspapers.com
pugilistica.com
wikipedia.org
worthpoint.com
youtube.com

Magazine

The Ring

Newspapers

Akron Beacon Journal (Akron, OH)
Anaconda Standard (Anaconda, MT)
Anderson Daily Bulletin (Anderson, IN)
Anderson Herald (Anderson, IN)
Arkansas Democrat (Little Rock, AR)
Atlanta Journal (Atlanta, GA)
Boston Post (Boston, MA)
Bozeman Courier (Bozeman, MT)
Brazil Daily Times (Brazil, IN)
Buffalo Commercial (Buffalo, NY)
Buffalo Courier (Buffalo, NY)
Buffalo Enquirer (Buffalo, NY)
Buffalo News (Buffalo, NY)
Buffalo Times (Buffalo, NY)
Butte Daily Post (Butte, MT)
Call-Leader (Elwood, IN)
Cincinnati Enquirer (Cincinnati, OH)
Cincinnati Post (Cincinnati, OH)
Commercial Appeal (Memphis, TN)
Daily Arkansas Gazette (Little Rock, AR)
Daily Free Press (Kinston, NC)
Daily Oklahoman (Oklahoma City, OK)
Des Moines Register (Des Moines, IA)
Dispatch (Columbus, OH)
Evansville Courier and Press (Evansville, IN)
Evansville Journal (Evansville, IN)
Evansville Press (Evansville, IN)
Evening Standard (Ogden City, UT)
Evening Star (Washington, DC)
Evening World (New York, NY)
Fort Wayne Daily News (Fort Wayne, IN)
Fort Wayne Journal-Gazette (Fort Wayne, IN)
Fort Wayne Sentinel (Fort Wayne, IN)
Fort Worth Star-Telegram (Fort Worth, TX)
Fresno Morning Republican (Fresno, CA)
Gazette (Cedar Rapids, IA)
Harrisburg Daily Independent (Harrisburg, PA)
Huntington Herald (Huntington, CT)
Indiana Daily Times (Indianapolis, IN)
Indianapolis News (Indianapolis, IN)
Indianapolis Star (Indianapolis, IN)
Jersey Observer and Jersey Journal (Secaucus, NJ)

Lincoln Journal Star (Lincoln, NE)
Logansport Pharos-Tribune (Logansport, IN)
Manhattan Mercury (Manhattan, KS)
Miami Herald (Miami, FL)
Miami News (Miami, FL)
Miami Tribune (Miami, FL)
Miles City Star (Miles City, MT)
Muncie Evening Press (Muncie, IN)
Nashville Banner (Nashville, TN)
New Castle News (New Castle, PA)
New York Herald (New York, NY)
News-Journal (New Castle, DE)
Oakland Tribune (Oakland, CA)
Palladium-Item (Richmond, IN)
Palm Beach Post (West Palm Beach, FL)
Philadelphia Inquirer (Philadelphia, PA)
Pittsburgh Post (Pittsburgh, PA)
Pittsburgh Post-Gazette (Pittsburgh, PA)
Pittsburgh Press (Pittsburgh, PA)
Pomona Progress (Pomona, CA)
Press and Sun-Bulletin (Binghamton, NY)
Princeton Daily Clarion (Princeton, IN)
Reporter-Times (Martinsville, IN)
Republic (Columbus, IN)
Richmond Item (Richmond, IN)
Rochester Democrat and Chronicle (Rochester, NY)
Rushville Republican (Rushville, IN)
St. Louis Dispatch (St. Louis, MO)
Salt Lake Herald-Republican (Salt Lake City, UT)
San Francisco Bulletin (San Francisco, CA)
San Francisco Chronicle (San Francisco, CA)
San Francisco Examiner (San Francisco, CA)
Seattle Star (Seattle, WA)
Seattle Union Record (Seattle, WA)
South Bend News-Times (South Bend, IN)
South Bend Times (South Bend, IN)
South Bend Tribune (South Bend, IN)
Springfield News-Leader (Springfield, MO)
Standard Union (Brooklyn, NY)
Star Press (Muncie, IN)
Star-Phoenix (Saskatoon, Saskatchewan, Canada)
Times (Munster, IN)
Times Union (Albany, NY)
Times-Democrat (New Orleans, LA)
Topeka Daily Capital (Topeka, KS)
Town Talk (Alexandria, LA)
Tribune (Seymour, IN)
Tulsa Tribune (Tulsa, OK)
Tulsa World (Tulsa, OK)
Washington Post (Washington, DC)
Washington Times (Washington, DC)
Wichita Falls Times (Wichita Falls, TX)
Wilkes-Barre Times Leader (Wilkes-Barre, PA)

Organizations—Research

Associated Press
Bureau of Labor Statistics' Consumer Price Index (CPI)
International Boxing Hall of Fame
International Boxing Research Organization (IBRO)
The Smithsonian Institution
United Press International
United States Census Bureau

Index

Numbers in ***bold italics*** indicate pages with illustrations

Ahearn, Young 96, 98–***99***, 107, 168
Allen, Whitey 116
Anderson, Andre 102–103, 145, 161, 225*n*11
Ashe, George "Kid" 78–79
Attell, Abe 12, 17, 59, 61

Baker, Harry 83
Barnsback, Eddie 154, 165, 172
battle royal 18, 220*n*41
Berger, Billy 36, 43–44, 57
Berry, Jack (Jim) *see* Wiggam, Howard
Block, Ted 152, 154
Braddock, James J. 193
Brennan, Willie "KO" 72–***73***
Brill, Izzy 14–15, 18, 20
Britt, Jimmy 23
Britton, Jack 54, 80, 155, 179, 181
Bronson, Ray ***16***, 17–18, 21–24, 28–***30***, 39, 57, 76, 134–135, 177, 179; biography 19
Brown, Fortville "Kid" 13
Brown, George "KO" ***37***, 51–52, 64, ***66***, 86, 91–95, 155
Brown, Pete "Frisco" 172–173
Burns, Tommy 12, 16, 64, 83–84, 104, 159

Canning, J.J. 193
Cantwell, Frank 42–43, 62–63, 79; arrest 63–64
Caponi, Tony 78–79
Carpentier, Georges 35, 75–76, 80, 164, 181
Carroll, Buck 32
Chip, George 34–36, 40–41, 46–47, 52–55, 57–58, 65, 67–68, 74–75, 80, 103, 105, 109, 132, 135, 138, 143–***144***, 151; biography ***35***
Christie, Gus 35, 67, 69–70, 78, 80,-81 82, 89, 109, 119, 125, 146, 152
Clabby, Jimmy 29, 35, 78, 80, 82, 94, 100, 107, 109, 132
Claiborne, Marshall 83–84
Clancy, Bud ***168***–169
Clark, Jeff 75
Clark, Tommy 15
Clark, William "Billy" 46
Clarke (Clark), Grant Kid 57–58, 68
Clifford, Jack 137
Coakley, Glenn 50–51
Coffey, Jim 108, 121
Coffey, Walter 57, 59
Coffroth, Jimmy 49, 53, 58, 62
Cole, Freddie 32
The Color Line 38, 88–89
Conners, Battling 68
Conners, Young 20
Coogan, George 102
Cooley, Jimmy 23, 26–27
Corbett, James J. 27, 38, 49, 67, 75, 112, 116, 156, 159, 165, 174, 195
Coulon, Johnny 169
Cowler, Tom 112–114, 120, 140, 166, 195
Cox, Joe 175
Cox, Sid 22
Crouse, Albert "Buck" 52, 55, 74
Curley, Don 144, 146
Curley, Jack 114
Cutler, Marty 102

Daly (Dailey), Jack 150
Dalton, Kid 30
Danforth, Tommy 83
Darcy, Les 118, 128–130, ***131***–133, 227*n*1, 227*n*8; death 135; first American battle 128–129; New York State litigation 133
Davidson, Wick 13
Dawson, Tommy 18
Day, Cecil 18
DeLane, Tom 15
dementia pugilistica 190–191
Dempsey, Jack 1, 103, 113, 145, ***157***, ***160***, 162–164, 169, 171; Dempsey versus Willard 156–159, 160–161
Denham, Jack 173–176; symbolism 175
Denning, Jack 71
Dennis, Robert 136
Devere, Bob 118
Dillon, Jack ***23***, ***26***, ***30***, ***31***, 39, 44, ***49***, 54, 59, ***72***, 86–87, ***88***, 114, 118, ***124***–***125***, ***144***, ***168***, ***170***, ***174***; automobiles ***77***, 79, 90, 96, 104, 122, 187; back-to-back beatings 139; baseball 65; *Best of Burlesque* 42; bootleg boxing 14; café (Hialeah) 187; champion prediction 29; comparison to Dempsey 159; comparison to Willard 7–8; Crabbs event and arrest 122; on Dempsey in army 164; depression 161; Dillon Stables

235

10; early challenges 13; education 9; excessive demands 33; fake identity 191–192; faking fight 95; family structure 9, fight articles (Roberts) 25–26; fighting heart 160; hardest punch 145; horseshoe punch *30*; hypnotic eyes *41*; institutionalization 193–194; (ring) introduction Dempsey-Miske 169; Jack Dillon Benefit 178–182; Jack Dillon's Bar and Café 126; jewelry stolen 134; keeping silent 59; legal woes 178, 181–182, 184–185, 188–190, 193; lunacy petition 192; matching issues 112; Murbarger (first bout with) 67; Musical Extravaganza 181; name 12; name change 190; opponent's size 145; puts pen to paper 145; raw deal (Klaus) 62; restaurant 187; rub on Willard 117; sparring partners 18; style comparison 32; teenage delinquency 43; temperament 18; vaudeville 115–116; weight disadvantages *161*; white hope 84; WWI draft registration 135–136
Dillon, Mrs. Jack (Grace Reed) 97, 105–106, 111, 142; death 189; wedding 89
Dillon, Mrs. Jack (identity unconfirmed) 61–62
Dillon, Tommy (fighter) 9, 61, 69, 81, 97, 111, 127, 153, 189; identity crisis 77
Dillon, Tommy (referee, politician) 77–79, 92–93
Dime, Jimmy 34
division champions: year 1915 110; year 1916 127
Donahue, Harry 40
Donnelly, Young 23, 28
Donovan, Billy 65–66
Donovan, Larry 25
Duffy, Jack 152
Durlacher, Louis H. 55

Earp, Wyatt 63
Edwards, Billy 172
Einert, Gus "Sailor" 93
English, Larry 100
Epstein, Solly 144, 146, 177
Erne, Ralph Young 48, 51, 54, 150

Farb, Nate 21, 24, *31*, 40, 43, 61, 89, 167
Farmer, Frank 109–110, 149, 152
Fisher, Jack 125
Fitzgerald, Richard "Dick" 29
Fitzgerald, Willie 25, 27–28
Fitzsimmons, Robert "Bob" 49, 56, 67, 69, 101
Fitzsimmons, Young 165–168, 171
Florida State Hospital 193–*194*, *195*, 231n34
Flynn, Dan "Porky" 52, 99–100, 103, 110, 112–*113*
Flynn, Jack 68
Flynn, Jim "Fireman" 83–*85*, 86, 94–*95*, 100–101, 110, 116, 121–122; biography 84
Foley, Harry 170, 172, 176
Fulton, Fred 132, 136

Gans, Joe 15–16, 44–45
Gardiner, George 83–84
Gardner, Jimmy 42–43, 46–47, 54, 57, 69, 222n23
Gavigan, Tommy 71

Gibbons, Mike 35, 72, 94, 100, 102, 107, 124–*125*, *126*, 129, 132, 138–140, 151, 155, 164, 179
Gibbons, Tommy 113, *126*, 179
Gilbert, Dick "Fighting" 86, 96
Gilbert, Yankee 106, 110
Gilmore, Harry 40
Glover, Mike 42
Goldman, Charley 150–*151*
Gorman, Joe Kid 65
Graham, Jack 51
Grande, Charles "Sailor" 106, 123
Gray, Young Kid 20
Greb, Harry 5, 48, 107, 113, 128, *137*–138, 142–143, 145–*146*, 147, 152–153, 162, 179, 181; biography 137
Griffin (Griffith), Kid 18–19
Griffith (Griffiths), Billy 55–56, 222n7
Griffiths, Johnny 155

Haack, Billy 155, 228n9; class act 155–156
Halstead, Battling 164–165, 169–170
Hanlon, Jack 42
Hansen (Hanson), Vic 81–82, 86, 115
Harper, Ben 14
Harrison, Phil 155–156, 161–162, 166
Hart, Marvin 24, 220n57
Harter, Edwin Steve 106, 127, 139–141, 143, 147–149, 165–166, 178
Hemingway, Ernest 103
Hendricks, Neal 51
Hennings, Joe 28
Herrick, Jack 33–34, 36–37, 47, 51, 53
Herring, James "Red" 170, 172,
Hialeah, Florida 6, *186*–190, 192–193
Hicks, Freddie 30–31, 83
Hoe, Frank 100
Hot Springs, Arkansas 83, 86, 97, 130–131, 133, *141*, 143, 154–155, 165–166, 169–172, 175
Houck, Leo 35, 44, 51, 53, 54–*56*, 71–*72*, 79–81, 107; 224n29; biography 54
Howard, Jimmy 68
Howard, Johnny 101, 105, 111
Hoy, Kid 57
Humphries, Charles 18
Hurtz, Walter 34

Indiana 8; Anderson 21–*22*, 27–29, 32, 64, 90, 109, 134, 137, 181, 187; Broad Ripple 21, 78–79, 93, 138, 149, 181, 184; Evansville 30, 46, 50–51, 56–57, 63, 69, 73, 98, 102, 105, 118, 126, 136, 182; Frankfort 9, 23, 62, 81, 122, 190; Muncie 28, 32, 48, 91, 101, 105–106, 110–112, 117, 122, 143, 148, 151; Peru 79; Richmond 63, 65, 74, 139, 162; Terre Haute 20–21, 46–47, 50, 65, 91, 93, 97, 136, 138, 177, 179–180; Vincennes 50, 51, 93

Jackson, Peter "Young" 69
Jeannette, Joe 100
Jeffries, Jack 81
Jeffries, James J. 27, 32, 49, 59, 84, 124, 145
Johnson, Jack 15–16, 27, 47, 83–84, *85*, 89–90, 101–103, 108, 114, 120, 148, 158, 179–180

Johnson, Jim "Battling" 113
Johnston, James J. 103
Jones, Tom 68, 114

Kauff, Benny. 163, 229*n*1
Kaufman, Al 89, 159
Kelly (Kelley), Hugo 55, 64, 75
Kelly, Jimmy 13
Kelly, Walter 80
Kennedy, James "Big Jim" 49
Ketchel, Stanley 12, 15–16, 36, 44–45, 52, 58, 64, 65, 76, 99, 101; contenders following death 34–35; death 34; Fifth Anniversary of Death 107
Kid, Zulu 105, 140
Kilbane, Johnny 15
Klaus, Frank 35–36, 42, 46–47, 50, 53–55, 59, *60*–63, 65, 69, 75–76, 80–81, 100–101, 183; biography 52; Fifth Anniversary 107
Krohn, Harry 152

Laffy (Laffey), Jack 15
Langford, Sam 12, 38, 47, 83–84, 100–101, 103, 183
Lardner, Rex 12
Lark, Pat 4, 15, 18–19
Lavin, Paddy 48, 57–58
legal boxing exhibition 20, 32–33
Leslie, Jack 181
Lester, Jack 85–86, 103–*104*, 113
Levinsky, Battling 5, 51, 54, 71, *74*–75, 80, 82, 85–*88*, 89–90, 94, 97, 100–101, 103, 107, 113–118, 122–123, 126–127, 129–130, 134, 146, 154, 164; versus Dillon X 123–124–125
Levinson, Sol 87
Lewis, Harry 45, 52, 54, 80
Lewis, Willie 119
Logan, Frank 71
London, Jack 101
Long, Bobby 20
Loughrey, Young 42, 44
Louis, Joe 193

Mace, Joe. 91, 93
Mack, Johnny 183
MacKinnon (McKinnon), Bill 71, 77–78
Madison Square Garden 5, 62–63, 96, 108–*109*, 132–133, 223*n*38
Malone, Teddy 15
Mansfield (Greenberg), Harry 39–40
Mantell, Frank 46, 70, 93–94, 100–101, 104, 149
Martin, Bob "Big" 164
Martin, Ed "Denver" 113
Martin, Terry 46,
Masterson, Bat 63, 112
May, Rube 28–29
Mayfield, Billy. 46
McAree (McCrea), Joe 17
McAuliffe, Jack 159
McCarey, Thomas 55
McCarney, Billy 159
McCarron, Jack 133–135
McCarty, Luther 84, 120, 224*n*17

McCarty, Tom 101, 106
McCoy, Al 124–126, 130, *132*–133, 138, 140, 150–*151*, 154–155; biography 150
McCune, Tom 67
McFarland, Packy (Packey) 21–23
McGoorty, Eddie 22, 35, 37–39, *40*, 50, 52–53, 55, 59, 66, 75, 80, 94, 107, 145, 148, 155
McGovern, Terry 145
McIntosh, Hugh 80
McMahon, Patsy 143–144, 146, 149–150, 163–166, 170, 172, 175, 178
McMahon, Tom "Bearcat" 103–104, 106–107, 134
Meehan, Willie 139
Mellody, Honey 29, 44
Mellody, Jimmy 44
Meyers, Earl 125
middleweights 1907 summary 12; 1913 summary 75
Miller, Walk 175
Miske, Billy 113, 117–118, 126–127, 129–130, 140–141, 148, 150, 164, 169, 171
Moha, Bob 41, 47–*48*, *49*, 55, 67, 74, 91–*92*, 128–129, 134
Moir, Gunner 105
Monaghan, Walter 80
Moran, Frank 5, 108–109, 113–*115*, 117–121, 127, 140, 145, 156, 159–160, 189, 195; battle against Dillon 119–121, 226*n*32; biography 119
Moran, Jack 133, 170
Morgan, Dan "Dumb" 75, 82, 224*n*1
Morgan, Jack 32–33
Morris, Carl 94
Morrow, Howard 30–*31*, 93
Munger, Ford 23
Murbarger, Sam 14, 65, 66, 78, 80–81, 93–95, 97, 99, 102, 104, 112–113, 116–119, 121, 123–126, 142; biography 66–67; calling out middleweights 94; final split with Dillon 126–127; first split with Dillon 78; initial promotion 65–66; marriage 121, 226*n*35; move to New York City 104, 108
Murphy, Jimmy 70
Murphy, Tommy "Harlem" 59, 149
Murray, Billy "Fighting" 102

Nelson, Battling 15, 64, 159
Nelson, Terry 20
Nig (Goldman), Alex "Kid" 43
Norton, Al 89, 110

O'Brien, Jack "Philadelphia" 64
O'Dowd, Mike 113, 151
O'Neil, Tim 123
O'Rourke, Tom 130, 226*n*25
O'Sullivan, Tim *131*
Otto, Young 54, 150
Owens, Walter 21; death 134, 144

Palzer, Al 120
Papke, Billy 12, 15–16, 34, 36, 38, 44, 49, 52, 60, 64–65, 71–72, 75, 80, 83–84, 107, 183, 221*n*30
Parson, Willie 13

Index

Patterson, Lee 19
Pelkey, Arthur 84, 101
Perry, Jim 33
Petroskey, Ed "Sailor" 58, 81, 91
Pickerd, Walter 189
Pollack, Harry 114
Potter, Lem (Lee) 15
Price, Amanda (Sigler, mother) 9, 162; death 190
Price, Chester B. (brother) 9, 219*n*19; death 10–12
Price, Ernest C. *see* Dillon, Jack
Price, James A. (uncle) 8–9
Price, John (grandfather) 8
Price, Paul W. (brother) 9, 162, 188, 190; death 192
Price, Russell C. (brother) 162, 190; *see also* Dillon, Tommy
Price, Sarah (grandmother) 8
Price, Winfield Scott (father) 8, 9

Ramsey, Harry 67, 69
Redmond, Jack 22–23
Reddy, Bill 150
Reed, Ralph (stepson) 89, 106, 182, 225*n*20
Reeves, Everett "Barber" 21
referee error (Bezenah v. Cole) 21
Rickard, Tex 124, 130–**131**
Riley, Jack 167
Roberts, Jasper "Jap" 25–26
Rogers, Al 71, 73
Roman, Paul 165
Rowlands, Len 136
Runyon, Damon 190
Ryan, Jack 32
Ryan, Tommy 30, 64,
Ryan, William Billy 151

Savage, Jim 107
Saylor, Milburn "Young" 14–15, 39, 168
Scanlon, Tommy 21
Schuster, Billy 62
Scott, Bill "Steamboat" 147–148
Scott, Winfield 8
Shank, Nig 65,
Simms (Sims), Kid 17
Smith, Dave 35
Smith, Ed "Gunboat" 84–85, 88, 90, 94, 100–103, 108, 113, 116, 119–120, 130–132, 134, 183; biography 101; White heavyweight title 101–102
Smith, Edward (referee) 90, 150, 155
Smith, Homer 147

Smith, Jeff 80, 135, 138
Smith, Ray "Sergeant" 136–137
Sparks, Kid 22–23
Stanley, Joe 140
Stevens, Jack 46, 51
Stolkin, Bob 68, 78–79
Stone, Kid 44
Stout, Harry 50, 87, 102
Sullivan, Jack "Twin" 71
Sullivan, Jimmy "Kid" 20–21
Sullivan, John L. 116
Sullivan, Mike "Twin" 29, 44–**45**, 64, 84
Sweeney, Robert KO 167

Taylor, Bud 177
Thomas, Joe 29, 65
Thompson, Tommy 175
Tracey, John 24
Truesdale, Clint 25, **26**, 29, 38
Tunney, Gene 166

Wagner, Emmett Kid 67
Walker, Hugh 139, 141–143, 146, 148–150
Walker Law 6, 163, 177, 227*n*32
Walsh, Tommy 92
Walters, James Jimmy 33, 35–36, 38, 40, 43, 81–83, 87, 91
Walters, Joe 149, 176, 183–184
Warner, Ed 175
Watts, Jimmy 21, 122, 181, 184–185, 192–193
Weinert, Charlie "Young" 96, **108**–109, 116, 140, 166, 195
Weiss, Pat 167–168
Wells, Bombardier Billy 101
Welsh, Freddie 18–19, 23, 110
Welsh, Jack 61–62
White, Charlie 169
White, Frank 17
White City Park 21
Wiggam, Howard 56–57, 133, 184
Wiggins, Chuck 176
Willard, Jess 6–7, 85, 101–103, 108–111, 114–**115**, 117, 121, 124, 127, 136, 140, 145, 148; Dillon on Willard 157–**158**, **160**; releasing Dillon 193; Summer 1919 (Dempsey versus Willard) 156–160
Williams, Barney *see* Battling Levinsky
Williams, Jack "Kid" 79
Williams, Larry 123
Wolgast, Ad 22–23, 28, 32

York (Yorke), Bob 152

www.ingramcontent.com/pod-product-compliance
Lightning Source LLC
Chambersburg PA
CBHW060340010526
44117CB00017B/2902